D1265121

THE CASTRO OBSESSION

Other Titles of Interest from Potomac Books, Inc.

Cuba: From Columbus to Castro, Fifth Edition by Jaime Suchlicki

Decision for Disaster: Betrayal at the Bay of Pigs by Grayston L. Lynch

The Kennedy Presidency: An Oral History of the Era by Deborah Hart Strober and Gerald S. Strober

THE CASTRO OBSESSION

U.S. COVERT OPERATIONS AGAINST CUBA

1959–1965

DON BOHNING

Potomac Books, Inc.
Washington, D.C.

Library of Congress Cataloging-in-Publication Data

Bohning, Don, 1933–
     The Castro obsession : U.S. covert operations against Cuba, 1959–1965 / Don Bohning. — 1st ed.
        v.   cm.
     Includes bibliographical references and index.
     Contents: The beginnings—Evolution of a disaster—Fixing blame—Bobby takes charge—Mongoose—"Nutty schemes"—Mongoose redux—Perpetual intrigue—A new beginning—Accommodation or assassination—"Let Cubans be Cubans"—Fading fast—A last hurrah—LBJ cashes out.
     ISBN 1-57488-675-4 (alk. paper)
     1. United States—Foreign relations—Cuba.   2. Cuba—Foreign relations—United States.   3. Subversive activities—Cuba—History—20th century.   4. Espionage, American—Cuba—History—20th century.   5. United States—Foreign relations—1953–1961.   6. United States—Foreign relations—1961–1963.   7. United States—Foreign relations—1963–1969.   8. Spies—United States—Interviews.   9. United States. Central Intelligence Agency—Biography.   10. Exiles—United States—Interviews. I. Title.

E183.8.C9B55   2005
327.1273'07291'09046—dc22   2005001483

Printed in Canada on acid-free paper that meets the American National Standards Institute Z39–48 Standard.

Potomac Books, Inc.
22841 Quicksilver Drive
Dulles, Virginia 20166

First Edition

10   9   8   7   6   5   4   3   2   1

For
Gerry, Terry, Lee, and Lori
and
special thanks to
Jake Esterline

CONTENTS

PREFACE

I was a naive young reporter from South Dakota by way of Arizona, and had just begun work for the *Miami Herald* in the Hollywood, Florida, bureau a few miles north of Miami. Having arrived in South Florida with an interest in Latin America, I had more than a passing, but not intimate, awareness of events unfolding in Cuba. The newspaper itself carried a daily diet of stories that reflected the growing concern about Cuba in the Cold War context. "No Aid? So what—Cuba," read a page-one headline July 10, 1959, my first day at work. "Says It Gets None Anyway," added a subhead. An adjacent story from Guatemala proclaimed: "Guatemala Has Open Door for Commies—Jail." Soon to come was the Bay of Pigs, then the missile crisis. The Hollywood office fronted the railroad tracks. From there we watched an endless string of southbound freight trains passing by with military equipment headed to Miami and the Florida Keys for a possible invasion of Cuba. But it wasn't until the spring of 1964, when I began work on the *Herald*'s Latin America desk, that I realized how much more bubbled beneath the surface. This book is a result of a latent but lingering curiosity to know more about what was happening in that period, abetted by several fortuitous events years later.

It was not uncommon in those earlier days for reporters on certain beats involving foreign affairs to talk with CIA officers, much as one would talk to the political officer in a U.S. embassy. The *Herald*'s executives were aware of the contacts. In the interest of full disclosure, the first CIA official I ever knowingly met was John Dimmer. Dimmer succeeded Ted Shackley in mid-1965 as chief of JMWAVE, the Miami Station that was located on the University of Miami's South Campus and served as the frontline command post for the secret war against Cuba. Dimmer stayed only briefly. Paul Henzie, later to serve on Jimmy Carter's National Security Council staff, succeeded Dimmer. Jake Esterline took over in early 1968 to complete the dismantling and relocating of JMWAVE. By the time Esterline departed in 1972, we had become friends, and we kept in touch after his retirement. I later learned from another source that he had been chief of the CIA's Cuba Project, that resulted in the Bay of Pigs. Esterline retired, first to the U.S. Virgin Islands, in part because he had been told he might be on a Cuban hit list for his role in the Bay of Pigs, an apparently erroneous warning. He then moved to North Carolina in the 1980s.

I wanted to do a story about his career for the *Herald*. He agreed to talk. The story appeared in the *Herald's* Sunday magazine in January 1995. That prompted a telephone call from Jim Blight, a professor of international relations at Brown University's Watson Institute for International Studies. Blight, working with Peter Kornbluh of the National Security Archive, a private, Washington-based research organization, was preparing a conference on the Bay of Pigs and Operation Mongoose in the spring. He had seen the story, and he wanted my assistance enlisting Esterline's participation. Sam Halpern, another CIA veteran actively involved in the post–Bay of Pigs covert war, also participated. I was invited to the conference as an observer. I realized then how much was not known about the covert campaign against Cuba. Even today, no comprehensive chronology of events is available for the six years from 1959 to 1965, the period of the most intense covert activity. This book is an attempt to fill that historical void.

The initial idea had been to collaborate with Esterline on a book about his career, focusing heavily on the Bay of Pigs, with the cooperation of Jack Hawkins, the Marine colonel and paramilitary chief for the Cuba Project. That approach changed suddenly on a Saturday afternoon in mid-October 1999 when Esterline died of a heart attack. The scope of the project was broadened to cover the period from pre–Bay of Pigs until the mid-1960s. Thousands of pages of declassified documents had become available over the previous decade; many of them were made available to me by the National Security Archive. And a few of the key participants were still alive and willing to talk. This book relies heavily on both interviews and documents to help the reader understand the context in which decisions were made.

While Esterline's untimely death changed the focus, his contributions, along with those of Jack Hawkins, provide new insights into the Bay of Pigs failure. I am particularly grateful to Jack Hawkins for the many observations he provided in interviews, letters, and written analyses. Peter Kornbluh and Tom Blanton of the National Security Archive were invaluable in making available documents and conference invitations. The staff at the Johnson Library in Austin, Texas, and particularly Senior Archivist Regina Greenwell, were most helpful and courteous.

Sam Halpern, executive assistant to both Bill Harvey and Desmond FitzGerald in the post–Bay of Pigs period, willingly consented to two informative interviews and proved an essential and willing contact for fact checking. Other former CIA officials who made themselves available include Ted Shackley, who I met for the first time in 1999, and who consented to two interviews before his death in December 2002; Tom Parrott, an aide to Gen. Maxwell Taylor when Taylor served as President Kennedy's military representative in the White House, and who kept minutes for the Special Group that approved covert proposals; Nestor Sanchez, case officer for Rolando Cubela, the temperamental revolutionary "asset" inside Cuba who the CIA hoped would lead an internal coup against Castro; Robert Reynolds, sent to Miami as CIA station chief before the Bay of Pigs and who arranged for JMWAVE's location on University of Miami property; Jim Flannery, an aide to Richard Bissell at the time of the Bay of Pigs; Justin Gleichauf of the agency's overt office in Miami and the first real CIA man to arrive in South Florida permanently after Batista's fall on New Year's Day, 1959; and Manuel "Manny" Chavez, the Air Force intelligence officer detached to Gleichauf's office in Miami.

This account would have been woefully inadequate without the Cuban exile perspective from Erneido Oliva, Rafael Quintero, and Carlos Obregon. All three dedicated a big chunk of their lives to serve as soldiers in the secret war. Oliva distinguished himself as the second in command of the Bay of Pigs brigade. He later became the highest-ranking Cuban in the U.S. Army Reserve as a major general and deputy commander of the Washington, D.C., National Guard. Quintero was among the first to join the ranks of exiles for what was to become the Bay of Pigs, was infiltrated into Cuba to report in advance of the invasion, and returned again during Operation Mongoose. As deputy to exile leader Manuel Artime, he provided invaluable insight for understanding the little-known "autonomous operations." Obregon, today the Miami representative for a South American publishing company, joined the CIA in the fall of 1961, becoming an infiltration team leader with numerous missions to Cuba.

John Crimmins, the State Department's coordinator of Cuban affairs and an acquaintance since the 1960s, provided a copy of the unpublished manuscript written by his late colleague, Robert Hurwitch, as well as his own observations. George Volsky, the enigmatic Polish-born exile from Cuba who worked for both the United States Information Agency and

PREFACE

the *New York Times* in Miami during the period covered in this book,
helped with local flavor.

I owe a particular debt of gratitude to several people at the *Miami Herald* for giving me the opportunities that made this book a reality, among them Lee Hills, George Beebe, Al Neuharth, John McMullan, Larry Jinks, and Jim Buchanan. Special appreciation also goes to former *Miami Herald* researcher Liz Donovan for her invaluable assistance, not only during my years at the newspaper, but after my retirement. Last, but certainly not least, I am grateful to George McGovern, my college adviser, who made me aware of a world beyond South Dakota.

INTRODUCTION

From Fidel Castro's rise to power in Cuba on New Year's Day of 1959 until the mid-1960s, the U.S. government resorted to economic and political destabilization, propaganda, manipulation, sabotage, and assassination plots to remove him. It was one of the most extensive, sustained, and ultimately futile covert action programs by one country against the government of another in the post–World War II era. Instead of ridding the hemisphere of Castro, the covert campaign undoubtedly contributed to maintaining and consolidating his control over Cuba. During more than forty years, he has outlasted nine U.S. presidents, from Eisenhower to Clinton.

The failed attempts to rid Cuba of Castro also transformed the face of South Florida, which became an area of anti-Castro ferment and upheaval. By the end of 1962 the CIA station at an abandoned Navy air facility south of Miami had become the largest in the world outside its Langley, Virginia, headquarters. Thousands of Cuban exiles were on the payroll. Thousands of others who weren't, attempted to give the impression they were. It gave them cachet and helped them raise funds. The same applied to scores of would-be soldiers of fortune who drifted in and out of the area, hoping to get a piece of the anti-Castro action. Some had previously fought with Castro against Fulgencio Batista, the corrupt Cuban dictator who fled the island on the first day of 1959.

The American public saw only the tip of the covert iceberg. The broader outlines emerged piecemeal in newspapers, magazines, and books over the ensuing decades. But only in recent years—with the declassification of thousands of once-secret documents and, as time passed, a greater willingness by surviving participants to talk about their actions—has the depth and extent of Washington's anti-Castro covert activities become apparent.

Drawing on those documents, the work of previous researchers, and scores of interviews since 1995 with people involved, this book is an effort to provide a comprehensive account of what happened, how it happened, why it happened, and how, after John F. Kennedy's assassination, anti-Castro activities gradually lost momentum as President Johnson turned his attention to Vietnam.

Even now, four decades later, there remain questions to be answered, decisions to be explained, "facts" to be corrected, lessons to be learned, and information yet to be revealed about the secret war against Castro. Some of the details may never be known, not having been committed to paper but taken to the grave by those involved.

In hindsight, given what is known today, some may wonder how our leaders could have sanctioned such activities in good conscience. The answer is simple. The tenor of the times was vastly different. The Cold War was at its hottest. Almost uniformly, the American mentality toward the Communist threat was one of "us against them." The media, opposition politicians, dissidents, and virtually anyone else who today would openly challenge such activities were, with rare exceptions, quiet. The prevailing atmosphere among policy makers and the public was that communism had to be stopped. And to do so, the ends justified the means, covert action among them.

Such was the case with Cuba under Castro. He was seen as another enemy in the war against communism. But he was much closer to home, and that made him, and Cuba, even more dangerous.

The war against Castro was a secret war that would have been impossible to wage just a few years later. As the United States became enmeshed in Vietnam, the antiwar movement exploded in streets and on campuses across the country. Then came U.S.–supported efforts in 1970 to prevent Marxist Salvador Allende from becoming president of Chile, followed in 1973 by a U.S.–encouraged coup in which Allende died, apparently by his own hand. In between, Watergate occurred. The times had changed, helped along by congressional hearings in the mid-1970s that exposed both the U.S. role in Chile and officially sanctioned assassination plots against foreign leaders, including Castro. With the media and the public less tolerant of such activities, the hearings made it more difficult for Washington to justify and wage secret wars. America and Americans had lost their innocence.

It wasn't until 1975 that the scope of covert efforts to oust Castro became publicly exposed in Senate hearings led by the late senator Frank Church, an Idaho Democrat. The hearings were closed, but the committee subsequently published an interim report entitled *Alleged Assassination Plots Involving Foreign Leaders*. The Church Committee report, as it became widely known, remains among the most useful and authoritative documents available on not only the assassination attempts but also the framework within which they occurred citing "concrete evidence of at least eight plots involving the CIA to assassinate Fidel Castro from 1960 to 1965."[1] Among these plots was the Bay of Pigs, for which assassination was a closely held part of the plan, though unknown even to its project director and paramilitary planner.

And for the first time, the public heard of Operation Mongoose, code name for the initial post–Bay of Pigs attempt by the Kennedy administration to remove Castro. Its arsenal ran the gamut of dirty tricks: from paramilitary activities and sabotage to psychological, political, and economic warfare; all aimed at provoking an internal uprising.

The Church Committee report defined covert action as an "activity meant to further the sponsoring nation's foreign policy objectives, and to be concealed in order to permit that nation to plausibly deny responsibility."[2] From 1955 to 1970, it noted,

> the basic authority for covert operations was a directive from the National Security Council, NSC 5412/2. This directive instructed the CIA to counter, reduce and discredit 'International Communism' throughout the world in a manner consistent with United States foreign and military policies. It also directed the CIA to undertake covert operations to achieve this end and defined covert operations as any covert activities as related to propaganda, economic warfare, political action (including sabotage, demolition and assistance to resistance movements) and all activities compatible with the directive. In 1962, the CIA's General Counsel rendered the opinion that the Agency's activities were 'not inhibited by any limitations other than those broadly set forth in NSC 5412.'[3]

The committee, too, noted the prevailing atmosphere in which the alleged assassination plots and other covert activities occurred.

> It was considered necessary to wage a relentless cold war against Communist expansion wherever it appeared in the 'back alleys of the world.' This called for a full range of covert activities in response to the operations of Communist clandestine services.[4]

Suddenly, with Castro's rise to power in Cuba, the Cold War and the Communist threat it posed could no longer be viewed in the abstract of some faraway place; it was at America's doorstep. Cuba had become one of the battlefields in the "back alley" war against communism, a responsibility that fell largely to the Central Intelligence Agency, created by President Truman in the immediate post–World War II period. And at the time, it was a war that had overwhelming popular support.

As the late Jake Esterline, the CIA's project chief for the failed Bay of Pigs, summarized in a 1995 interview with the author, communism was considered the mortal enemy of America, to be confronted at every turn. Dictators and human rights were secondary considerations. This attitude, in his view, didn't really change until the last half of the 1960s when protests began to build against Vietnam.

For Esterline, the CIA's activities in Latin America during his heyday were a logical follow-up to World War II and the spreading fear of communism. "When the Second World War ended and the Cold War started, the issue of survival was more clearly drawn" than it is today. "There may be just as many enemies today but the issues are not clearly drawn."[5]

It's also important to remember, said Esterline, that the CIA "was simply an agency of U.S. policy," and not the rogue elephant it has sometimes been described as. "They never did these things on their own. They were an instrument of U.S. policy from beginning to end" and as "a secret arm of U.S policy could not respond as to why they were doing these things."

By the time Castro and Cuba came along, the CIA was already flying high, responsible for "regime changes" in Iran (1953) and Guatemala (1954), and savoring other lesser-known successes. Esterline, himself a veteran of guerrilla warfare in Burma during World War II as a member of the Office of Strategic Services, the CIA's precursor, describes this atmosphere:

I really guess that as a result of our [the United States's] success in the Second World War there was kind of a . . . I've heard the word John Wayne used . . . derring-do, and maybe that is a good way to sum it up. There was quite a derring-do attitude, 'Well, hell, we can do anything if we want to.' And I feel that related to people like our elitist group in the agency headed by Allen Dulles and his boys.

I think those that left at the end of the war and returned to private life, then were jerked back suddenly, as I was, from other endeavors, probably had lost a little bit of their derring-do but the enthusiasm of others caused us to be swept up in it again. And I suppose that the happenstance of the

Guatemalan success, plus apparently some successes in other parts of the world that I was not necessarily familiar with, made this in a certain group of people within the DDP (as the CIA's clandestine service was known at the time) kind of fashionable.[6]

So again, as he had done earlier with Jacobo Arbenz, the left-leaning president of Guatemala in 1954, President Eisenhower turned to the CIA to deal with Castro and Cuba.

The single concern—and debate—in Washington, even before Castro came to power, was whether he was a Communist. The people who thought he was were enough in number to warrant two feeble attempts to prevent him from taking power. William D. Pawley, a Miami business-man who owned the Havana bus company, who had been U.S. ambassa-dor to Peru and Brazil under Eisenhower, and who was a friend of Batista, initiated the first effort. With Batista's collapse imminent, Pawley received State Department approval to go to Cuba. There, he tried to persuade Batista to turn power over to a junta that "would be unfriendly to him, but satisfactory to us." Pawley met with Batista for three hours in Havana on December 9, 1958, offering, among other things, exile for the Cuban leader and his family in Daytona Beach, Florida, where Batista had a home. Batista rejected Pawley's entreaties.[7] The next effort came in the waning days of December, shortly before Batista fled. It involved a CIA subsidized and supported plan by anti-Batista exile Justo Carrillo and his small Montecristo Movement to spring Col. Ramon Barquin from a Cuban jail on the Isle of Pines. Barquin, a popular and liberal officer, had been imprisoned after an unsuccessful coup d'etat against Batista. The plan was that, once freed, he would head a provisional government to forestall a Castro takeover. That attempt fared no better than had Paw-ley's.[8]

Still, after taking control in January 1959, enough uncertainty re-mained in Washington to give Castro the opportunity to prove he wasn't a Communist. But by the fall of 1959, most U.S. officials had been con-vinced that if he wasn't a Communist, he was increasingly under Com-munist influence, and so the plotting began. On March 17, 1960, Eisenhower approved an elaborate covert action plan designed to oust him. It culminated some thirteen months later—after a change of admin-istrations and many modifications to the original plan—in the Bay of Pigs invasion by a U.S. trained and supported Cuban exile brigade.

The invasion's failure fell like a cold shower on the CIA. The inevitable bureaucratic recriminations erupted. There was plenty of blame to go around. President Kennedy publicly accepted the blame, but privately blamed the CIA and the military Joint Chiefs. They, in turn, blamed the president, along with Secretary of State Dean Rusk and his State Department, for imposing too many limitations on the operation in an attempt to make U.S. involvement "plausibly deniable," another catch phrase in the lexicon of covert action.

Again, the Church Committee report offers an authoritative definition of "plausible deniability" and how its interpretation is twisted to satisfy needs of the moment.

> Non-attribution to the United States for covert operations was the original and principal purpose of the so-called doctrine of 'plausible denial.' Evidence before the Committee clearly demonstrates that this concept, designed to protect the United States and its operatives from the consequences of disclosures, has been expanded to mask decisions of the President and his senior staff members. A further consequence of the expansion of this doctrine is that subordinates, in an effort to permit their superiors to 'plausibly deny' operations, fail to fully inform them about those operations.
>
> 'Plausible denial' has shaped the processes for approving and evaluating covert actions. For example, the 40 Committee and its predecessor, the Special Group, have served as 'circuit breakers' for Presidents, thus avoiding consideration of covert action by the Oval Office.
>
> 'Plausible denial' can also lead to the use of euphemism and circumlocution, which are designed to allow the President and other senior officials to deny knowledge of an operation should it be disclosed. The converse may also occur; a President could communicate his desires for a sensitive operation in an indirect, circumlocutious manner. An additional possibility is that the President may, in fact, not be fully and accurately informed about a sensitive operation because he failed to receive the 'circumlocutious' message. The evidence . . . reveals that serious problems of assessing intent and ensuring both control and accountability may result from the use of 'plausible denial.'[9]

The doctrine of "plausible denial" has kept alive one of the lingering questions of Kennedy's attempts to rid the Caribbean of Castro: Did the president and/or his brother Bobby know and approve of the assassination efforts?

Kennedy loyalist and historian Arthur Schlesinger, a special assistant to President Kennedy, insists that the Kennedys did not approve, and were not even aware, of the assassination plots, most of which came during the Kennedy administration. Others, including many within the CIA, are just as certain that the Kennedys not only had knowledge of the assassination plots, but encouraged them, perhaps in an "indirect, circumlocutious manner."

Whether they did or did not know of the assassinations, it is clear that failure at the Bay of Pigs intensified, rather than ended, the covert anti-Castro effort, with Bobby Kennedy, the president's brother and attorney general, leading the charge. There seems little doubt that the intensified effort was fueled, at least in part, by the Kennedys' desire to extract revenge for the Bay of Pigs defeat.

Bobby, in a memo to the president written the day the Bay of Pigs invasion collapsed, was already urging a new campaign to deal with Castro.[10] The next day, Defense Secretary Robert McNamara, in a memo to Gen. Lyman Lemnitzer, chairman of the Joint Chiefs of Staff, wrote that the president had asked the Defense Department to "develop a plan for the overthrow of the Castro government by the application of U.S. military force." McNamara cautioned, however, "the request for this study should not be interpreted as an indication military action against Cuba is probable."[11]

Next, the National Security Council [NSC] "agreed that the United States should not undertake military intervention in Cuba now, but should do nothing that would foreclose the possibility of military action in the future." The NSC also named White House aide Richard Goodwin to head a Cuba Task Force.[12]

The Cuba debate, led by Goodwin's task force, received substantial input from Bobby Kennedy, who by now was aggressively involved in the Cuba problem. Low-level covert operations continued, including assistance to the Cuban underground, pretty much on automatic pilot throughout the summer of 1961. A detailed plan to overthrow Castro finally emerged in early November. Under the code name Operation Mongoose, all the relevant U.S. government departments and agencies—not only the CIA—were mobilized for the renewed anti-Castro campaign.

Reflecting his distrust of the CIA after the Bay of Pigs, President Kennedy named Brig. Gen. Edward Lansdale the Mongoose Operation chief. Lansdale, then working from the Pentagon, was a quirky and flamboyant officer with a reputation for expertise in counterinsurgency. Bill Harvey, almost as notorious as Lansdale in his own right, was to take charge of the CIA's Cuba Task Force under Mongoose. The president's ubiquitous brother, Bobby, took on the dual roles of attorney general and Mongoose czar. He made sure Cuba became the administration's highest priority.

Under Lansdale's grand scheme, everything that came under the Mongoose umbrella was to be done by the numbers, including Castro's fall the following October. The basic concept of the entire operation was to "bring about the revolt of the Cuban people. The revolt will overthrow the Communist regime and institute a new government with which the United States can live in peace."[13]

At the Pentagon, Operation Northwoods, apparently the code name for the Defense Department's slice of Mongoose, produced a flurry of sometimes-bizarre proposals designed to provide an excuse for deposing Castro.

Reading the documents some forty years later, it's difficult to see how grown men could have taken either Lansdale or Mongoose seriously. Yet, until November 1962, they constituted the Kennedy administration's Cuba policy. Mongoose culminated, not with the popular revolt Lansdale envisioned, but with resolution of the Cuban Missile Crisis.

The missile crisis and the end of Mongoose also brought an end to Cuba policy involvement by Lansdale and Harvey. As part of the crisis resolution, Kennedy secretly pledged that the United States would not invade Cuba, but there was no such restriction on the covert campaign against Castro.

Desmond FitzGerald, an elitist Ivy League veteran of the OSS [SP], took over the CIA's Cuba program, renaming it the Special Affairs Staff, or SAS. The CIA's operational activities (i.e., intelligence gathering, psychological warfare, underground support, and even sabotage) continued, much as they had under Mongoose and with no greater success.

This time Bobby Kennedy took direct charge of the war against Cuba, with the CIA as his principal operational weapon. The new program had no known code name, instead relying heavily on Bobby's philosophy to "let Cubans be Cubans." In addition to its own efforts, the CIA provided the intelligence, the logistical support, and the cash while Bobby provided the supervision for two selected exile organizations led by Manuel Artime and Manuel Ray. In the bureaucratic jargon of declassified documents, these organizations are known as the "Autonomous Groups."

The CIA's post-Mongoose program under FitzGerald also had an assassination component. As with the other assassination plots, no "smoking gun" has yet been found to show that either of the Kennedys was aware of it, but FitzGerald certainly was.

Ironically, while the administration was still trying to overthrow Castro, back-channel discussions were under way to normalize U.S.-Cuban relations, only to be abruptly interrupted by Kennedy's assassination. With Kennedy's death and Lyndon Johnson's swearing in, covert activities began to languish, although the so-called Autonomous Groups continued to operate. Exile frenzy surrounding the Ray and Artime ventures reached a crescendo as May 20, 1964, the anniversary of Cuban independence, approached. But nothing happened. With the Johnson administration showing little enthusiasm, covert activity—except for intelligence gathering—gradually sputtered to a halt over the next year or so.

In April 1965, Johnson—albeit under different circumstances—did what Kennedy had declined to do at the Bay of Pigs for fear of the wrath of the hemisphere. He ordered U.S. troops into the Dominican Republic, ostensibly to protect Americans and end the bloodshed of a civil war, but primarily to halt what Johnson viewed as the possibility of a Communist takeover of another Caribbean island nation.

CHAPTER 1

THE BEGINNINGS

By the autumn of 1959, less than a year after Fulgencio Batista fled into exile, it was clear that peaceful coexistence between Washington and Cuba was impossible. Fidel Castro's government had become increasingly and belligerently anti–United States. Any lingering doubts were erased by events of October: Castro announced the creation of the Revolutionary Armed Forces, headed by his brother, Raul. Huber Matos, a popular anti-Communist guerrilla commander, was arrested on charges of treason. Cuban Air Force Maj. Pedro Diaz Lanz, who had defected to Florida in July, returned for a clandestine leaflet drop over Havana, denouncing Castro as a Communist.

Despite deteriorating relations, debate continued in the United States as to whether Castro was a Communist and, if so, when had the transformation occurred from revolutionary to Marxist revolutionary? For some, like Earl E. T. Smith, a former U.S. ambassador to Cuba under Batista, there was no doubt that Castro had always been a Communist. Others, such as Herbert Matthews of the *New York Times*, saw him as a reformer, pushed into communism by U.S. pressures.

Both of these positions seem naive, based more on the ideological persuasions of their adherents than realistic appraisal. Declassified Soviet-era KGB documents show that Fidel's brother, Raul, joined the Communist Party in the early 1950s, while a student at the University of Havana, although Fidel didn't find out until 1962.[1] There was also little doubt about the Communist leanings of Argentina-born Ernesto "Che" Guevara, another Castro comrade who had been in Guatemala at the time of the 1954 Arbenz overthrow. But Fidel himself remained an ideological enigma well into the first year of his rule.

Fidel's transformation probably lies somewhere between the two ideological extremes, and is best explained by the more realistic assessments of Theodore Draper and Andres Suarez, two of the foremost students of the Cuban Revolution's early years. Both portray Castro, above all, as a calculating opportunist who became a Communist because it suited his purpose. And both saw the failure of the Bay of Pigs as an important watershed in furthering his purpose of imposing one-man rule. According to Draper,

> Once power came into his hands, he refused to permit anything that might lessen or restrict it. He would not tolerate the functioning of a government that was not a façade of his personal rule or of a party that might develop a life of its own. His power and his promises were from the first incompatible, and this contradiction forced him to seek a basis for his regime wholly at variance with that of the anti-Batista revolution. He did not have the disciplined and experienced cadres, the ideology, and the international support to switch revolutions in full view of the audience. Only the Cuban and Russian Communists could make them available to him.
>
> Only the ingenuous can still believe that Fidel Castro walked into a Communist trap or that he gave up the democratic road because the United States did not give him enough support in his early months in power. The Communists and Fidel walked toward each other, each with his eyes open, each filling a need in the other.[2]

Suarez offers a similar assessment.

> He [Castro] has changed his main ideas in accordance with circumstances: First he was a 'democrat,' then he was a 'humanist,' later he was a 'socialist' and at the moment he is a 'Marxist Leninist.' He has founded and dismantled organizations. But what he has never abandoned is his personal leadership and the stratagem to impose it, his weapons, and his handful of followers, devoid of ideology and education and with no known professional training, who first in the Sierra and later in the command posts of the Revolutionary Armed Forces . . . have carried out the constantly changing orders of their chief.[3]

In response to escalating tensions as 1959 progressed, Philip Bonsal, the U.S. ambassador in Havana, fired off an October 23 cable to the State Department, declaring the "situation here has deteriorated considerably past week." He cited Washington's attempt to block the British sale of jets to Cuba, possible punitive reduction of Cuba's sugar quota, and "alleged air bombings of Habana and other points in Cuba, by planes allegedly based in Florida. Intrinsic damaging effect these developments greatly inflated for present at least by hostile manner in which Castro has treated them in his TV appearances."[4]

11

At the end of October 1959, a program agreed on by the State Department and the CIA went forward to President Eisenhower, recommending approval to "support elements in Cuba opposed to the Castro Government while making Castro's downfall seem to be the result of his own mistakes." It gave birth to the first recorded covert action program against Cuba after Castro's seizure of control.[5]

In December 1959, the CIA prepared to activate a two-phase operation. The first phase called for recruitment of some thirty-five Cubans, "preferably with previous military experience, for an intensive training program which would qualify them to become instructors in various paramilitary skills, including leadership, sabotage, communications, etc."

In the second stage, the new instructors would train—in some Latin American country—a group of Cuban recruits "who would be organized into small teams similar to the U.S. Army Special Forces concept, and infiltrated with communicators, into areas where it had been determined numbers of dissidents existed who required specialized skills and leadership and military supplies."[6]

From this bare beginning emerged—after many twists and turns—the ill-fated April 1961 invasion of Cuba by a 1,500-member Cuban exile brigade; one funded, trained, and directed by the U.S. Central Intelligence Agency. When it was executed with such disastrous consequences three months into the Kennedy administration, it bore little resemblance to the far less ambitious covert action campaign officially approved by President Eisenhower on March 17, 1960, the more formal forerunner to the Bay of Pigs.

The controversial October 1961 CIA Inspector General's Report on the operation, declassified in 1998, read:

> Originally the heart of the plan was a long, slow clandestine build-up of guerrilla forces, to be trained and developed in Cuba by a cadre of Cubans whom the Agency would recruit, train and infiltrate into Cuba. But thirteen months later the Agency sponsored an overt assault-type landing of 1,500 combat-trained and heavily armed soldiers. Most of them were unversed in guerrilla warfare. They were expected to maintain themselves for a period of time (some said a week) sufficient to administer a 'shock' and thereby, it was hoped, to trigger an uprising.[7]

> Between the plan approved by President Eisenhower . . . and the invasion plan actually carried out on April 17, 1961 . . . there was a radical change in concept.

Throughout the shifting clandestine effort to rid the hemisphere of Castro, the one constant under both Eisenhower and Kennedy and the major reason for failure was the caveat of "plausible deniability." Maintaining the façade that the U.S. government was not involved became increasingly difficult as the plan moved from infiltration to invasion. To preserve the fiction of non-attribution, political decisions invariably took precedence over tactical ones when the two conflicted.

This meant that the brigade could not be trained in the United States; no U.S. air base could be used for overflights of Cuba to supply arms to agent teams nor logistical support to the brigade when it landed; no U.S. air base could be used for tactical air operations against Cuba; less sophisticated aircraft and weapons available on the open market had to be used; and the brigade landing site had to have an airstrip from which its B-26s could fly sorties against Cuban forces. It also resulted in the cancellation of air strikes against Castro's air force in conjunction with the brigade landing, another significant factor in the defeat. Finally, it meant the CIA had to cobble together and maintain the constantly squabbling Cuban exile leaders organized as a front for the operation, each of whom regarded himself as a future leader of the island.

The difficulties compounded on January 3, 1961, with the rupture of diplomatic relations between Washington and Havana. Loss of the embassy in Cuba deprived agency planners of a major source of on-the-ground intelligence and reduced contact with the internal resistance. The break in relations came during the uncertainty generated by the interregnum between John F. Kennedy's November 1960 presidential election victory and his inauguration on Janury 20, 1961.

A deteriorating relationship between the two countries had made diplomatic severance inevitable, the only uncertainty being when and why. Washington recalled Bonsal from Havana in late October 1960 for "extended consultations," effectively ending his tenure in Cuba. In mid-December, Daniel Braddock, the embassy chief in Bonsal's absence, sent a lengthy cable to Washington arguing the pros and cons of a diplomatic break. He concluded that relations should be "severed at the moment most advantageous for our purposes, and in any event not without prior consultation and coordination with friendly Latin American countries."[8] Washington agreed.

But an advantageous break wasn't to be. It came less than three weeks later, provoked by Castro's January 2, 1961, speech in which he demanded the United States reduce its embassy staff. Wayne Smith—then

13

a junior Foreign Service officer who later returned to Havana to head the diplomatic mission established under President Jimmy Carter—was monitoring from the embassy what had been a dull speech when, unexpectedly, Castro referred to the embassy as a "nest of spies," firing up the restless crowd. Invigorated by the audience response, Castro followed up with a demand that the embassy reduce its staff to eleven, the same number as the essentially nonfunctioning Cuban embassy had in Washington. U.S. embassy officials scrambled to determine whether the number included only accredited diplomats or support staff as well. When told the reduction order meant everybody, Washington decided the mission would no longer be able to function and broke relations the next day.

Smith wrote later that he was "convinced" the reference to a "nest of spies" was an "off-the-cuff remark, not a theme Castro intended to weave into his speech." But, with the crowd responding enthusiastically, Castro went further by demanding the embassy reduction.[9] Bonsal concurred. "I suspect," he wrote, "that Castro's demand was a notion that came to him while he was orating; once the words were out of his mouth he could not retreat. Nor did the United States, once it was determined that Castro meant what he said, have any choice other than to close the Embassy in Havana."[10]

These and other factors involved with the planning, execution, and defeat at the Bay of Pigs have been recounted in detail in scores of books, articles, and declassified documents in the intervening years. The late Peter Wyden's *Bay of Pigs: The Untold Story,* published in 1979, remains the most thorough and authoritative account of the many treatises available. Among declassified documents, the most comprehensive are the scathing *Inspector General's Survey of the Cuban Operation, October 1961,* compiled by Lyman Kirkpatrick, the CIA's inspector general at the time, and the so-called Taylor Commission report, the product of a probe ordered by President Kennedy to dissect the invasion's failure. Headed by Gen. Maxwell Taylor, the president's military adviser, the Taylor Commission included CIA Director Allen Dulles, Adm. Arleigh Burke, and Attorney General Robert Kennedy.

Less chronicled is how a guerrilla operation evolved over thirteen agonizing months into an invasion at the Bay of Pigs. The frustrations of the two professionals most directly responsible for planning the operation grew accordingly during those months amid the ever-changing political ground rules imposed for the sake of "plausible deniability." The roles of Jake Esterline and Jack Hawkins—the project chief and chief of the paramilitary staff, respectively—have been largely lost in the historical debate over the search to place blame. Also lost are accounts of their failed last-ditch effort to cancel the invasion.

Esterline was a veteran CIA officer and the Cuba Task Force chief largely responsible for drafting the March 17, 1960, plan approved by Eisenhower. Hawkins, a Marine colonel, was brought in during the late summer of 1960 as the paramilitary chief when the project began its metamorphosis from a simple guerrilla operation to a much more complex amphibious invasion. Both Esterline and Hawkins were eminently qualified for their jobs, and while both had strong personalities, they got along well together. As greater details became known in later years, both came to view Richard Bissell, the CIA's brainy, egocentric, ambitious, and secretive chief of clandestine operations as among those most responsible for the operation's failure.

Jacob D. "Jake" Esterline, a.k.a. Jake Engler, became a spy more by accident than by design. A gruff country boy who grew up near Lewistown, in rural south central Pennsylvania, he at various times considered careers as an accountant, a lawyer, and a baritone singer. Enrolled as an accounting student at Philadelphia's Temple University in 1938, he left college for World War II before he finished his degree and wound up with a second lieutenant's commission from Officer Candidate School at Fort Benning, Georgia. He and several classmates were recruited by the Office of Strategic Services, precursor to the Central Intelligence Agency, and sent to Washington's Congressional Country Club where the OSS did its training.

A three-month training course completed, Esterline was sent to India in early 1943. He was then infiltrated into Burma to train Burmese guerrillas in an effort to stop the advancing Japanese army. After returning to Calcutta for leave time, he parachuted into the China–Burma border area, taking command of a Burmese guerrilla unit. The war over, Esterline returned home, took a reserve commission in the U.S. Army, and finished his accounting degree from Temple. He then took dual jobs at a family law firm in northern Pennsylvania, where he was a taxman, and at a local corporation. His plan was to become a country lawyer and accountant.

Again war interrupted, this time in Korea. Recalled by the military he chose, instead, to take up a standing offer with the recently minted Central Intelligence Agency, for which he had been recommended by his OSS commanding officer. After initial CIA training, he was assigned as the first chief instructor at the agency's guerrilla warfare school at Fort Benning. Nine months later, in late 1952, he was transferred as chief of training to the CIA's new super-secret training center, known as The Farm, near Williamsburg, Virginia.

Given his World War II guerrilla bonafides, Esterline caught the eye of Col. J. C. King, a former army officer and FBI agent who had worked in Latin America and headed the CIA's Western Hemisphere covert operations. Guatemala was becoming a problem, and the Eisenhower administration had selected the CIA to do something about leftist president Jacobo Arbenz, who seemed to be moving the country toward communism. Esterline was named to head the Washington task force on the Guatemala problem. With the CIA secretly orchestrating the show, a coup led by Carlos Castillo Armas ousted the Arbenz government in June 1954. Castillo, a renegade Guatemalan colonel, was installed as the new president.

Three months later Esterline became CIA station chief in Guatemala, a post he held until 1957. He then transferred to Caracas as chief of the CIA's Venezuela station, where he was to witness Castro's mass appeal firsthand during the Cuban leader's initial trip abroad in March 1959. Thousands of Venezuelans turned out to greet the bearded revolutionary as the reincarnation of Simón Bolívar.

Frank Wisner, Esterline's old CIA boss and friend from the Guatemala operation, stopped by Caracas en route to a conference in Rio later the same year. Esterline recounted that Wisner asked if "I would be interested in getting back into harness, as he put it in our conversation, in connection with an operation against Cuba. I told him at the time I would certainly think about it."

Subsequently, Colonel King, still chief of covert action for the CIA's Western Hemisphere Division, contacted Esterline about a return to CIA headquarters in Washington "to begin to form a task force that would come to grips with the Cuban situation." Esterline accepted. He ended his tour in Caracas in December 1959, a year early, taking leave time in the U.S. Virgin Islands. He returned to Washington in January 1960, becoming head of the newly created WH/4 Task Force for Cuba within the CIA's Western Hemisphere Division.[11]

Jack Hawkins joined the project eight months later, September 1, 1960, at a time when the original concept of a guerrilla-type operation to mobilize internal resistance was evolving into one that would include a small "strike force." A request had gone to the Marine Corps for an officer

16

experienced in amphibious warfare. Gen. David M. Shoup, the Marine Corps commandant, personally selected Hawkins. He was assigned as chief of the paramilitary staff, a post for which he had impeccable credentials. His military experience included both guerrilla and amphibious operations.

Hawkins was born in tiny Roxton, Texas, in 1920, and his family moved to Ft. Worth where he graduated from high school in 1933. He went on to the U.S. Naval Academy, graduating in 1939 as a Marine second lieutenant. After a stint at the Marine Corps Basic School for Officers, he was ordered to China, where he served with the Fourth Marines in Shanghai. The regiment moved to the Philippines shortly before the Japanese attacked Pearl Harbor.

By then a first lieutenant, Hawkins fought the Japanese at Bataan and Corregidor before his capture in May 1942. He spent nearly eleven months in a Japanese prisoner-of-war camp on Mindanao before he and several companions escaped. After a tortuous trek through the jungles, they made contact with, and joined, a Philippine guerrilla force operating on the island. Their prison escape brought the first news to the outside world of the atrocities committed by the Japanese against American and Filipino prisoners, which resulted in thousands of deaths. Hawkins spent seven more months on Mindanao as a guerrilla leader before being taken to Australia by a U.S. submarine. He detailed the gripping account of his capture, imprisonment, escape, and guerrilla campaign in his book *Never Say Die*, published in 1961.

Hawkins had considerable experience—both practical and theoretical—in amphibious operations like the Bay of Pigs. He also took a senior course in 1944 at the Marine Corps Schools and, from 1950 to 1954, was an instructor for the same course. In 1959–60, as a student at the Naval War College, he wrote a thesis on the future of amphibious warfare.

During World War II, as a lieutenant colonel and assistant operations officer in the First Marine Division, he was directly involved in planning the 1945 amphibious landing in Okinawa. Again, in 1950, as a battalion commander, Hawkins planned the battalion landing plan at Inchon, South Korea, and the eventual capture of Seoul. Contrary to some accounts, Hawkins did not participate in the Iwo Jima operation.

Between World War II and the Korean War, he served three years in Venezuela as adviser to the Venezuelan Marine Corps before returning to Camp Lejeune, North Carolina, and then Korea. Promoted to full colonel in 1955, he gained still further amphibious experience with the Commander Amphibious Forces, Atlantic, at Little Creek, Virginia.

After graduating from the Naval War College in 1960, he was assigned to the staff of the Marine Corps Schools, Quantico, Virginia, for three years, a tour interrupted by his temporary assignment to the Cuba Task Force.[12]

Among the decorations awarded Hawkins during his active duty career were the Distinguished Service Cross, the Silver Star Medal, the Bronze Star Medal with Combat V, and the Navy Commendation Medal with Combat V. There are those, Esterline among them, who believed that had it not been for the Bay of Pigs, Hawkins would have become a general and perhaps Marine Corps commandant.

Hawkins refused all public comment on the Bay of Pigs until 1996, the same year he and Esterline renewed contact for the first time since 1961. If there is a flaw in Wyden's otherwise excellent book on the Bay of Pigs, it is his obvious pique with Hawkins for refusing to discuss the operation, which is reflected in several gratuitous comments in the book regarding Hawkins and a list at the end entitled "The People Who Made This Book." The list concludes with "some who could have helped chose not to do so. They had their reasons." The three so identified include "Colonel Jack Hawkins [who] refused to discuss any aspects of his role as the military commander and then carefully informed the CIA that he had done so." The other two are Jose "Pepe" Perez-San Roman, the Cuban brigade commander who later committed suicide, and "The CIA bureaucracy of the present."[13]

Richard Bissell, head honcho of the Cuba Project for the CIA, was known by colleagues as "the smartest man in Washington." Few would refute this description. Lyman Kirkpatrick, who was to become a bitter Bissell adversary within the agency, once cited him as one of the most brilliant individuals ever to serve in intelligence. Among the Ivy League elitists who dominated the CIA in its early years, Bissell's best-known career achievement was overseeing development of the U-2 reconnaissance aircraft.

Prior to that, he had worked with Averill Harriman in implementing the Marshall Plan for Europe; served as deputy administrator of the European Cooperation Act; been with the Ford Foundation, simultaneously serving with a group of CIA consultants who met regularly at Princeton University; taught at the Massachusetts Institute of Technology; and been a member of the American Delegation to the postwar Yalta and Potsdam summit conferences that brought together Roosevelt, Churchill, and Stalin. However, his resume contained no military experience or experience as a field operative.

Bissell joined the CIA in 1954 as special assistant to Director Allen Dulles. In that role he became involved with PBSUCCESS, the covert operation that brought about the ouster of Arbenz in Guatemala. In late 1958, Dulles named him chief of the CIA's clandestine service, succeeding Frank Wisner and beating out Richard Helms for the job.

As clandestine service chief, he became entangled in unsuccessful assassination plots against the Congo's Patrice Lumumba and Castro. More importantly, he was Esterline's and Hawkins's immediate superior in what became the Bay of Pigs disaster, a project tightly held and controlled by Bissell. Esterline and Hawkins later complained that Bissell made, or agreed to make, changes without advising either of his two top subordinates responsible for planning and executing the project. The Bay of Pigs failure cost Bissell the post of CIA director—a position he had been promised by John F. Kennedy.[14]

Both Esterline and Hawkins came to believe that Bissell, in his desire to push ahead with the Bay of Pigs at all costs, failed to express their concerns about the operation in its late stages to either CIA Director Allen Dulles or President Kennedy. Said Esterline: "I don't think he was being honest. I don't think he was being honest up—I mean with Kennedy and maybe with Dulles too; and I don't think he was being honest down—in dealing with his two principal aides, Esterline and Hawkins. I don't believe he was leveling with us."[15]

"By the time I got back to Washington it was pretty damn clear in my mind what had to be involved in any kind of operation against Cuba and Castro, regardless of who did it," Esterline recalled many years later. "To that end, under instructions of my longtime boss, J. C. King, I put together a first basic plan which suggested a few lines of action that should be very carefully adhered to if we were to avoid any kind of real disaster in Cuba."[16]

One of the first priorities, according to Esterline, was to increase the intelligence available in areas outside and inside Cuba, including intelligence concerning whether there was "any significant anti-Castro group, and, if so, how viable were they; how capable they would be of defending themselves against what was becoming an ever-increasing, Soviet-style overrunning of the countryside. We knew from the very beginning that the only thing we could hope to do in and around Havana was to try and create good agents and sources who could give us reporting on what the government might be doing in terms of possible Soviet support."

He also knew from his guerrilla experience in the Far East "what the conditions have to be to survive and . . . whether we can put people some-place in Cuba to see if they can survive for one month, three months, six months, become active and still survive. That's paramount."

King accepted Esterline's ideas "and from that I developed what became the Trinidad Plan where I thought maybe we could test the water . . . [but] I vowed when I accepted this assignment that I would not let myself get put into a situation in which we would get into a disaster. And yet that's exactly what we moved into and I was too stupid to say to Mr. Bissell, 'Sorry Sir, I'm not your man. Get somebody else.'"

Development of the Trinidad Plan began with the search for new recruits in addition to those already available, particularly, Esterline said,

> people who were well motivated, tied in [to the island] and who had the gumption to come out, be trained, and go back in. In that time period, before diplomatic relations had been broken, we still had a station in Cuba. We were able to move with more flexibility in these kinds of things. We began to develop the cadres that we would train very well in the United States, then put into [the area around Trinidad] and task them with things to do and see whether they could survive; if there was enough goodwill and spirit among the people there to allow us to do something like that.
>
> We had no idea at that point whether Cuba was so totally lost to our control or whether there was still a chance. In retrospect, I believe our plan was pretty sound. That will never be proved one way or the other because the plan was taken away from us before it ever had a chance to evolve by Bissell's decision to go for more, much more, and create an invasion force.

The reason the Trinidad area had been selected for the original plan, said Esterline, is that an operation could be mounted there and, "if it hadn't succeeded it would have looked like just one more exile effort to do something that didn't work. It wouldn't have become a national disaster."[17]

The Trinidad Plan emerged as part of *A Plan of Covert Action Against Cuba,* which Esterline began drafting when the CIA's Cuba Task Force was created on January 18, 1960. The plan became official policy on March 17, 1960, when President Eisenhower approved it. And, as Hawkins noted in his May 5, 1961, after-action report, written for the Clandestine Services Historical Board, it was the only written policy directive ever approved "throughout the life of the project [culminating with the Bay of Pigs] . . . at the national level to guide the project . . . and it was general in content."[18]

Its basic components were:

- formation of a Cuban exile organization to attract Cuban loyalties, to direct opposition activities, and to provide cover for agency operations
- a propaganda offensive in the name of the opposition
- creation inside Cuba of a clandestine intelligence collection and action apparatus to be responsible to the direction of the exile organization
- development outside Cuba of a small paramilitary force to be introduced into Cuba to organize, train, and lead resistance groups.

The initial staffing chart for the Cuba Task Force—known as WH/4 within the agency's Western Hemisphere Division—called for forty people, including eighteen in Washington, twenty at the Havana Station, and two in Santiago, at Cuba's eastern tip. By April 16, 1961, the Task Force had been "expanded to 588 . . . becoming one of the largest branches in the Clandestine Services, larger than some divisions."[19]

The task force total did not include air operations personnel who reported directly to Bissell, another source of ongoing frustration for Esterline and Hawkins. They had to go through Bissell to incorporate air activity into their planning.

By the end of June 1960, a Miami Base had been opened; a civilian exile front organization, the Democratic Revolutionary Front (FRD) had been formed; Radio Swan, the clandestine propaganda station, was on the air; and twenty-nine Cubans arrived in Panama for training in small unit infiltration.

A task force briefing paper prepared separately in August for the president and the Joint Chiefs of Staff estimated that by November 1, 1960, there were expected to be "500 paramilitary trainees and 37 radio operators ready for action. It was expected that this group would be available for use as infiltration teams or as an invasion force." But it also made the point to the Joint Chiefs that "obviously the successful implementation of any large-scale paramilitary operations is dependent upon widespread guerrilla resistance throughout the area."

The briefing paper outlined the plan of operations:

The initial phase of paramilitary operations envisages the development, support and guidance of dissident groups in three areas of Cuba: Pinar del Rio, Escambray and Sierra Maestra. These groups will be organized for concerted guerrilla action against the regime.

The second phase will be initiated by a combined sea-air assault by FRD forces on the Isle of Pines coordinated with general guerrilla activity on the main island of Cuba. This will establish a close-in staging base for future operations.

The last phase will be air assault on the Havana area with the guerrilla forces in Cuba moving on the ground from these areas into the Havana area also.[20]

When the document was approved, says the Taylor Commission report, "It is apparent . . . the concept of paramilitary action was limited to the recruitment of a cadre of leaders and the training of a number of paramilitary cadres for subsequent use as guerrillas in Cuba."

There are no precise dates for when the guerrilla/internal resistance concept, originally drafted by Esterline as the Trinidad Plan, became a guerrilla operation with a strike force and then an invasion plan. According to the Taylor Commission, "sometime in the summer of 1960 the paramilitary concept for the operation began to change. It appears that leaders in the CIA Task Force . . . were the first to entertain the thought of a Cuban strike force to land on the Cuban coast in supplementation of the guerrilla action contemplated." The first thought was to create a 200- to 300-man infantry force for "contingency deployment with other paramilitary operations."[21]

The Trinidad area—on the south coast of Cuba below the Escambray Mountains where indigenous Cuban guerrillas were active—remained the preferred landing site throughout the changing concepts. The operation was referred to as the Trinidad Plan until President Kennedy ordered a change in March 1961, to make it "less spectacular." It is apparent, however, that the concept already was beginning to change, with Bissell as the principal architect, when Hawkins joined the task force in September 1960.

In early November 1960, according to the Taylor Commission's postmortem, a cable went from the CIA in Washington to the project officer in Guatemala directing "a reduction of the guerrilla teams in training to 60 men and introduction of conventional training for the remainder as an amphibious and airborne assault force. From that time on, the training emphasis was placed on the assault mission and there is no evidence that the members of the assault force received any further preparation for guerrilla-type operations."[22]

Hawkins, in his after-action report, noted:

Action was begun on 4 November 1960, to recruit, organize, equip and train a larger ground force than the small 200 to 300 men contingency force originally contemplated. It was planned at the time that this force would reach strength of about 1,500. As this 'Strike Force,' as it came to be known, was developed over the ensuing months, many difficulties were encountered as a result of slowness in recruiting, political bickering among Cuban exile groups, lack of adequate training facilities and personnel, uncertainties with regard to whether Guatemala could continue to be used as a base, and lack of approved national policy on such questions as to what size force was desired, where and how it was to be trained, and whether such a force was actually ever to be employed.[23]

"From that time on," according to the Taylor Commission, "the training emphasis was placed on the assault mission and there is no evidence that the members of the assault force received any further preparation for guerrilla-type operations. The men became deeply imbued with the importance of the landing operation and its superiority over any form of guerrilla action to the point where it would have been difficult later to persuade them to return to a guerrilla-type mission."[24]

Bissell wrote in his memoirs, *Reflections of a Cold Warrior*, of growing problems with guerrilla infiltrations; squabbles within the exile community and the front organization itself; increasing repression by the Castro government; declining propaganda effectiveness and other difficulties.[25]

As a result, according to Bissell, in late 1960 the initial covert action program approved by Eisenhower "underwent a metamorphosis . . . [and] our reliance shifted to the invasion force being trained in Guatemala." Bissell said he discussed it with Jack Hawkins, telling him that the five hundred in training would have to be expanded by another one thousand to fifteen hundred but "Hawkins appeared not to share my sense of urgency about a further buildup."

Shortly after, Hawkins laid out clearly in a lengthy and prophetic January 4, 1961, memorandum what he believed necessary to assure success of an invasion. It was addressed to Esterline under the subject: "Policy

Decisions Required for Conduct of Strike Operations Against Government of Cuba."[26]

Among the decisions required, said Hawkins, was one by the incoming president, Kennedy, on whether he concurred with the operation and its timing. If approved, Hawkins recommended it take place before March 1, 1961, citing as reasons: (1) pressures on the Guatemala government over training there; (2) Cuban trainees in the camps were "becoming restive and if not committed to action soon there will probably be a general lowering of morale" and even "large-scale desertions . . . with attendant possibilities of surfacing the entire program"; (3) time was working against the operation in a military sense with Cuban pilots being trained in Czechoslovakia as part of a military buildup with arms and equipment from Soviet Bloc countries; and (4) Cuban government progress in turning the island into a Communist-style police state.

Perhaps the most significant and prescient topic Hawkins raised related to air support. "The question has been raised in some quarters," he wrote, "as to whether amphibious/airborne operation could not be mounted without tactical air preparation or support or with minimal air support. It is axiomatic in amphibious operations that control of the air and sea in the objective area is absolutely required."

He recommended "(1) that the air preparation commence not later than dawn of D minus 1 day; (2) that any move to curtail the number of aircraft to be employed from those available be firmly resisted; (3) that the operation be abandoned if policy does not provide for use of adequate tactical air support."

When Hawkins read from his memorandum before the Taylor Commission's postmortem, CIA Director Allen Dulles asked "what disposition" had been made of it. Hawkins replied that it was sent to Esterline, who said he had directed it "to higher authority." General Taylor then asked Esterline to identify "higher authority." Esterline said the paper went to J. C. King, Bissell, and Tracy Barnes, Bissell's deputy. Bissell, in the same set of questioning, responded that the paper "did not go much further than his [Bissell's] office." Bissell offered no indication of what attention he might have given it, but it was evident from the context of the testimony that the Hawkins memo went to no one of any "higher authority" than Bissell himself.[27]

As the project evolved in late 1960 and early 1961, Esterline and Hawkins moved to accommodate both the ever-changing demands of the operation and the change in the presidency. But they did so without knowledge of Richard Bissell's "magic bullet": a plot, in collusion with the Mafia, to assassinate Fidel Castro.

Esterline became peripherally aware of the assassination attempt in late 1960, but only because, as the task force chief, he was responsible for the Cuba Project's budget. It wasn't until many years later that he concluded Bissell's assassination plan was linked to the Bay of Pigs. He did not tell Hawkins what he had learned about the assassination plot until after the invasion failed.

Given his accounting background, he was meticulous in keeping track of where funds went. "We were never wanting for money, but we tried to be careful and abstemious about how we spent it. I was always a dog on that." If it hadn't been for that financial "doggedness," it's unlikely he would have known that Bissell was pursuing a two-track policy against Castro: one track of which included the assassination plot involving the Mafia.

Sometime in the fall of 1960 Esterline received a mysterious request "for a large amount of money. . . . It could have been $50,000 or $150,000, I just don't remember. But it was a big amount, way above what would normally be signed off on . . . without questioning." The request came from J. C. King, who had been marginalized from the Cuba Project by Dulles and Bissell.

"I looked at it and I thought, 'no way. I'm not going to sign this,'" said Esterline. He sent the request back to King. "I got it back from him in due course and he said this is one you have to sign and do it promptly, because we need the money. I called him and said, 'J.C., I'm not going to sign this thing. If it's something you can't tell me about, then you better get somebody here that you can tell about it.'"

King said he would get back to Esterline, which he did within the next day or so. King said he had gotten clearance to tell Esterline, but he could not tell anyone else. "And what he briefed me on . . . really couldn't believe I was hearing it," Esterline said.[28] What he heard were the broad outlines of an assassination plot against Castro, involving the Mafia, for which Esterline eventually signed over about $200,000.

After he became CIA director, Richard Helms ordered the agency's inspector general to do a report on CIA involvement in assassinations. Declassified in 1993, it noted that the "first seriously-pursued CIA plan to assassinate Castro had its inception in August 1960. It involved the use of members of the criminal underworld with contacts inside Cuba."

The report added: "Richard Bissell, Deputy Director for Plans, asked

Sheffield Edwards, Director of Security, if Edwards could establish contact with the U.S. gambling syndicate that was active in Cuba. The objective clearly was the assassination of Castro, although Edwards claims that there was a studied avoidance of the term in his conversation with Bissell. Bissell recalls that the idea originated with J. C. King, then Chief of WH Division, although King now recalls having had only limited knowledge of such a plan and at a much later date—about mid-1962."[29] Esterline's account of his conversation with King belies King's claim of when he became aware of the plot.

The various accounts agree on the plot's details. They consisted of a plan for the Mafia, financed by the CIA, to poison Castro with a lethal pill, also provided by the CIA, and passed by the Mafia to underworld contacts in Cuba. Two separate attempts were aborted, and the plot was abandoned shortly after the Bay of Pigs failed.

Four decades later, however, it is still disputed as to who originated the Mafia-linked plot and how directly it was linked to the Bay of Pigs invasion. Bissell, the key figure who died in 1994, gave widely varying answers at different times to both questions, although the preponderance of evidence indicates that the plot originated with him and that it was linked to the Bay of Pigs invasion.

The CIA inspector general's 1967 report on assassinations said, "the plots that were hatched in late 1960 and early 1961 were aggressively pursued and were viewed by at least some of the participants as being merely one aspect of the over-all active effort to overthrow the regime that culminated in the Bay of Pigs."

Bissell, in his memoirs, wrote that as brigade plans advanced "I hoped the Mafia would achieve success. My philosophy during my last two or three years in the agency was very definitely that the end justified the means."[30] But historian Michael R. Beschloss wrote in 1985 that "Richard Bissell said years later that Track Two was 'intended to parallel' the invasion preparations: 'Assassination was intended to reinforce the plan. There was the thought that Castro would be dead before the landing.' If Castro were killed, Bissell said, 'it could have made Track One' either unnecessary or much easier."[31]

As for who originated the assassination plot, Bissell was quoted in a 1975 interview with CIA historian Jack Pfeiffer as saying that "I remember an initial session with [Shef] Edwards, I don't know who originally had the notion that it might be possible to work through, or in some way with, or in a supporting role with the Mafia. Shef apparently did bring this idea to me to the best of my recollection."[32]

In his memoirs, Bissell offered a slightly different version, saying again that he thought he first heard about the Mafia assassination plan from Edwards, adding that the plot did not originate with him and "I had no desire to become personally involved in its implementation."[33]

Edwards, in a Memorandum for the Record, dated May 14, 1962, and prepared at the request of Attorney General Robert Kennedy, said categorically that in August 1960 he "was approached by Mr. Richard Bissell then Deputy Director for Plans at CIA to explore mounting this sensitive operation against Fidel Castro." Edwards then described the evolution of the assassination plot.[34]

"There's no question about it. If that whole specter of an assassination using the Mafia hadn't been on the horizon, there would have been more preparation [for the invasion]," Esterline concluded. "If Bissell and others hadn't felt they had that magic bullet I don't think we would have had all the hair-splitting over air support."

In briefing him about the assassination plot, Esterline said, King had told him "this is so sensitive, so hush, hush . . . you dare not brief Dick Bissell on this because he's not cleared. I looked at him and I said, 'how can that be? I work for him directly. . . . This is a hell of a mess. How am I supposed to work in good faith with a man and not tell him?' He said 'well, you have to do it.' I didn't discuss it with Bissell. As time went on, I was pretty damn sure that Bissell was not being straight with us on a number of things." After he forced King to tell him the outlines of the plot, Esterline said he got a fuller briefing from Edwards.

It wasn't until many years later that Esterline said he discovered what he believed to be the truth: "I was concerned about not being honest with him [Bissell], but the sonofagun . . . was one of the architects of the whole damn thing. And he wanted it to look that way to me, I presume, because he thought . . . that if I thought they had some magic bullet they would not properly support those valiant Cubans . . . we were sending to Cuba. And that certainly was Hawkins's reaction when he found out sometime later, after the invasion."[35]

President Kennedy took office January 20, 1961. Eisenhower had broken diplomatic relations seventeen days earlier. Preparations for the Cuba Project continued, although Kennedy would not give a final go-head until early April, even then reserving the right to call it off up until the day before. Meanwhile, much to and fro on details—many related to "plausible deniability"—continued between agency planners and the State Department, particularly with Dean Rusk, the new secretary of state.

It was in one of these meetings, said Esterline, that "I shot myself in the foot," getting banned by Bissell from attending further sessions after insulting Secretary Rusk. As Esterline later described it, the problem related to the airstrip in the Trinidad area, which had significant impact on the so-called Trinidad Plan that was then still viable. There had been a dispute between Esterline/Hawkins and Bissell over the fact that the air section of the Cuba Project, headed by Col. Stan Beerli, who had worked with Bissell on the U-2 project, was not only in a separate building from the task force but also kept under Bissell's direct control.

The Cuba Task Force, from the beginning, had wanted B-25s for the exile air force as opposed to B-26s, because B-25s were much more flexible and reliable. Bissell and Beerli insisted on B-26s. When Esterline asked why, the response was, "because they're [the B-26s] more deniable"; the B-26s were more easily available on the open market. Esterline continued to object about the use of B-26s and the lack of task force control over the air section. But, as Esterline put it, he "was whistling in the dark every time I tried to do anything involving air . . . our exchanges got pretty vitriolic at various points . . . and I am sure Beerli hated my guts . . . but there wasn't a damn thing we could do about it because we had no control of air and they chose to ignore us."

"The coup de grace, certainly for the Trinidad Plan," said Esterline, "came when our air people advised the State Department . . . that the airstrip at Trinidad" was 100 to 200 feet too short for the B-26s, even though it initially had been believed able to accommodate them. "I'm not sure how much too short, but that immediately put the whole Trinidad Plan in question which was the basis for my development of the program [of] 'testing' and avoid disaster." As originally conceived by Esterline, he saw the more modest Trinidad Plan of infiltration and guerrilla buildup as one that would "test" the situation in terms of survival and expansion, without the risk an assault such as the Bay of Pigs entailed.

At a subsequent meeting with Rusk, Esterline said he

was trying to defend the B-26s, because I had already lost the battle on B-25s. I said that we had to have a potential airport and Trinidad was the only place that had one that really was good enough and was viable for guerrilla warfare. And the Secretary [Rusk] said to me, 'well, if your airstrip isn't long enough why don't you clandestinely airdrop bulldozers and lengthen it?' I lost my cool. I said, 'Mr. Secretary, if I made a suggestion like that to Mr. Dulles he should summarily fire me, because, hell, we don't even know whether we can survive there in terms of putting people on the island. How in the world could we drop bulldozers in and lengthen an airstrip?' Needless to say, we lost the argument and we lost the airstrip and the Trinidad Plan went out the window. And that's the point that Jake Esterline should have asked for reassignment. But I didn't.

Then, said Esterline, Bissell advised him that "Mr. Dulles said I was no longer to attend any high level meetings in the State Department or the White House because I was just too blunt and brusque in my dealings with people at that level. Therefore, Hawkins would attend in my place. Mad as it made me, I had to accept that because I had been rude to the Secretary of State when he goaded me into losing my temper about the bulldozer episode." It occurred to him many years later, Esterline said, that it wasn't Dulles who banned him from the meetings, but it was Bissell in "another one of his lies. . . . He didn't want my strident voice there because he knew he couldn't control me the way he was able to control Hawkins or any of his other military people, because he controlled their efficiency reports." At the same time, concluded Esterline, "at some point during this period, perhaps even before the selection of the Bay of Pigs, [Bissell] had already made an agreement with the President that he never thought to tell anybody about . . . that this operation would be low-keyed, would not use excessive air power."

Sidelined by Bissell, said Esterline, he took himself out of the day-to-day planning, concentrating instead on administrative and other projects, but kept himself available to Hawkins for any help needed in developing the plan.[36] Esterline said he and Bissell never spoke after the Bay of Pigs. Bissell mentions Esterline once, and only in passing, in the fifty-two pages of his memoirs dedicated to the Bay of Pigs.

Even though he had been taken out of the high-level planning sessions, in early March 1961, Esterline was dispatched on an unprecedented visit to Guatemala to pacify President Miguel Ydigoras Fuentes, who was under increasing pressure related to the Cuban brigade training in the country.

When the project got under way, said Esterline, an oral agreement was made with Ydigoras "to handle all this training in Guatemala which he was understandably very nervous about." As the brigade grew bigger and stayed longer than anticipated, added Esterline, "it was becoming a real problem and he would just not deal with the ambassador. He wanted a representative of the State Department to come down. He was afraid the thing was going to blow on these 1,500 to 2,000 Cubans who at the time we had training there. And he damned well wanted a piece of paper to protect him with the international community."

The State Department didn't want anything to do with it. Esterline, who had served in Guatemala earlier as CIA station chief, was a known quantity to Ydigoras, although neither knew the other personally. Esterline was asked to go and, in effect, execute a status of forces agreement with Ydigoras. He got the agreement, saying to Ydigoras, "I hope this thing won't become a public issue, this thing we're signing, in the next year or so. He looked at me and said, 'Mr. Esterline, Jacobo, if this thing surfaces it won't be Ydigoras Fuentes in Guatemala. It will be you, or more likely, some of your friends up there in Washington.' I thanked him, took my paper, duly boarded the plane and returned to Washington to find that we had a whole new ballgame."[37]

CHAPTER 2

EVOLUTION OF A DISASTER

Returning to Washington from his mission to pacify Guatemalan president Miguel Ydigoras, Esterline found yet another major alteration of his original design for a covert operation, one that brought a major change in its dynamics. The plan already had evolved from a guerrilla infiltration to an amphibious invasion, and Bissell had marginalized him in the process. Now the landing site had shifted from Trinidad to the Bay of Pigs, upon President Kennedy's order made under pressure from the State Department to find a "less spectacular" locale that would better mask U.S. involvement.

Esterline said the old Cuba and Latin America hands on the task force were

> in a state of shock because of the choice the paramilitary staff had made. I must say, though, that the paramilitary staff made the only choice they could. . . . It was the only airport that could handle B-26s and, unfortunately, it was called the *Bahia de Cochinos* [Bay of Pigs], and was located in a damn swamp. The old Cuba hands were upset because they couldn't understand how any kind of guerrilla warfare could be fought in a swamp. Although it might be protected from Castro, it made it almost impossible to break out of the swamp and get to the Escambray Mountains, a couple of days or more to the east. But that was the decision that had to be because of the damn B-26s. And Dave Phillips [head of the project's propaganda section] hit it right when he said 'how can you expect to have an operation succeed when it's called the Bay of Pigs?'[1]

To meet the new criteria imposed on the operation, Hawkins and his staff worked around the clock for three days, poring over maps of Cuba in search of a suitable site: a less populated area, in which a landing strip for exile air sorties against Cuban defenders could be seized by the brigade on the first day of the operation. They came up with several possibilities, but the only plausible alternative was the Bay of Pigs, still on the island's south coast but eighty miles to the west of Trinidad, on the swamp-filled Zapata Peninsula. Once the new site was selected, they had to revise the plans. The new code name became Operation Zapata; the Pentagon, appropriately, called it Bumpy Road.

"As soon as I felt sure we would be able to finish them on schedule, I found time for serious thinking about whether a landing at the Bay of Pigs could accomplish the assigned mission of overthrowing the Castro government," Hawkins said. "My conclusion was that it could not. We could seize a beachhead and hold it for several days and possibly longer, but operations beyond the beachhead would not be possible."[2]

Hawkins shared his misgivings with Esterline, who had reached essentially the same conclusion. By then, it was Saturday afternoon, April 8, 1961, at Quarters Eye—the operation's headquarters on Ohio Avenue off the Mall in Washington—where the Cuba Project planning was under way.

"Jake said that we had to talk to Bissell immediately and persuade him to stop the operation," said Hawkins. "We learned that Bissell had already left and was at home. Jake telephoned him and made an appointment to meet at his home on the following morning; Sunday."

The next day, April 9, 1961, a sunny Sunday morning, Esterline and Hawkins drove together to Bissell's home in northwest Washington's Cleveland Park neighborhood. The subsequent three-hour meeting, which has never been fully recounted nor even acknowledged by Bissell, could have altered the course of history had Bissell heeded what they had to say.

At the request of the author for specifics on the meeting with Bissell, Hawkins provided a detailed account of his and Esterline's misgivings about the operation in a letter dated August 27, 2001. With Bissell and Esterline dead and nothing committed to paper, there is no way to know forty years later if—or how forcefully and in what detail—all the concerns cited by Hawkins were presented to Bissell. In general terms, however, Hawkins's account of the meeting is consistent with his own previous comments and Esterline's comments in a June 1995 interview with the author and in a now-declassified 1975 interview with CIA historian Jack Pfeiffer.

As Hawkins noted in his letter:

"Both Jake and I had war experience as infantry battalion commanders in extended combat and understood the capabilities of a reinforced infantry battalion, and also its limitations, in offensive combat, alone and unsupported, against larger enemy forces." The exile brigade, with its 1,500 men, a tank platoon, and heavy mortars was equivalent to a reinforced U.S. infantry battalion. On that basis, said Hawkins, he and Esterline concluded:

- The Brigade could not break out through the few narrow passages through the great swamp behind the beachhead. Castro would be able to prevent egress with his greatly superior numbers of troops, tanks and artillery.
- Even if the Brigade succeeded in breaking out, it would not be able to fight its way over 80 miles of flat, open country against Castro's much larger forces in order to reach the Escambray mountains. Only in these mountains could the Brigade survive for a long time, perhaps long enough to overthrow Castro.
- The Brigade could hold a beachhead behind the swamp for at least several days and possibly longer providing that Castro's fighters and bombers had been completely eliminated, but would be overwhelmed eventually by the larger forces opposing them.
- Since the Brigade could survive at the beachhead for only a limited time, it could not cause Castro's overthrow except in the unlikely event that large elements of Castro's armed forces would immediately turn against him.
- The 16 B-26 bombers of the exile air force and the limited number of Cuban exile pilots were inadequate to ensure complete destruction of Castro's fighters and bombers (about 16) in a single surprise attack on the three airfields where these aircraft were based.
- If any of Castro's fighters and bombers survived the first attack, they could defeat the landing by sinking the assault ships and maintaining control of the air over the beachhead. Surviving fighters would make further operations of our B-26 aircraft over the beachhead suicidal. They could also prevent aerial resupply of the landing force by cargo aircraft, essential for continued operations.
- A landing at the Bay of Pigs could not cause Castro's overthrow and would result in loss of the landing force within a short time after landing.[3]

And as Hawkins described the meeting with Bissell:

He ushered us into the living room where the three of us sat down and promptly entered into the business of our urgently arranged meeting. The atmosphere was calm, serious, polite and mutually respectful. There were no heated discussions, but opinions were firmly stated without reservation by us all. In all of my extensive dealings with Bissell I found him to be courteous and friendly, never abrupt, abrasive or overbearing.

Jake and I presented our conclusions about the upcoming operation. We recommended unequivocally that Bissell take immediate action to stop the operation. Both Jake and I said that if the operation was not to be stopped we wanted to resign from our duties since we did not want to take any further part in what we believed would be a terrible disaster.

Bissell did not attempt to refute our arguments about the military pitfalls of landing at the Bay of Pigs. He took the position, however, that it was too late to stop the operation and was adamant that it had to go forward. Although Jake and I both believed that Kennedy would welcome a recommendation from the CIA to cancel the Bay of Pigs landing, we did not argue the point with Bissell for he had already made it clear that he would not try to stop it.

Bissell did address the question we had raised about the inadequacy of the exile air force for eliminating all of Castro's aircraft in a single attack. He said that he would take the matter up with the president and believed that he could persuade him to allow a greater number of aircraft in the first strike.

He earnestly asked us not to abandon him at this late date, saying that there was no one to take our place. Jake and I reluctantly agreed, but Jake exacted a promise from him that he would take immediate action with the president to use more aircraft and increase the power of the attack on the opposing air force.

It was thirty-seven years later, said Hawkins, when he and Esterline learned from declassified documents—as the National Security Archive in Washington brought them together for the first time since the Bay of Pigs—that

Bissell promptly reneged on this solemn promise. Within the next two or three days he agreed with Kennedy to cut the attacking force in half, from 16 to 8 aircraft! He never informed us that he had agreed with the president to do this. We were allowed to believe that Kennedy had acted arbitrarily in making the cut when we were finally notified about it late in the afternoon on the day prior to the attack on the following morning.

I have never seen any written acknowledgement by Bissell that our urgent Sunday meeting took place, much less that Jake and I had tried to persuade him to stop the landing. I did note in a draft of his memoirs an admission that he had not given enough thought to the fact that moving the landing to the Bay of Pigs had eliminated the possibility of guerrilla warfare in the Escambray. That was one of the points we made with him at our meeting. I was informed a few years ago by Janet Weininger, daughter of one of our National Guard pilots killed in the Bay of Pigs action, that Bissell had said to her during a personal interview, 'I should have listened to Esterline and Hawkins.' I am sure he was remembering our Sunday meeting when he said that.[4]

In the presidential briefing memorandum dated April 12, 1961, referred to by Hawkins, Bissell said that "the plans for air operations have been modified for operations on a limited scale on D-2 and again on D-Day itself instead of placing reliance on a larger strike coordinated with the landings on D-Day."[5]

The air operations were apparently modified even more after that briefing paper was prepared. In his memoirs, Bissell wrote that on the Friday before the invasion, Kennedy gave "a fairly ambiguous instruction" to downplay the scope of the invasion with a more limited air strike than the one scheduled. "I was simply directed to reduce the scale and make it 'minimal.' He left it to me to determine exactly what that meant, and I responded by cutting the planned sixteen aircraft to eight."[6]

Wyden, in his 1979 book on the Bay of Pigs, offered a slightly different account for cutting back on the air operations, a decision he implied came after President Kennedy read that day's column by James "Scotty" Reston in the *New York Times*, imploring the public and administration to give greater consideration to the implications of an invasion of Cuba.

"In the White House," wrote Wyden, "Kennedy picked up the phone and called Bissell. He said the Saturday air strikes could go forward. Then, 'almost as an afterthought,' he asked how many aircraft would participate." When Bissell told him sixteen, Kennedy said "minimal," without specifying a number. "That was left to Bissell, who thought the informality of this decision-making was 'rather odd,' especially after all the 'agonizing' weeks of hassle in the Cabinet Room. He did not question the President's decision. He was too pleased to hear that the strikes could go at all. That made it less likely than ever that the President might scrub the entire project. He passed the word to Stan Beerli: only six planes were to fly."[7]

The recollections by Esterline—who died in 1999—of the meeting with Bissell were less explicit than those of Hawkins as far as the specific concerns addressed and whether they recommended the operation be called off. But in his 1995 interview with the author, Esterline left the clear impression that he was doubtful about the operation's success.

"We were being emasculated in the critical hours of the Bay of Pigs and that's when Hawkins and I went to Bissell and said 'you better get somebody else. . . . We can't do what you're asking because there are too many things happening to us externally.' We made a bad mistake by not sticking to our guns and staying resigned. . . . We wanted out of the project. He [Bissell] needed different leadership. . . . Because of the way they kept limiting us and taking things away from us, we couldn't guarantee any success," said Esterline.

Esterline said he debated with himself

many times over the years. I've said to myself 'if we stuck with it, if we walked off the project . . . it would have gone on and they would have gotten somebody in there and it would have become a bigger mess.' I guess what Hawkins and I both felt was that if we had just been able to fight, if we had been able to learn several months earlier there were going to be these restrictions put on us, we would have gotten out in a gentlemanly manner and said 'we think you better use somebody else. We don't think that we're going to be able to do what you want.' But unfortunately we didn't have that luxury of time. We didn't discover the problems, the limitations we were going to have until it was too late to quit. You just can't walk away and leave the ship to sink.[8]

In his posthumously published memoirs, Bissell made no mention of the Sunday meeting with Esterline and Hawkins. In a 1975 interview, CIA historian Jack B. Pfeiffer asked Bissell directly: "Did Jake Esterline and Hawkins ever threaten to resign from the operation, to your knowledge?"

Bissell's response was evasive: "I have little doubt that both of them did at one time or another. I think that Jack Hawkins' moment of greatest unhappiness was when I didn't put Beerli [Air Section Chief] under him. I don't remember Jack ever saying that he flatly was going to resign, although it seems to me when I think back on it, that there may have been occasions when we were waiting around for one of the White House meetings, and Jack would say, 'well, if they are going to take all the air cover away I am going to ask to be relieved' and words to that effect. I don't remember Jack ever coming to me and objecting so strongly to some decision of mine that he made noises of that sort."

Of Esterline, Bissell said, "Jake, I guess, got mad occasionally. I don't remember the specific issues of which Jake got mad at me and threatened to resign."[9]

Pfeiffer's four-volume internal history of the invasion is among the most significant documents of the Bay of Pigs operation yet to be declassified. Pfeiffer himself wanted to see his work declassified and before his death sued the CIA unsuccessfully for its release.

Bissell did write in his memoirs that he recalled a meeting with Hawkins regarding the change of landing site. He also remembered Hawkins saying that his group had come up with an alternative plan that was better than the original in some ways to meet Kennedy's requirements for a landing with "less noise." "What we did not think or talk about much—but should have—was the fact that it hindered the possibility of guerrilla action in the event of an initial setback," wrote Bissell.[10]

Hawkins refuted this statement, and given the fact that he and Esterline went to Bissell's house eight days before the landing to protest the change in landing site, it does seem unlikely Bissell would make such a comment that he attributed to Hawkins, about the landing site being better.

"I never made such a statement to him [Bissell] nor conveyed such thoughts using other words or means," Hawkins said. "Also untrue is the assertion . . . that he did not get from me or others on his staff a feeling that a change from Trinidad made the outcome more uncertain. He could not possibly have forgotten what transpired at the urgent meeting at his home on a Sunday morning when Esterline and I explained in detail why a landing at the Bay of Pigs had no chance of success, would end in disaster and should be canceled. It is truly reprehensible that he never acknowledged, insofar as I know, that this meeting took place."[11]

Hawkins also disputed Bissell's comments to Pfeiffer regarding his and Esterline's threats to resign.

I mentioned resigning to Bissell only once—at the Sunday meeting at his home on April 9, 1961. It is clear that Bissell deliberately avoided ever mentioning this meeting. It is inconceivable that he did not remember the meeting and what transpired there. Jake and I urgently requested the meeting by telephone to Bissell, who had gone home from his office late on Saturday evening, April 8th. Both the time and venue for the meeting were out of the ordinary, taking place on Sunday morning, the next day, at Bissell's home. The subject for discussion was of momentous importance—our recommendation to cancel the Bay of Pigs landing since we had concluded a landing at the site, selected hastily at the last minute to satisfy political rather than military requirements, would fail disastrously. Jake and I both said that we wished to resign if the landing was not canceled.[12]

The concerns Esterline and Hawkins expressed that fateful Sunday morning apparently went no further than Bissell. Four days later, however, he made sure President Kennedy immediately saw a message Hawkins sent from Puerto Cabezas, Nicaragua, where the Cuban brigade was preparing to board the invasion vessels.

Early Thursday, April 13, Esterline sent Hawkins an "emergency precedence" cable asking "if your experiences the last few days in anyway changed your evaluation of the Brigade" and telling Hawkins that "the President has stated that under no conditions will U.S. intervene with any U.S. forces."

Esterline's cable was sent at the request of Bissell, who had dispatched Hawkins to Guatemala and Nicaragua.

Hawkins responded: "My observations the last few days have increased my confidence in the ability of this force to accomplish not only initial combat missions but also the ultimate objective of Castro's overthrow."

He described the brigade in glowing terms, and observed: "They say it is Cuban tradition to join a winner and they have supreme confidence they will win all engagements against the best Castro has to offer. I share their confidence."

Hawkins then described the brigade as "well organized and . . . more heavily armed and better equipped in some respects than U.S. infantry units. The men have received intensive training in the use of their weapons, including more firing experience than U.S. troops would normally receive" and called it "a formidable force."

"The Brigade officers," said Hawkins, "do not expect help from U.S. Armed Forces. They ask only for continued delivery of supplies. This can be done covertly."

He concluded by saying that "this Cuban Air Force is motivated, strong, well trained, armed to the teeth, and ready. I believe profoundly that it would be a serious mistake for the United States to deter it from its intended purpose."[13]

The cable has subsequently been cited as a major factor in President Kennedy's decision to give the go-ahead for the operation. Robert Kennedy later said he believed that Hawkins's cable, more than any single factor, persuaded the president to go ahead.[14]

Four decades later, historian Arthur Schlesinger Jr., a Kennedy aide at the time of the Bay of Pigs and one of the few in the White House then who opposed the invasion, referred to the "fatuous" cable sent by Hawkins at a 2001 Bay of Pigs conference in Havana.[15]

Hawkins has defended his cable in various forums, including interviews and written material, since 1996, when he first began speaking publicly about the Bay of Pigs.

His most detailed explanation came in a letter to Peter Kornbluh of the National Security Archive in Washington, the private, nonprofit organization responsible for getting large amounts of Cuban-related documents declassified by the U.S. government.[16] He acknowledged in the letter that his cable "seems inconsistent," given the fact that he and Esterline had, only days before, gone to Bissell's home to tell him the operation was doomed and they wanted to resign from the project. Hawkins's explanation of his cable:

> The mission in Central America assigned me by Bissell was to determine the state of morale and readiness for battle of the Cuban forces. The mission was *not* to determine whether or not the operation should go forward. That question had already been decided by Bissell in the affirmative despite the contrary advice Esterline and I had given him. My duty was to carry out my orders to the best of my ability.
>
> I found the Cuban forces in a high state of morale and readiness. Speaking to the officers in Spanish, I learned that they wanted to fight *now* and were unwilling to remain in the camps any longer. I knew also that the host countries, Guatemala and Nicaragua, were becoming restive and wanted the Cubans to leave. Under these circumstances, I thought the best thing I could do was to get the operation under way before there was a collapse of morale or serious difficulties arose with the host countries.
>
> With these thoughts in mind, I couched my message in terms calculated to get the action going without further delay.
>
> As I drafted the cable, I thought how very sad it was that these men could not be heading to the protective mountains of the Sierra Escambray, where they could hold out and fight for a long time, perhaps long enough with the help of the air arm to topple Castro, instead of to the forbidding swamps of Zapata.
>
> Had I known before setting off for Central America that the President, in concert with Bissell, would at the last minute cut by half the number of aircraft to participate in the first strike, and then, when the troops were actually nearing the beaches, the President would suddenly and unexpectedly cancel the second air strike altogether, I would not have made the trip. Instead, I would have asked General [David] Shoup, the Commandant of

the Marine Corps, to recall me from my temporary assignment with the CIA so that I would be spared from further involvement in such a disgraceful betrayal of the Cuban fighting men.

Hawkins's explanation has remained consistent in interviews and other forums since he began speaking out on the Bay of Pigs, including a brief, undated paper entitled: *MY INSPECTION TRIP TO GUATEMALA*.

Hawkins, in a letter to the author accompanying a copy of the undated paper, also accused Bissell of "departing from the norms of command and staff procedure" by not providing such "vital information" as the cutback in the air strikes to Esterline, as Cuba Project chief, and Hawkins, as the chief of the paramilitary section.[17]

Referring to the Sunday meeting at Bissell's home, Hawkins said:

It seems reasonable to conclude that Bissell deliberately kept us in the dark until the last minute, knowing that Esterline and I would be outraged by what had happened and might make another last-ditch effort to stop the operation as we had done a short while before.

Bissell would not agree to try to stop the operation, which he could easily have done. It was obvious that the President was reluctant to conduct the operation and probably would have welcomed advice from Bissell to cancel it. . . . If Bissell had consulted Esterline and me before agreeing to such drastic changes to the air plan, as he should have done, we might have been able to avert the catastrophe which lay ahead.

Jacob Esterline was a forceful man with considerable clout in the Western Hemisphere Division headed by Col. J. C. King, and had much experience in the kind of thing we were doing. If there had been time enough to act, I believe he would have gone to extreme measures to prevent the operations from being undertaken without adequate air support.

As for himself, said Hawkins, "I would have had time to consult with General Shoup, the Commandant of the Marine Corps, who had personally assigned me to the mission, explain the untenable military situation which had developed and recommend to him that he propose to the Joint Chiefs of Staff that they intervene by informing the President that the plan as modified by changing the landing site from Trinidad to the Bay of Pigs and greatly reducing planned air support was no longer viable. It was indefensible for Bissell to make drastically weakening changes in the operation plan at the last moment without consulting Esterline, the Chief of the Cuba Project, or even informing him. If he had not taken this unwise course, the tragedy at the Bay of Pigs might have been avoided."

In Guatemala, meanwhile, one of the more puzzling incidents of the Bay of Pigs operation—one unlikely ever to be explained—was occurring. It involved the activities of Army Lt. Col. Frank Egan, the on-site paramilitary operations chief who reported to Hawkins. Egan was already with the Cuba Project in Washington when the transformation began in November 1960 from a guerrilla operation to an invasion. He then was assigned to Base Trax in Guatemala to direct the brigade training.

In early April, according to Haynes Johnson's 1964 book on the Bay of Pigs—the earliest published account of the incident—Egan spoke privately with the brigade's ranking officers, Cmdr. Jose "Pepe" Perez-San Roman and Deputy Cmdr. Erneido Oliva.

He told them there were forces in the Kennedy administration trying to block the invasion and that "Frank," as he was identified, might be ordered to stop it. If the operation was cancelled, he said, the brigade should take the American trainers as "prisoners," and the Cuban Brigade would then be given the plans to proceed with the invasion on their own. Separately, but later the same day, Frank gave Manuel Artime, the exile front's civilian representative to the brigade, the same message.

According to Haynes Johnson's account, "Frank never said who opposed the invasion—it was 'forces in the administration' or 'politicians,' or 'chiefs above.' He did say that if he received the order to stop the invasion 'I have also orders from my bosses, my commanders, to continue anyway.'" If indeed he did receive such orders, he didn't identify who might have given them.[18]

Oliva, the brigade's second in command who became an invasion hero for his leadership after the landing, provided a similar, but more extensive, account to the author in 1998. This account appears in his unpublished memoirs.

There is little question of Oliva's credibility and credentials. After his capture, imprisonment, and release from Cuba, Oliva not only became close to Bobby Kennedy, but rose to the rank of brigadier general in the U.S. Army Reserves and deputy commander of the Washington, D.C., National Guard, before retiring. After his release from a Cuban prison, he gained an impeccable reputation among those with whom he worked, including former Secretary of State Al Haig Jr., then a Pentagon aide.[19]

As recounted by Oliva, as the invasion drew closer, Egan and his staff began holding regular secret briefings with Oliva and Perez-San Roman. During these briefings, wrote Oliva, "we learned that we would establish and hold a beachhead until the president of the Revolutionary Council arrived in Cuba, set up a provisional government and asked for assistance from the United States and other Latin American countries.

"There would be no problems, Frank assured us, because 'everything had been arranged in' Washington. Once the provisional government has been formally recognized, the Free World, including the United States, would supply the brigade with whatever it would need."

One afternoon later in April, wrote Oliva,

Frank called the brigade commander and I to his headquarters. When we arrived, I found him very gloomy. He also sounded a little upset when he said: 'there are forces in the administration trying to block the invasion, and if I receive such an order, I will secretly inform you. If this happens, you will come here and make some kind of show, as if you are putting us [all American advisers] in prison, and you go ahead with the plans as we have discussed. We will give you the whole plan, even if we are your prisoners.'

Frank was very specific in his instructions. We were to post an armed brigade soldier at each door of the American advisers' quarters, cut outside communications and continue training until we were told when, and how, to leave for 'Trampolin' [Puerto Cabezas, Nicaragua, the brigade's departure point]. Frank then smiled and said, 'At the end we will win.' Pepe and I were disturbed by this revelation, but we trusted Frank and his military advisers. They were outstanding professional soldiers who, fortunately, had replaced the European, Chinese and White Russian mercenaries originally contracted by the CIA to train us. Frank had treated us very fairly and seemed committed to the liberation of Cuba. At the beginning, we thought that what he had said must be a scheme to mislead Castro's intelligence apparatus.

Oliva acknowledged that there would have been problems in carrying out such a scheme, including "explaining to the *brigadistas* why we were placing our American advisers under house arrest," as well as logistical difficulties involved in getting the troops to the staging area and on to Cuba.

Pepe and I did not discuss Frank's instructions with anyone. However, late that evening, Frank called Artime and, privately, told him the same thing. Manolo called me to an isolated area behind one of the barracks and asked me if I had been told by Frank that someone was trying to stop the invasion. 'Why do you ask?' I said. 'Well,' he replied, 'that is what Frank told me.'

When I answered affirmatively to his question, he told me that he could not believe what Frank said. He was as stunned as I had been. He then went to headquarters to 'check notes with Pepe,' looking concerned. Frank never said who in the Kennedy Administration was opposing the invasion plans—he only referred to them as 'forces in the Administration,' or later on, 'politicians' or 'chiefs above.' 'I also have orders from my bosses, my commanders, to continue anyway,' he said on one occasion when the same topic was discussed.

Oliva said that he, Artime, and Perez-San Roman all agreed,

We did not have the contacts nor the political, financial or military muscle to accomplish such an enterprise.

After more than ten secret meetings with Frank, most of them attended also by Manolo, we arrived at the following conclusions:

1. The forces that would land in Cuba would be much, much larger than the brigade;
2. We would have the complete support of the United States Government;
3. The invasion was going to take place even if the 'politicians' in Washington tried to stop it;
4. Most important of all, the invasion was going to succeed and we would liberate our homeland.[20]

Hawkins and Esterline said they had been unaware of Egan's activities as related by Oliva, adding that, given the logistical problems involved, they did not see how such a plan could be carried out.

A possible clue is contained in Esterline's November 1975 interview with CIA historian Pfeiffer, who asked:

"Do you know anything about Dick Drain's [Esterline's chief of operations for the Cuba Project] diary . . . for example, he says that on the 3rd of April 1963, that you felt that Ydigoras [Guatemalan president] and possibly with Somoza [Nicaraguan president] might run this operation anyway. Did you really think that if the United States said 'no,' that if Kennedy said 'no,' the Brigade can't go, etc., that there was a possibility that Ydigoras and Somoza would pick up? Or was this just emotional?"

Esterline responded: "No, no, no. I felt, I guess I was reflecting Alejos [brothers Carlos and Roberto Alejos, on whose Guatemalan coffee plantation the brigade training was taking place], who was my right hand man . . . no, it was more likely Alejos. It was something that Alejos more than

Ydigoras would have said to me, that they weren't just going to let this thing fizzle like this . . . because they had taken all the risk. As far as they were concerned . . . they had all those people in there, training them and what not, and goddamn it, if we weren't going to do it, they would do it. Well, the answer is, how are you going to get them there?"[21]

Oliva remained convinced that Egan was not acting on his own when he discussed the takeover plan with the two brigade officers and Artime.

"I don't think he would do something like that in isolation," said Oliva. "He was loyal and professional to his superiors . . . whoever told him that. I don't think that's something that, 'hey, Frank thinks that this is the way it should be. Let's do it.' He knew the same way that I did, that I could not have moved from Guatemala without the support of the Navy. So how can he say take over the camp and we'll give you the plans."[22]

Hawkins disagreed that anyone higher up in Washington might have been involved, insisting, "I cannot believe that Bissell or any other responsible official at the CIA could countenance such a hare-brained scheme. If there was such a plan, Egan had to be acting on his own initiative."

Hawkins said that Egan, on one of his trips to Washington, "remarked to me that the Cubans might refuse to turn the ships around if so ordered by the President."

Hawkins said he "dismissed the idea," noting that the Cubans "were entirely dependent upon U.S. support . . . possibly Egan made this remark to determine what my reaction would be. He said no more about it."

But, said Hawkins, there were decisions made that caused him to suspect Bissell and Egan were communicating directly with each other about "important questions of policy." Among those decisions were the increase in size of the landing force from seven hundred to fifteen hundred, organization of a parachute unit, and a platoon of tanks, none of which "was recommended by Jake or me.

"In fact, I offered my opinion to Bissell that it would be difficult to recruit, train, land and support such a force in Cuba and the use of tanks and parachute troops would brand the venture as a U.S. undertaking. He [Bissell] was firm in his decisions, however, and I pressed the matter no further."

Bissell not being a military man, said Hawkins, "it seems unlikely that he would conceive the idea of using tanks or parachute troops, although he might have originated the idea of using a larger number of troops.

Someone must have recommended these things to him and the most likely person had to be Egan who was directly responsible for organizing and training the Cubans in Guatemala and was familiar from his Army experience with the employment of tanks and parachute troops. Egan never made these recommendations to Jake or me. If the recommendations were indeed his, and I think they were, they must have been made directly to Bissell orally in his office."[23]

Jim Flannery, one of Bissell's three assistants during the Bay of Pigs period, said he didn't even remember Egan and "never saw him in Bissell's office. If they met, it had to be somewhere else." Bissell, said Flannery, "could have come up with the additional troops, tanks, paratroopers' angles all by himself. He didn't need Egan for those ideas."[24]

Egan died December 11, 1999, in Ventura, California, at age seventy-six. His obituary, appearing in the local newspaper, made no mention of his role with the brigade and the Bay of Pigs. It did note that he was a veteran of "World War II, the Korean conflict and the Vietnam War." Hawkins and Oliva, both of whom knew Egan well, said there was no question that the man described in the obituary was the man they had known from the Bay of Pigs.

Hawkins said he had last heard from Egan not long after the Bay of Pigs, when Egan contacted him to ask for a letter of recommendation for a promotion to full colonel. Hawkins said he wrote "a good letter to have in his file." The obituary indicated Egan never got the promotion and retired as a lieutenant colonel.

Although Pfeiffer had indicated in other interviews that he intended to interview Egan for his history of the Bay of Pigs, he apparently never did. Pfeiffer is also dead.

Egan's only known recorded comments regarding the Bay of Pigs came on May 1, 1961, in testimony before the Taylor Commission, in which he described the sequence of events leading to his arrival in Guatemala, the brigade readiness, Cuban spies, and other matters.

The only question linked to the possibility of the invasion being called off indirectly confirmed what he told brigade leaders: "What would have happened if the operation had been called off after the first part of April?"

Egan's response: "It would have depended upon the posture they were in at the time. If it had been called off after they were actually on the way they would have taken over and kept going. I was informed that if the operation was called off they would take over. They said that as a friend we want you to direct all your people not to resist if this comes about, because we don't want anybody to get hurt. Consequently, I had all our people turn in their side arms. I would say that after the 1st of April it was a go operation."[25]

Allen Dulles called Johnson's account about Egan a "myth" in his book *The Craft of Intelligence*, published in 1965, adding that "Frank has denied the story." Dulles wrote that he knew Frank and "from what Frank has recently said, I am prone to believe this was all a misunderstanding which the [Haynes] Johnson book has built up into a grave incident seemingly only to discredit the CIA."[26]

The so-called disposal problem of the Cuban Brigade were the invasion to be called off figured in Kennedy's decision to go ahead with the plan, but again the president's decision was based on political, and not tactical, reasons.

In his book *A Thousand Days: John F. Kennedy in the White House*, historian Arthur Schlesinger, a special assistant to Kennedy in 1961, quoted Allen Dulles as saying at the March 11 meeting that resulted in a change of the landing site: "Don't forget that we have a disposal problem. If we have to take these men out of Guatemala, we will have to transfer them to the United States, and we can't have them wandering around the country telling everyone what they have been doing."

Confronted by Dulles's arguments, Schlesinger added, "Kennedy tentatively agreed that the simplest thing, after all, might be to let the Cubans go where they yearned to go—to Cuba. Then he tried to turn the meeting towards a consideration of how this could be done with the least political risk." One answer was to change the landing site.[27]

Oliva left no doubt that he believed there would have been a serious problem with any last-minute effort to call off the invasion:

> If you were an American advisor who had come to me and said 'take all the weapons of your men and put them in the supply area, armor room. Go home,' I would have called you some bad words and said we are not going anywhere. We are going to keep on training and we are going to fight whoever is in our way.
>
> I knew that we could not go to Cuba from there because I didn't have the means to transport our troops. But the problem that we would have created in Guatemala would have been so great, Cubans fighting the Guatemalan army, taking over Guatemala, something to that effect. . . .

The same brigadistas who fought in the Bay of Pigs, in Playa Larga, and Playa Giron, would have fought against the Guatemalan army. . . . The Americans were the advisors and they were fifteen, maybe twenty. That would not stop us because we were the guys with the weapons. . . . We have something that kept us together. It wasn't only training. . . . We want to fight the Communists. Whether we fought in Guatemala or whatever. What I am telling you is that the disposal problem you mentioned was more than a problem; it was a BIG problem. I think Kennedy made the right decision to say, 'hey, let them go to Cuba,' instead of bringing them back to Miami.[28]

Esterline believed it would have been a resolvable problem but said nobody ever asked either him or Hawkins. "These Cubans were very practical people. We would have worked out a solution for them. As a matter of fact, I ended up working out solutions for all kinds of them the last five years I worked . . . when I went down to Miami to gradually retire those Cuban operations which nobody was backing and didn't have much interest in." This reference was to the late 1960s when, as CIA station chief in Miami, he completed the shutdown, except for intelligence gathering, of what had become a mammoth post–Bay of Pigs covert anti-Castro operation.

Apart from the change in landing site, if the Bay of Pigs were doomed by a single decision, it came Sunday night, April 16, when President Kennedy, at Rusk's urging, called off a second air strike timed to coincide with the next morning's brigade landing in Cuba.

It was a decision provoked by U.S. ambassador Adlai Stevenson's anger and embarrassment after his staunch defense before at the UN against charges of U.S. aggression following Saturday's first strike. Not having been adequately briefed in advance of the U.S. role in the project, Stevenson's defense was not only too convincing; it was untrue.

At 9:30 P.M. that Sunday evening, Gen. Charles Cabell, the CIA's deputy director, was in Quarters Eye when he received a telephone call from McGeorge Bundy, President Kennedy's national security assistant. The message: "The President has directed that the air strikes scheduled for tomorrow morning be canceled."

Cabell was further told—again in the name of plausible deniability— that air strikes would not resume until after the landing forces had seized the airstrip within the beachhead so the B-26s would be able to operate from Cuban soil. Bundy said he was leaving immediately for New York to calm Stevenson down and any further discussion on the matter should be with Rusk, who "had the proxy of the President, who was going to Glen Ora," his Virginia retreat.

Recognizing the implications of the cancellation and too late to halt the operation, Cabell called Bissell at home and Rusk at the State Department, both of whom agreed to meet with him immediately. Cabell and Bissell arrived at the State Department at 10:15 P.M.

They made the case for air strikes to Rusk, who remained adamant but agreed to call the president at Glen Ora. Rusk, said Cabell, "gave the President an astonishingly complete and accurate account of my stated implications and effects of the cancellation order." But Kennedy stuck by his decision. Rusk offered them the phone to make their case directly with the president, but both declined.[29]

Cabell was greeted by a firestorm of anger when he returned to Quarters Eye and delivered the message. Hawkins, according to Bissell, yelled, "Goddamn it, this is criminal negligence," to which Esterline added, "This is the goddamndest thing I have ever heard of." It was the only time in his memoirs Bissell mentioned Esterline. Bissell also acknowledged that it was "probably out of cowardice" that he let Cabell face the music at Quarters Eye by "delivering the bad news."[30]

Many years later, Esterline said the incident was one he would never forget. He, too, noted that only a week earlier, in their meeting with Bissell at his home, "he solemnly pledged to Hawkins and I that he would ensure that we would get the total number of planes. He would go to the President and explain why it simply had to be. That we would get the number of planes we had to have before the task force got too close to Cuba to be recalled. Of course, the rest is painful history, which has been written about."

What he found "most unacceptable," said Esterline, "is that they [Bissell and Cabell] were offered the opportunity to speak with the President and they elected not to. . . . Bissell knew damn well what we were saying had to be right."

In 1998 Esterline vividly recounted his reaction to that fateful Sunday night when Cabell returned from his meeting with Rusk and delivered the message to the task force team gathered at Quarters Eye:

'Listen,' I said, 'General, what do you mean? Where's Bissell?' He said, 'well, Mr. Bissell couldn't come back, but they sent me to tell you that you're not going to get all the planes you want.' I blew my top, which was another futile exercise. I said, 'General, you can't do this. You have those damn B-26s we didn't want. You can't expect those planes . . . a small number of planes to cover all those targets. You're going to end up with at least one Cuban jet and possibly another Sea Fury that are going to remain intact, and those two planes are enough to destroy our B-26s and destroy our ships deck-loaded with gasoline.'

Jack Hawkins went into great and painful detail with General Cabell, telling him exactly what had to be done to save the task force and the General simply said 'there is nothing we can do.' . . . We didn't find out until sometime later that they didn't even exercise the last choice that they had to get to the President and talk to him. Well, we know now that Bissell already had this agreement with President Kennedy that we never knew about. We should have surmised something like that, because Kennedy had been in the service and he couldn't have been that much of a dope if he had had all the facts presented to him on a regular basis.

The rest of the night, said Esterline, was a fog.

I simply can't remember. . . . I'm sure I remained in the building. Jack and his paramilitary staff and my principal personal aide, Richard Drain, engaged in frantic planning of one sort or another, getting information and instructions out to the brigade. I can't remember what instructions went out, but I am sure they were as graphic as we could make them.

Everything we sent had to be relayed. We didn't have any direct channels and we could not send cables to the air arm. That was another thing Bissell had denied us; the right to send any air cables. So I don't know what was done about air cables. But I'm sure that Jack and the staff got out as much information to the brigade, which was now on the high seas, as was possible.

The next morning, about 8 o'clock, I sat down at my desk and wrote out in very, very scathing terms, my resignation from CIA, expressing absolute disgust with the events of the last month, with particular emphasis on this shameful performance last night. . . . I didn't want to be part of an agency that conducted itself like this.

I finished it and typed it up. I went over to see my boss, J. C. King, who was in another building at the time. I said 'J. C., our operation is about to be destroyed because of the goddamndest things that I'll never understand. And I just don't want to be part of it or the agency.' I handed him the resignation and started to leave. He said, 'wait,' and read it. And he said 'I don't want you to do this. . . . You can't quit at this point because there may still be something you can do to help.' 'Well,' I said, 'I don't know what it could be.' I said, 'I was at the point of jail last night. I was about to strangle General Cabell when he walked in and gave us the news. And Bissell wasn't man enough to come in himself.'

He said, 'calm down, calm down now. . . . I'm going to put this resignation on ice. I'm not going to put it through now because it won't accomplish anything. It won't make things any better. Go back and see what you can do to help,' so I said 'yes sir,' and that's exactly what I did. I went back, but I was still in a state of shock over what happened the night before, and I confess that my mind is blank on the next three days.

Even today, it's like when you were in a bad accident like that and your memory, from the time the thing happened and for quite a period of time after that, isn't very good. I'm afraid that's the situation I'm in. I know they sent me on leave but I'm not quite sure how I got reconstituted and functioning, but I did, and within a very short time, after the usual meetings with various inspectors and what not.[31]

Esterline took leave time and went to Miami where he was seen going around town commiserating with families of brigade members, who by then were dead or imprisoned in Cuba. Manny Chavez, an Air Force intelligence officer assigned to the CIA's overt office in Miami and an Esterline friend since the Guatemala coup in 1954, recounted in his unpublished memoirs:

"About a week after the defeat of Brigade 2506 Jake Esterline called me from Washington and asked me to meet him at Miami International Airport late that afternoon. As Jake walked out at the arrival gate he looked tired and distraught. He threw his arms around me and cried as he said, 'Manny, I tried to call it off. It was not my fault. We were screwed by Kennedy. They made me send these men to their slaughter. I will never forget this as long as I live. How could I be responsible for the lives of so many people who had faith in me?' Jake was emotionally depressed. He then asked me to take him to one of the CIA safe houses in Coconut Grove [Miami], where he stayed about a week to try to recover from this tragic event. He told me he wanted to contact each of the mothers and fathers, wives and children of the men of the brigade to personally apologize for what had happened."[32]

"He was in a deep state of shock," said Jay Gleichauf, who headed the CIA's overt office in Miami at the time. "I talked to him briefly. There was no question about it. He was very much overcome by the way that [Bay of Pigs] turned out. This one time I saw him, he was just gray. The spirit was gone out of him. He was trying to pull himself out but it was very difficult. He was like a ghost."[33]

CHAPTER 3

FIXING BLAME

V ictory has a thousand fathers and defeat is an orphan," President Kennedy told a press conference in assuming responsibility for the Bay of Pigs failure. And, added the president, he was "the responsible officer of the government." Although publicly accepting the responsibility for what historian Theodore Draper called a "perfect failure," Kennedy didn't accept the blame. Nor did he accept defeat gracefully, as subsequent events showed.

The sniping began almost before the Cuban Brigade's surrender ended the shooting. Privately, Kennedy was furious with the Central Intelligence Agency and the Joint Chiefs of Staff, and quickly made his anger known through surrogates. Kennedy loyalists, including Arthur Schlesinger Jr. and Theodore Sorensen, lashed out at both the generals and the spies, accusing them of providing the president with bad or incomplete information and advice. They also contended that Kennedy's predecessor had foisted a program on the idealistic and inexperienced young president that he couldn't stop even if he had wanted to.

Hindsight, based on the greater information now available, indicates they were at least partially right. Communications and sharing of information among the various Kennedy administration players—inadvertently in some cases, deliberately in others—left much to be desired. It's now clear that had officials with direct access to the president—namely Richard Bissell—been more candid in their briefings, Kennedy might well have called off the invasion. Adding to the problem was the fact that only the concept of the project, not the details, was committed to writing, a sure recipe for miscommunication.

The CIA, the Pentagon, and their defenders were just as insistent that Kennedy administration officials, including the president and Secretary of State Dean Rusk, made success impossible by imposing ever-increasing political restrictions on the operation in an effort to keep "secret" what was an already obvious U.S. role. Political restrictions resulted in two critical—and fatal—decisions ordered by Kennedy: the change in landing site to make it "less spectacular" and the last-minute cancellation, at Rusk's urging, of the D-Day air strikes.

Part of the problem also, acknowledged even by Kennedy partisans, was the loose organizational structure of a new and inexperienced White House staff that didn't lend itself to making sure the president was kept fully informed. Even today, more than forty years later, the debate continues over responsibility for failure as new perspectives emerge.

Tom Parrott, a veteran CIA official who served as an assistant to CIA Director Allen Dulles during the planning for the Bay of Pigs, contended that histories of the project gloss over the depth of White House responsibility for the Bay of Pigs failure without ever really presenting the agency's side of the story. His opinion was widely shared by CIA officials involved.

"I've always deplored the fact that in the face of Schlesinger's book and Sorensen's book . . . [both] totally wrong . . . just apologia for Kennedy, but they are going to go down in history as the word because there's nobody else left to tell the truth. Bissell didn't do it [in his posthumous memoirs]. And Dulles wouldn't do it," complained Parrott, who was assigned in mid-July 1961 as a White House aide to Gen. Maxwell Taylor, the president's newly minted representative for military and intelligence matters.[1]

Gen. Charles Cabell, the CIA's deputy director, provided the exception with his memoirs, *A Man of Intelligence: Memoirs of War, Peace and the CIA*, which was harshly critical of Kennedy and his entire administration. Edited and published posthumously by his son in 1997, some twenty-six years after Cabell died, the memoirs attracted scant attention.

Bissell, in his memoirs, cited an unpublished document found in the Allen Dulles Papers at Princeton University, in which the CIA director was implicitly critical of President Kennedy and "deplored" the version of events by Sorensen and Schlesinger. According to Bissell, Dulles observed that: "Great actions require great determination to succeed, a willingness to risk some unpleasant political repercussions, and a willingness to provide the basic military necessities. At the decisive moment of the Bay of Pigs operation, all three of these were lacking." Dulles wrote in the same paper about the Sorensen and Schlesinger histories of the 1960s: "I deplore the way this is being done. In effect, an attempt is now being made to write history and only part of the story is available. If what is so written goes entirely unanswered and without critical examination, it will go down as the history of the event. It is not the true story."[2]

As the various governmental institutions and individuals involved sniped at each other over responsibility for the failure in the days following the event, two formal inquiries got under way, each adding its own perspective.

President Kennedy appointed one, the so-called Taylor Commission, or Cuba Study Group. To head the commission and also serve as the president's military and intelligence adviser, Kennedy brought in from retirement Gen. Maxwell Taylor, a former chairman of the Joint Chiefs of Staff under President Eisenhower. Joining Taylor on the commission were the president's brother and attorney general, Bobby Kennedy, CIA Director Allen Dulles, and Adm. Arleigh Burke of the Joint Chiefs of Staff. The dichotomy of the group was apparent in the final report in which Dulles and Burke dissented—in an implicit criticism of President Kennedy's last-minute cancellation of air support—from a section suggesting that even with control of the air, a beachhead invasion "could not have survived long without substantial help from the Cuban population or without overt U.S. assistance," neither of which ever materialized.

The Burke-Dulles dissent appeared as a footnote to the report. It read:

Admiral Burke and Mr. Dulles consider that there is insufficient evidence to support the conjectures in this paragraph. The well-motivated CEF [Cuban Expeditionary Force] fought extremely well without air cover and with a shortage of ammunition. They inflicted very severe losses on the less well-trained Cuban militia. Consequently, it is reasonable to believe that if the CEF had had ammunition and air cover, they could have held the beachhead for a much longer time, destroyed much of the enemy artillery and tanks on the roads before they reached the beachhead, prevented observation of the fire of the artillery that might have been placed in position and destroyed many more of the local militia en route to the area. A local success by the landing party, coupled with CEF aircraft overlying Cuba with visible control of the air, could well have caused a chain reaction of success throughout Cuba with resultant defection of some of the militia, an increasing support from the populace and eventual success of the operation.[3]

"My feeling is that Bobby was determined to pin the blame on anybody except Jack, and Arleigh Burke did not go along with all that," said Parrott. "Dulles, of course, was in an anomalous position. And Taylor, I think, was in a tough spot, too, because he was brand new in the job and I think he realized the pressure."

Although Dulles and Burke were half the commission, "they didn't have the firepower," said Parrott. And as the first among equals, Bobby Kennedy "was out for blood."[4]

Even with Bobby's influence, the Taylor Commission report was far more evenhanded than the one by Lyman Kirkpatrick, the CIA's inspector general, who apparently used the occasion to exorcise some personal demons.

The Taylor report at least offered an indication of White House disorganization related to the project. The report cited as the last of eleven "immediate causes" of failure: "The Executive Branch of the government was not organizationally prepared to cope with this kind of paramilitary operation. There was no single authority short of the President capable of coordinating the actions of CIA, State, Defense, and USIA. Top level direction was given through ad hoc meetings of senior officials without consideration of operational plans in writing with no arrangement for recording conclusions and decisions reached."[5]

So controversial was the Kirkpatrick report that it was not declassified until February 1998, nearly thirty-seven years after its completion in the fall of 1961. Only twenty copies were made; nineteen were recalled and destroyed. The remaining copy was locked in the CIA director's office safe.

The report's existence—and the fact that it was critical—had long been known, but when finally released most news accounts focused only on its scathing indictment of the agency. They made bare mention, if any, of the report's controversial background and the lengthy rebuttal from Bissell, Kirkpatrick's rival, attached to it.

Typical of the many articles appearing on the report's declassification was one in the February 22, 1998, edition of the *New York Times*, which ran under the headline: "C.I.A Bares Its Bungling in Report on Bay of Pigs Invasion." Only two paragraphs, buried in a lengthy story, accompanied by excerpts from the report, made any reference to its controversial nature, and the first contained two significant errors. It read:

"The C.I.A.'s leaders believed that it was President John F. Kennedy's failure to approve an attack on Cuba's air force to coincide with the landing of the commandos that caused the deaths of 1,500 raiders. And in their rebuttals to the report by Mr. Kirkpatrick, they wrote that his depiction of 'unmitigated and almost willful bumbling and disaster'—in the words of Gen. Charles P. Cabell, then Deputy Director of Central Intelligence—was motivated by personal malice. Mr. Kirkpatrick had wanted to be the agency's spymaster, but his career advancement stalled when he contracted polio in the early 1950's."

It was not President Kennedy's "failure to *approve* an attack on Cuba's air force," but his decision within hours of the landing to *call off* an air strike that already had been approved, a fact noted deeper in the story. Nor did "nearly 1,500 raiders" die in the landing. Only 114 died and another 1,189 were captured, while 150 either failed to land or never shipped out. No mention was made of Bissell's rebuttal. With the exception of Cabell, briefly quoted a second time later in the story, no other mention was made suggesting the torrid controversy that Kirkpatrick had stirred with his report.

Perhaps the most measured CIA response to Kirkpatrick came from John McCone, a businessman without an intelligence background, who succeeded Dulles as CIA director. In a January 19, 1962, cover letter transmitting a copy of the report and its rebuttals to the chairman of the president's Foreign Intelligence Advisory Board, McCone said: "It is my personal opinion as a result of examinations I have made of this operation after the fact, that both the report and the rebuttals are extreme. I believe an accurate appraisal of the Cuban effort and the reasons for failure rest some place in between the two points of view expressed."[6]

Jake Esterline, who was on the original distribution list of twenty people, commented at the time of its declassification, that "any good that could have come from the report was lost because of the vitriolic manner in which Kirkpatrick wrote it."[7]

Sam Halpern, a retired senior agency officer who had no role in the Bay of Pigs, but knew Kirkpatrick well and had worked with him, described the report as "basically Kirk's vendetta against Bissell, aiming for the highest job [CIA director]. He had been a real rising star. Once he had polio [he was stricken on an overseas trip in July 1952] he got sidetracked and became a bitter man."[8]

Author Peter Grose, in his biography of Allen Dulles, wrote that "Kirkpatrick had once been a player in the Great Game [to succeed Dulles]; as he was repeatedly passed over for higher responsibility, colleagues came to sense that bitterness came to dominate his capacity for judgment. Pursuing his investigation with a vigor that also seemed to include the settling of old scores, the inspector general produced a 170-page critique even more scathing against his CIA colleagues, implicitly including Allen, than the Taylor report."

Then, says Grose, Kirkpatrick "made a fatal misstep in the game of bureaucracy. Completing his work the week before McCone was to be sworn in, he handed the report personally to the new man. McCone read the text on the plane to California, where he went to close out his private affairs over the Thanksgiving weekend. He telephoned Kirkpatrick the morning after his arrival. The document, he said, must go to Allen, who was still the director of central intelligence, and it must go to him 'immediately.' Allen, predictably, was outraged, both at Kirkpatrick's ugly personal judgments and at the seemingly devious manner in which he had presented them to the new director rather than to the executive who had commissioned it."[9]

Tom Parrott had this to say:

Kirkpatrick was a good friend of mine. I probably knew him longer than anybody in the agency, because I was in college with him . . . but I'm convinced that by the time of that report he was a bitter, disillusioned guy. Bitter anyway, and with probably some good reason. He was intensely ambitious. It was just incredible.

And he had maneuvered himself into a position where he was all set to go . . . then he took this trip early in that capacity [head of the intelligence side of the CIA's clandestine services] to view his empire around the world and got polio and that was it . . . so he was bitter, and very disappointed, of course. So when he saw all these people, and this is my view, going by him like [Richard] Helms and then Bissell being brought in from the outside and being put in jobs that Kirk would have liked to have had . . . I just think that his report was dishonest and biased. I honestly think that Kirk was just almost demented at that point.[10]

Bissell, the most obvious target of much of the report's criticism, said in a 1967 oral history interview that he thought the document was "a typical report that uses hindsight illegitimately for criticism . . . and, in effect, criticized the participants for judgments that allegedly turned out to be incorrect after the fact, rather than trying to assess them on the basis of the evidence available to those who made them when they made them."

Bissell added that Kirkpatrick "was known to be, to I think everyone that knew him, extremely ambitious. He was an individual who, as I felt well before this incident, was not above using the reports and his analysis of situations to exert an influence in the direction that he chose; and these directions were, not always but sometimes, tied up with his own personal ambitions. I think in this case he had a number of purposes he was trying to serve, more or less of that character."[11]

Kirkpatrick, defending his work in another 1967 oral history interview, said that "the report was tailored quite specifically to just what CIA had done and how it had done it, and we avoided any political decisions that might have been made in the White House or the Pentagon or in the State Department or Congress because we were tailoring our report strictly to CIA successes or failures. What it boiled down to, in simple terms, in a report that ran about a hundred and fifty pages, was that by trying to do it [the Cuba Project] in a compartmented unit outside the regular structure of the Agency, it had failed to take advantage of the best talent in the Agency."

When the report was finished, said Kirkpatrick, "it was a very, very difficult decision on my part as to what to do with it and how to do it because it couldn't help but be a highly critical report on the Agency's operations. Mr. Dulles by then had announced his retirement; the President had appointed John McCone; and I probably handled it the wrong way, in retrospect. . . . I decided to show it to John McCone first [within a week of being sworn in as director] and asked him how he thought I should handle it."

McCone replied, telling him, "I think you better hand this to Mr. Dulles immediately."

"I told him when I gave it to him [McCone]," Kirkpatrick said, "that I realized that this would both shock and hurt Allen Dulles because it did indicate such very serious failings in the Agency's operation: poor organization, poor use of personnel, overoptimism of the success of the operation, failure to use the intelligence side of the Agency—the intelligence side, I mean the Research and Analysis Directorate."

Kirkpatrick said he gave Dulles and General Cabell copies of the report the next day "and they were both exceedingly shocked and upset, irritated and annoyed and mad and everything else because Mr. Dulles, I believe, used the term to McCone when he saw him that it was a hatchet job. And McCone talked to me and said, 'Mr. Dulles thinks this was a hatchet job. I want you to reread it and write me a memorandum as to what you think now, looking at it again.'" Kirkpatrick said he reread the report and sent McCone a one-paragraph memo saying, "On rereading it several months after the report was finished, it's my observation that, if anything, this is a moderate report and is not as severe as it should be."[12]

While critical of the "vitriolic manner" in which Kirkpatrick wrote the report, Esterline did say that it reinforced the conclusion that he and Col. Jack Hawkins had reached in recent years: Bissell had lied to them—

especially regarding air cover—and, at the least, withheld information from President Kennedy.

Esterline said it was now clear that "Bissell lied constantly or withheld vital information. We know now that Bissell had already agreed with President Kennedy that the expected air support would not be forthcoming."

"It's difficult to take positions after all these years on people who are now dead," said Esterline, "but what has emerged to me in depth . . . is the intensity of the rivalry between these two men [Kirkpatrick and Bissell]. That, coupled with my increased knowledge of both, has disillusioned me with both."[13]

Much has been heard, and written, about the activities and views of top officials and their partisans in the White House and, to a lesser extent, the CIA and the Pentagon, regarding the Bay of Pigs. But only in recent years did Esterline and Hawkins, the two men most directly charged with planning and carrying out the operation, decide to publicly make known their thoughts on what went wrong and who was responsible.[14]

After reading declassified documents and comparing notes, Esterline and Hawkins came to the belated conclusion that their boss, Richard Bissell, should be added to their list of those most responsible for failure of the Bay of Pigs. The other two on the list were President Kennedy and Secretary of State Rusk.

They both became convinced that Bissell, who had virtually complete control over the Cuba Project, presented only selective information to the president reflecting their concerns about the operation, and they concluded, he never gave them access to the full scope of the operation either. This belief was reinforced by Bissell's memoirs.

"Of the two, he [Bissell] was the bigger schemer than Kennedy," said Esterline.

Hawkins, in a 1997 memo, offered his "Reflections on the Actions of Richard Bissell," including the Cuba Project head's responsibilities, management style, crucial mistakes, and reasons for what he did.[15]

Hawkins noted that Bissell, as the CIA's deputy director/plans, originated plans for "covert operations against Cuba and was the driving force behind their execution. He had virtually free rein within the CIA to direct the project as he saw fit." CIA Director Allen Dulles, said Hawkins, "exercised oversight but did not play an active day-to-day role."

Hawkins called Bissell's management style "unconventional in that he often bypassed the established chain of command and control and dealt

58

directly with individuals, field activities and other agencies. Sometimes his own staff was not aware of what he was doing through his own channels. The lack of coordination with his staff caused misunderstanding and confusion."

As for his "mistakes," said Hawkins, the most fundamental was "his failure to realize that a successful landing operation which might lead to the overthrow of Castro had become infeasible as political authority imposed successive, fatally crippling restrictions."

Tom Parrott recalled Bissell saying long afterward, in Parrott's presence, "that he should have told Kennedy that with the change from Trinidad—and particularly to such an inhospitable place—the operation was no longer feasible."[16]

Among Bissell's mistakes, Hawkins contended, were:

- Not responding to a staff study—after the landing site was changed in March 1961 from Trinidad to the Bay of Pigs to meet presidential criteria—reported to him that the new site was the only one meeting the requirement that it have a landing strip which could accommodate B-26s. It also said that the new site "could neither hold a beachhead nor advance beyond it. Mr. Bissell should have reported the results of this study to the President immediately." Instead, he ordered staff preparation for a landing at the Bay of Pigs and "persuaded the President to approve it."

- Ignoring the "emphatic advice" from Esterline and Hawkins, "both of whom had extensive combat experience, that a landing at the Bay of Pigs . . . would result in disaster if allowed to proceed. If he had informed the President of this opinion, the Bay of Pigs disaster would probably have been avoided." Not only did he fail to inform the president, he apparently never acknowledged publicly that the two top planners had urged cancellation of the operation only a week prior to the invasion.

- Failure "throughout the planning period to make it clear to the President why it was essential to destroy Castro's air force completely before the landing, and that further air operations would be required until the mission was accomplished or had failed." Even though well aware of such necessities "he did not make the importance of this clear to the President." Lacking military experience himself, he would have been better served to have his military staff brief the president on "this and other important military considerations."

- During the preparatory phase, Bissell "tended to act more as an advocate trying to win approval of his plan from the President than a careful advisor. He accentuated positive aspects of the plan but played down, or did not mention, shortcomings, risks, possible adverse consequences or failure." Hawkins noted that he accompanied Bissell to meetings at the White House with the president and Cabinet members, but "was not present at his briefings of the President. His briefing papers were not coordinated with Mr. Esterline nor me and we had no way of knowing what had been said."

- Not until 1996, when Hawkins and Esterline obtained a declassified copy of Bissell's "final briefing paper for the President, dated April 12, 1961, three days before the first scheduled air attack," did they learn he had not given the president an accurate picture of what the operation entailed. "The tenor of the briefing was to assure the President that the landing would be a quiet operation, less like an invasion, as the President desired. This was not true. The Bay of Pigs landing was an invasion, far from quiet."

- Hawkins and Esterline learned from the same paper that Bissell and the president "had reached agreement several days before the first air attack was to be launched to cut the number of our attacking aircraft in half, from sixteen to eight, and did not inform" them until the day before the attack, "thereby ensuring that we would have no time to react effectively against the decision. Mr. Bissell had promised us at our urgently requested Sunday meeting that planned air attacks would not be reduced."

- The ultimate mistake, said Hawkins, came a few hours before the landing was to begin, when Bissell declined to speak personally to the president "to explain the probably disastrous consequences of the President's last-minute order canceling the scheduled dawn air attack against Castro's remaining military aircraft. He was offered that opportunity by the Secretary of State, and the President was waiting on the telephone, but Mr. Bissell did not act. The Cuban Brigade was abandoned to its fate."

Hawkins then offered what he acknowledged as "conjecture" about why Bissell acted as he did, and suggested "several factors which may have influenced him." Among the reasons for Bissell's actions were:

- **Overconfidence.** Too much confidence in his own judgment and abilities, given recent successes in developing the U-2 spy plane and his role in the 1954 overthrow of Guatemalan president Jacobo Arbenz. Hawkins speculated that Bissell's confidence in his own intellectual ability may have "prompted him to substitute his own judgment for that of others who were more qualified in certain fields."

- **Career considerations**. Success in getting rid of Castro would "probably ensure" his promotion to CIA director, succeeding Allen Dulles.
- **Faulty intelligence**. Too heavy a reliance on reports from the Cuban exile community for information about conditions in Cuba. "The Cuban exiles were bitterly opposed to Castro and would be inclined to slant their reports in ways calculated to benefit their own interests. CIA intelligence about Cuba was overly optimistic."
- **Lack of military experience**. Bissell had no military training, nor experience, yet assumed the burden of advising the president about military plans for operations against Castro. "A better approach would have been to have his military staff handle military portions of his briefings. This change of procedure alone might have averted the Bay of Pigs disaster."
- **Momentum**. "Operations of this kind generate a momentum of their own and are hard to stop once started. There is a large and ever-growing investment of human effort, not to mention government funds. Other agencies and other countries become involved. The originator of such an operation naturally hesitates to give up for fear of appearing incompetent or ridiculous."
- **Possibility of U.S. intervention**. Bissell "may have believed that in the end, if failure seemed imminent, the President would feel compelled to intervene with U.S. forces. Some involved people did believe that. Having listened to what the President had to say on numerous occasions, I believed the exact opposite. Perhaps Mr. Bissell did not interpret the President's remarks in the same way that I did, or knew something that I was unaware of, but I doubt that this was the case."
- **Disposal problem**. If the operation were to be called off and the brigade disbanded, there was fear of "political embarrassment. This was considered at high levels of government." Hawkins said he "did not know" Bissell's views on the subject, but that he "doubted that many problems would have been encountered."
- **Clandestine service tactics**. Hawkins, a military officer, observed "the practice of secrecy and deception is necessary in the everyday lives of persons in the clandestine service, even in their social relationships. For some individuals, and I do not think this is widespread, the habitual use of deceptive tactics in professional activities may spill over into dealings with other agencies of government and even with their own colleagues. Those who cross the line in this

regard may feel that deception is justified in the interest of advancing what they regard as an important agenda."[17]

Hawkins concluded his "reflections" of Bissell with the observation that, "to some extent Mr. Bissell misled, sometimes by silence and omission, both the President and his own staff in dealing with important matters. Was this the result of misunderstanding on his part of the military realities, or the result of his uncoordinated, one-man-show management style, or was it conscious resort to deceptive tactics commonly employed in the clandestine service? Or was it all three?"[18]

Bissell, who died in 1994, did little to provide any clear answers either in his posthumously published memoirs or his many interviews related to the Bay of Pigs. Instead of clarifications, a comparison of his public remarks shows a maze of contradictions regarding his actions.

"If there was anyone I wanted in the room, it was Richard Bissell," said Jorge Dominguez, a Cuba scholar at Harvard University, in commenting on discussions at a spring 1996 Bay of Pigs Conference at St. Simon's Island, Georgia. "No one made the point bluntly, but the impression was that Bissell deceived his superiors . . . the fact that Bissell didn't write stuff down for the record. One of the ways you are truthful to those above and below you is to say 'this is where you are.' It's almost impossible to find Bissell's written record. If he was not being deceptive, he was hoarding information in such a way that he risked being deceptive."[19]

British historian Lawrence Freedman wrote "as D Day approached, presidential input was largely driven by Kennedy's misconceived preoccupation with deniability. Bissell agreed with all of the President's demands to trim the operation without ever warning of the consequences for its integrity. This exasperated the staff, which saw all the dangers. All modifications requested were immediately delivered. Faced with such responsiveness, the administration could not be churlish."[20]

Of the three factors that Hawkins suggested might have influenced Bissell's actions, the most accurate seems to be his "uncoordinated, one-man-show management style." This explains why Bissell paid no heed to, and told no one about the Esterline and Hawkins visit to his home eight days before the invasion to warn him it was doomed to failure. Or why he didn't make it clear to the president that the change in landing site essentially ruled out the "guerrilla option" for the Cuban Brigade. And why he didn't insist on talking with the president himself when offered the chance to argue for restoration of the critical invasion day air strikes.

Or why he apparently ignored a prescient January 4, 1961, memo by Hawkins—with its emphasis on air cover—that outlined what was required to make the operation a success.

Jim Flannery noted after reading Hawkins's memos cited above that "I am now persuaded that Bissell did play games with Jake and Hawkins, especially in the final briefing [of the president April 12, 1961]. But what doesn't make sense was that he was shooting himself in the foot with the lies and he must have known it.

"He didn't need a Cuban success to put him in the Director's chair. He didn't need to go forward with the Bay of Pigs unless there was some private understanding with JFK," said Flannery. "It just doesn't make sense. Something's missing. And I'll bet that 'something' was between Kennedy and Bissell."[21]

Esterline shared such speculation.

"I'll never forget that last meeting with Bissell [at his home eight days before the invasion] in which he solemnly pledged to Hawkins and I that he would ensure that we would get the total number of planes. He would go to the president and explain why it simply had to be; that we would get the number of planes we had to have before the task force got too close to Cuba to be recalled," said Esterline. "Of course, the rest is painful history that has been written about."

What Esterline found most unacceptable was that neither Cabell nor Bissell took the opportunity offered to appeal directly to the president when he confirmed cancellation of the D-Day air strikes. "That was unacceptable because Bissell knew damn well what we were saying [regarding need for the strikes] had to be right. Of course, again, now we know why he didn't. He had already made an agreement with President Kennedy that he felt he had to live with, for better or for worse."[22]

Giving some credence to a private agreement between Kennedy and Bissell is the fact that Secret Service logs show Bissell, by himself or with others, at thirteen off-the-record Oval Office meetings with Kennedy in the first three months of 1961.[23]

Taking note of the meetings, Hawkins said it raised two unanswered questions: "'What did Bissell tell Kennedy in their numerous private meetings?' and 'Why did he keep us [Hawkins and Esterline] in the dark about his private relations with the president?'"[24]

Flannery's description of Bissell during the Bay of Pigs reinforces the "uncoordinated, one-man-management style" approach suggested by Hawkins. Bissell had, said Flannery, "lots of staff complexes and personnel at his beck and call . . . but none that he used in a conventional sense. For planning, etc., Jake had a project staff in Quarters Eye, but I'm not sure how much Bissell used them or paid attention to them, especially on important matters. In essence, Bissell was his own staff, just as he was his own deputy and chief of operations."

Even before reading Hawkins's memos, Flannery had come to the conclusion that "Bissell's most serious mistakes were not in what he did, but in what he did not do." High among them was mending his relationship with Richard Helms, his deputy and a CIA veteran seen as "keeper of the flame on behalf of a pretty tight-knit group of old pros . . . most of whom dated back to wartime service with the OSS and military intelligence."

Bissell was named to replace Frank Wisner as the CIA's deputy director/plans. As Wisner's chief of operations, Flannery wrote in a private paper, Helms "had become Wisner's de facto deputy. Few matters from within the Clandestine Services found their way to Wisner's desk without having passed through Helms. . . . Bissell came in as an outsider and new broom exuding change. I suspect he even carried a bit of a chip on his shoulder." Bissell had come in leaving "no doubt in anyone's mind that he was going to be his own deputy and chief of operations . . . and most documents and matters would come directly to him. No wonder Bissell and Helms didn't hit it off. As a matter of fact, I can't recall a single occasion when Bissell had Helms into his office, though they were next door to each other. If they had any business to transact, they did so by telephone or notes." Said Flannery:

A prime example of the depth of their estrangement was the Cuban operation. To keep up with developments in the project, Helms had me give him a briefing every Friday. That was fine until the latter stages when, from my position on the sidelines, I could no longer keep up with mounting developments. So, one Saturday afternoon when Bissell was not being harassed and seemed relaxed and in a good mood, I told him I had been briefing Helms on the Cuban project for some time, but it had reached the point where I couldn't be sure I wasn't missing important details, and I thought he might wish to cut Helms in on some of the meetings concerning the operation . . .

He extended me the courtesy of exposing me to a fifteen minute discourse that came down to the fact that one of his great weaknesses was an inability to work with a deputy so I should continue briefing Helms as well as I could. And that was that. The tragedy was that, temperaments aside, Bissell and Helms could have complemented each other in many ways and would have made a great team. In generic terms, Bissell was a problem solver and innovator with an anarchist streak while Helms was an organization man who made the system function in an orderly fashion without any rocking the boat. Almost as important, Helms knew where all the skeletons from the past were buried and the strengths, weaknesses, and idiosyncrasies of most of our operational people. . . .

He could have used Helms' vast knowledge of the organization and its people to considerable advantage . . . not to speak of Helms' keen operational instincts and judgment as well. If Bissell was prone to use anyone as his deputy, it was Tracy Barnes and especially on the Cuban project. But Barnes had neither the stature within the Clandestine Service nor the operational acumen of Helms.[25]

Rather than clarify his role, the recent declassification of documents, reflections by former colleagues, and many contradictions in his own statements have only served to make Bissell a greater enigma.

As journalist and author Evan Thomas wrote, one of the big questions of the Bay of Pigs is why McGeorge Bundy, Kennedy's national security adviser and a former Bissell student at Yale "did not do more to ride herd on Bissell or clear up a series of ruinous misunderstandings between the CIA and Bissell's flaws. 'If Dick has a fault,' Bundy wrote JFK in February, 'it is that he does not look at all sides of the question.' "[26]

In reassessing responsibility for failure of the Bay of Pigs, the one area where there is little dispute by all involved, although from differing perspectives, is what British historian Freedman succinctly described as the conflict between "deniability" and "viability."[27]

Or, as the Taylor Commission observed: "A paramilitary operation of the magnitude of Zapata should not be prepared or conducted in such a way that all U.S. support and connection with it could be plausibly denied.

"Once the need for the operation was established, its success should have had the primary consideration of all agencies of government," the Taylor report concluded. "Operational restrictions designed to protect its covert character should have been accepted only if they did not impair the chance of success. As it was, the leaders of the operation were obliged to fit their plan inside changing ground rules laid down for military considerations, which often had serious operational disadvantages."[28]

Bissell, in his memoirs, admitted that as an advocate for the operation, he was worried about what might happen if he told Kennedy that the U.S. role in the invasion could not be hidden, so it might as well be done openly. Among the conditions Kennedy had placed on the invasion was one "that hard evidence of direct involvement by the U.S. government had to be concealed and, if exposed, plausibly explained or denied. . . . If the United States was sure to be held responsible, then it made no sense to pay a price in terms of impaired operational capability for a result that could not be obtained. Yet that is exactly what we did. It was a major error."[29]

Bissell had made the same point in an earlier interview, saying "the concept of this as an operation, responsibility for which could be plausibly disclaimed by the U.S. Government, had lost its validity many weeks before the invasion itself took place. It was this fact, as I now believe it to have been, that really, it seems to me, was never faced by those of us in the CIA who were advocating the operation and deeply committed to it emotionally, or by someone like Rusk, who was on the whole opposed to it, or by the President or others in the circle of advisors. The one thing that seemed to be taken sort of for granted throughout was that if anything was going to be done, it would be done within this original concept. My feeling is that if the breakdown of that concept had been faced, some other possible courses of action would have been considered."[30]

Even Kennedy loyalist Arthur Schlesinger, while deflecting any blame away from the president, wrote that "if it was to be a covert operation for which we could plausibly disclaim responsibility, it should have been, at most, a guerrilla operation. Once it grew into a concentrated amphibious operation, it was clearly beyond the limits of disownability."[31]

Hawkins cited seven politically imposed restrictions "in the unrealistic and mistaken belief that 'plausible deniability' could be maintained on an operation of this scale. The principal advocate of these restrictions was the Department of State whose position prevailed."

The restrictions: "(1) U.S. bases could not be used for training Cuban forces; (2) No U.S. air base could be used for overflights of Cuba to supply arms to agent teams for guerrilla forces nor to provide logistical support to the brigade when it landed; (3) No U.S. air base could be used for tactical air operations nor for logistical overflight missions; (4) American contract pilots could not be employed for tactical air operations nor for logistical overflight missions; (5) Only half of the sixteen available B-26 bombers could be used in the initial effort to destroy Castro's air force in a surprise attack; (6) Important military targets could not be attacked in the initial strike due to the limit imposed on number of aircraft to be employed, and; (7) Cancellation . . . while the troops were approaching the beach area to land, of the air attack which was to eliminate Castro's air force, ensured that the unwitting landing force would meet with disaster."

"Political considerations were allowed to restrict military operations to such an extent that success was not possible," Hawkins concluded.[32]

For Esterline, with hindsight, the critical period on which success of the invasion hinged began in late March when

> we were beginning to get our legs cut off all the time . . . about the kind of weapons, boats and planes we could have. . . . The whole thrust of our air program was that well before the invasion force was nearing Cuba, we felt that we could still catch those planes on the ground. . . . We knew we couldn't destroy them in the air. . . . Every time we'd plan a raid and we would submit the plans with the number and kind of planes we thought were necessary for targeting, invariably somebody would say, 'that's too many, that's too much noise,' and they'd cut down the number of planes we could use. There was always some political factor that seemed to say 'no, you can't have that much.'
>
> I'll always regret that I wasn't more forceful, couldn't have been more forceful, or couldn't have been more successful in fighting to preserve the advantage that I thought was necessary that political forces finally shot down. But that is the echo of anybody who's ever tried to do anything in history.[33]

CHAPTER 4

BOBBY TAKES CHARGE

Bobby Kennedy was angry. The Bay of Pigs invasion effort had collapsed a day earlier. The Kennedy Cabinet meeting in an April 20, 1961, emergency session at the White House "was about as grim as any meeting I can remember in all my experience in government, which is saying a good deal," Chester Bowles, the undersecretary of state who was sitting in for Dean Rusk, recorded in his notes of the meeting.

"Lyndon Johnson, Bob McNamara and Bobby Kennedy joined us. Bobby continued his tough, savage comments, most of them directed against the Department of State for reasons which are difficult to understand. When I took exception to some of the more extreme things he said by suggesting that the way to get out of our present jam was not to simply double up on everything we had done, he turned on me savagely," according to Bowles's notes.[1]

The outburst came, according to RFK biographer C. David Heymann, after Bowles—described by Heymann as Kennedy's favorite whipping boy—read a State Department paper saying that Castro couldn't be ousted from office with anything less than a full-scale invasion.

"That's the most meaningless, worthless thing I've ever heard," Bobby said. "You people are so anxious to protect your own asses that you're afraid to do anything. All you want to do is dump the whole thing on the president. We'd be better off if you just quit and left foreign policy to someone else."[2]

Bobby's tirade continued two days later at a National Security Council meeting on Cuba, according to Bowles, when again Bobby "took the lead as at the previous meeting, slamming into anyone who suggested that we go slowly and try to move calmly and not repeat previous mistakes.

"The atmosphere was almost as emotional as the Cabinet meeting two days earlier, the difference being that on this occasion the emphasis was on specific proposals to harass Castro. . . . The President limited himself largely to asking questions—questions, however, which led in one direction." Bowles said he "left the meeting with a feeling of intense alarm, tempered somewhat with the hope that this represented largely an emotional reaction of a group of people who were not used to setbacks or defeats and whose pride and confidence had been deeply wounded."[3]

As subsequent events were to suggest, no one's pride and confidence were more deeply wounded by the Bay of Pigs than the Kennedy brothers'.

Preoccupied with his duties as the new attorney general, Bobby had been absent from preinvasion decisions involving Cuba and the Bay of Pigs. His only exposure came in a January briefing by the Pentagon and the State Department just after his brother's inauguration and, at the request of the president, a briefing by Richard Bissell a week before the invasion.[4] Bobby's role changed dramatically with the brigade's defeat.

"To understand the Kennedy administration's obsession with Cuba, it is important to understand the Kennedys, especially Robert. From their perspective, Castro won the first round at the Bay of Pigs," Bissell reflected in his memoirs. "He had defeated the Kennedy team; they were bitter and could not tolerate his getting away with it. The president and his brother were ready to avenge their personal embarrassment by overthrowing their enemy at any cost."[5]

Six months later that obsession culminated with Operation Mongoose, a multiagency covert action program of propaganda, economic sabotage, and infiltration of exile units to foment an uprising in Cuba, directed by Air Force Brig. Gen. Edward Lansdale, a somewhat quirky and flamboyant officer who had made a reputation in the Philippines as a counterinsurgency expert. But the last word on Mongoose—and everybody involved knew it—rested with the attorney general.

Bobby had given the first clue of his new role in formulating Cuba policy on April 19, a day before the brigade's collapse was a *fait accompli,* in a handwritten memo to the president, planting the seeds for a new secret war—and what many people view as the beginning of a Kennedy vendetta—against Castro. The memo declared in part:

> The alternative to the steps that were taken this past week [Bay of Pigs] would have been to sit and wait and hope that in the future some fortuitous event would occur to change the situation. This, it was decided, should not be done. The immediate failure of the rebels' activities in Cuba

69

does not permit us, it seems to me, to return to the status quo with our policy toward Cuba being one of waiting and hoping for good luck. The events of the last few days make this inconceivable.

Therefore, equally important to working out a plan to extricate ourselves gracefully from the situation in Cuba is developing a policy in light of what we expect we will be facing a year or two years from now! Castro will be even more bombastic, will be more and more closely tied to Communism, will be better armed, and will be operating an even more tightly held state than if these events had not transpired. . . . Something forceful and determined must be done. Furthermore, serious attention must be given to this problem immediately and not wait for the situation in Cuba to revert back to a time of relative peace and calm with the U.S. having been beaten off with her tail between her legs.

What is going on in Cuba in the last few days must also be a tremendous strain on Castro. It seems to me that this is the time to decide what our long-term policies are going to be and what will be the results of these policies. The time has come for a showdown for in a year or two years the situation will be vastly worse. If we don't want Russia to set up missile bases in Cuba, we had better decide now what we are willing to do to stop it.[6]

In the same memo, hoping to galvanize concerted hemisphere action, Bobby wondered "if it was reported that one or two of Castro's MIGs attacked Guantanamo Bay and the United States made noises like this was an act of war and that we might very well have to take armed action ourselves, would it be possible to get the countries of Central and South America through OAS to take some action to prohibit the shipment of arms or ammunition from any outside force into Cuba?"[7]

By the time the National Security Council met again April 27, Bowles observed that the "climate is getting considerably better, and the emotional attitudes are falling back into line. If anyone had not attended the previous meetings, he would have thought the NSC meeting this morning had its share of fire and fury. However, it was in far lower key. . . . At this stage plans continue for all kinds of harassment to punish Castro for the humiliation he has brought to our door. However, the general feeling is that all this should be handled carefully, that there should not be too much publicity, that attitudes of others should be taken into account."[8]

President Kennedy had already asked the Defense Department to "develop a plan" for overthrowing Castro by military force, but he cautioned that his request "should not be interpreted as an indication that

U.S. military action against Cuba is probable." The request to Secretary of Defense Robert McNamara came the same day, April 20, that the president was telling the American Society of Newspaper Editors "our restraint is not inexhaustible."[9] All this occurred with the ultimate fate of the Cuban Brigade, how many had escaped, been captured, or killed, unknown.

Walt Rostow, then the deputy national security assistant, followed with his own advice to the president, warning "right now the greatest problem we face is not to have the whole of our foreign policy thrown off balance by what we feel and what we do about Cuba itself. We have suffered a serious setback; but it will be trivial compared to the consequences of not very soon gaining momentum along the lines which we have begun in the past three months."

Rostow then offered his assessment of the administration's existing foreign policy and his recommendations for regaining initiative and momentum. It came with what appeared to be implicit advice for Bobby to calm down, when he noted, "as I said to the Attorney General the other day, when you are in a fight and knocked off your feet, the most dangerous thing to do is to come out swinging wildly."[10]

Not only was Bobby taking control of the new clandestine effort against Castro, the president also named him to the Taylor board of inquiry into the Bay of Pigs. Presumably the appointment was made, in part, to assure that the board's findings, if not favorable, were at least acceptable to the White House. In its mid-June final report, the Taylor group reinforced the views of those like Bobby Kennedy who were all for action now. The report noted "the general feeling that there can be no long-term living with Castro as a neighbor." It recommended that "the Cuban situation be reappraised in the light of all presently known factors and new guidance be provided for political, military, economic and propaganda action against Castro."[11]

As Heymann observed, "on the [Taylor] committee and off, RFK took it upon himself to shift fault for the failure." Hanson Baldwin, then military editor of the *New York Times,* told Heymann about a telephone conversation he had with the attorney general: "I talked to Bobby Kennedy over the phone and, of course, he was trying to get the onus off his brother. . . . He said: 'Well, have you looked at the role of the Joint Chiefs of Staff in this? They're the ones to blame. You ought to investigate that.' And I said 'I have and I will.' In fact, I'd talked to all the Joint Chiefs . . .

and it was pretty clear that it was a botched-up operation all around. [John] Kennedy had lost his nerve. He never really understood what he was doing, I guess. He took it on too soon."[12]

The next significant date in the evolution of the administration's post–Bay of Pigs Cuba policy came at a May 5 meeting of the National Security Council, during which it was formally agreed, and later approved by the president, that "U.S. policy toward Cuba should aim at the downfall of Castro." The National Security Council also decided "that the United States should not undertake military intervention in Cuba now, but should do nothing that would foreclose the possibility of military intervention in the future." Richard Goodwin, assistant to the special counsel to the president, was to continue as chairman of the Cuba Task Force. Notes of the meeting recorded that "it was decided that sooner or later we probably would have to intervene in Cuba, but that now is not the time." Secretary of State Rusk "wanted to hold off on covert actions a little while at least. CIA and the task group will look at all covert proposals for Cuba." The formation of a Cuban Freedom Brigade was rejected, but approval was given for "the induction of Cuban volunteers into the U.S. military forces."[13]

The historical record indicates that the drafting of, and reaching agreement on, a new covert action plan against Cuba occupied much of the rest of the spring and summer. Bissell, still in charge of the CIA's covert operations, convened his agency troops on May 9, telling them "there is an urgent need to decide what we are going to do next—what people and facilities we are going to use . . . planning and carrying out sabotage operations which would call for the use of a minimum of people . . . also think of training programs for resistance and underground types." He cited the need for "an outline proposal for covert action" to be drafted within a week.[14] The result was a May 19 document, entitled "Program of Covert Action Aimed at Weakening the Castro Regime," premised on three basic assumptions: (1) There would be no intervention of U.S. armed forces except in response to aggressive military action by Cuba directed at the United States; (2) There would be no organizing and training of a Cuban exile military force for action against Cuba; but (3) The United States would permit and provide "covert support of Cuban clandestine activities and the carrying out of covert unilateral activities . . . including the use of maritime and air facilities within the United States as the bases for staging sabotage, in-exfiltration, supply, raider and propaganda (including leaflet dropping) operations."

The objective was to "plan, implement and sustain a program of covert action designed to exploit the economic, political and psychological vulnerabilities of the Castro regime. It is neither expected nor argued that the successful execution of this covert program will in itself result in the overthrow of the Castro regime" except "only as the covert contribution to an overall national program designed to accelerate the moral and physical disintegration of the Castro government."

The proposal broke the covert program into Short Term Tasks and Long Term Tasks. Identified as Short Term Tasks were: Operational Intelligence Collection; Sabotage Operations against Selected Targets; Operations in Support of Guerrilla Activities; Operations Directed at Defection of Castro Officials; Operations Directed at Destroying the Popular Image of Castro; and Operations Aimed at Strengthening the Prestige and Acceptability of the Revolutionary Council. The Long Term Tasks were: Political Action, Intelligence, Counterintelligence, and Psychological.[15]

Even as the debate over a covert action plan continued, "occasional operations were mounted during the summer but there was no overall strategy and little activity."[16] Bobby's impatience and frustration were growing with the lack of progress toward an acceptable plan. He reflected his unhappiness in a June 1 memorandum complaining: "The Cuba matter is being allowed to slide, mostly because nobody really has an answer to Castro. Not many are really prepared to send American troops in there at the present time but maybe that is the answer. Only time will tell."[17]

In July a refined covert action program was presented to the Special Group, the select high-level committee representing State, Defense, CIA, and the White House that dealt with and approved covert activities. The paper cited as its basic objective: "to provide support to a U.S. program to develop opposition to Castro and to help bring about a regime acceptable to the U.S." The Special Group agreed that "sabotage operations, particularly, require a close policy look" and that "any major operations in this field would be subject to further approval by the Special Group."[18]

Richard Goodwin followed with an August 22 memo to President Kennedy, recommending that the United States "continue and step up covert activities, aimed, in the first instance, at destruction of economic units, and diversion of resources into anti-underground activities. This would be done by Cuban members of Cuban groups with political aims and ideologies."[19] Another Goodwin memo followed after a meeting of his task force, citing among the decisions taken: "Covert activities would now be directed toward the destruction of targets important to the economy, e.g., refineries, plants using U.S. equipment, etc. This would be done within the general framework of covert operations—which is based on the principle that paramilitary activities ought to be carried out through Cuban revolutionary groups which have a potential for establishing an effective political opposition to Castro within Cuba. Within that principle we will do all we can to identify and suggest targets whose destruction will have the maximum economic impact."[20]

An irritating distraction from the efforts to develop a new covert plan arrived at the White House with the September 1961 issue of *Fortune* magazine, which carried a lengthy article by Charles J. V. Murphy, *Fortune's* Washington bureau chief, titled "Cuba: The Record Set Straight." The story essentially shifted blame from the CIA to the White House for the Bay of Pigs failure. The White House was furious. President Kennedy wanted the article rebutted and to find out the source of the story, said Tom Parrott, a CIA official transferred to the White House from the agency to serve as an aide to General Taylor.[21]

Parrott described the president's reaction to the Murphy article:

Kennedy, Jack Kennedy, told people in the White House to go over the thing, very, very carefully and note all the mistakes. Taylor was then supposed to take that thing [the list of mistakes] and go up and see *Time* and *Life* and make the case that Murphy's thing was wrong. It's the kind of thing that ordinarily I would have gone along with Taylor because he was quite meticulous about division of labor and anything that had to do with intelligence or Cuba, I was in on it. But in that one he recognized I couldn't because of my association with Dulles . . . so he took his executive officer, a colonel, up to New York. The colonel told me afterwards it was pathetic; that this list was so trivial that it just didn't make any sense. Taylor was very embarrassed, he felt, trying to make this case. And obviously the *Time* and *Life* people didn't think it was a very good case, but Taylor had to go through with it but he didn't like it.

The source of the story remains a matter of speculation. Dino Brugioni, a CIA photo interpreter, wrote that Murphy told Brugioni and his boss, Art Lundahl, while they were working with Murphy on another story, that the leaker was Admiral Burke, a member of the Taylor Commission on the Bay of Pigs. "The admiral felt that the president had 'chickened out' in not calling for Navy fighter aircraft to cover the Bay of Pigs invasion," wrote Brugioni. "Murphy said that Burke had nothing but contempt for President Kennedy and his 'bagman' at the Department of

Defense, McNamara." According to Brugioni, President Kennedy was "furious" with the story, suspecting General Cabell as the source of the leak and "asked for his resignation. Cabell tried to explain that he was not the source of the leak, but to no avail." Cabell resigned January 31, 1962.[22]

Tom Parrott believed Bissell "may have supplemented" the information Burke provided to Murphy. Parrott said he had

> discovered that Bobby K. had written a memo to brother Jack, saying Murphy's source undoubtedly was Cabell, and perhaps Bissell. I wasn't supposed to have been privy to this memo, but I felt it was so vindictive that I should alert the suspects. Cabell's response was that he had had no contact whatever with Murphy. Bissell's was 'I didn't tell him anything he didn't already know.'
>
> I was so fed up at one point with all the false and exaggerated venom that was coming out of the White House crew, that I stuck my neck out with Taylor. I said that I understood that Admiral Burke had said that Murphy's article was an accurate depiction of what had happened. Taylor fixed me with an icy stare, and I figured I was on my way out of the White House and back to CIA. Then he said, 'It *was* pretty accurate.'[23]

By the fall of 1961, Goodwin also was reflecting frustration in the slow development of an acceptable covert action operation. In a November 1 memorandum to the president that had obviously been influenced by Bobby Kennedy, Goodwin expressed his belief that "the concept of a 'command operation' for Cuba, as discussed with you by the Attorney General, is the only effective way to handle an all-out attack on the Cuban problem. Since I understand you are favorably disposed toward the idea I will not discuss why the present disorganized and uncoordinated operation cannot do the job effectively.

"The beauty of such an operation over the next few months is that we cannot lose. If the best happens we will unseat Castro," said Goodwin. "If not, then at least we will emerge with a stronger underground, better propaganda and a far clearer idea of the dimensions of the problem." And, said Goodwin, the "most effective commander of such an operation" would be the attorney general. The only downside to having Bobby Kennedy head it, he added, "is that he might become too closely identified with what might not be a successful operation."[24]

Two days later, November 3, President Kennedy convened a meeting of about twenty people dealing with Cuban matters at the White House, at which he authorized development of the new covert program. Bobby

Kennedy's handwritten notes of the fifty-five-minute session are the only known record of the meeting. In the notes, he wrote that McNamara had said he would make Lansdale available to him, who he then "assigned . . . to make survey of situation in Cuba—the problem and our assets. My idea is to stir things up on island with espionage, sabotage, general disorder, run & operated by Cubans themselves with every group but Batista-ites [sic] & Communists. Do not know if we will be successful in overthrowing Castro but we have nothing to lose in my estimate."[25] The same day a National Intelligence Estimate on Cuba began by stating that "the Castro regime has sufficient popular support and repressive capabilities to cope with any internal threat likely to develop within the foreseeable future."[26]

The next day, November 4, a top level meeting was convened in the White House attended by Bobby Kennedy, Defense Secretary McNamara, Paul Nitze, the assistant secretary of defense for international security affairs, Secretary of State Rusk, Lansdale, Alexis Johnson, the deputy undersecretary of state for security affairs, Goodwin, and Bissell. A memorandum for the record written by Bissell, reported that "there seemed to be general acceptance" of (a) the "need for close operational coordination of all arms of the U.S. government that could contribute to the operation," and (b) "that responsibility for its direction should be lodged in a task force . . . partly for the express purpose of making possible denial that this was another exclusively CIA undertaking."

Bissell presented a rundown of current and planned CIA activities against Cuba, noting, among other things, that "our approach to date has been to build up competent CIA controlled and independent Cuban capabilities and to set as their priority task the creation of one or more competent resistance organizations within the Island. . . . Meanwhile, however, we are encouraging minor sabotage and planning for larger scale action."[27] The CIA gave a further indication of what was to come in a November 8 paper, which said, "It is now planned to support in the next few months larger scale infiltrations of men and arms for sabotage and perhaps ultimately guerrilla activities when well-conceived operations are proposed by reputable opposition leaders now outside the country or are requested by the resistance leadership from within. In most cases the sponsorship and ultimate responsibility for such operations will rest with Cubans and the Agency's role will be that of furnishing support in the form of funds, training, equipment, communications, frequently the facilities to conduct the actual infiltration itself, and resupply following infiltration if required and feasible."[28]

What became Operation Mongoose was born, but the man who may have inspired its conception—*New York Times* correspondent Tad Szulc—wasn't in attendance at its birth. Bob Hurwitch, the State Department official with the Cuba portfolio and among those at the briefing, gave the following account of Szulc's role in his unpublished memoirs, made available by John Crimmins, one of Hurwitch's former State Department colleagues. Much of Hurwitch's attention at the time had been devoted to working with Bobby Kennedy on the release of more than eleven hundred Bay of Pigs Brigade members still in Cuban prisons. But as he wrote in his memoirs:

> While our operation [prisoner release] was quietly moving ahead, my jour-
> nalist friend, Tad Szulc of the NY Times, surprisingly telephoned to ask if
> he could drop by our home in the Virginia suburbs the next evening. Puz-
> zled, for we had always met before in my office or for luncheon in town, I
> wondered what he was up to. Tad is an excellent newspaperman, a creative
> writer, who had especially good contacts with the Cuban exiles. His under-
> standing of the 'art of the possible,' however, sometimes became distorted
> by some strong romantic notions. I have always liked Tad, and found him
> to be a decent, warm human being. Over a drink the next evening, Tad
> revealed some thinking he had been doing about the Cuban situation. 'If
> the communists could successfully launch wars of national liberation, why
> couldn't we, the U.S.?' he enquired. Wars of national liberation, to be suc-
> cessful, I countered, required highly motivated, well-organized, armed
> opposition from within which was not the case in Cuba. Tad countered
> that some of his Cuban exile contacts believed that the time was ripe, and
> that he was trying the thought out on several people, including Dick Good-
> win at the White House. I paid little attention to Tad's proposal, which I
> thought impractical in the absence of a situation in Cuba warranting such
> action. Tad followed this visit by another several days later, on the same
> theme. Tad reported that he was making good progress with his project,
> and might even have a meeting with President Kennedy on the subject.
> Foolishly, I thought he was boasting, and concentrated upon liberating the
> Bay of Pigs prisoners. Within a week, there was a high-level, inter-agency
> meeting at the White House which I attended. There, we were given a
> recital of Tad's project (without identifying it as such), and informed that
> a Task Force would be established under the overall supervision of the
> Attorney General, and under the daily operational control of Air Force
> General Lansdale. Flabbergasted by this turn of events, I was speechless and

regrettably failed to object to what had seemed to me a doomed, romantic adventure.[29]

Hurwitch's account of the origins of Mongoose suggest it was more than a coincidence that Goodwin asked Szulc to meet with Bobby Kennedy on November 8, five days after the White House meeting, to discuss the Cuba situation "off-the-record." Szulc did so "as a friend of Goodwin's, not as a reporter," Szulc told the Church Committee in 1975.

"During the meeting with Robert Kennedy, the discussion centered on 'the situation in Cuba following the [Bay of Pigs] invasion [and] the pros and cons of some different possible actions by the United States Government in that context.'" according to the committee report.

"At the close of the meeting, Robert Kennedy asked Szulc to meet with the President. The next day Szulc, accompanied by Goodwin, met with President Kennedy for over an hour in the Oval Office. Szulc recalled that the President discussed 'a number of his views on Cuba in the wake of the Bay of Pigs, asked me a number of questions concerning my conversations with Premier Castro, and . . . what the United States could [or] might do . . . either in a hostile way or in establishing some kind of dialogue.'"

Although the meeting lasted an hour, the only public attention it received was the widely reported question to Szulc by Kennedy: "What would you think if I ordered Castro to be assassinated?"[30]

Neither Goodwin nor Szulc, who died in 2001, acknowledged his role in inspiring Mongoose, although Goodwin related in his 1988 book sentiments regarding Mongoose similar to those Szulc expressed to Hurwitch.

"Bobby," Goodwin said, "was also the point man for his brother's desire to construct an apparatus to counter what was then perceived as the newest technique in the communist arsenal—subversion, guerrilla armies, 'wars of national liberation.' (Not wholly an illusion, proclaimed by Chairman Khrushchev himself as the way to mastery of the third world.) Operation Mongoose, the virtual apotheosis of the Special Forces with their distinctive green berets, a strengthened capacity for covert operations—all these reflected the optimistic, unshakable confidence of the early Kennedy days."[31]

CHAPTER 5

MONGOOSE

I n a fitting irony, the University of Miami's sprawling 1,572-acre South Campus research center that once housed the CIA's forward outpost for Operation Mongoose among its nondescript wood office buildings is now home to the Miami-Dade County Metrozoo.

Attorney General Bobby Kennedy served as the chief Mongoose zoo-keeper, overseeing the clandestine, interagency war against Fidel Castro from Washington, through his designated surrogate and the project's chief of operations, Air Force Brig. Gen. Edward Lansdale. Mongoose lasted a year—from the end of November 1961 until the missile crisis of 1962 condemned it to an unmourned death. It achieved little for the estimated $50 million that was spent on it.

In retrospect, virtually everything about Mongoose was shrouded in a zoolike atmosphere, beginning with its conception, perhaps from the seeds of a journalist's idea, to its cryptonym to the unrealistic and often zany proposals to rid Cuba of Castro, which were put forward under pressure by otherwise serious and intelligent officials. Two of its most significant players—Lansdale and the CIA's Bill Harvey—came to the project with controversial and flamboyant reputations; reputations which they upheld during the course of Mongoose.

But even today, more than four decades and thousands of declassified documents later, Operation Mongoose retains an oddly mystifying quality of a bygone era, cloaked in hyperbole by some and romanticism by others, both of which belie the facts.

There is still a perception in some quarters that it was solely a CIA operation when, in fact, it was seen with disdain by not only many of those in the agency who were privy to Mongoose secrets, but elsewhere in the government as well. Bob Hurwitch, the State Department's representative to the so-called Caribbean Survey Team [Mongoose] wrote that "the entire operation was pathetic, and I ruefully longed for a way to turn it off."[1] At the conclusion of a 1996 conference on the Bay of Pigs and

Mongoose attended by former CIA and Kennedy administration officials and academics, Arthur Schlesinger was asked if he had learned anything new. "Yeah," he responded, "the CIA didn't like Mongoose any better than we did," referring to himself and some other White House aides.[2]

In February 1962, just as Mongoose was becoming operational, CIA Director John McCone designated Dick Helms as the agency official responsible for Cuba. Helms offered this assessment of Mongoose in his posthumously published memoirs:

> We had been busting our britches on the MONGOOSE operation, but aside from a marked improvement in intelligence collection—which was a considerable achievement—there was damn-all to show for it. Despite our maximum effort we had not inspired any resistance activity worth the name in Cuba; the—in my opinion—ill-advised sabotage operations were but pinpricks. The political emigration was less than unified. Propaganda was, at the least, ongoing. It was the ouster of Castro and his unelected government that interested the President; the increase in intelligence was a by-product, no matter how helpful it was to the all-important production of sound National Intelligence Estimates. The agency's operational arm was stretched taut and thin. Our response to President Kennedy's demands had already resulted in what must have been the largest peacetime secret intelligence operation in history—some four to five thousand staff and contract personnel, acres of real estate, and a flotilla-size private navy.

Concluded Helms: "For all the White House pressure, and the combined efforts of everyone involved, Operation MONGOOSE never quite lived up to the dictionary definition, 'an agile mammal.'"[3]

The creation of Mongoose, by most accounts, except those from a handful of Kennedy loyalists, came in response to the obsession of the Kennedy brothers with exacting revenge from Fidel Castro for the defeat at the Bay of Pigs.

As Sam Halpern, a veteran of the OSS assigned as deputy director of the CIA's Caribbean Desk in October 1961, just before Operation Mongoose became official policy, put it: "One thing that I am still kind of confused about—and I've tried for a long time to figure out the answer—is what made these two gentlemen—both the president and the attorney general—so full of hysteria, paranoia and obsession about Cuba. . . . It seems to me there has got to be something more to this, other than the fact that they got bloody noses at the Bay of Pigs. Maybe their father convinced them to. . . . Don't get mad, get even. I mean: to make Cuba the number-one priority of the agency, at the expense of everything else; then to put Bobby in charge of the operation and this—this boy, really, this hot-tempered boy—to try to run it and do the personal bidding of his brother. Unbelievable."[4]

To Halpern goes credit, or blame, for the code name Mongoose. A short time after he arrived at the CIA's Cuba Desk, he received a request from Lansdale, who knew Halpern from the Philippines in the 1950s. Lansdale wanted a cryptonym for the new operation, telling Halpern it was easier for him to get one from CIA than to go through the bureaucracy at the Pentagon, where Lansdale was located.[5]

"So I picked up the phone and called an old friend of mine from OSS days in World War Two who was the cryptic reference officer in charge of cryptonyms and pseudonyms," Halpern recalled. "I said 'Charlotte [Gilbert], I need a cryptonym from the other side of the world. I want to confuse people in the building for about 30 seconds.' She said, 'how about the MO diagraph?' I said 'that's fine with me.' The MO diagraph indicated Thailand in those days. She sent me a list of about a half a dozen . . . from the dictionary at random that weren't being used at that moment." Mongoose was among them.

"I didn't know what the hell a mongoose was and I didn't bother to look it up. . . . I had no idea of the legend about the mongoose and the snake. I picked mongoose. It sounded good to me and it makes good sense. I picked up the phone and called Ed [Lansdale] and said 'the crypt you want is mongoose.' He said 'spell it,' so I spelled it for him and then Ed began to use it. We named it but we in the agency never used it internally . . . but he used it for every other part of the government and he used it when he sent papers to us, all stamped Operation Mongoose."

Mongoose, said Halpern, "was a special activity and from that point of view, whoever knew about Mongoose was kind of in a club all by themselves . . . the Mongoose brotherhood. . . . You could talk about it. Ed used it with the Special Group [high-level group that approved covert activities] and everybody started talking about Mongoose. It could have been any other name . . . but it just happened to be Mongoose."

The name itself had "no relation to anything," Halpern said, except that "Thailand is on the other side of the globe and I figured if we had wanted to use a crypt for Cuba at that time we would have had to use AM, like the AMLASH Operation. That identifies the crypt as belonging to the Cuba activity. It doesn't tell you what it is, but you look at it out of the blue, if somebody throws AMLASH at you, the AM means it has to do with Cuba." According to Halpern, the first time the name Mongoose surfaced publicly was during the Church Committee's 1975 Senate hearings on alleged assassinations.

Shortly after his arrival on the Caribbean desk, or Branch 4, of the Western Hemisphere Affairs Division, Halpern and his boss, Ghosn Zogby, were called in by Bissell, who was in his last weeks as head of the clandestine services. He told them he "had just been chewed out in the Cabinet room of the White House by the president and the attorney general for sitting on his ass and doing nothing about Cuba."[6]

"The new marching orders," said Halpern, "were to get rid of Castro and the Castro regime. I asked Dick Bissell, 'what are the limitations?' Bissell said very clearly, 'as far as I know, none.' As far as I was concerned there were none. The whole idea was to come up with some ideas how to get rid of him. The first thing we had to do was start writing papers for the Special Group."

The Special Group consisted of the number-two men in all the agencies involved. It met in the White House as necessary to approve covert action programs. When Bobby Kennedy and General Taylor were added solely for Cuba matters, it became the Special Group Augmented, or SGA.

"The problems of trying to write papers . . . at that point were innumerable and I told Helms, 'Look, we don't have a pot to piss in. We don't know what the hell's going on in Cuba. How the hell can we do something about it until we get some intelligence? We've got to find out what's going on. . . . We need answers before you can plan anything. We just can't plan in a vacuum. I kept yelling like that. . . . I don't know what kind of an impact I made, maybe none, but we were still told to write papers."

The one thing they did not have a problem with, said Halpern, was funding. "When you are running an operation and the president of the United States is personally, directly involved . . . money is no object. We never had to worry about money. If we wanted to spend a half-million bucks on something, we spent it. We never worried about where it was coming from. Nobody knows where the hell it's coming from. Nobody cares. The president directs it; you do it. So when somebody asks how much does Mongoose cost, there's no way to tell."[7]

It was nearing the end of 1961. The program had been approved, but it was still very much in its embryonic stages. Lansdale had taken over as its chief of operations, working from the Pentagon, in part to keep him from being "tainted" by the CIA, which he already had alienated with criticism of the Bay of Pigs.

"Ed Lansdale was a great sparkplug on this but basically it was Bobby Kennedy who did everything. Bobby Kennedy was a guy who was pushing, pushing Ed for all of this kind of stuff," said Halpern. "And the thing is that Mongoose, or what later became Mongoose, was never, never, never designed, either by Ed Lansdale or Bobby Kennedy, to be solely a CIA operation. Every agency in town had their Mongoose compartment, all very highly secret. You know, don't touch; burn before reading and all that kind of nonsense." Those agencies directly involved in Mongoose were the CIA, the State and Defense Departments, and the United States Information Agency, with the Department of Justice (FBI) participating as required.[8]

Kennedy and Lansdale, according to Halpern, had expected each of the participating agencies to detail men, money, and material to the operation, but McCone, the new CIA director, Secretary of State Rusk and Secretary of Defense McNamara, all resisted. "Ed didn't like it because his responsibilities and authority would be diminished."

During this same late 1961 time frame Ted Shackley—an up-and-coming young CIA operative who had returned from Europe to agency headquarters, where he was dealing with Eastern Europe—was told by his boss to talk to Bill Harvey. Although Harvey did not formally take charge of the CIA's Cuba task force until February 1962, Cuba already was in his sights.

Shackley had worked for Harvey in Berlin, where the hard-charging, heavy-drinking CIA veteran made his reputation by engineering a six-hundred-yard tunnel into East Berlin to spy on the Soviets. And he was about to work for him again. When he met with Harvey in 1961, said Shackley, "He said, 'Do me a favor. Go to Miami. Spend whatever time necessary. Write me a report. Tell me with no BS what it is one needs to do from a tactical operational level if we're going to design a program for Cuba.' I think by December of 1961, somebody already was talking with Harvey about doing something on Cuba," and he wanted an assessment "to see if it was something he should tackle." Shackley went to Miami that same month, where he spent three weeks working on his report.[9]

Shackley said he looked at Cuba as a "new problem" in terms of an intelligence collection target, asking himself: "What do we know? What do we need to know? What are we doing operationally? What should we do that we are not doing? And what would it take in terms of manpower and money to do it?" Shackley wrote his report, went back to Washington, edited it, and turned it in to Harvey. "He read it. I chatted one day on it with him, and I said good-bye. My job was over. I went back to what I was doing."

For Shackley, the return to his old position at headquarters was short-lived. "In late January 1962 my boss said I had two calls, one from Harvey and one from McCone. I think that was a Friday afternoon." Both callers said they wanted Shackley in Miami the following Monday morning to begin a new assignment as deputy station chief. The old station chief departed shortly after Shackley arrived, and he became head of JMWAVE, code name for the Miami Station, a position he kept until June 1965.

During the short lifetime of Mongoose, JMWAVE grew to be the largest station in the world outside headquarters in Langley, Virginia. Eventually some four hundred clandestine service officers toiled there, overseeing the activities of thousands of Cuban exiles added to the payroll for everything from propaganda to sabotage. Some three to four hundred front companies were created throughout South Florida. The agency owned or leased marinas, boats, planes, "safe houses," and scores of other properties in addition to operating the third largest navy in the Caribbean, after the United States and Cuba.

For Bissell, it was hard to understand decades later that the cautious president, who canceled the air strikes at the Bay of Pigs, had aggressively, through his brother, hammered on the CIA to do more. "If the Kennedys felt this strongly about waging war against Castro," wrote Bissell, "relaxing the constraints that crippled the planners at the Bay of Pigs would have been much easier in the long run . . . than undertaking a successor project in the hope of achieving the same results." Bissell concluded that the debate was still open on whether Mongoose was a good operation and served the long-term interests of the United States.[10]

History suggests that Mongoose was neither a "good operation" nor "served the long-term interests of the United States." And it certainly did not achieve its objective, as stated by Lansdale, of bringing about the downfall of Castro by "a popular movement of Cubans from *within* Cuba," with support from the United States. The option of U.S. military intervention, if necessary, always loomed in the background.

"I guess I would describe it as really an amorphous exercise that wasn't going to go anywhere and it didn't go anywhere," said Tom Parrott, who kept minutes for the high-level SGA that had Mongoose oversight responsibilities. "The objective was once described, I think, to keep the pot simmering, or something like that. But nothing really concrete came out of it that amounted to anything. Lansdale was totally incompetent in that job. He sold himself to the Kennedy boys as the greatest thing since James Bond . . . [but] they were just spinning their wheels."[11]

The passage of time exposed the folly of the operation, but in late 1961 Mongoose was still in its early stages of development. Reservations about the operation never reached the top, or if they did, they were ignored. Declassified documents reflected widespread skepticism, however. Asked how enthusiastic the CIA was about Mongoose, Halpern replied: "We weren't, from the director on down, we weren't, I'll tell you. Hell, I fought it all I could. You do what you're told to do, but the thing was silly."[12]

Bissell recalled that when the "Kennedys wanted action, they wanted it fast." Looking for a quick solution, Bobby "was impressed by Lansdale's name and reputation, more so than any concrete plans Lansdale evolved." Bissell remembered attending Mongoose meetings "where Lansdale outlined his approach, but . . . I thought his ideas impractical and never had much faith they would be successful. I was under a stern injunction, however, to do everything possible to assist him."[13]

Halpern described Lansdale as a "con man, absolutely perfect. He's the man in the gray flannel suit from Madison Avenue in New York. I think he could sell refrigerators to Eskimos or . . . the Brooklyn Bridge to people who don't have cars. I betcha he could sell that, too. He was very good. You got to give him credit for that."[14]

Parrott, as White House keeper of the minutes for the Special Group, said that he "had a little network of people that I dealt with in State, Defense, and CIA on coordinating things before these meetings. And we . . . I guess about four of us . . . came up with a name for Lansdale because we didn't want to use the name so much on a lot of nonsecure phones. So we called him the FM, the Field Marshal. It was really pretty bad and it [Mongoose] was not effective, obviously."[15]

One of the more colorful assessments of Lansdale came from Al Haig, who became involved with Cuba post-Mongoose, in February 1963, as an aide to Army Secretary Cyrus Vance and working directly for Joe Califano, the Army's general counsel. "I was told to go up and see Ed Lansdale when I joined Vance. I went up to see him and he's the strangest duck I ever talked to. It was something else. He was telling me about the Philippines. That's all he wanted to talk about. I didn't get anything on Cuba. I went back to Joe and said, 'That's a complete waste of time.' I said, 'That guy's a dingbat.' I thought he was then, and to this day, I think he was."[16]

But Lansdale moved ahead, self-confident and unfazed. In a December 7 memorandum—referring to an earlier presidential memorandum—Lansdale noted it had been decided "that the United States will use all available assets in a project to help Cuba overthrow the Communist regime." He complained that the past "orientation and programming" of the CIA regarding Cuba had been "definitely out of phase with the objective of establishing a popular movement within Cuba to overthrow Castro and the Communist regime. In the main, CIA thinking has been to apply militant force covertly (such as action teams for 'smash and grab' raids on up to armed resistance groups), in the hope that a popular uprising would possibly harass the regime. The early task, then, has been to re-orient this 180°, with militant (sabotage, etc.) actions to be considered as part of the support of the popular movement we are generating. The basic strategy of building our action upon a genuine internal popular movement is underlined; this will apply the major lesson to be learned from earlier operations in Indonesia and Cuba."

Lansdale then listed four "tasks assigned to the representative of the Director of Central Intelligence" along with four "bold new actions to help the popular movement for CIA executive follow through." Included among the tasks were tightening and reorienting its Cuba activities "with a hard look at operational effectiveness, especially the management and programs of the field station in Florida." Another task was the formation of a "nucleus for a popular Cuban movement" and a "program for this Cuban nucleus to use."

The final task called for "special support projects" to be "readied for use on call. These projects (such as operations to scuttle shipping and otherwise hamper the regime) will be timed to support actions by the movement and to permit the movement to take credit for them." Lansdale's memo also cited what he expected of the State and Defense Departments and the U.S. Information Agency for the Mongoose program.[17]

As described by Halpern, it was a time of both frenzy and frustration for the CIA operatives involved with Mongoose.

We were struggling like hell over the Thanksgiving holiday and Christmas and New Year's trying to make sense out of these vague ideas about how to get rid of Castro. . . . It was murder. It was just flat out trying to make

86

sense out of what the hell we could offer them, and I kept saying, 'All we can offer them is we'll get some intelligence and when we get the intelligence, after that then maybe we can come up with a plan, but not before.'

I remember arguing, I think with Bissell, before we got Ed's papers . . . and we could have done a better job than Ed on that . . . if you want just talk and smoke and mirrors, we can do it, but it's silly if we sit down and write a piece of paper for the president of the United States, which is who you're writing for when you write for the Special Group, and we can't produce. I said, 'We'll be in worse shape than we are now. This is crazy. Nobody likes us anyway. After the Bay of Pigs, we're all a bunch of dummies. And if we promise something and can't produce it, this is going to be a garden tea party compared to what will happen to us afterwards. . . . They'll cut us to ribbons.'[18]

In a January 11, 1962, progress report to the Special Group, Lansdale indicated problems with recruiting "suitable Cubans to accomplish the initial task of infiltration." He also reported that "the prevailing policy on sabotage is still in effect, i.e., that no actions which would be dangerous to the population will be undertaken, nor will major demolitions be done at this stage."[19] On the diplomatic and economic side, the State Department was laying the groundwork for hemisphere isolation of the Castro government at an upcoming OAS foreign ministers meeting and preparing for the imposition by President Kennedy of a full trade embargo against Cuba, both overt elements of Operation Mongoose, which occurred in February 1962.[20]

In a January 18 "Program Review" of Mongoose, Lansdale laid out a "target schedule" for thirty-two "tasks" to be achieved by the CIA, State and Defense Departments, and the U.S. Information Agency in the areas of intelligence, political, economic, psychological, and military action. Many of them were creative, others obviously unrealistic, unachievable, and even idiotic. Some examples:

Task 5: CIA to submit plan by 1 February for defection of top Cuban government officials, to fracture the regime from within. The effort must be imaginative and bold enough to consider a 'name' defector to be worth at least a million U.S. dollars. This can be a key to our political action goal and must be mounted without delay as a major CIA project. . . .

Task 17: State to report by 15 February on feasibility of harassing Bloc shipping by refusing entry to U.S. ports (statedly for security reasons), if vessels have called at Cuban ports. . . .

Task 25: USIA to submit plan by 15 February for the most effective psychological exploitation of actions undertaken in the Project, towards the end result of awakening world sympathy for the Cuban people (as a David) battling against the Communist regime (as a Goliath) and towards stimulating Cubans inside Cuba to join 'the cause.'. . . .

Task 28: By 15 February CIA will report on plans and actions for propaganda support of the popular movement inside Cuba. Included will be exactly what is planned for use by the movement inside Cuba, and feasibility of using smuggled food packets (such as the 'I Shall Return' cigarette packets to Philippine guerrillas in World War II) as morale boosters in generating popular support. . . . .

Task 29: Defense to submit contingency plan for U.S. military force to support the Cuban popular movement, including a statement of conditions under which Defense believes such action would be required to win the Project's goal and believes such action would not necessarily lead to general war. Due 28 February.

In the same paper, Lansdale gave several further indications that U.S. military intervention—a theme that runs continuously through the life of Mongoose—was seriously contemplated under the right conditions. He concluded a section headed "Concept of Operation" by declaring: "The climactic moment of revolt will come from an angry reaction of the people to a government action (sparked by an incident), or from a fracturing of the leadership cadre within the regime, or both. (A major goal of the Project must be to bring this about.) The popular movement will capitalize on this climactic moment by initiating an open revolt. Areas will be taken and held. If necessary, the popular movement will appeal for help to the free nations of the Western Hemisphere. The United States, if possible in concert with other Western Hemisphere nations, will then give open support to the Cuban peoples' revolt. Such support will include military force, as necessary."[21]

A day later, on January 19, Bobby Kennedy convened a meeting with CIA and Defense Department representatives, telling them in no uncertain terms that solving the Cuba problem "carries the top priority in the United States Government—all else is secondary—no time, money, effort or manpower is to be spared. There can be no misunderstanding on the involvement of the agencies concerned or on their responsibility to carry out this job. The agency heads understand that you are to have full backing on what you need."

He then noted, ominously, that "yesterday . . . the President indicated to the Attorney General that 'the final chapter on Cuba has not been written'—it's got to be done and will be done." He concluded by exhorting those present to address themselves "unfailingly" and "with every resource at your command" to the "32 tasks" given them by Lansdale.[22]

At the CIA Halpern's ongoing insistence on the need for intelligence before planning was beginning to bear fruit. "We're in January of '62 and we're still trying to come up with some decent papers for the Special Group Augmented," said Halpern. "We're going crazy trying to write something people will accept without promising the moon. . . . We just can't do it. First of all, we have got to have intelligence. That's what we kept on screaming bloody murder on. I kept saying to Dick Helms [the CIA's Cuba representative for Mongoose] particularly, that we need some senior people in this operation. This is a political operation in the city of Washington, D.C. It's got nothing to do with the security of the United States. We need somebody with some whammy up on the Hill."[23]

By mid-January, Helms agreed that they needed more clout in dealing with Cuba, said Halpern, "but he also takes a look at the [internal bureaucratic] problem and he says, 'What else do you have besides Cuba?' And we told him we had all the other islands. He picked up the phone and he called J. C. King and right then and there Cuba was taken out of Branch 4, which made sense, particularly with the pressure from outside. Cuba was now alone and organized as a one-country task force."

The clout arrived in early February 1962 in the form of Bill Harvey, who took charge of the agency's Cuba operation, under Helms. "Lansdale was very happy that somebody with Bill Harvey's background and name . . . was in charge and not a Zogby or a Halpern. Bill comes over and sets up Task Force W, and we send out a book message to all stations that by presidential order 'Cuba is number one priority around the world. And fellows you need to put your shoulder to the wheel kind of thing.' Cuba was number one as far as the president was concerned. Cuba was it."

Shackley arrived in Miami and, said Halpern,

We start building what amounts to an intelligence collection activity plus some sabotage that goes along with it, simply because the powers that be wanted 'boom and bang'; that was the phrase used by everybody. Finally, I think, and the record is quite clear on this, the Special Group itself, after looking at Lansdale's original charges to all of the various agencies in town, also decides that it ought to be basically intelligence operations with sabotage in there but not the major activity, just secondary.

The Special Group says, let's turn this into basically an intelligence collection operation first. We'll worry about sabotage second, instead of the other way around. So we start getting and using, not only people in Miami whom we recruit and send back into the island to collect intelligence. We also use every other possibility . . . foreigners from around the world visiting Cuba . . . diplomats who travel, diplomats who stay in . . . everything. We were able, over a period of several months, to start getting some decent information about what was going on.

On March 2, the Special Group agreed that "the immediate objective of the U.S. during March, April, and May will be the acquisition of intelligence and that other U.S. actions must be inconspicuous and consistent with the overall policy of isolating Castro and of neutralizing his influence in the Western Hemisphere."[24]

By February 20, Lansdale was ready to unveil the "firm time-table" he had promised in his January 18 paper assigning tasks. It was a doozy, containing a thirty-nine-page action plan to begin in March and neatly divided into six phases. They were:

Phase I, *Action*, March 1962. Start moving in.

Phase II, *Build-up*, April–July 1962. Activating the necessary operations inside Cuba for revolution and concurrently applying the vital political, economic, and military-type support from outside Cuba.

Phase III, *Readiness*, 1 August 1962, check for final policy decision.

Phase IV, *Resistance*, August–September 1962, move into guerrilla operations.

Phase V, *Revolt*, first two weeks of October 1962. Open revolt and overthrow of the Communist regime.

Phase VI, *Final*, during month of October 1962. Establishment of new government.

Lansdale again raised the question in the paper on U.S. intervention, noting "a vital decision, still to be made, is on the use of open U.S. force to aid the Cuban people in winning their liberty. If conditions and assets permitting a revolt are achieved in Cuba, and if U.S. help is required to sustain this condition, will the U.S. respond promptly with military force to aid the Cuban revolt?"[25]

So unrealistic does Lansdale's plan appear—at least outside the netherworld of spooks and spies—anybody reading the plan today might wonder if he were living on another planet or perpetrating a joke. The plan is divided into seven categories, entitled: (A) Basic Action Plan Inside Cuba; (B) Political Support Plan; (C) Economic Support Plan; (D) Psychological Support Plan; (E) Military Support Plan; (F) Sabotage Support Plan; and (G) Intelligence Support Plan. Each category is then broken down by months into descriptions of project actions within Cuba, their purpose, and considerations.

In April, for example, the first action listed under Operation in Cuba reads:

"Establish up to five more agent operations in key areas selected by CIA." The purpose: "Report on resistance potential and lay groundwork for additional agent operations." Considerations: "These additional teams should provide current reporting on major Cuban areas, so broad political action program can be planned. Risk to teams will continue high, but mission is essential."

And the next to last action cited for August: "Cuban paramilitary teams infiltrated to bases in the hills." The purpose: "To provide a trained guerrilla cadre upon which to form guerrilla units." Considerations: "The paramilitary teams must be capable of initiating minor harassment and reprisal actions, as well as organizing and training guerrilla units. Popular support is essential."[26]

Again, from Halpern's view, "We took one look at this list of stuff we had to do . . . the CIA had its part, the military had its part, and everybody else had their parts to do, and it made no sense at all. But that's a beautiful plan on a piece of paper. It looks marvelous, except it has no relation to reality. If you take a look at that thing, and you're supposed to recruit ten agents this week and fourteen new sources and you're going to get sabotage sources and psychological warriors. . . . You don't find people overnight in blocs of ten, ten there and fifteen here, twenty there. Look at the plan. Just look at that. . . . It's crazy. And we were under orders and we had to write papers." Neither did Halpern see it as a coincidence that under Lansdale's by-the-numbers schedule, the climax was to come in late October. Lansdale "just thought that because there were elections for Congress the next week in this country. . . . You don't have to be a magician or brain surgeon to figure [the connection between] a big victory parade in Havana and the next week elections come on."[27]

On the same day Lansdale was unveiling his plan, a State Department official, in a memo to a superior, dared question the entire concept as outlined in Lansdale's January 18 "Program Review." Roger Hilsman, director of the State Department's Bureau of Intelligence and Research, in a memo to Alexis Johnson, the deputy undersecretary of state for political affairs, expressed "serious misgivings." Hilsman questioned whether the CIA could build up the popular movement within Cuba called for by Mongoose, observing "on the contrary, the evidence points toward the present regime's tightening up its controls. This leads me to conclude, as others have, that unless a popular uprising in Cuba is promptly supported by overt U.S. military action, it would probably lead to another Hungary. Briefly, I do not believe we can unseat the present regime in Havana by anything short of outright military intervention." There is no indication Hilsman's warning was heeded.[28]

Mongoose moved ahead. For those involved, the pressure from the top to produce was becoming intense. As Bissell noted, so great was Bobby's involvement in supervising Mongoose "he might as well have been director for plans for the operation."[29]

Former Defense Secretary Robert McNamara, in 1975 testimony before the Church Committee, remembered "we were hysterical about Castro at the time of the Bay of Pigs and thereafter, and there was pressure from JFK and RFK to do something about Castro." Helms characterized the atmosphere surrounding Mongoose as "pretty intense, and I remember vividly it was very intense. . . . [N]utty schemes were born of the intensity of the pressure. And we were quite frustrated."[30]

CHAPTER 6

"NUTTY SCHEMES"

I n his Church Committee testimony Richard Helms didn't elaborate what he meant by the "nutty schemes" he said the pressure to rid Cuba of Castro engendered, but the historical record provides abundant examples. They ranged from the silly to the sublime, with the outrageous sandwiched among them, and they did not include the numerous assassination plots against Castro, which the author dealt with separately. Some proposals now seem more like practical jokes than ideas that were seriously contemplated. Many, but not all, were encompassed within Operation Mongoose. Of those under Mongoose, a large number originated within the Pentagon—under the code name Operation North-woods—as justification to invade Cuba. The CIA, too, offered its share of schemes, beginning well before and continuing well after Mongoose, but apart from the assassination schemes, most were markedly subtler in their approach than proposals from the Pentagon. Such "nutty schemes" were embodied in, but not necessarily born of, the character of their leaders— from the Kennedy brothers to Mongoose Operations chief Ed Lansdale, from the CIA's Bill Harvey to the generals at the Pentagon—and a mentality shaped by the Cold War.

Bob Hurwitch, the State Department's representative to the Caribbean Survey Group, a more sedate title for the multiagency Mongoose working group, saw Lansdale as "a graduate of the Madison Avenue advertising world. He had achieved fame, probably justifiably so, for a successful, innovative program in the Philippines, working closely with President Magsaysay. Cutting a dashing Air Force figure, very clever about imagery including his own, Lansdale became the darling of many who became 'experts' in foreign affairs vicariously."

Hurwitch noted that, "Although he is said to have failed in his efforts in Vietnam, he had sufficient support to obtain his assignment despite his total lack of experience in Latin America, in general, and Cuba, in particular. One of Lansdale's more 'imaginative' ideas was to put someone to work to write a stirring song in Cuban rhythms that would be smuggled into Cuba and adopted by the opposition to Castro as a stimulus to morale. Every advertising man seems to believe that human beings can be motivated to do anything provided the correct influences are brought to bear. But wars of national liberation succeed when political convictions are strong; to attempt to inculcate such motivation from the outside seemed futile to me."[1]

Historian Ronald Steel, in a profile of Bobby Kennedy, described Lansdale as "Bobby's kind of man. He combined anti-communist fervor with a skill for knocking heads together and spilling blood in a noble cause."[2]

Tom Parrott spoke of Lansdale with considerable disdain, calling him "a creature of the Kennedy brothers. They thought he was God . . . just the greatest thing that ever happened. He really didn't come through on anything.[3]

"I'll give you one example of Lansdale's perspicacity," Parrott said in his 1975 testimony before the Church Committee. "He had a wonderful plan for getting rid of Castro. This plan consisted of spreading the word that the Second Coming of Christ was imminent and that Christ was against Castro [who] was anti-Christ. And you would spread the word around Cuba, and then on whatever date it was, that there would be a manifestation of this thing. And at that time—this is absolutely true—and at that time just over the horizon there would be an American submarine which would surface off of Cuba and send up some star shells. And this would be the manifestation of the Second Coming and Castro would be overthrown. . . . Well, some wag called this operation—and somebody dubbed this—'Elimination by Illumination.'"[4] Lansdale was later to refer to Parrott as a "jerk," claiming the story was "absolutely untrue."[5]

As for Harvey, he was nearing the end of his run after the Berlin Tunnel operation, which turned out not to be the success it had initially appeared. It was disclosed in 1997 that the Soviet KGB had known about the tunnel from the beginning, thanks to George Blake, the British intelligence traitor. Harvey reflected his "cowboy" character in Task Force W, the name he gave the CIA's reorganized Cuba unit. The W, according to Sam Halpern, referred to William Walker, the mid–nineteenth-century American freebooter who took over Nicaragua and was eventually captured and executed by a Honduran firing squad. Parrott, who had known Harvey in Germany, says that by the time he took over the Cuba operation, "poor guy, he was on his way to becoming an alcoholic, a real alcoholic, which he did become. And if the meetings were after lunch . . . these high-powered meetings with the [Cabinet] Secretaries there and everything, he was plastered at that time. They didn't know it but I knew it.

"I remember one time my boss, Max Taylor, said 'will you tell your friend Harvey to cease, desist, from mumbling into his umbilicus' and he [Taylor] would go '*xewhfuwtrd xneytgnectya, uygngkhy.*' Another time I was coming back from a meeting with [McGeorge] Bundy and Bundy said 'your friend' . . . it was always my friend . . . said 'your friend Harvey does not inspire confidence.' He was way over his head in many ways."

Parrott recalls the time in Germany when Harvey—well known for having at least one pistol, and sometimes two, stuck in his pants—was leaning over in a Berlin nightclub "and a gun fell out on the table. The waitress said, 'Sir, I think this is yours.'"[6]

Sam Halpern, who worked with both Lansdale and Harvey during his CIA career, had this to say about their roles in Mongoose: "On the main characters of this soap opera: Ed Lansdale and Bill Harvey never saw eye to eye. Then nobody I know ever saw eye to eye with Ed Lansdale on anything. Ed realizes right away that, in Bill Harvey, he has a tough guy to work with. No love is lost between the two. They somehow work together, though, and as the documents show, we did produce what Ed asked for—in terms of paperwork at least."[7]

In this milieu, under the trickle down pressure from above, numerous "nutty schemes" were hatched; that is, "nutty" as seen from the perspective of historical hindsight. Most found their way to, and some originated with, Lansdale, as the chief operations officer for Mongoose.

For example, a day after he outlined his "32 tasks" to the various agencies involved in Mongoose, he added Number 33, which called for the use of chemical warfare to immobilize Cuban sugar workers during harvest with a nonlethal chemical that would sicken them for up to forty-eight hours. According to the Church Committee, this task was initially approved for planning purposes with the notation that it would require "policy determination" before final approval. A study showed the plan was not feasible, and it was canceled without ever going before the Special Group Augmented for debate.[8]

It was neither Lansdale nor Harvey, but Bobby Kennedy who was responsible for what folks at the CIA considered one "nutty" scheme. "We had one officer assigned to do nothing but meet members of the Mafia, who Bobby would identify and tell the officer, in effect, where the meeting was and what time, what place, and everything else," according to Halpern, Harvey's executive assistant. "And that was kind of a 'no no' most of the time because we want to control the meeting place . . . who the hell we see and where we see 'em. But in this case Bobby insisted that we meet Joe Pacachaluka or whoever at such and such a place. Bobby's idea was that the Mafia must have left 'stay behinds' in Cuba and as a result they must know what is going on. So it would be a good intelligence source. It was nonsense. This was simply, allegedly, intelligence collection. We assigned a case officer who dutifully went where he was told and we never disseminated a single solitary line from any of the stuff that this guy picked up. It was hogwash."[9] It was Bobby Kennedy, as well, who was the first to suggest—in a handwritten note to his brother as the Bay of Pigs collapsed—the possibility of a staged attack on Guantánamo Bay Naval Base to help rally hemisphere support against Cuba with the Organization of American States.

By far the most bizarre proposals were spawned by the Pentagon in response to the pressures of Lansdale and Mongoose, as indicated by documents released in 1997 and 1998 by the JFK Assassination Records Review Board. Their proposals also reflected the Pentagon's gung ho attitude regarding Cuba at the time. Many of the ideas were generated in response to Lansdale's January 18, 1962, dictum outlining his "32 tasks" for the various agencies involved in Mongoose.

On January 30, Brig. Gen. William H. Craig, the Defense Department representative to the Caribbean Survey Group offered up for Lansdale's consideration the first of his numerous "nutty schemes," Operation Bounty, to create "distrust and apprehension in the Cuban Communist Hierarchy." The concept called for "a system of financial rewards, commensurate with position and stature, for killing or delivering alive known Communists." Craig's idea consisted of dropping leaflets in Cuba offering rewards ranging from $5,000 for an "informer" to $100,000 for "government officials," but only two cents for Castro. Lansdale testified before the Church Committee that the price on Castro's head was intended to "denigrate" him "in the eyes of the Cuban people." Lansdale told the committee he "tabled" the idea because he "did not think it was something that should be seriously undertaken or considered."[10]

That didn't inhibit Craig. Three days later, in a February 2 memorandum to Lansdale, he proposed another dozen "nutty" ideas for "further consideration in furtherance of the objectives of the Cuba Project," to which he added: "I think some of them have promise and should you desire our group to develop them in more detail, they will do so."[11]

Each of the proposals came complete with an operation code name, objective, and concept. Among the rather exotic code names offered were: Operation 'NO LOVE LOST,' Operation SMASHER, Operation FREE RIDE, Operation TURN ABOUT, Operation DEFECTOR, Operation BREAK-UP, Operation COVER-UP, Operation DIRTY TRICK, Operation FULL-UP, Operation PHANTOM, Operation BINGO, Operation GOOD TIMES, Operation HEAT IS ON, Operation INVISIBLE BOMB, Operation HORN SWOGGLE, and Operation TRUE BLUE. Each suggested operation came complete with a blurb about its "objective" and its "concept." Some examples:

Operation NO LOVE LOST

Objective: To confuse and harass Castro Cuban Pilots by use of radio conversations.

Concept: Fly Cuban refugee pilot in sterile aircraft in proximity of Cuba at periodic intervals while communication monitoring Cuban air/ground frequencies used for airdrome control. Cuban refugee pilot in sterile aircraft would personally know many of the pilots still flying for Castro. Refugee pilot would get into argument with Castro pilots over radio thus distracting, confusing, etc. Would be real trouble for Castro pilots in actual weather conditions. Argument could go, 'I'll get you, you Red son-of-a-gun,' and call by name if appropriate. . . .

Operation FREE RIDE

Objective: The objective is to create unrest and dissension amongst the Cuban people.

Concept: This is to be accomplished by airdropping valid Pan American or KLM one-way airline tickets good for passage to Mexico City, Caracas, etc. (none to the U.S.). Tickets could be intermixed with other leaflets to be dropped. The number of tickets dropped could be increased. The validity of the tickets would have to be restricted to a time period.

Operation DIRTY TRICK

Objective: The objective is to provide irrevocable proof that should the

MERCURY manned orbit flight fail the fault lies with the Communists et al. in Cuba.

Concept: This to be accomplished by manufacturing various pieces of evidence that would prove electronic interference on the part of the Cubans.

Operation GOOD TIMES

Objective: To disillusion the Cuban population with Castro image, by distributing fake photographic material.

Concept: Prepare a desired photograph, such as an obese Castro with two beauties in any situation desired, ostensibly within a room in the Castro residence, lavishly furnished, and a table brimming over with the most delectable Cuban food with an underlying caption (appropriately Cuban) such as "My ration is different." Make as many prints as desired on sterile paper and then distribute them over the countryside by air drops or agents. This should put even a Commie Dictator in the proper perspective with the unprivileged masses.

"These and other suggestions were passed along to Brigadier General Lansdale, who was in charge of Mongoose," observed historian and scholar Anna Nelson, a member of the JFK Assassination Records Review Board. "They were far too unrealistic to be taken seriously, but are instructive for what they reveal about the pressure on the military services and others in the Survey Group to come up with new ideas."

"A quite different plan was also presented to the Survey Group by the Defense Department," Nelson noted. "This plan relied on the Defense Department to harass Castro by using the technique of 'cover and deception' C&D. The cover and deception plans were designed to piggy-back on military exercises so they could provide credible evidence of the possibility of military intervention."[12]

Defense's plan came as a collection of far more serious "nutty schemes" as contained in a March 13, 1962, memorandum prepared by the ubiquitous Craig and transmitted by Gen. Lyman Lemnitzer, chairman of the Joint Chiefs, to the secretary of defense. The subject: "Justification for US Military Intervention in Cuba."[13]

The memorandum, as Lemnitzer described in his cover letter, responded to a request from Lansdale for a "brief but precise description of pretexts which would provide justification for US military intervention in Cuba." The paper and its enclosures, prepared some days earlier by

Brigadier General Craig, contained a litany of overly imaginative suggestions.

"The suggested courses of action . . . are based on the premise that US military intervention will result from a period of heightened US-Cuban tensions which place the United States in the position of suffering justifiable grievances," Craig said. "World opinion, and the United Nations forum should be favorably affected by developing the international image of the Cuban government as rash and irresponsible, and as an alarming and unpredictable threat to the peace of the Western Hemisphere." He added that "harassment plus deceptive actions to convince the Cubans of imminent invasion would be emphasized. Our military posture throughout execution will allow a rapid change from exercise to intervention if Cuban response justifies."

It is obvious from the preliminary context in which the proposals were presented that the "pretexts for invasion" were far from ever being realized, but the fact these proposals were even considered at an official level is mind-boggling in itself. Among Craig's ideas were:

- A series of coordinated incidents in and around Guantánamo Naval Base that appeared to be carried out by "hostile Cuban forces." Incidents could include such staged activity as an attack on the base by friendly Cubans in uniform; the capture of "saboteurs" inside the base; the detonation of ammunition inside the base; and sink a ship near the harbor entrance complete with funerals for mock victims.
- A "Remember the Maine" incident, which could take several forms, including the blowing up of a US ship in Guantánamo Bay, and blaming of Cuba; the blowing up of a drone (unmanned) vessel anywhere in Cuban waters, followed by an air/sea rescue operation covered by U.S. fighters to "evacuate" remaining members of nonexistent crew. "Casualty lists in US newspapers would cause a helpful wave of national indignation." "Remember the Maine" became a rallying cry when the United States went to war against Spain in 1898 and blamed Spain for sinking an American warship in Havana Harbor.
- A "Communist Cuban terror campaign in the Miami area, in other Florida cities and even in Washington" aimed at Cuban refugees seeking haven in the United States or "we could sink a boatload of Cubans en route to Florida (real or simulated.) We could foster attempts on lives of Cuban refugees in the United States even to the extent of wounding in instances to be widely publicized."

- A "Cuban-based, Castro-supported" filibuster against a neighboring country. "We know that Castro is backing subversive efforts clandestinely." and "these efforts can be magnified and additional ones contrived for exposure."
- The use of MIG type aircraft piloted by Americans to provide "additional provocation, harassment of civil air, attacks on surface shipping and destruction of US military drone aircraft by MIG type planes would be useful as complementary actions."
- An elaborate scheme for a simulated attack on a passenger plane "which will demonstrate convincingly that a Cuban aircraft has attacked and shot down a chartered civil airliner en route from the United States to Jamaica, Guatemala, Panama or Venezuela." Such a flight plan would route the plane over Cuba. "The passengers could be a group of college students off on a holiday or any grouping of persons with a common interest to support chartering a non-scheduled flight."

The plane itself would be a drone "painted and numbered as an exact duplicate for a civil registered aircraft belonging to a CIA proprietary organization in Miami." It would be a duplicate "substituted for the actual civil aircraft . . . loaded with the selected passengers, all boarded under carefully prepared aliases. Take off times of the drone aircraft and the actual aircraft will be scheduled to allow a rendezvous south of Florida."

The passenger-carrying plane would then descend to minimum altitude and go to an auxiliary field at Eglin Air Force Base in the Florida Panhandle "where arrangements will be made to evacuate the passengers." The drone would fly the filed flight plan and, when over Cuba, transmit a distress message saying it was under attack by a Cuban MIG. That would, in turn, be interrupted with destruction of the aircraft by radio signal. "This will allow ICAO [International Civil Aviation Organization] radio station in the Western Hemisphere to tell the US what has happened to the aircraft instead of the US trying to 'sell' the incident."

Craig concluded by noting that the Joint Chiefs of Staff had cited the need for a provocation to justify intervention if "covert efforts to foster an internal Cuban rebellion are unsuccessful." He referred to a March 7, 1962, document by the Joint Chiefs declaring that if there is a "determination that a credible internal revolt is impossible" during the coming months a decision will be needed "to develop a Cuban 'provocation' as justification for positive US military action."

Not long after Craig's proposals came a campaign designed to turn the symbol of internal resistance from a fish to a worm, an idea that apparently originated with the CIA's Harvey. Described by author Jon Elliston, as gleaned from Assassination Records Review Board documents, the CIA decided its propaganda slogan should be *Gusano Libre,* or Free Worm. The CIA had used the fish as the symbol of internal resistance at the time of the Bay of Pigs. *Gusano* was a derogatory term used by the Castro Cubans for "counterrevolutionaries." Lt. Col. James Patchell, an army officer who helped plan propaganda for Mongoose, suggested ways the agency could exploit the worm idea, such as "relating it to such expressions as the 'worm will turn.'" That still left the problem of gaining acceptance of the symbol by the internal Cuban opposition.[14]

Harvey, in an August 1962 memorandum to Lansdale, said the "CIA plans a coordinated campaign to popularize, exploit and encourage the use of '*Gusano Libre*' as the symbol of the resistance to the Castro regime," but he wanted to leave the impression it was a "spontaneous internal development and not an exile one." Therefore, Harvey said, the CIA wanted the next "Voice of Free Cuba" submarine operation planned for mid-August "to announce that the '*Gusano Libre*' has become the symbol of popular resistance to the Castro regime, calling upon the people of Cuba to show their defiance of the government by scrawling this symbol in public places." After the warmup, said Harvey, "actions will be taken to provide the people in Cuba with pictures of 'El Gusano Libre' as well as instructions on how to draw" the symbol. "A small bulletin entitled 'El Gusano Libre' will be prepared for inside distribution. Gusano Libre pins, armbands, seals, pencils, balloons, etc., can obviously be produced for inside distribution via mail, legal travelers and propaganda balloons." The new symbol didn't sell.[15] The State Department, in a briefing paper apparently prepared by Hurwitch for Secretary Rusk in advance of an SGA meeting, derisively noted that "the Agency is pushing ahead with its 'Gusano Libre' theme. . . . I doubt whether 'worms of the world unite' will cause people to revolt; I should put it in the nuisance category at this stage."[16]

Lt. Col. Manuel "Manny" Chavez, an Air Force intelligence officer assigned to the overt CIA station in Miami, but also a regular commuter to Washington to confer with Lansdale on Mongoose, offered one of the more innovative ideas. Chavez said he had been interviewing a recently arrived female Cuban refugee in midsummer 1962 who described the increasing shortages on the island, among them toilet paper and sanitary napkins.

"This interview prompted me to come up with a brilliant idea," wrote Chavez. "It was true, we had been receiving many reports about the drastic shortage of paper. Within a few days, I had to go to Washington, so I wrote down my idea and presented it at one of the [Mongoose] conferences. . . . My idea was simple. Because there was a shortage of toilet paper, which was the result of government inefficiency, I suggested that we send in black (covert) flights and airdrop cases of toilet paper to the interior towns. The people would cheer and know that they were getting support from outside the island. However, to make it an effective psychological impact, my recommendation was to print a picture of Fidel Castro and Nikita Khrushchev on alternate sheets. This would absolutely drive Castro mad, knowing that the suffering Cuban people were finally smiling. The idea was accepted and plans were made to carry it out, until President Kennedy put the squash on it."[17]

The CIA came along with another rather strange request to Lansdale seeking approval "to establish a sea borne balloon launching facility" to bomb Cuba with anti-Castro and anti-Soviet propaganda. The idea had been floated some months earlier, but more fully detailed in a memo dated September 17, 1962 (but stamped October 10). The memo described the project as one in which "helium-inflated balloons will be launched at night from a foreign flag ship in international waters at least ten miles off the coast of Cuba." The ship would avoid U.S. ports to "the extent practicable and will particularly avoid the Miami area." It would be chartered by a respected Cuban exile "politically acceptable to a broad segment of the Cuban exile community" with the CIA selecting a candidate who met the criteria. While a "respected Cuban exile" would be the ostensible sponsor of the operation, the CIA was to make all the arrangements and set the guidelines. The CIA cautioned, however, that meeting their guidelines "may not be possible in view of the extent of Cuban exile participation."

The estimated cost of getting the balloon off and running was $50,000 (1962 prices). The subsequent cost would be $22,000 for a six-month period to "launch 1,000 balloons per month exclusive of the propaganda material to be delivered. Each balloon ready for launching, including the balloon itself, timer, ballast and helium, but exclusive of the propaganda material to be delivered, cost approximately $15.50. The one-time cost of the chartered vessel is estimated at approximately $10,000. The recurring monthly costs for operation of a type of vessel as will be required for this operation amounts to approximately $11,000."

The project proposal warned "there is a remote possibility that a child could be injured by a free falling timer which weighs two-tenths of a pound, an empty cardboard container which carries the leaflets or by a four pound bundle of leaflets." And, finally, as a precaution against aircraft being brought down, "it is contemplated that the propaganda balloons will be launched only during hours of the night when there are no scheduled aircraft in flight over Cuba."[18]

This project was slowed, but not halted, by the missile crisis. During a September 27, 1962, meeting of the Special Group Augmented, "the Group concluded that the concept as outlined could be considered approved, subject to the presentation of a detailed plan of action in line with today's discussion."[19] At the SGA's October 16 meeting "the balloon proposition was approved, subject to resolution of what flag the vessel would sail under."[20] The balloon project remained on the SGA agenda as late as October 26, as the missile crisis neared a climax. Minutes of the meeting noted, "CIA should continue to develop the balloon propaganda facilities, although it was recognized that by the target date of 1 December this capability might no longer be needed because of other methods of delivery."[21]

Although Mongoose effectively died during the missile crisis, the balloon idea did not, resurfacing at a January 25, 1963, meeting of the National Security Council's Executive Committee. A record of the meeting by Bromley Smith, the council's executive secretary, reports that there was a "discussion of the dropping of propaganda leaflets from free traveling balloons," despite the facts that it had no apparent advocates and President Kennedy "decided that balloons should not be used."[22]

By April 3, however, the balloon proposal had been resuscitated once again, topping the agenda for the new Cuban Coordinating Committee, which had replaced the Mongoose Cuban Survey Group. The first item, "Balloon Operations Over Havana," referred to a CIA proposal to release balloons "containing 300,000 to 500,000 leaflets on May Day (before daylight)." The leaflets would "(1) attack Castro's henchmen, and (2) contain cartoons illustrating sabotage techniques." A final decision on balloon operations was scheduled for another review the week before May Day.[23] But again President Kennedy stepped in, according to an April 9 presidential action memo from Joseph Califano, special assistant to Army

Secretary Cyrus Vance, that said "the President rejected the balloon item on the recommendation of Ed Murrow," then director of USIA.[24]

Not all the "nutty ideas" were confined to Operation Mongoose. One of the most bizarre came in a memorandum dated—presumably by coincidence—Valentine's Day 1963, from the Office of the Chief of Naval Operations to Califano. Responding to Califano's "verbal request" of the previous day, the memo offered suggestions on how to "Restrict Travel to Cuba for Subversive Training," providing seven possible actions, each followed by a consideration of the consequences.

The first action went directly to the point, proposing under action: "Liquidate selection trainees after return from Cuba." It was tempered by the consideration: "Value of this action lies in destroying a potentially dangerous individual while simultaneously serving a warning to other potential trainees. It is politically risky and contrary to our morale [sic] precepts. Could boomerang by creating martyrs."

One of the more novel suggestions under action was to: "Attach incendiary device to bats and drop over training centers. Bats retire to attics during daylight. Incendiaries ignite by timers and start fires." And under consideration: "Politically risky. Since bats would have to be air dropped, risk of retaliatory action against essential U.S. photo recon aircraft is increased."

And, finally, under action came this possibility: "Substitute aerosol insecticide bombs with aerosol bombs containing phosphorescent dyes which are very difficult to remove from skin. Individual travelers would be marked for a significant length of time." The consideration: "This has some psychological and intelligence value. Should be relatively simple and inexpensive to accomplish. Probably effective on a one-time basis only unless dye effect could be delayed and spray otherwise be made to look and smell like real insecticide."[25]

Perhaps the nuttiest scheme of all was a proposal entitled "War Between Cuba and Another LA [Latin American] State," which appears to be part of a broader Defense Department document of uncertain date in 1963. Also unclear is the context in which the proposal was made. The objective, as outlined, was "to capitalize on the contingency of war breaking out between Cuba and another LA state by using the 'obligation' to support an ally to overthrow Castro." Next came the scenarios under which "the war or outbreak of hostilities between Castro and another state could come." Five were cited:

104

- A contrived "Cuban" attack on an OAS member could be set up and the attacked state could be urged to "take measures of self-defense and request assistance from the U.S. and OAS. . . .
- "An actual Cuban attack or Cuban identified subversive action could trigger the same response."
- "A contrived Cuban attack on Jamaica, one of three Guineas [sic], or Trinidad-Tobago could be set up and the U.S. and the mother country come to the defense of the attacked state while referring the political action to the UN."
- "An actual attack on one of the foregoing states could result in similar action."
- "A revolution in Haiti could be set up with the assistance of Cubans-in-exile masquerading as Haitians (or with other appropriate commitment) in exchange for the understanding that the new regime would recognize and provide a base for a Cuban government and would provide assistance including use of force in support of action against the Castro regime."

After going into detail regarding the possible scenarios and how the United States might react, the document concluded "that any contrived situation carries greater risks than benefits. . . . This course should probably only be pursued when the situation vis-à-vis Cuba had preceded [sic] to the point that two-thirds of the OAS membership were judged ready to authorize such covert action. Manifestly that time has not arrived."[26]

Lieutenant Colonel Patchell's imaginative mind went to work again in a May 13, 1963, paper proposing "the creation of an imaginary Cuban leader," in part to fill the vacuum created by the end of U.S. support to the Cuban Revolutionary Council, originally set up as a front for the failed Bay of Pigs invasion. Such a fictional leader, Patchell argued, would "serve to reduce the bickering among exiles" and "as a focal point for resistance directed against Castro by Cubans and Latin Americans." Virtually any name would do, said Patchell, as long as it was "acceptable and meaningful in Spanish." Among those suggested were "The Little Bull," "The Friendly Worm," or "The Tough Peasant."

It's possible, said Patchell, that the Castro regime might claim capture or pursuit of the imaginary leader or even suggest he was a fraud. "Such action would only serve to further publicize the actions of the individual and so long as resistance in general continued the fame of our 'Cuban Kilroy' would spread. Humorous antics could be credited to our imaginary friend and rumors of his exploits of bravery (ala Zorro) could be circulated."

"Eventually," predicted Patchell, "a member of the resistance in Cuba may gain sufficient stature to assume or be given the title of this imaginary hero," depending "in large measure on individual leadership ability to 'fill the boots' of this anti-Castro image."[27] There is no indication such a leader ever emerged.

"Nutty schemes" preceded Mongoose, as well, dating back to the March–August 1960 pre–Bay of Pigs period. The early schemes apparently were "aimed only at discrediting Castro personally by influencing his behaviour [sic] or by altering his appearance," according to the CIA Inspector General's report on assassination plots prepared in 1967. One such scheme cited was to "contaminate the air of the radio station where Castro broadcast his speeches with an aerosol spray of a chemical that produces lysergic acid (LSD). Nothing came of the idea . . . because the chemical could not be relied upon to be effective."

Jake Esterline told the inspector general's investigators that he recalled a plot involving a "box of cigars that had been treated with some sort of chemical. . . . His recollection was that the chemical was intended to produce temporary personality disorientation. . . . The thought was to somehow contrive to have Castro smoke one before making a speech and then to make a public spectacle of himself." Although Esterline said when he was interviewed a second time by investigators that he "no longer remembered the intended effect of the cigars, he was positive they were not lethal."

Another scheme involved "thallium salts, a chemical used by women as a depilatory—the thought being to destroy Castro's image as 'The Beard' by causing his beard to fall out." The plan apparently originated in connection with a trip Castro was expected to make abroad. The idea was to dust thallium powder—which can be administered either orally or by absorption through the skin—"into Castro's shoes when they were put out at night to be shined. The scheme progressed as far as procuring the chemical and testing it on animals," but Castro didn't make the trip and the plan was abandoned.

The inspector general's investigators said they found "no evidence that any of these schemes was approved at any level higher than division, if that. We think it most likely that no higher-level approvals were sought, because none of the schemes progressed to the point where approval to launch would have been needed."[28]

CHAPTER 7

MONGOOSE REDUX

Aided by Sam Halpern's constant prodding, the original emphasis for Operation Mongoose underwent an overhaul in March 1962. The Special Group dictated that focus of Phase I be intelligence-collection. At Phase I's end in July a decision would be made on the details for Phase II, although Mongoose's underlying premise remained one of igniting a popular revolt within Cuba. As Mongoose moved forward, the suggestion of overt U.S. military intervention increasingly laced the debate. And since the Soviets and Cubans surely were listening to and watching Mongoose's progress, the greater threat of intervention undoubtedly helped fuel Moscow's decision to install missiles in Cuba.

As Halpern remembered it, "the Special Group says 'let's turn this into basically an intelligence collection operation first. We'll worry about sabotage second, instead of the other way around.' So we start getting and using, not only people in Miami whom we recruit and send back into the island to collect intelligence. We also use every other possibility to collect intelligence . . . foreigners from around the world who visit Cuba, travel to Cuba, diplomats who travel, diplomats who stay in . . . everything. But we were able over a period of several months to start getting some decent information."[1]

Lansdale was not pleased, said Halpern. The Special Group "limited Ed basically to an intelligence operation with some sabotage thrown in here and there and everywhere . . . nickel and dime stuff."

Lansdale issued the new Mongoose Phase I guidelines in mid-March, saying the operation would now "be developed on the following assumptions:

> a. In undertaking to cause the overthrow of the target government, the U.S. will make maximum use of indigenous resources, internal and external, but recognizes the final success will require decisive U.S. military intervention.

b. Such indigenous resources as are developed will be used to prepare
for and justify this intervention, and thereafter to facilitate and support it.

The guidelines declared that the "immediate priority objective of U.S.
efforts during the coming months will be the acquisition of hard intelligence on the target area. . . . All other political, economic and covert
actions will be undertaken short of those reasonably calculated to inspire
a revolt within the target area, or other development which would require
U.S. armed intervention."[2]

Lansdale clearly was not happy with the emphasis on intelligence collection and away from that of fueling a popular revolt. In a memorandum
for the record of a March 16 Special Group meeting with President Kennedy, Lansdale reported that McCone, the CIA director, "asked me if I
were in agreement with the concept contained in the 'Guidelines.' I commented that they didn't fit the conditions inside Cuba that were becoming more apparent to the operational people. . . . I felt we needed much
more freedom to work on the revolutionary possibilities than is possible
under the guidelines."

The issue of military intervention again came up at the same session as
Lansdale briefed the president and suggested that if "conditions [in Cuba]
arose that would need quick exploitation . . . we would have to be ready
. . . to supply arms and equipment; it is possible that this could be done
without U.S. military intervention, but we must be ready to intervene
with U.S. forces, if necessary."

General Lemnitzer of the Joint Chiefs chimed in that "the military had
contingency plans for U.S. intervention" and plans "for creating plausible
pretexts to use force, with the pretexts either attacks on U.S. aircraft or a
Cuban action in Latin America for which we would retaliate." To that,
wrote Lansdale, "the President said bluntly that we were not discussing
the use of U.S. military force, that General Lemnitzer might find the U.S.
so engaged in Berlin or elsewhere that he couldn't use the contemplated
4 divisions in Cuba. So, we cannot say that we are able now to make a
decision on the use of U.S. military force."[3]

The Defense Department and the Joint Chiefs, too, were unhappy
about the new Mongoose guidelines, as indicated in a briefing paper prepared for Bobby Kennedy. It was presented to Kennedy on March 21 by
Brig. Gen. William H. Craig, the Pentagon's representative to the multiagency Mongoose working group. It declared in part: "We feel that there
is an alarming lack of appreciation that time is running out. . . . We are

concerned that the new proposal de-emphasizes the time factor by waiting until July before the decision is made as to what to do next."[4]

At the CIA, which now had the lead role in Phase I, there also was
grumbling—from Harvey in particular—about a limitation that any
"major operation going beyond the collection of intelligence be approved
in advance by the Special Group." In a memorandum to McCone, Harvey
complained that the "tight controls exercised by the Special Group and
the present time-consuming coordination and briefing procedures
should, if at all possible, be made less restrictive and less stultifying."

Sam Halpern, Harvey's executive assistant, was asked in his 1975
Church Committee testimony to describe the degree of detail required in
papers forwarded to the Special Group. "Well, to use my word, it was
nauseating details," Halpern replied. "It went down to such things as the
gradients of the beach, and the composition of the sand on the beach in
many cases. Every single solitary thing was in those plans, full detail,
times, events, weaponry, how it was going to happen, who was going to
do what, when it was going to happen, and what contingency plans were
for emergencies, the full details of every single thing we did."[5]

In Miami Ted Shackley echoed similar sentiments. Washington and the
Kennedys, said Shackley, "wanted things in excruciating detail, dates,
times, everything, and it was unnecessary. You could never tell when they
were going to inject themselves."[6]

Tom Parrott had a different take. Parrott said Harvey "complained bitterly to Dick Helms . . . that Taylor was a 'dead hand' who wouldn't allow
him to do anything. I was called in and asked if I couldn't do something
to goose Taylor up. Well, point of fact was that Taylor, being a good military guy, wanted to just have the facts. He didn't want to approve a concept. He wasn't going to approve a concept. He wanted to know what
kind of beach they were going over and what their exit plan was and all
the rest of it. Well, Harvey didn't think that way; Harvey just thought in
concepts. . . . Taylor would not approve a lot of these operations because
he said they just weren't staffed out. The committee's [Special Group] job
was to weigh the political risks, plus the other risks, and he said he
couldn't do that until he had a better idea of what they were going to do."

At the same time, said Parrott, the Mongoose objective "was always a
little foggy to me other than the feeling that Jack [Kennedy] had been
humiliated by Castro. And he was just damn well going to get back at him
so Bobby rushed off with the ball, which he was very inclined to do. I
think there was a certain amount of flailing around. Not a great deal was

accomplished under Mongoose. I don't think anybody was really happy with it."[7]

Although the emphasis of Phase I was intelligence collection, it did not preclude sabotage operations. But those few approved by the Special Group Augmented were largely futile efforts, often criticized by Bobby Kennedy for making too much "noise," even as he pressed for more of them. According to Sam Halpern:

> If you look back at that program, boom and bang [sabotage] seemed to be the order of the day. We eventually did organize teams that could do sabotage. Cuban exiles were recruited and sent back in. We never did anything major. . . . We tried to do some damage. The Matahambre Mine [a copper mine in western Cuba, the target of three failed sabotage attempts] is one of the things he [Lansdale] finally picked on. When Ed was targeting stuff like that, we had to come up with a sabotage team, and we did but, again, the first thing was getting intelligence. . . .
>
> After Bill Harvey takes over in early '62, we did have a small success, in a culvert we blew up or something . . . maybe we knocked out some transformer. It was a minor thing but it made headlines in Cuba and it made the headlines in Miami . . . and the attorney general gets on the phone to Bill Harvey. . . . This is to give you some idea of sabotage operations directed by the White House. . . . Bill gets chewed out by Bobby Kennedy on the phone. Harvey tells the attorney general that people are going to talk about it; it's going to be on the radio, it's going to be on television. That's the facts of life. You can't hide these things. What we keep secret is how it happens and who did it, not the fact of an explosion. It finally sunk in somewhere along the way over a period of time. Intelligence collection is one thing. You can do that quietly and nobody is any wiser, if it works right, but not if you are going out to do boom and bang. Boom and bang means publicity and you better be ready for it.[8]

It was obvious by April that Mongoose—except for the intelligence collection element—was treading water with the guidelines under which it was operating and the limitations set by the Special Group Augmented. McCone raised the issue at an April 12 meeting, noting that the "original concept was to have a situation within Cuba developed by August, and that the present plan of action would not bring this about." Rather than expanding the program, the SGA "decided to eliminate the August date but not to eliminate the original intention of the effort."[9]

At another meeting two weeks later, McCone "expressed dissatisfaction with progress; stated nothing had been accomplished in putting Cubans in the Army for training and that no actions had been taken on matters decided two weeks ago." McCone added that he "was very disagreeable." He recommended "more action, acceptance of attribution if necessary; establishment of training facilities; training of guerrillas and a more dynamic effort in the infiltration of both agents and guerrillas."[10]

In an apparent response to McCone, Lansdale issued an "Operation Mongoose Priority Operations Schedule" of "tasks" for the May 21–June 30 period. One of these tasks called for many more activist undertakings by the various agencies involved. For the CIA, he wanted "a sabotage operation . . . to make a psychological impact upon the regime and public, which symbolizes popular resistance to the regime and which causes talk encouraging to resistance." The agency should, said Lansdale, "select a feasible sabotage operation, a 'showy' one against the regime but not against the people, and present a specific proposal for approval." The CIA also was to "make a special effort to step-up the infiltration of teams" and "penetrate black market operations in Cuba for economic sabotage."

Around this time—May 29, 1962—a high-ranking Soviet delegation, posing as an agricultural mission, but including Marshal Sergei Biryuzov, head of the USSR's Strategic Rocket Forces, and two nuclear ballistic missile specialists, arrived in Havana. They were there to propose installation of strategic missiles on the island. The Cuban leadership agreed to the plan. Raul Castro and Che Guevara went to Moscow in early July to formalize the agreement.[11] Missiles began to arrive in Cuba secretly during the first half of September under a Moscow project code-named Operation Anadyr.

A plethora of books has appeared during the intervening four decades, each providing ever more detail on the missile deployment, crisis, and withdrawal, as greater information is gleaned from newly declassified documents and various forums bringing participants and scholars together. Among the more revealing works are *One Hell of a Gamble*, by scholars Aleksandr Fursenko and Timothy Naftali; *Operation Anadyr*, by Gen. Anatoli I. Gribkov and Gen. William Y. Smith, military men directly involved in either side of the crisis; and *Cuba and the Missile Crisis*, by Carlos Lechuga, Cuba's UN ambassador at the time.

All three accounts cite a fear in both Moscow and Havana of a U.S. invasion of Cuba coupled with a Soviet effort to redress the nuclear missile imbalance that, by then, was seventeen to one in favor of the United States, as major reasons for the deployment of missiles. Although Operation Mongoose did not become public until years later, there is little doubt the activity it generated contributed to the invasion fears.

Mongoose was getting well under way when Soviet premier Nikita Khrushchev's son-in-law, Aleksei Adzhubei, after a stop in Cuba, met with President Kennedy in Washington on January 30, 1962. Kennedy hinted in their conversation that the United States might show force in Cuba as the Soviets had done in Hungary in 1956, when they forcefully put down an anti-Russian rebellion. Adzhubei reported on the meeting to Khrushchev, raising concerns that had been allayed earlier, when Kennedy told Khrushchev at their June 1961 Vienna summit that the Bay of Pigs had been a mistake. "It was this report [by Adzhubei] which triggered the whole [missile crisis] situation," Castro told French journalist Jean Daniel during a November 1963 interview in Havana, an account of which appeared in that year's December edition of *The New Republic*.

"Six months before these missiles were installed in Cuba, we had received an accumulation of information that a new invasion was being prepared under sponsorship of the Central Intelligence Agency," Castro told Daniel. "We also knew the Pentagon was vesting the CIA preparations with the mantle of its authority, but we had doubts as to the attitude of the president." Then came Adzhubei's report, which Castro said he had received a week after the Adzhubei-Kennedy meeting.

"To be sure," Castro told Daniel, "the actual word 'invasion' was not mentioned and Adzhubei, at the time, lacking any background information, could not draw the same conclusions as we did. But when we communicated to Khrushchev all our previous information, the Russians too began to interpret the Kennedy-Adzhubei conversation as we saw it and they went to the source of our information. By the end of the month, the Russian and Cuban governments had reached the *definite conviction* that an invasion might take place from one moment to the next."[12]

An instant analysis of Daniel's article by the State Department's Bureau of Intelligence and Research, noted, "Castro's remarks to Daniel regarding the origins of the missile deployment, in our view, tend on the whole to confirm our reconstruction of it.

"We have no doubt that Castro, and probably the Soviets too, were increasingly worried in the late winter and spring of 1962 about the possibility of a new US invasion attempt. Castro, as the more directly involved party, may well have placed an ominous interpretation on President Kennedy's remarks to Adzhubei . . . regarding the parallelism between the Soviet attitude toward Hungary and ours toward Cuba." The assessment concludes that the decision to deploy missiles "almost certainly goes back to the spring, which was a time of heightened Cuban concern about invasion, of Soviet-Cuban efforts to agree on what to do about the danger and of Soviet wrestling with the larger strategic issue of the US-Soviet military balance."[13]

As part of Mongoose, the Pentagon had begun to formulate contingency plans for invading Cuba, including the February revision of OPLAN 314–61 by the Atlantic Command. As Fursenko and Naftali, who had access to declassified Soviet documents, wrote in *One Hell of a Gamble*, a KGB report went almost immediately to top Soviet officials warning that "military specialists of the USA had revised an operational plan against Cuba, which, according to this information, went to Kennedy." The report did not specifically refer to OPLAN 314, "but stated that activity of the land forces would 'be supported by military air assets based in Florida and Texas.'"[14]

"If Soviet agents picked up rumblings of these [invasion] plans, perhaps they, and Nikita Khrushchev, would consider them evidence of intent. So much the better," concluded Gen. William Gray. "Pleased at the Kremlin's attention focused on Castro's survival rather than on exporting revolution, the Pentagon made no effort to hide the two-week, 40,000-man Marine and Navy maneuvers that engaged forces from North Carolina to the Caribbean in April 1962. The action culminated with an amphibious assault on the island of Vieques off the coast of Puerto Rico. . . . U.S. press accounts of these maneuvers alone would give Soviet intelligence enough information to feed Kruschchev's anxiety about American plans and Castro's future."[15]

Mongoose had helped trigger the law of unintended consequences. Khrushchev moved to consider the installation of missiles in Cuba, as early as March or April, depending on which account one reads. He convened a May 20 meeting with ranking Kremlin officials and Alexsandr Alekseev, the Soviet ambassador-designate to Cuba who was close to Castro. The Defense Council approved the decision the next day, a decision Khrushchev himself apparently had already made.[16] The Soviet delegation went to Havana the following week to discuss and reach agreement with Cuban officials over the deployment.

Castro, at a 1992 missile crisis conference in Havana, offered his rationale for accepting the missiles: "If it had involved only the defense of Cuba, we wouldn't have agreed to having the nuclear missiles installed— not out of fear of the dangers that might ensue, but because of how they might harm the revolution, the image [the Cuban] revolution had in Latin America, since the installation of those weapons would turn Cuba into a Soviet military base. However, I believe that the installation of those missiles in Cuban territory strengthened the socialist camp and helped to even up the balance of power."[17]

No one knew it at the time, but Khrushchev's May 1962 decision to deploy the missiles meant the effective end of Mongoose five months later, without the Havana victory parade Lansdale had envisioned.

But Lansdale had more immediate problems. The State Department's lack of enthusiasm for Mongoose had become increasingly apparent. In a petulant May 31 memorandum to the SGA, Lansdale complained that the State Department reaction to the latest assigned tasks "has been disappointing to me so far. Apparently, my schedule of targets for special efforts is accepted only as it may fit into long-range, existing programs already underway."[18]

The State Department's Hurwitch complained a week later, in his notes of a Mongoose meeting, that "Lansdale and to a greater extent General Craig harbor notion that we can order other nations to do our bidding. When we point out reluctance certain governments follow our lead, they urge a major psychological and political campaign within the country among labor, student and political groups to 'force' the government to change its mind. . . . General Craig particularly remains convinced that Department is emphasizing 'long range goals in the hemisphere' as compared to 'priority for Cuba.' "[19]

As might be expected, of the agencies involved in Mongoose, the Defense Department—with the high-level exception of Secretary Robert McNamara, who publicly expressed his misgivings much later—was by far the most gung ho. The Pentagon apparently saw a potential opportunity to resolve the "Cuba problem" by an invasion, especially if a rationale, manufactured or otherwise, could be found. The State Department, as reflected in Hurwitch's comments, was by far the least enthusiastic and most cautious, as it had been with the Bay of Pigs. In Mongoose and the Bay of Pigs, it is apparent that State was worried about how unilateral actions against Cuba would impact on the department's broader diplomatic mission in the rest of Latin America and the world. The CIA— despite its desire to bring down Castro—appeared to be ambivalent toward Mongoose. Working level personnel, such as Sam Halpern, viewed the operation from the beginning as an exercise in futility. Many in the agency also resented Lansdale and, particularly, Bobby Kennedy, who the professional spies regarded as an unwanted and overbearing interloper. At the White House, Arthur Schlesinger made it clear that he thought the whole operation was stupid. But, as noted, it was his colleague, Richard Goodwin, who emerged as the principal architect of the program. At an October 2002 conference in Havana on the missile crisis, Schlesinger characterized Mongoose as "silly and stupid," adding, "it's well understood as a consequence of Operation Mongoose that the Cubans had a legitimate fear of an American invasion." McNamara, at the same conference, conceded that he "didn't think Mongoose was worth a damn, but I didn't say, 'Don't do it.' "[20]

In any event, Lansdale finally enlisted Bobby Kennedy to bring the recalcitrant State Department into line. A June 8 memorandum of a Mongoose meeting notes that Lansdale, "with certain support from the Attorney General, requested more active participation by the Department of State. The meeting agreed that the Department would furnish real support, appoint a full-time senior officer, and present action proposals."[21]

In mid-July "four possible courses of action regarding Cuba" were presented for consideration by agencies involved in Mongoose. They were:

a. Cancel operational plans; treat Cuba as a Bloc nation; protect hemisphere from it or

b. Exert all possible diplomatic, economic, psychological, and other pressures to overthrow the Castro-Communist regime without overt U. S. military commitment, or

c. Commit U.S. to help Cubans overthrow the Castro-Communist regime, with step-by-step phasing to ensure success, including the use of U.S. military force if required at the end, or

d. Use a provocation and overthrow the Castro-Communist regime by U.S. military force.[22]

Hurwitch recommended State Department support for Course B. He also complained, "preliminary discussion of these courses of action . . . reveals that the CIA and Defense representatives favor prior commitment to employ U.S. military force." In his opinion, Hurwitch said, "the concentration of attention upon the employment of U.S. military force against Cuba runs counter to the basic concept of Mongoose, which is to bring down the Castro regime from within."[23]

At dinner the same evening, Bobby Kennedy told John McCone "the last six months' effort had been worthwhile inasmuch as we had gained a very substantial amount of intelligence which was lacking, but that the effort was disappointing inasmuch as the program had not advanced to the point we had hoped. He urged intensified effort but seemed inclined to let the situation 'worsen' before recommending drastic action."[24]

The time arrived for a Mongoose report card on Phase I. The four agencies directly involved—CIA, State, Defense, and USIA—were asked to submit to Lansdale a review of their activity and comment on the four possible courses of action for the next phase. The Phase I results were obviously disappointing.

"At the close of Phase I my concern is strong that time is running out for the U.S. to make a free choice on Cuba, based largely on what is happening to the will of the Cuban people," Lansdale wrote in the covering memo of his review. "Rightly or wrongly, the Cubans have looked to the U.S. for guidance on what to aspire to and do next. . . . We have been unable to surface the Cuban resistance potential to a point where we can measure it realistically. The only way this can be done, accurately, is when resistance actually has a rallying point of freedom fighters who appear to the Cuban people to have some chance of winning, and that means at least an implication that U.S. is in support. . . . There was little opportunity for the Cuban people to join an active resistance in April 1961; there is less opportunity today."[25]

In a memo to Assistant Secretary of State Ed Martin accompanying Lansdale's Phase I review and comment on the four possible future courses of action, Hurwitch made clear the differing positions of the agencies involved. He began by telling Martin "you will be interested to see that DOD would like to see the Monroe Doctrine re-affirmed," adding:

I think the essence of the positions [on the four possible courses of action] lies in the following:
1. CIA believes that if assurances were given of US intervention, a revolt could be mounted by late 1963, but would be destroyed at best within a matter of a few days if it is not supported by substantial military force. No mention is made of the nature or magnitude of the revolt.
2. Defense states it needs eighteen (or perhaps twelve) days of preparation, although some units might be available in as soon as five days.
3. State believes it needs a virtual civil war situation in Cuba before

intervention in Cuba with US military force might be considered politically feasible.

These three conditions do not appear to be easily reconciled.[26]

In response to a request from the SGA, on August 8 Lansdale submitted a paper for a "possible stepped up Course B" as Phase II of Mongoose. The basic Course B called for increased "diplomatic, economic, psychological, and other pressures to overthrow the Castro-Communist regime without overt U. S. military commitment." As Lansdale described the stepped up Course B under Phase II, "the major difference from Phase I . . . would be the removal of the restrictions . . . which kept our actions 'short of those reasonably calculated to inspire a revolt within the target area.'"

What this essentially meant was that the heavy load would fall to the CIA, with accelerated covert actions. But, as Lansdale also noted, "the CIA operational people who would implement a stepped up Course B as Phase II of Operation Mongoose, do not believe this course of action by itself would bring the overthrow of the regime in Cuba; they believe that the use of military force in the final stage must be anticipated, for success."[27] The CIA estimated it would need a $40 million budget for 1963 to implement its role in Phase II, and another $60 million in fiscal 1964, with CIA personnel assigned full-time to Mongoose increasing to six hundred. None of the estimated budget would be reimbursable to the Defense Department for its support role.[28]

The initial SGA action was to decide, instead, on a "CIA variant," or modified Course B, proposed by McCone, which "posted limited actions to avoid inciting a revolt and sought a split between Castro and 'old-line Communists' rather than Castro's overthrow."[29] The SGA—presumably under Bobby Kennedy's influence—also made it clear to Lansdale that Phase II should "afford full attention to the desirability of the Cubans liberating Cuba with our help . . . distinguished from the concept of our employing the Cubans in programs where we are seeking to liberate Cuba." This, added Lansdale in a memorandum to Harvey, "will require an imaginative and bold approach to the whole concept of the management, use, and potential values in the Cuban exiles in the U.S. and other countries."[30] The initial action hinted at things to come and Bobby Kennedy's "let Cubans be Cubans" approach to post–missile crisis covert anti-Castro activity.

In advising President Kennedy of approval for Phase II, General Taylor made two things clear: it was not designed with U.S. military intervention in mind, barring "an unanticipated revolt," and there was "no reason to hope" it would bring about Castro's overthrow from within. "As we look ahead in the Mongoose program," said Taylor, "we have considered several alternative courses of action. . . . For the coming period, we favor a somewhat more aggressive program than the one carried out in Phase I." He noted also that "from what we know now we perceive no likelihood of an overthrow of the [Cuban] government by internal means and without the direct use of military force."[31]

In hindsight—given Castro's crackdown, including decimation of existing internal resistance and stepped up internal security measures in the immediate aftermath of the Bay of Pigs—it should have been evident that anything short of direct U.S. military intervention to oust the dictator was likely to fail. In fact, Jack Hawkins warned three weeks after the ill-fated Bay of Pigs, in his May 5, 1961, after-action report, that: "A Communist-style police state is now firmly entrenched in Cuba, which will not be overthrown by means short of United States military power. Further efforts to develop armed internal resistance, or to organize Cuban exile forces, should not be made except in connection with a planned overt intervention by United States forces."

The Phase II guidelines retained the "eventual objective" of overthrowing Castro but had only the immediate goal of "containment, undermining . . . discrediting [and] isolating" Cuba. They called for selective sabotage, continued efforts to create friction among the Cuban leadership, and a continued priority on intelligence collection. They acknowledged that the "noise level" might rise, but also emphasized "the importance of maintaining non-attributability remains unchanged." The guidelines said, "a revolt is not sought at this time," even as they declared that the Joint Chiefs would "maintain plans for U.S. military intervention."[32]

Approval of Phase II brought with it even greater skepticism and friction among the various Mongoose players, who disagreed over the use of Guantánamo, the "noise level," the degree of sabotage, and what actions needed prior approval. "In general," McCone wrote in a memorandum of an August 16, 1962, Special Group Augmented session, "the meeting [at which Phase II was discussed] was unsatisfactory, lacked both purpose and direction and left me with the feeling that very considerable reservation exists as to just where we are going with Operation Mongoose." Further reflecting the acrimony among participants, he concluded, "a detailed plan of operation specifying the acts of sabotage, planned infiltrations, propaganda effort, etc., should be presented by Lansdale at the earliest moment. Harvey should straighten out any differences between Lansdale and CIA, with the assistance of Helms or others. McCone should discuss this subject privately with the Attorney General."[33]

Days later alarm bells sounded over intelligence reports of a massive Soviet military buildup in Cuba and the interconnected implications for other Cold War pressure points such as Berlin. Soon after, on August 31, Senator Kenneth Keating, a respected New York Republican, began an ongoing barrage of public attacks on what he called "a look-the-other-way" policy by the Kennedy administration on Cuba. He first cited refugee reports, then "reliable reports," on the flow of Soviet military equipment and personnel into Cuba, as well as "ominous reports" of "missile bases." According to General Smith, an aide to General Taylor, "his [Keating's] information corresponded very closely to the reports the administration was receiving through regular intelligence channels. The Senator never revealed his sources . . . but there can be little doubt that he had solid, inside information, far more complete than what government channels were providing to officials such as myself."[34]

"There was general agreement that the situation was critical and the most dynamic action was indicated," wrote McCone of an August 21 meeting in the secretary of state's office. And "there was discussion of various courses of action open to us in case the Soviets place MRBM missiles on Cuban territory." Bobby Kennedy "queried the meeting as to what other aggressive steps could be taken, questioning the feasibility of provoking an action against Guantánamo which would permit us to retaliate, or involving a third country in some way," suggestions previously considered under Mongoose to justify military intervention.

McNamara urged more "aggressive action in the fields of intelligence, sabotage and guerrilla warfare, utilizing the Cubans and do such other things as might be indicated to divide the Castro Regime." McCone countered, "all of these things could be done" but "efforts to date with agent teams had been disappointing. Sabotage activities were planned on a priority basis and in all probability, we would witness more failures than successes."[35]

In Miami Ted Shackley had been working hard to increase the CIA station's intelligence collection and improve the paramilitary capability. "While all this was unfolding," Shackley said, "we were in fact successful in collecting intelligence and detailed the Soviet building up in Cuba. We did not start out looking for the Soviet buildup but detected it and focused on it. In the early days we saw cruise missiles coming in, then detected bigger missiles, then SAMS [surface-to-air-missiles]. And we also picked up shipments of manpower into Cuba, ostensibly for the agricultural sector as opposed to troops. That was rubbish.

"We in Miami were closer to being right about the Soviet building up and the number of troops in Cuba. We did produce the agent report that described this trapezoid [-shaped restricted area]. . . . When this report came in it added to the fire for the U-2 flights and a guy in the Pentagon interpreted it."[36]

The Soviets, said Shackley, "started building up in early 1962 with so-called agricultural technicians. We were concerned early on that these were Russian military and not agricultural technicians. We got into a polemic with DDI [Deputy Director of Intelligence Ray Cline]. They couldn't see the Russians doing that. It was a never-ending battle with DDI; a constant never-ending battle. In hindsight, we [Miami Station] were more correct than they were. We estimated forty-five thousand to forty-eight thousand Russian military in Cuba and it turned out there were about forty-five thousand. The first missiles were cruise missiles for coastal defense and they [U-2s] were able to get pictures to make the case that missiles were there and the photo interpreters supported it."[37]

On the night of August 24, Shackley suddenly had another problem to deal with. As tensions over Cuba escalated with the discovery of the Soviet military buildup, a group of young Cubans from the exile Revolutionary Student Directorate (DRE by its Spanish acronym) penetrated Havana harbor in two motorboats armed with .20 caliber guns. Getting within a half-mile of shore, they opened fire for several minutes against seaside buildings in the Miramar section of the city, before fleeing back out to sea.

Cuba protested the attack to the United Nations as an instance of U.S.-sponsored aggression and "within the senior levels of the Kennedy administration a debate developed involving President Kennedy, the attorney general, and Under Secretary of State Ball, and others over whether to arrest and prosecute the Cuban exiles involved after they returned to Florida. President Kennedy decided to issue a statement deploring such 'spur of the moment' raids as counter-productive, and warning against any future raids."[38]

Although the raid was not U.S. sponsored, the CIA had been supporting the DRE. The raid, said Shackley, "came at a time when we were in talks separating ourselves [the CIA] from them. The DRE was an uncontrollable group. These guys were not disciplined. It was in the process of parting company with them when the raid on Havana occurred. We could not work with the DRE, which also was getting a lot of help from the private sector."[39] A CIA document dated April 22, 1963, shows the DRE receiving a $51,000 subsidy during an uncertain time frame.[40]

The late Enrique Baloyra, a former DRE militant, recalled the attack at a 1996 conference, noting that there was a "payroll" for members "and each person was supposed to be getting x number of dollars per month. But what happened is that we would be paid half of that, and the other half would be used to buy weapons and organize things on our own. This is how in August of 1962—the 24th to be exact—that the directorate was able to shell Havana from the harbor. There was a big brouhaha in the station in Miami because, obviously, somebody got on the phone and asked what the hell was going on. And the poor bastard who was on the Miami side had no idea. And the organic matter hit the fan. There was much confusion about that."[41]

Ultimately, the missile crisis brought Mongoose to an end, but the initial reaction to Soviet military buildup gave the operation new impetus. A National Security Action memorandum of August 23 said the "line of activity projected for Operation Mongoose Plan B plus should be developed with all possible speed." It ordered "a study of the advantages and disadvantages of action to liberate Cuba by blockade or invasion or other action beyond Mongoose B plus, in the context of an aggravated Berlin crisis."[42] A State Department intelligence analysis of August 25 suggested that the "most likely Soviet motivation in providing military assistance and personnel to Cuba is to enhance the Cuban regime's defense capabilities against an external threat. . . . It is fairly certain that the Cuban regime fears more than anything else an attack by the US, or other forces strongly, if indirectly supported by the US."[43] Still, no one at the time, it seems, even considered that the activities of Mongoose might have been at least partially responsible for the Soviet military buildup in Cuba.

Arthur Schlesinger weighed in with a September 5 memorandum to President Kennedy expressing his concern about reports of an "internal uprising" in Cuba and the impact on upcoming midterm elections if the CIA were allowed to run amok. "All this points to the absolute importance of making sure that there is no premature insurrection in Cuba," warned Schlesinger. "I would therefore hope that CIA be given the clear-cut and definite responsibility to make sure that no such premature insur-rection takes place. I think that the instruction should be issued in these terms, so that the top leadership of CIA will be impelled to check the situation all the way down the line. . . . It is indispensable to be sure that no one down the line is encouraging Cubans into rash action."[44]

CIA Director John McCone appeared to be the only one at the top levels of the U.S. government who believed installation of medium-range ballistic missiles would follow soon as part of Soviet military buildup. He was on a honeymoon in France when a U-2 flight on August 29 con-firmed construction of SAM sites. He expressed his concern in a series of cables to CIA Deputy Director Marshall Carter, but analysts concluded the Soviets wouldn't risk such an action.[45]

Mongoose activities during late August and through September focused mostly on intelligence collection activities related to the Soviet military buildup. At the same time, the operational schedule Lansdale had laid out in mid-August for Phase II was fine-tuned, and various contingencies began preparation. According to notes of a September 14 Mongoose meeting, "the Attorney General expressed concern that activities by cer-tain Cuban exiles are reaching the point where the Government may be forced to take action against them rather than to simply state that 'we are investigating.' The Agency is requested to see what it can do to help reduce the noise level of these activities."[46]

The Mongoose emphasis on intelligence collection was paying off, said Halpern. "I'd like to pat myself on the shoulder from time to time and say I held out long enough that finally people agreed, and Harvey and Shackley were the right guys for an intelligence operation. We did a fine job of finding out what was going on inside, leading up to the fact that by September of '62 we had an agent . . . who was able to tell us about strange goings on in a certain part of Pinar del Rio province," recalled Halpern. "The report simply said 'there are between four little towns,' which he plotted on a map, where there are strange goings on. Everybody is being moved out, men, women, and children.' The report we got from this agent naming those four towns was disseminated September 18." After bureaucratic delays, a U-2 reconnaissance flight was made directly over western Cuba from south to north on October 14, providing the first verification of offensive missiles on the island. "That's the only decent thing Mongoose ever did . . . because we turned it into a decent collection operation, and Shackley and his people get full marks for this as far as I'm concerned," said Halpern. The agent report—apparently the same one referred to by Shackley—was declassified and released in 1992 for a thirtieth anniversary missile crisis conference.[47]

With confirmation of the missiles still ten days away, Bobby Kennedy was back on the warpath at an October 4 Mongoose meeting, complaining bitterly about the lack of sabotage, according to a memorandum of the session by McCone. "The Attorney General reported on discussions with the President on Cuba; dissatisfied with lack of action in the sabotage field, went on to stress that nothing was moving forward, commented that one attempted effort had failed, expressed general concern over developing situation." McCone countered that he, too, had "observed a lack of forward motion due principally to 'hesitancy' in government circles to engage in any activities which would involve attribution to the United States." Kennedy, according to McCone, "took sharp exception, stating the Special Group had not withheld approval of any specified actions, to his knowledge, but to the contrary had urged and insisted upon action by the Lansdale operating group." A heated exchange followed "which finally was clarifying inasmuch as it resulted in a reaffirmation of a determination to move forward." Lansdale was told to come up with some ideas, despite their noise level; among them were a plan for mining harbors and a study of "the possibility of capturing Castro forces for interrogation."[48] A week later Lansdale followed up with a memorandum to the SGA with "action proposals," including one for sabotage of Cuban-owned ships.[49]

The October 14 U-2 flight dramatically changed the dynamics of the operation, although it did not initially alter Bobby Kennedy's aggressive approach toward Castro and Cuba, as indicated by a Mongoose meeting on the afternoon of October 16. Invoking his brother's position again and repeating his earlier message, "the Attorney General opened the meeting by expressing the 'general dissatisfaction of the President' with Operation Mongoose," recorded Richard Helms. "He pointed out that the Operation had been underway for a year, that the results were discouraging, that there had been no act of sabotage and that even the one which had been attempted had failed twice. He indicated there had been noticeable improvement during the year in the collection of intelligence but that other actions had failed to influence significantly the course of events in Cuba. . . . The Attorney General then stated that in view of this lack of progress, he was going to give Operation Mongoose more personal attention." To do so, he said he would begin daily Mongoose meetings.[50]

Later the same day, at a high-level White House meeting on the crisis, Bobby hinted at the possibility of a provoked or staged attack to justify removing the missiles from Cuba: "One other thing is whether . . . whether there is some *other* way we can get involved in this through, uh, Guantánamo Bay, or something, er, or whether there's some ship that, you know, sink the Maine again or something."[51]

During the same time frame, Rafael Quintero was among sixty CIA exile operatives trained in radio communications waiting in Miami-area safe houses to be parachuted into Cuba to report on troop movements, missiles, and other information if an invasion order was given. Quintero had previously come to know Bobby Kennedy through Roberto San Roman and the efforts to obtain the release of Bay of Pigs invasion troops still imprisoned in Cuba. The imprisoned troops included Roberto's brother, Pepe San Roman, the Brigade 2506 commander. Quintero and Roberto San Roman had, at Bobby's request, gone to New York to make the first contact with attorney James Donovan and then put Donovan in touch with Ernesto Freyre, who headed the Families Committee. After that, again at Bobby's request, they traveled to Latin America to make the exile case for release of the prisoners. Quintero had met and briefed Kennedy previously on the situation in Cuba after slipping in and out of the island twice between December 1960 and April 1962.

While in the safe house, said Quintero, he received a call from Roberto San Roman, telling him that the attorney general wanted to see them in Washington. "We personally talked with [Bobby] Kennedy," said Quintero, "and he told us that 'this time it's for sure . . . and you Cubans, if you really want to help . . .' Nobody will believe this, but this is true. Roberto and I were present. He [Bobby] said 'what you have to do is get yourself a boat and try to sink one of those Russian ships trying to break the blockade . . . on your own.' Not CIA. You guys. You Cubans do it, which was impossible really. San Roman didn't have the capability to do it, really, so he thought I could get the people together. So we came back and I said to my guy [CIA case officer] this is what I had been told." Quintero is still puzzled by what the intent was, except possibly for the exiles to provoke a confrontation such as Bobby had suggested by "sinking the Maine again or something."[52]

According to author Evan Thomas, a provocation is exactly what Bobby had in mind. Bobby had called San Roman earlier in the crisis without telling him about the Soviet missiles, sounding him out about the "sinking the Maine" provocation. San Roman told Thomas that he and Bobby had "discussed creating a provocation, a way of drawing in the Cubans and the Americans. Bobby asked me, 'What do you think you can do to provoke a situation?' I said we could badly damage a Russian ship approaching port."[53] San Roman apparently never told Quintero the full story. The attack never materialized.

Events of the next few days leading up to the peaceful resolution of the crisis are well chronicled, including the month of wrangling over details and Castro's resistance of resolution through late November. There is no need to repeat them here. What is worth repeating, however, is Kennedy's pledge, in an October 27 letter to Khrushchev, not to invade Cuba, part of the agreement for a verified withdrawal of the missiles. The pledge reads: "We, on our part, would agree . . . to give assurances against an invasion of Cuba and I am confident that other nations of the Western Hemisphere would be prepared to do likewise."[54] Although never formalized in a written agreement, the no-invasion pledge, with its post–missile crisis implications for Cuba, U.S. policies toward Cuba, and Cuban exiles, was kept. There are those who argued that the agreement was voided by Castro's refusal to allow on-site inspections, but its validity has never been tested.

For Quintero, and many Cuban exiles, Washington's action in the missile crisis was a greater betrayal than the Bay of Pigs. The exiles were convinced that this conflict would be the end of Fidel Castro. "Talk about the word treason at the Bay of Pigs, this was even bigger for us, the people involved," said Quintero. "It was even bigger because we knew that maybe we were not going to come out alive from this one. Right in the middle of a fight, nobody is going to make a point of saving the life of one guy, but we didn't mind. Remember, at that time I was 22, 23 years old, full of patriotism. . . . I lost a lot of my idealism. That was bigger for me than the Bay of Pigs, because the Bay of Pigs I could understand."

As for Mongoose, the missile crisis brought it one step closer to an agonizingly slow but unlamented end. Bob Hurwitch at the State Department tried to give the operation a push into the grave during the height of the crisis. He had become personally close to Bobby Kennedy as a result of their efforts to gain freedom for the Bay of Pigs prisoners in Cuba, whose plight became subsumed by the threat of nuclear war.

As Hurwitch recounted in his unpublished memoirs, "I saw [Bobby]

Kennedy in the State Department on his way to see Rusk. After coming out, I took Bob aside and observed that we should shelve Operation Mongoose. He looked at me first, blankly, and then suspiciously. I elaborated this was not the time to risk muddying the waters of our head-to-head showdown with the Soviets by encouraging exile raids against Cuba. If we were caught, the Soviets would gleefully justify their missile actions as reasonable defense measures to protect their Cuban ally. Bob saw the point, and Mongoose eventually died, without ceremony or mourning."[55]

President Kennedy, at an October 26 meeting of the Ex Comm, the high-level group dealing with the crisis, suggested "the Mongoose operation be reconstituted, possibly as a subcommittee of the Executive Committee, and oriented toward post-Castro Cuban problems. The President stressed the importance of tying together all existing groups engaged in covert activities in order to integrate our planning." At the same meeting McCone said he "had stood down a CIA operation which involved sending into Cuba by submarine ten teams involving fifty people. He said he did not believe it should be done by CIA unilaterally."[56] But Harvey, the chief of Task Force W, had already dispatched three agent teams, an action which was to bring down the wrath of Bobby Kennedy and cost Harvey his job.

At a Mongoose meeting later the same day, there was considerable discussion of the dispatch of agent teams into Cuba. "As a result . . . it was agreed that all plans for dispatch should be suspended pending further examination; instructions were issued during the course of the meeting designed to recall the three teams already on the way." McCone and Harvey said during the discussion that dispatching the teams had been a "unilateral decision by the CIA," regarded as "within its sphere of responsibility, and particularly with respect to the first three teams had considered that it was a continuation of previously approved operations."[57] That didn't satisfy Bobby Kennedy.

Harvey recounted to the Church Committee in 1975 that he had a "confrontation" with Bobby Kennedy at the height of the missile crisis concerning his order that agent teams be sent into Cuba to support any conventional military action that might occur. Harvey told the committee that Kennedy "took a great deal of exception" to the order and McCone ordered him to halt the agent operations. McCone's assistant, Walter Elder, told the committee that although Harvey had attempted to get guidance from top officials during the missile crisis, he "earned another black mark as not being fully under control."[58] Shortly after the crisis ended, McCone posted Harvey to Rome as the agency's station chief there.

"I thought it was quite unfair to Harvey at the time," Tom Parrott said. "That was the approximate cause of his getting fired, but I thought that particular thing was not fair to him because he had dispatched this team before the ban was on and there was no way for him to recall them. But it was a good excuse. They were fed up with Bill by that time. Poor guy."[59]

On October 30 Lansdale ordered a halt to all sabotage operations by Task Force W, effectively ending Mongoose,[60] although it resurfaced November 29 in discussion at the end of an Ex Comm meeting. McCone, in a memorandum for the record, said he thought that the operation's "future activity should be restricted to intelligence gathering . . . in a most intense manner." To do so, he said the CIA was prepared to present a plan utilizing the Caribbean Admission Center, a refugee interrogation center opened near Miami earlier in 1962 as part of Mongoose. McCone added, "the form of Mongoose organization should be modified and this was agreed, but no new organization was discussed."[61]

Even without the missile crisis, it seems likely that Mongoose eventually would have floundered to an ignominious and unmourned end. It had failed to achieve even minimal expectations, outside of intelligence gathering. Many of its participants, institutional and individual, had little enthusiasm for the Mongoose program. And there was a general antipathy among them for Ed Lansdale and Bobby Kennedy, its two leaders and principal proponents.

If there was a burial for Mongoose, it came in a January 4, 1963, memorandum by McGeorge Bundy to President Kennedy, responding to a request for a reorganization plan to deal with Cuba. "The time is ripe for such a reorganization," wrote Bundy, "because we seem to be winding up the [missile crisis] negotiations in New York, the [Bay of Pigs] prisoners are out, and there is well nigh universal agreement that Mongoose is at a dead end." The reorganization, as suggested by Bundy, was to result in a coordinator for Cuban affairs within the State Department, with a deputy coordinator based in Miami. "If a Coordinator for Cuban Affairs is established, then we think the Mongoose office should be disbanded and responsibility for covert operations should be a part of the work of the Coordinator and his associates from other departments, reporting on covert activities to the Special Group in the normal way. . . . Such a change," Bundy concluded, "would liberate General Lansdale for many other tasks in which his services are uniquely valuable."[62]

Meanwhile, as Bob Hurwitch observed, "one of the consequences of the Cuban Missile Crisis and of the demise of Mongoose was the virtual shutdown of exile anti-Castro activities such as infiltration of agents into Cuba and coastal raids."[63] It was but a temporary lull, however, for the Kennedys were not about to let Castro off the hook.

CHAPTER 8

MIAMI: PERPETUAL
INTRIGUE

For South Florida, first Mongoose and then the Cuban Missile Crisis intensified a frenzied decade that began in the mid-1950s when Castro's eighty-two-member guerrilla band landed in southeastern Cuba. Mongoose increased the already substantial population of CIA agents, Cuban exiles, wannabe soldiers of fortune, and assorted other adventurers who were involved—or wanted to be—in the secret war against Castro. Then along came the Cuban Missile Crisis to make Miami the hottest spot in the Cold War—apart from the three capitals involved—and further fuel the perpetual intrigue simmering beneath the city surface.

An alphabet soup of Cuban exile groups numbering in the hundreds had sprung up, each trying to outdo the other in anti-Castro militancy. A handful of such organizations had no more members than the leader who announced its existence. To fuel fund-raising, the groups called press conferences and issued war communiqués proclaiming actions against Cuba that most often never occurred. Stirring an already boiling pot was JMWAVE, the secluded Miami headquarters of the CIA's frontline command post in Washington's "back alley" war against Castro.

JMWAVE's activities reached a peak in late 1962 and early 1963, before and during the missile crisis and its immediate aftermath. Functioning under the cover of Zenith Technical Enterprises, Inc., JMWAVE operated from Building 25 at the University of Miami's secluded South Campus, a former U.S. Navy installation. Ted Shackley, a rising CIA star, was in charge as station chief from early 1962 through mid-1965. Some three hundred to four hundred agents toiled under Shackley's leadership, making JMWAVE the largest CIA station in the world after the headquarters in Langley, Virginia. Additional CIA officers worked the Cuba account at Langley and elsewhere.

With its estimated budget of $50 million a year (in 1960s dollars), the Miami Station's economic impact on South Florida was tremendous. CIA front companies numbered "maybe three hundred or four hundred at one time or another. . . . We had three or four people working on real estate to manage those companies designed to hold properties," said Shackley. "We could only use properties for short periods of time. We couldn't stay in any one place very long." The properties included marinas, hunting camps, merchant shipping, airlines, a motel, leasing and transportation firms, exile-operated publishing outfits, "safe houses" strung throughout the area, and, of course, Zenith Technical Enterprises. The station itself had more than a hundred cars under lease. It ran the third largest navy in the Caribbean, after the United States and Cuba. Shackley estimated there were up to fifteen thousand Cubans "connected to us in one way or another."

The tenor of the times and the threat next door contributed to a tolerant, and even cooperative, South Florida attitude toward JMWAVE activities. "There was, first and foremost, a great deal of patriotism in South Florida," recalled Shackley. "When we needed things, we were dealing with people who had a memory of the Korean War and World War II. There was a strong anti-Castro feeling among Americans. And the influx of Cubans in late 1961 and early 1962 were the cream. What's important to understand is that it made it easy to work in that environment, a pro-government environment. I can't remember going to a businessman and asking him for cooperation who was not pleased to cooperate with the government and help."[1]

When authors David Wise and Thomas B. Ross blew the Zenith cover, identifying the company as a CIA front in the June 16, 1964, edition of *Look* magazine—a prelude to their book *The Invisible Government*, published later the same year—the agency promptly changed the station's cover name to Melmar Corporation and went about business as usual from the same location.[2] "We couldn't hide. We were stuck with the plant at the South campus," said Shackley. "We made other changes [in addition to the name] that reduced efficiency but enhanced security." He cited as an example the shifting of a "mother ship" used in actions against Cuba to Tampa from Fort Lauderdale or West Palm Beach ports.

Gene Cohen, University of Miami vice president and treasurer at the time, denied knowing that Zenith was a CIA cover. "As far as we're concerned, the university is leasing space to an organization we consider a good tenant which pays rent promptly," said Cohen. "There's nothing to indicate a connection with the CIA."[3] As the still naive young reporter who spoke with Cohen and wrote the story appearing in the *Miami Herald*, the author typed notes showing that Cohen added "off the record" that it probably wouldn't have made any difference if the university did know Zenith was a CIA operation since "we're all on the same side," reflecting the near-universal South Florida attitude at the time.

Maybe Cohen didn't know, but university president Henry King Stanford certainly did, said Shackley. "He knew who we were and what we were doing. I would meet him occasionally but only when we had a problem. I didn't see him often."[4]

The *Look* article identified three other Miami corporations as CIA covers. They were Double-Chek, Gibraltar Steamship, and Vanguard Service. Double-Chek recruited the Alabama Air National Guard pilots for the Bay of Pigs. Gibraltar Steamship operated Radio Swan, the clandestine CIA station broadcasting to Cuba from Swan Island in the western Caribbean. It was listed under the same telephone number as Vanguard Service in a downtown Miami office building.

Bradley Ayers, an Army Ranger captain detached to the JMWAVE station in the spring of 1963 to help with training commando teams, later described its activities in a "tell all" book entitled *The War That Never Was*. He recounted the first meeting with Shackley in his office at Zenith.

> Monday morning we met the station chief, Ted Morley [Shackley]. As we sat in his outer office, waiting a little nervously, I saw that they had missed no detail in setting up the false front of Zenith Technical Enterprises. There were phony sales and production charts on the walls and business licenses from the state and federal government. A notice to salesmen, pinned near the door, advised them of the calling hours for various departments. The crowning touch was a certificate of award from the United Givers' Fund to Zenith for outstanding participation in its annual fund drive.
>
> When we were finally shown into Morley's office, I was immediately impressed by the tall young executive. The wisdom and professional skill demanded by his post and the strategic and diplomatic delicacy of the station's mission made it imperative that the position be filled by someone attuned to the political goals. The station chief would have to be close to the President, a member of the inner circle; and Morley seemed the kind of man Kennedy might have personally appointed.[5]

Ayers was to become so emotionally involved, both in the Cuban exile cause and with a Cuban refugee woman, that Shackley terminated him.

However, according to Cuban exiles who were trained by the agency, his book offers an accurate portrayal of CIA operations in South Florida at the time. Shackley, in an interview, recalled Ayers as a "strange guy," although acknowledging that Ayers's portrayal of the station activities was generally accurate as far as it went. "He was assigned to do training . . . real gung ho. He came with the impression he was going to train and then lead a team into Cuba. That was always a problem with the Special Forces. When they found they were not going to lead a team they became enamored of the Cuban cause. He started messing around with some female down there. We could see problems and ordered him to return to his parent unit. He was basically a good guy, but they go native." Shackley said that the station "maybe had fifteen or so military trainers at any one time."[6]

While JMWAVE was by far the biggest, it was not the first CIA presence in Miami. That distinction belonged to Justin F. "Jay" Gleichauf, who arrived shortly after Cuban dictator Fulgencio Batista fled into exile on New Year's Day of 1959. Gleichauf told his story more than forty years later in an unclassified edition of a CIA publication.[7] "I had no inkling [when Batista fell] that within two weeks I would be in Miami as head— and sole staffer—of a newly authorized office of the Domestic Contacts Division in the Directorate of Intelligence," Gleichauf wrote. "The Headquarters briefing was short and not particularly enlightening as to my new duties: 'Basically, use your own good judgment.'"

Gleichauf opened an overt CIA office at 299 Alhambra Circle, a well-known, east-west street in Coral Gables, an upscale area abutting Miami on the south, and adjacent to what later would become known as Little Havana because of its overwhelmingly Cuban population. When he arrived in Miami, Gleichauf said, the "first wave of Cuban refugees had landed, some on their yachts, with jewels and *objets d'art*. Palm Beach became a safe haven for 'Batistianos,' including Batista's son-in-law. In contacts with them, I was never impressed with their opposition to Castro, although one offered the services of the captain of his yacht, who said he would 'do anything' CIA desired."

The basic function of the new office was to be a Cuba "listening post." To aid his effort, Gleichauf listed a CIA number—but no address—in the phone book and passed out business cards with his home number, resulting in calls from a "motley collection of weirdos" as well as some irate Castro supporters.

With no direct air service from Cuba to Central or South America, said Gleichauf, "all shipments to the area had to pass through the Pan American Airways base in Miami. Every night I would head for the PAA base warehouse and pick up 17 copies of every newspaper, magazine, or other printed matter en route [from Cuba] south. . . . Nothing could be done with the many tins of propaganda film heading south, but I was informed that quite a number were 'accidentally' run over by a fork-lift truck."

Representatives of companies that had business interests in Cuba, including an aircraft maintenance and repair firm that still held a contract to service Cuba's air force and Cubana, the country's national airline, were also a fertile field for cultivation. Gleichauf put out the word and shortly thereafter Pedro Diaz Lanz, commander of the Cuban Air Force, became one of the first major defectors from the Castro regime in July 1959, as did his brother, the Cuban Air Force inspector general, and several top Cubana pilots.

"Initially, Headquarters directed me to contact a number of self-proclaimed influential political figures who boasted strong support which could be converted into armed resistance once CIA gave them the 'green light' (read dollars)," Gleichauf recalled.

"There were scores of other opportunists in the Miami area, including gun merchants eager to sell equipment to the literally hundreds of 'resistance' groups in the area. Newsphotos were common of grim-faced men in fatigues, holding rifles. There were also lots of would-be Mata Haris, eager to do anything for the cause. And I ran across a lot of soldiers of fortune looking for a fast buck."

Many of those soldiers of fortune found the *Time-Life* bureau, in a downtown Miami office complex overlooking the mouth of the Miami River, a hospitable place to hang out. One, Gerry Patrick Hemming, a six-foot five-inch ex-Marine, had fought with Castro's rebels before breaking with Fidel and organizing a shadowy outfit called Intercontinental Penetration Force based in the Florida Keys. At one point, Hemming contacted the president's military aide in a letter written on the *Time-Life* bureau's stationery, seeking "advice and constructive criticism." There is no indication any was forthcoming.[8]

Among the more notorious of the would-be adventurers to surface was Frank Fiorini, another onetime fighter with Cuban rebels who switched sides to join the battle against Castro. He later changed his name to Frank Sturgis and become nationally infamous as one of the 1972 Watergate burglars. Sturgis, remembered Gleichauf, "was held in low esteem."[9] He generally had a reputation among those who dealt with him as being one of the more reckless and least credible of the freelance warriors who invaded South Florida for the war against Castro.

Robert K. "Bob" Brown, a U.S. Army Special Forces officer who seemed to come and go from military service with regularity, was another to appear on the local scene. Brown, with a master's degree in political science from the University of Colorado, delighted in ferreting out and exposing CIA front companies. He wrote an unpublished manuscript on the subject that circulated widely in certain local circles. Brown went on to found *Soldier of Fortune* magazine in 1975.

For most adventure seekers, the greatest adventure—meriting a badge of honor—was arrest by U.S. officials for violation of the Neutrality Act or on customs or immigration charges. John Dorschner later wrote of the adventurers collectively in a 1976 article for the *Miami Herald's* Sunday magazine, observing: "They are romantics, and they tell fantastic stories of adventure, perhaps half of which are true. The fabricated escapades, the dreams, are as much a part of their milieu as the adventure themselves. 'One wonders where fact and fantasy divide,' a *Washington Star* reporter wrote about the life of Watergate burglar Frank Fiorini Sturgis, and the comment holds true for the group as a whole."[10]

Many made their local home at Nellie Hamilton's boardinghouse on Southwest Fourth Street in what is now the heart of Miami's Little Havana. "In Nellie's side yard," as Dorschner recounted one story, "Jerry [sic] Patrick Hemming used to drill commandos, and the men hid weapons in her storage shack. Once, Nellie emerged carrying a hand grenade by the ring. 'What's this, boys?' she asked. [Ralph] Edens [one of her tenants] gingerly took the grenade away from her. Nellie professed not to know what the 'boys' were up to, but a *Herald* writer once quoted an unnamed CIA agent as calling her 'Mother Hubbard and her commandos.'"[11]

The American freelancers, as did many of the multitude of Cuban exile groups, often tried to leave the impression they were connected with the CIA, which would give them cachet in the Miami community. Few of either the soldiers of fortune or the exile groups actually were subsidized by—or even worked with—the agency as an institution. Some, however, may have had links with individual CIA case officers who were working with or encouraging them. A declassified CIA document dated April 23, 1963, shows eight exile organizations were receiving money, and only two—the Revolutionary Student Directorate (DRE) and the Movement for Revolutionary Recovery (MRR)—were engaged in paramilitary activities against Cuba. The biggest recipient was the Cuban Revolutionary Council, formed by the CIA as a front group for the Bay of Pigs invasion. It broke with the agency in April 1963.[11]

Among the more widely known militant Miami exile groups of the day, in addition to the DRE and the MRR, were Alpha 66, the Second National Front of the Escambray, Commandos L, the Insurrectional Revolutionary Recovery Movement (MIRR), the Thirtieth of November Movement, and the Peoples Revolutionary Movement (MRP), which later was joined with other groups to become the Cuban Revolutionary Junta (JURE). The JURE, headed by Manuel Ray, and the MRR, headed by Manuel Artime, were both supported by the U.S. government in the post–missile crisis period but operated as so-called autonomous groups.

Many exiles would travel to Washington, seeking to meet with anybody involved in Cuban affairs, starting with the president. "That was kind of amusing in a way," recalled Tom Parrott of the exile delegations constantly knocking on the White House door. "They would come in to see Taylor. . . . They wanted to see the president, of course. And lacking the president, they wanted to see Bobby, and they ended up seeing Taylor and they'd end up seeing me. They were all saying 'we don't want to have anything to do with the CIA; absolutely nothing to do with the CIA at all. So, of course, I would find out what they had. . . . None of them turned out to have anything. They all professed all kinds of assets inside of Cuba and so forth but you could tell that they were phonies. But of course the minute they left, I'd get on the phone to the CIA and ask, 'What do you have on these people?' "[12]

Parrott recalled a visit by one exile in particular, Marcos Garcia Kohly. "He claimed to have all kinds of support and he came to see Taylor. We talked to him for a little bit and then I took him over. He had a big scrapbook to show all the people supporting him inside Cuba and if he came back he could be the leader. He could replace Castro. It was pretty ridiculous. He had things like the Women's Club of Santiago and, you know, the Boy Scouts of some other place, that kind of thing. There was nothing. I do remember that in this scrapbook as we leafed through, there was a ten-peso note. . . . It was there to keep in touch and this was the currency they had in Cuba. Well, the next thing I know he is being prosecuted in New York for counterfeiting Cuban currency and he said I had authorized him to do it. I wasn't aware that I was authorized to let anybody counterfeit any kind of currency. It got to be quite a thing, and it [Parrott's alleged authorization] was part of his defense," said Parrott, who doesn't know how the case turned out.[13]

There was "something like seven hundred exile groups," recalled Gleichauf. "One guy was head of something called AAA, and claimed they had five thousand men under arms. They were ready to go as soon as they got the green light . . . made a lot of promises. It turned out to be completely ineffectual. It was all bull. The green light was money. It was a racket, one guy and his brother-in-law and existed only on paper. Most existed only to raise money."[14]

George Volsky, employed by the U.S. Information Agency's Miami office in the early 1960s and also as a local correspondent for the *New York Times*, had similar recollections. "There were Cuban groups which did all kinds of things which were not very effectual at all. And the CIA knew exactly what they were doing and let them do it so the government could say 'well, we allowed Cubans to do it.' Otherwise they would be . . . the usual big mouth . . . they would say 'the United States doesn't let us do anything against Castro. . . . They are keeping Castro in because they don't allow us to do anything.'"

Volsky, a Polish-born refugee who wound up in Cuba in the late 1940s, then fled to the United States after being jailed in Havana during the Bay of Pigs, cited, as an example, a boat seizure on the Miami River that he witnessed. "It was laughable," he said. "There was a boat full of weapons, hundreds. Maybe 10 percent were operational and all the others were some old revolvers and rifles bought by these people. The operation worked like this. They would go around [in the exile community] and say we are going to Cuba, we are going to invade and so on. They would get, say, $10,000 and buy for $2,000 all this junk then call the Coast Guard and tell them a boat is leaving for Cuba. The Coast Guard would seize them and then they would say 'the United States doesn't allow us to go to Cuba and all the money was there [for purchase of the seized weapons]' when it actually was only a fraction. So it was a big joke."

Volsky recalled a visit to the offices of Alpha 66, one of the more militant exile groups, not long after an action that involved an arrest for an aborted raid against Cuba. "As a result they started getting money . . . one, two, five dollars in letters because they had asked for support. I went to their office and they were actually putting money into a sock. I saw it. There were a lot of those kinds of operations. A lot of loud mouths, but they were just like mosquitoes biting Castro and maybe even less."[15]

Volsky was himself involved in one unsuccessful clandestine anti-

Castro operation, led by a Cuban exile, Nestor Moreno, and reluctantly supported by Shackley's JMWAVE, on orders from Washington. Code-named AMTRUNK, the aim was for exile infiltrators to subvert and organize Cuban military officers. It had no known success.[16]

Those Cuban exiles recruited and trained by the CIA as part of infiltration and commando teams or as support personnel for JMWAVE operations were much more discreet. Typical is the experience of Carlos Obregon, today the Miami representative for a Venezuelan publishing firm, who toiled in the shadows for the CIA from 1961 to 1970. A native of Havana, Obregon arrived in Miami in January 1961 on a commercial flight from Cuba. In late summer of the same year his CIA career began with his recruitment as a militant young exile member of the DRE, a group of mostly ex-university students active first against Batista and then against Castro.

The CIA had asked the DRE leadership to select some fifteen members for training in clandestine warfare, and Obregon was among those selected. In early October of 1961 the CIA trimmed the group to about a dozen, and Obregon was among them too. They were taken to a motel near Homestead, just south of Miami on the fringe of the Florida Everglades, to begin their training. There, CIA-trained Cuban instructors taught the group infiltration and exfiltration procedures; recruitment, training, and handling of agents; basic map reading; and small weapons and explosives. The course was cut short after two weeks, with the CIA complaining that the local press had been nosing around.

The trainees were temporarily relocated to the Miami Beach area. A short time later they were taken to a site near North Key Largo at the top of the Florida Keys where training resumed in what was then a much less populated area. The training site, said Obregon, consisted of a four-bedroom stucco house located along the highway and two smaller wooden buildings, next to the Atlantic Ocean, a hundred yards or so from the main house.

On some days during the latter stages of the Key Largo exercise, the group was split into smaller units and taken for a full day's training at a site in the Everglades. To get there, they were driven by car to an abandoned U.S. Navy airfield southwest of Fort Lauderdale—now the campus of Nova Southeastern University—then flown to the site by small plane. There they received instructions in the operation and use of various types of pistols, submachine guns, and C3 and C4 explosives. An American named Larry, and Roy, a Cuban assistant, conducted the training. Training ended in mid-December and the group was put on standby through the holidays. Most were housed at a DRE "safe house" near downtown Miami, doing very little until early 1962, when Obregon's first direct involvement with the CIA began. He successfully underwent a polygraph test before reporting to a CIA "safe house" on Krome Avenue near Homestead. Then he was assigned to a radio operator course and spent two months learning Morse code and the operation of two radios, the RS1 and RS6. Finishing the course in the second quarter of 1962, Obregon was assigned to a team and flown to what he later learned was "The Farm," the CIA's super-secret training facility near Williamsburg, Virginia. At the end of six weeks' classroom and field training at "The Farm," a team "was well-prepared to begin to operate in Cuba," Obregon said.

Then it was back to Miami for maritime training, including learning to operate small boats, rubber rafts, and electronic navigational equipment; and the uses of infrared light and the metascope in infiltration and exfiltration operations. Classroom training was at a "safe house" near the main entrance to Everglades National Park. Field training was in the Flamingo area at the park's southernmost land tip and it included nighttime infiltration and exfiltration exercises under circumstances that might be encountered in Cuba.

By late summer 1962 training was completed and the team was put on standby, meeting occasionally with its CIA case officer to discuss the situation in Cuba while awaiting the first infiltration assignment. On October 21, 1962, the team was told to report to a "safe house" in the Homestead area and await instructions. They did not yet know that Soviet offensive missiles had been detected in Cuba. Their case officer joined them that night, as President Kennedy announced the discovery and the Cuban Missile Crisis exploded.

The next morning the team was told it would be landed in Cuba "within the next two or three days. . . . The team was very eager and ready to move" in anticipation of a U.S. invasion. A recent Cuban arrival in Miami was to return to Cuba with them and act as guide in the Camaguey area. But the next day, a Friday, the case officer arrived to tell them the infiltration was on hold. The following Sunday the case officer "told us bluntly that all operations against Castro had been put on hold and we should pack up and go home. If there were a need for us, we would be contacted."

Disgusted, the other team members broke with the agency. "Although disappointed," Obregon decided to stay to do what he could to "unseat Castro." From then until 1967 he was a member of CIA infiltration teams that "periodically were sent to the island to build intelligence gathering networks, and to develop a paramilitary capability that would be available in case instructions were given to start a guerrilla operation." As both a radio operator and team leader, he estimated he made at least ten infiltration runs into Cuba.

"Most of the CIA infiltration teams that operated between late 1962 and 1967 were extremely well trained and had full support of the Agency," said Obregon. Most teams, of two to five members each, operated in the Cuban countryside, "setting up intelligence gathering networks. . . . The teams were built around a team leader and radio operator [who] were relatively well educated with at least a high school education." Many team leaders "had been small land or business owners," whose properties had been confiscated. Others were ex-university students. Many of the team members had been fishermen and/or farmers in Cuba.

"The team contact with the CIA was the case officer," said Obregon. With few exceptions, the case officers were Americans and career CIA employees, some of whom spoke Spanish, "although the majority did not. Assisting the case officer was a so-called principal agent (PA), who in all likelihood was a Cuban national."

The infiltration teams operated from "safe houses," mostly located in the Perrine-Homestead-Florida City areas, all immediately to the south of Miami en route to the Florida Keys, in the same general geographic area as JMWAVE. The "safe houses" were used as meeting places and sometimes for team training. On the day of an operation, team members would be picked up at their homes in the Miami area and taken to the "safe house." There, operational plans were reviewed and the latest U-2 photos of the infiltration area were examined. Required documentation and Cuban currency were provided.

From the "safe house" the team would be driven to the Florida Keys and taken in a small boat to the larger so-called mother ship, which, in turn, would tow an "operational vessel" that would take the team to the actual infiltration point. The operational vessels, all part of the CIA navy, were V-20s, Sea Crafts, Formulas, and Boston Whalers, said Obregon. During the latter stages of his participation in the CIA's Cuba covert action program, Obregon commanded a six-member team that was self-contained to include the operational vessel. Obregon and two others—a fisherman and a farmer—would "enter the island to run the networks that we had established" in Cuba's Las Villas Province. The other three members of the team would crew the operational vessel. Once it had dropped off the team, the operational vessels would return to the mother ship and head back to the Florida Keys.

Obregon's team operated on Cuba's north coast, not far from Florida, so they could leave the Florida Keys in the morning and be at the operational vessel's drop-off point by about 11 P.M. the same day. The trip from the drop-off point to the infiltration point usually took about an hour, said Obregon. The operational vessel would take him and his team about fifty yards from shore and drop them off. "After reaching shore, the team would move about 200 yards inside and wait for the following day to start moving inside in order to make contact with members of the networks," said Obregon. "The movement from the shore to the general area where the team would establish contact was very difficult through heavy mangroves, requiring extreme physical effort from team members." Each team member had a thirty-pound pack on his back. As the radio operator, Obregon's was even heavier. Team members also carried submachine guns and 9mm pistols.

When exfiltration was "called up," said Obregon, "the operational vessel would go to the exfiltration point to pick up the team, rendezvous with the mother vessel and head back to the [Florida] Keys. Sometimes the operational vessel could not make the rendezvous with the mother ship and had to get back to the Keys on its own." The length of time the team remained on the island varied, said Obregon, ranging from a couple of weeks to a month or more, depending on the operation.

"Central to every operation, once the locals had been recruited, was the establishment of a communication link between the local underground group and the CIA station in Miami. In order to establish this link, at least one member of the recently recruited group would be trained in the use and operation of a high speed radio to send coded messages to the CIA communication base."

During his nine years with the agency, said Obregon, he was "always paid in cash." But, in an indication of the cooperative local atmosphere described by Shackley, Obregon said that during 1962 and 1963, "I was advised to use M. R. Harrison Construction Company [a large and well-known Miami company] on credit applications as my place of employment. My position was timekeeper and interpreter. During this time and up to 1964, I was never issued a W-2 form for tax purposes." He began receiving W-2 forms in 1965, which continued until he left the agency in 1970. From 1965 through 1967, the W-2s came, as best he could recall nearly four decades later, in the name of South Allapattah Properties Incorporated, where he was again listed as timekeeper and interpreter. From 1968 to August 1970, he received the W-2s from a company named Marine Research.[17]

From the time of his arrival in January 1959 until the spring of 1960, Jay Gleichauf did double duty for the CIA on the overt and covert side. When President Eisenhower authorized the covert operation that evolved into the Bay of Pigs, a CIA colleague from the clandestine service joined him in Miami to open the Western Hemisphere Division's new Forward Operating Base (FOB). His duties were to coordinate "all support, training and preparatory activities for operations against Cuba," according to a heavily censored and undated CIA record of the Miami Station declassified in 1995.[18]

In describing the new covert operation, the document notes that the new Miami Station "simultaneously supported our busy Havana Station which was operating under difficult circumstances, including inhibiting surveillance of our officers by Castro security services. After the Station was closed in Havana when US diplomatic relations were broken with Castro's government in January 1961, it was envisioned that selected personnel assigned to the Miami Base would, upon the overthrow of the Castro government, become a nucleus to reopen the Havana Station. During the Bay of Pigs landing, the FOB provided support for the operation."

Bob Reynolds, Jake Esterline's deputy in Washington as the Cuba Project got under way in early 1960, remembered the decision to open the Miami Station. "Jake said to me one day, I want you to go to Miami. There was a real need for a station in Miami. Too many people from too many different organizations were sending people to Miami to meet this guy or that guy, to make this or that plan. . . . There was zero coordination . . . all within the agency. . . ." remembered Reynolds. "We definitely had to have a permanent representation down there. So we put one together under the temporary leadership of Ray O'Mara, who we called back from Bogota . . . a senior member of the agency . . . very good man. He had FBI experience during World War II and was now living in Bogota." O'Mara set up the new station and took initial charge of it, but with his temporary arrangement expiring, Reynolds said, "Jake needed somebody to go down and replace him on a permanent basis and he chose me."

Reynolds arrived in September 1960 and left a year later. The covert office, too, was initially in Coral Gables with "very thin cover," although Reynolds said he did not recall the address nor did he think it was then named JMWAVE. "We had no problems operating from this tiny office we had in Coral Gables . . . cars coming and going night and day, people dealing with members of the Cuban exile community all over the area, including down in the Keys . . . with our own little navy. It was amazing how freely we were able to operate without detection, and by that I mean you folks [the press]."

Reynolds said he had "not a clue" about the timing for the Bay of Pigs invasion "until the day after" it happened. "Why would they tell the Miami station? Our role involved recruiting *brigadistas* to go for training. Once we put them on an airplane for Guatemala, that was it." In addition to recruiting brigade members, Reynolds said the station was involved in propaganda, counterintelligence, and intelligence collection and "would occasionally send people in and out [of Cuba]."

By the time he departed Miami in the fall of 1961, the Bay of Pigs had failed. Tentative planning for a new covert campaign against Castro—one that became Operation Mongoose—already was under way. Before his departure, Reynolds said he arranged to relocate the covert office from Coral Gables to the old Richmond Naval Air Station, by then the University of Miami's secluded South Campus.[19]

Reynolds said he did not recall who at the University of Miami handled the arrangements with the agency to relocate the station there. "I had some very competent administrative people down there who set it all up and I've forgotten how the arrangements were made or with whom." By that time, said Reynolds, "we had a huge communications component and it seems to me that if I counted those in as being part of my command, we had about 160, of whom about half were communications people."

Bob Davis, the CIA station chief in Guatemala at the time of the Bay of Pigs, succeeded Reynolds for a brief period. When Reynolds left Miami he said he had an "extremely good working relationship" with Gleichauf, head of the overt office in Miami, "which I understand deteriorated after I left. I don't know if he [Davis] intentionally left relations with Jay's office slag or whether it was his successor."

After Davis's departure as chief, the covert station suffered from leadership and organizational problems. In December Bill Harvey sent Shackley, his Berlin protégé, to Miami to do a report. Six weeks later, Shackley was back in Miami as deputy station chief and became station chief shortly thereafter. Gleichauf suggested that the deterioration in the relationship between the two Miami CIA operations coincided with Shackley's arrival, describing his new clandestine counterpart as "a cold person . . . [who] delighted to drive around with his telephone in his ear dealing with manufactured crises."[20]

The declassified Miami Station review document described the change in locations only by noting: "In September 1961, the Miami Station was established at a new location, replacing the FOB. About 300 persons were assigned to the Station at one time; Headquarters responsibility was in an autonomous group until 1965, when the Western Hemisphere Division resumed charge."[21]

The station review does offer some insight as to JMWAVE activities, noting:

Utilizing former Cuban assets in Havana who had fled to the United States, indigenous Cuban organizations were formed to continue the overt struggle against the Castro government. In addition, a Cuban Intelligence Organization in exile was formed to collect information on the activities of militant autonomous Cuban exile groups in the United States who were not affiliated with the US Government effort against the Cuban regime.

The Cuban intelligence organization in exile participated in a number of activities including the issuance of anti-Castro publications, maintaining relations with anti-Castro governments and groups in the Caribbean and Latin American countries, and debriefing Cuban exiles arriving in the United States for positive foreign intelligence and counterintelligence to identify Cuban agents being infiltrated into the United States via the Cuban Freedom Flights and small boats. Allied with this effort [words blacked out] directed at Cuban government [words blacked out], which was manned by indigenous Cuban exiles. Close working relations were maintained with US Government agencies in the Miami area such as the FBI, INS, Coast Guard, Customs, Navy, Air Force, etc., to coordinate activities. A small support base was established in Key West.

During the period 1962–66 the Miami Station engaged in classical intelligence operations directed against the Cuban regime. Radio Americas was established and broadcast daily from Swan Island in the Caribbean. Psychological, economic and political activities were undertaken in an effort to undermine confidence in the Castro government and underscore the

Soviet presence and total Cuban dependence on the USSR. Maritime operations were also undertaken. Among other missions, Cubans who desired to escape from the Cuban mainland were assisted.

The Cuban Intelligence Organization was more commonly known within the local Cuban community and intelligence circles as Operation 40, a quasi-independent group headed by Joaquin Sanjenis, who gained somewhat of a legendary and controversial reputation among some exiles. The group was created in March 1961 and trained in intelligence matters by the CIA as part of the planning for what was to become the Bay of Pigs.

According to a Cuban exile who worked for Operation 40 for three years in the late 1960s, the group's initial objective was to take over administration of "the towns and cities liberated by the invasion force, roundup government officials and sympathizers and secure the files of the government's different intelligence services." Sanjenis was the overall boss. The top field officer was Vicente Leon, who was believed to have been a colonel in Cuba's pre-Castro police. Leon killed himself rather than surrender when he landed with the Bay of Pigs invaders as part of an Operation 40 advance team.

After the Bay of Pigs, Operation 40 turned its attention more to counterintelligence activities directed at suspected Castro agents who might have infiltrated into the local exile community. More controversially, it provided intelligence on the activities of local exile groups, some of which allowed local or federal authorities to thwart unsanctioned exile raids. Numerous declassified CIA Intelligence Information Cables on file at the Lyndon Baines Johnson Library in Austin, Texas, included the "source and appraisal of the cables." A variation of the following was often cited: "A member of a group of Cuban émigrés trained in the techniques of information collection. The group has provided useful reports for over two years. The information was obtained from a local representative of the JURE who has access to members of the JURE executive committee."

The exile who worked for the unit in the late 1960s said Operation 40 was "fairly compartmentalized," but "foremost to its existence was the collection of intelligence on Cuba. . . . Most of the information collected was from overt sources . . . primarily the hundreds of Cuban refugees coming to South Florida on Freedom Flights." The refugees were screened as they arrived. Those that might have useful information were interviewed separately. Intelligence reports were prepared on the basis of the information provided. Additional information was gleaned from Cuban publications arriving in the Operation 40 offices. The group monitored the activities of local Cuban exile groups as well. A large database of index cards was maintained, containing the names of Cubans both inside and outside the island. The database information was "extremely helpful" in determining recently arrived refugees who might have had a close association with the Castro government, said the exile that worked with the unit.

There were those in the exile community who held a darker view of the operation. One exile familiar with the operation said that "when the Bay of Pigs went kaput, they stayed as a group and Sanjenis became a very, very dangerous and powerful guy in Miami because he had a file on everybody . . . whose wife was whose lover, how much money, etc. . . . Some people tried to use that for blackmail. Actually, nobody knows where those files are. It's a big question mark." He said he had heard, without knowing whether it was true, "that they had something like 50,000 files on people and names." Operation 40 was shut down in late 1972 or early 1973, and the files were reportedly packed up and sent to Washington.[22]

For both Gleichauf and Shackley, activity in their respective offices reached a crescendo during the Cuban Missile Crisis, in which both facilities played a critical role.

Virtually since his arrival, Gleichauf had been pressing headquarters for "establishment of a formal reception and interrogation center similar to the Camp Kilmer [where Gleichauf had served] operation in 1957, where Hungarian Freedom Fighters and refugees were processed and interrogated."

His effort got a big push shortly before Christmas 1961 when George McManus, special assistant to CIA Director Allen Dulles visited Miami. By then, "refugees were coming in at the rate of 1,700 per week, via air, small boats and even rafts made of old truck-tire inner tubes." McManus told Gleichauf that Dulles wanted to know why there was so little reporting on Cuba. Gleichauf responded that with only four interrogators and no interviewing facilities, "we could not begin to cope with the influx." Manny Chavez, who was detached to Gleichauf's CIA office as one of the four interrogators, recalled that they had to await incoming refugees as they cleared customs and then hand them a card with a telephone number, asking them to call if they had information they wanted to relay.

Two weeks after McManus's visit, Gleichauf was in Washington working on the details for a processing center in Miami. President Kennedy
approved the project, and it became one of the many "tasks" assigned to
the CIA by General Lansdale as part of Operation Mongoose. The so-
called Caribbean Admissions Center opened in the spring of 1962, at a
former World War II military airbase in Opa-Locka, a northwest Miami
suburb. Although operating under the direction of Gleichauf's office, it
became a cooperative effort of numerous federal agencies and included a
military staff of about fifty, many of Hispanic heritage.

"We operated on a seven-day-a-week basis," Gleichauf said. "One
team screened arrivals for knowledgeability, and a second team conducted interrogations in depth." They were soon averaging 150 interrogations a day. By late summer, the Soviet military buildup was becoming
apparent from the questioning, and reports were beginning to surface of
"Soviet ships carrying large objects in crates, unloaded at night under
strict security. Frequently, regular Cuban stevedore crews were dismissed
and ordered out of the area, and the ships were unloaded by special steve-
dores."

By September, Gleichauf recounted, increased reports of missiles were
being forwarded to Washington, "scoffed at by analysts who judged that,
even if true, they would represent only defensive missiles. In their view
Khrushchev would never risk introducing offensive missiles in Cuba."

But, recalled Gleichauf,

On a Sunday afternoon in mid-September, a new arrival reported that six
days before his departure he had observed a large Soviet truck convoy at
night leaving the Havana dock area under tight security. The trucks towed
65-to-70-foot trailers carrying objects so large they extended over the trailers. The objects were covered, but they had large fins. One of our best men,
an army lieutenant colonel, was conducting the interview and immediately
recognized the potential significance of the information. He asked the refugee to sketch the object he had seen.

It compared with photos of the SS-4, a medium range ballistic missile
capable of hitting most of the eastern United States. He then asked the
refugee to identify the missile he had seen from various photos of several
types of Soviet missiles, and the refugee picked the SS-4. It was decided to
put the report, identifying a possible SS-4, on the teletype to Headquarters
immediately. It created a sensation. President Kennedy ordered a U-2
reconnaissance mission over the area, but heavy cloud cover hampered vis-
ibility until 14 October, when a flight proved conclusively that offensive

missiles were indeed present in Cuba, and that missile-site construction was proceeding on a crash basis.

"On September 17," said Gleichauf, "we obtained a second refugee report of the sighting of a large convoy in Pinar del Rio province, carrying several possible missiles. It dovetailed with the original report and helped to trigger the targeting of the 14 October U-2 flight. The Cuban missile crisis was on.

"Following confirmation of offensive missiles in Cuba, Florida quickly became an armed camp," said Gleichauf. "Military convoys clogged highways, the railroad line to Homestead Air Force Base was jammed with military supplies, and rockets sprouted along the Overseas Highway [to the Florida Keys]. The 82nd Airborne took over Opa-Locka Airbase, and we moved elsewhere on twenty-four-hours notice. As one of my last support activities for an expected invasion, I obtained 6,000 local road maps of Cuba from a major oil company, ideal because of detailed local information. But Khrushchev backed down, and the maps were not needed."[23]

Shackley, too, found himself preoccupied with the missile crisis, describing the ten days from October 21 to October 30 as one of three phases into which he divided his nearly three and a half years as JMWAVE station chief. The other two phases were from his takeover of the station in early 1962 until the missile crisis and the period from November 1, 1962, until his departure in June 1965.[24]

The first phase, said Shackley, began by

cleaning up the debris from the Bay of Pigs. There were a lot of unfinished administrative things . . . a nightmare of administrative things and housekeeping chores. Also within the general rubric of intelligence collection we had to find out what was happening in Cuba, to produce positive intelligence, and put the paramilitary program into shape to do what we perceived to be the mission of the time, to take in supplies, bring people out and put them back in and carry out a certain amount of sabotage operations.

At first the notion and scope of what Washington wanted in terms of paramilitary operations skewered the operation. They wanted X. If we did X, we could not do other things needed to keep the intelligence collection operation going, and at that time intelligence was the primary mission.

Then we had to reorganize the psychological warfare campaign against Cuba and create an effective counterintelligence program. And there were other things. . . . We had to come up with an assessment of prospects for overthrowing Castro; could it be done by exiles, popular revolt, military coup or somebody assassinating Castro, at some point? Then we had to engage in contingency planning . . . what to do if Castro is overthrown.

During this period, cleanup work probably was about 10 percent and 80 percent went toward positive intelligence, bringing the paramilitary program up to snuff and counterintelligence and the other 10 percent looking at the prospects of overthrowing Castro and developing contingence plans.

While all this was unfolding, what in fact happened is that we were successful in collecting intelligence and detailing the Soviet buildup in Cuba. We didn't start out looking for the Soviet buildup but we detected it and then focused on it. In the early days, we saw cruise missiles coming in, and the SAMs and we also picked up shipments of manpower into Cuba, ostensibly for the agricultural sector as opposed to troops. That was rubbish.

The first phase also meant playing a key role in Operation Mongoose under the leadership of Harvey, Lansdale and, at the top, Bobby Kennedy, all in Washington. In contrast to many other participants, Shackley said he did not detect skepticism about Mongoose among Miami Station personnel, "but I can see where they might in Washington where they may have had more interference."

He did, however, describe Lansdale as a "strange duck. He came to Miami on two or three occasions. One time we met most of the day. Another time he called and said he was coming down and would like to meet senior guys [of JMWAVE]. I had a dinner for him and he didn't show up. I found out he went to Homestead Air Force Base [near Miami] and met with some of his Air Force buddies. At seven the next morning he called to see if he could come by for breakfast. He never said a word about dinner the night before or what had happened."

The brief but hectic and intense second phase covering the immediate period of the missile crisis, said Shackley, consisted of an "all out effort to get intelligence on chances of hostilities; planning with the military what role we would play if U.S. troops went into Cuba; to put in pathfinders to mark beaches and drop zones for airborne troops; counterintelligence deployment with military police for prisoner of war and identifying Cuban intelligence agents; and bringing in people who could function in civil administration."

In the third phase, said Shackley, "the task was really to keep intelligence going; to see if the Soviets were really pulling out; what was happening inside; and expanding counterintelligence efforts. The Cubans were dispatching more and more agents to the United States. We were looking for information. And we were going to honor the agreement, the no-invasion pledge." At the same time, said Shackley, the "operational environment" had become much more difficult. "In the early days of 1962, Cuba was in a permissive operational environment. By the time I left in 1965 it had ceased to be a permissive environment. When we first started, there was a large refugee outflow and no dearth of material to work with. Castro had not yet created coastal defenses. Radars, boats and internal population controls including the Committees for the Defense of the Revolution and other programs borrowed from the Soviet system, increased.[25]

Despite the many constraints, the Kennedy brothers' continuing effort to rid Cuba of Castro didn't slow.

CHAPTER 9

A NEW BEGINNING

T he missile crisis was largely resolved by January 1963, after weeks of haggling between Moscow and Washington and resistance from a petulant Castro over the withdrawal verification process. The remaining 1,113 Bay of Pigs prisoners returned to the United States in late December 1962, exchanged for a $53 million ransom of food and medicines. President Kennedy welcomed them in Miami's Orange Bowl, promising to return the brigade's flag "in a free Havana." Mongoose was dead. Ed Lansdale had moved on. So had Bill Harvey. Desmond FitzGerald, an urbane agency veteran comfortable in the Kennedys' social circle, was soon to be the CIA's new top gun for Cuba. Task Force W became the Special Affairs Staff.

For the Kennedy administration, it was an opportune time to revamp Cuba policy, newly constrained by the no-invasion pledge given Moscow in return for the missile withdrawal. But the Kennedy obsession for neutralizing or, even better, deposing Castro, remained. President Kennedy already had determined that "an assurance covering invasion does not ban covert actions or economic blockade or tie our hands completely. We can't give the impression that Castro is home free."[1]

McGeorge Bundy's post–missile crisis draft proposal for a new Cuba policy reiterated that "our ultimate objective . . . remains the overthrow of the Castro regime. . . . Our immediate objectives are to weaken the regime. . . . A policy of containing, undermining, discrediting and isolating the Castro regime through the exercise of all feasible diplomatic, economic, psychological and other pressures will achieve these immediate objectives and could create propitious conditions in Cuba for further advance toward our ultimate objective." The proposal included a twelve-point program for covert action, ranging from sabotage to propaganda.[2]

The first signs of unhappiness with Mongoose and a new direction in Cuba policy had emerged even before the missile crisis erupted. Proposal for the new direction came from Walter Rostow, chairman of the State

Department's Policy Planning Council. He suggested, in early September 1962, implementation of a two-track covert Cuba policy, one that would place more of the burden, and the responsibility, on Cuban exiles. As Rostow described it in a memo to the president, "Track One would consist of a heightened effort to move along the present Mongoose lines. . . . Track Two would consist of an effort to engage Cubans more deeply, both within Cuba and abroad, in efforts for their own liberation." As Bundy saw it, such a policy would call for:

a. Authentic Cuban leadership with a considerable range of freedom to implement ideas and to assume risk.

b. Minimal U.S. direct participation: ideally, one truly wise U.S. adviser—available, but laying back; equipped to provide finance, but not monitoring every move; capable of earning their respect rather than commanding it by his control over money or equipment.

c. Basing outside the United States.

d. A link-up with the scattered and sporadic groups and operations now going forward of their own momentum in Cuba.

e. A plan of operation which aims at the overthrow of Castro primarily from within rather than by invasion from without.

f. A long enough time horizon to build the operation carefully and soundly.[3]

Ed Martin, assistant secretary of state for Inter-American affairs, followed with a similar but more detailed proposal, describing "a program of 'giving Cubans their heads' in an effort to effect the downfall from within." In summarizing his suggestion, Martin warned: "We should be cautious about grandiose schemes, a 'major' U.S. effort, and deep commitments to the exiles. We should experiment in this new venture on a small scale with patience and tolerance for high noise levels and mistakes." This warning proved prophetic.[4] The missile crisis erupted and any change of course in long-term Cuba policy succumbed to the immediacy of averting a nuclear holocaust.

The immediate post–missile crisis focus was on intelligence collection to verify the withdrawal of offensive weapons and resolution of the impasse with the Soviets over inspection. Sabotage was on hold. But in late November, President Kennedy asked the State Department "to prepare a plan which would keep the heat on Castro."[5] Bundy drafted a bureaucratic reorganization proposal for dealing with Cuba. "The time is ripe for such a reorganization," wrote Bundy in a January 4, 1963, memo to the president, "because we seem to be winding up the negotiations in New York [over verification of offensive weapons withdrawal], the prisoners are out, and there is well nigh universal agreement that Mongoose is at a dead end."[6] The main thrust of the reorganization proposal was to consolidate all Cuba activity—both overt and covert—within the State Department under a new coordinator for Cuban affairs. In his memo Bundy concluded: "The role of intelligence officers needs to be redefined. The large commitment of the CIA to Mongoose activities should be reexamined, and probably substantially reduced, and the role of CIA as apparent spokesman and agent of the United States Government for Cuban affairs should probably be reduced still further—although this in no sense reflects on the Agency, which has been trying to do what it was told to do."

The reorganization was set forth in a January 8, 1963, National Security Council memorandum. The first of two key documents in 1963 that shaped Washington's revamped approach to Cuba, the memo reflected the constraints imposed by the no-invasion pledge and Castro's refusal to allow on-site inspection to verify missile withdrawal. The other key document was the June 19 approval for an integrated covert operational program against Cuba drafted by the CIA.

The January bureaucratic reorganization gave the "day-to-day coordinating responsibility" to the newly created coordinator of Cuban affairs within the State Department who was to chair an Interdepartmental Committee on Cuba. The committee would consist of representatives from the Defense Department, the CIA, and other departments "as necessary in particular cases." The reorganization also gave the new coordinator "the same responsibility for covert actions as well as overt actions." But it still required covert activities to be approved by the Special Group "which will be guided by broader policy established by the President through the Executive Committee."[7] Sterling Cottrell, a career Foreign Service officer heading the Vietnamese task force but with broad experience and background in Latin America, became the first coordinator. Bob Hurwitch was his deputy.

An Office of the Coordinator opened in Miami a few weeks later, headed by John Crimmins, who soon replaced Cottrell as the top coordinator in Washington. The Miami office essentially served as a de facto embassy to the Cuban exile community and coordinated all the federal agencies there involved with Cuba. The CIA remained the principal instrument for covert activity, with the Defense Department playing a supporting role. But Bobby Kennedy was still the unofficial overseer, particularly of the covert program, constantly on the telephone with anyone and everyone involved, both U.S. officials and Cuban exiles.

"He was really running it," Tom Parrott said of Bobby. "He was a thorn in the side of FitzGerald and to some extent Helms. I knew FitzGerald extremely well, and he would just be seething sometimes about this. . . . Bobby was, as we all know, arrogant and overbearing, prone to hint not too subtly that if you don't do what I say, I'll tell my big brother on you . . . just generally difficult. I think he drove poor Des crazy. Was Bobby Kennedy obsessed? Absolutely. Oh, absolutely. He was particularly riding the people at the CIA all the time. No question about it, obsessed is the right word."[8]

Sam Halpern, who retained his position as executive assistant under FitzGerald in the revamped program, said the CIA's role remained essentially the same as under Mongoose, "except more sabotage, this time under the hand of Bobby Kennedy. He steps in and starts directing it, instead of indirectly; instead of doing it through Lansdale, he is doing it directly."[9]

Although the new policy theoretically was designed, in Martin's words, to "give Cubans their heads," it did not apply to those exile groups based in South Florida who were waging their own freelance war against Castro. And it especially did not apply in the still sensitive post–missile crisis period. Defense Secretary Robert McNamara raised the problem of the militant Alpha 66 group in an October 30, 1962, Ex Comm meeting, just as the agreement with Moscow was culminating. According to notes of the meeting, President Kennedy "stated that insofar as we had any control over the actions of Alpha 66, we should try to keep them from doing something that might upset the deal with the Russians."[10]

As Sam Halpern described it, "there were all these Cuban exile groups who were doing things all over, and we couldn't work with all these groups. We didn't try to. One of the first things Des had to do under Bobby's direction in January of 1963 was go down to Miami and, with the help of all the other government agencies in town . . . the Coast Guard, Immigration, Customs, the local police, FBI, everybody . . . the whole idea was to really put the clamps on all of these various Cuban exile groups who were doing things on their own because they were interfering with some of our activities. And you can't have boats at sea running across each other, going after the same targets. We didn't know what the hell they were doing. They didn't know what we were doing. So the whole idea was to shut them down. And hold them. Don't let them out. They were screaming bloody murder and they blamed CIA for it. But we were not the guys. . . . We were not involved. . . . We were involved only as far as the U.S. government, but it was Bobby Kennedy who wanted to clamp everything down. If there was going to be any activity against Cuba, he wanted to be the guy running it. He didn't want all these extra hangers on, not knowing what the hell they were up to."[11]

Despite the crackdown, the freelance exile raids remained an ongoing concern into the spring. The problem came to a head the night of March 17–18, 1963, when Alpha 66, along with the Second National Front of the Escambray, mounted attacks on a Soviet ship and Soviet installations in Cuba, drawing protests from both Moscow and Havana. This time the State and Justice departments went public in a joint March 30 statement announcing the crackdown, declaring that "law enforcement agencies are taking vigorous measures to assure that the pertinent laws of the United States are observed."[12]

The relationship was always a fitful one between the militant groups and the U.S. government, as described by Enrique Baloyra, a onetime member of the exile Student Directorate: "There is," he said, "a certain psychology involved in all this business, a psychology shared by groups like Alpha 66, and, later on, Omega 7. The basic assumption these people make is that you cannot trust the Yankees, so you have to operate in the shadows and totally disconnect yourselves from any American agency. Their philosophy was: 'We were not going to follow what you tell us to do. What is sensible for you is not necessarily sensible for us.'"[13]

If there was mistrust of the U.S. government, and particularly the CIA, on the part of the more militant exile elements, there was considerable disdain and frustration in Washington regarding South Florida's exile community. That disdain and frustration was reflected in various memorandums, including one by Gen. Chester Clifton, President Kennedy's military aide, to Bundy following a December 29, 1962, meeting of the Joint Chiefs in Palm Beach. The meeting was held the same day Kennedy paid tribute to the Bay of Pigs Brigade in Miami's Orange Bowl.

Clifton noted that the question had arisen regarding future dealings by the U.S. government with the 100,000 Cuban refugees already in the South Florida area. "It was suggested," wrote Clifton, "that whatever we do in Washington it is essential to establish a 'focal point' in the Miami area. Right now these various groups sit down there, stew in their own juice, elect committees, become emotionally upset, and then finally call

upon somebody in Washington to let off steam. If we are to get any benefit for future operations with this large group of people, it was suggested
that we have a continuing office down there so that these committees
could be guided and they would have a place to put in their requests and
let off steam before they get to such an emotional pitch."[14] Such attitudes
contributed to the approval a few days later for a State Department coordinator's office in Miami under the bureaucratic reorganization of Cuba
policy.

Although now cast in a revamped framework with new leaders, the first
few months of reorganization were devoted more to defining and refining
the new policy than reactivating covert operational activities, particularly
sabotage. The emphasis remained on intelligence collection and tightening Cuba's international isolation. Additional constraints were imposed
by the ongoing efforts of New York attorney James Donovan—who had
successfully negotiated the release of the Bay of Pigs prisoners—to gain
freedom for twenty-two natural-born American citizens still jailed in
Cuba. There was concern as well about provoking a surface-to-air missile
shoot-down by Cuba of U-2 surveillance flights over the island, which
were made in lieu of on-site inspections for weapons withdrawal.

And there was internal wrangling between the diplomats and the soldiers, with State wanting to exploit "appropriate opportunities" and
Defense favoring a more aggressive approach of applying "increasing
degrees" of pressure, including "open military support upon request of
indigenous forces" inside Cuba. A peripheral and ongoing debate centered on how best to utilize the returned Bay of Pigs invasion brigade,
with Bobby Kennedy pushing for an activist role, including the brigade's
participation in "selection of targets and methods of operation."[15]

"The brigade was the object of massaging all the time," recalled John
Crimmins, who succeeded Cottrell as Cuban affairs coordinator in April
of 1963. "They were always being sort of promised stuff then something
would go wrong. The brigade people would get restive, then have to be
cajoled, and conned again."[16]

In March 1963 President Kennedy formally designated Erneido Oliva,
the second in command at the Bay of Pigs, as the brigade's official representative. His liaison at the Pentagon was a young army officer named
Alexander Haig Jr. Haig had been assigned in February as military assistant to Secretary of the Army Cyrus Vance and worked directly for Joe
Califano, the army's general counsel. "The job included the duty of acting
in *loco parentis* to the rescued Cubans," wrote Haig. Califano "let me

know early on, in our first meeting on the subject, that the President himself and, even more to the point, his brother Robert, were taking a close personal interest in the rescued Cubans. Apparently one Kennedy or the other called Califano nearly every day to inquire about their welfare. It was their wish that every veteran be given a new start in life in the United States." His job, said Haig, "was to make sure they got it."[17]

In the meantime, thrust by the missile crisis into a broader international context, contingency plans for an invasion of Cuba had to be reconsidered. "The time will probably come when we will have to act again on Cuba," President Kennedy told his National Security Council. "Cuba might be our response in some future situation—the same way the Russians have used Berlin. We may decide that Cuba might be a more satisfactory response than a nuclear response."[18]

By early April, documents reflect a renewed interest—with apparent pressure from above—in stepped-up covert activities, particularly sabotage, and in more clearly defining the Cuba policy within the new bureaucratic framework. President Kennedy and his brother convened a White House meeting about Cuba on April 3 with a group from State, CIA, and Defense, including Cyrus Vance and the CIA's Richard Helms, along with McGeorge Bundy. The president pointedly asked FitzGerald if the exile raids accomplished anything. FitzGerald responded that they probably did nothing but "bolster morale." The president said he didn't object to such raids but so far they seemed to amount to nothing more than "froth," adding, "we cannot condone the holding of press conferences by exiles after such raids." Kennedy then asked if sabotage operations were under consideration. Bundy said no because "the Special Group had decided . . . that such activity is not worth the effort expended on it, in relation to the results that could be obtained in the intelligence field." Others at the session thought sabotage might have some impact in terms of economic damage and psychological effect. Bobby Kennedy, reflecting his fixation with paramilitary operations, wanted to know "whether it might be useful to consider commando-type raids by groups of from 100 to 500 men." FitzGerald said that "even if such groups could be landed it would probably be impossible for them to survive for any length of time." Kennedy then urged that the "CIA survey all possibilities for aggressive action in Cuba over the next six months."[19]

On April 11 the Cuba Coordinating Committee dedicated a session to covert operations. FitzGerald presented three sabotage targets for approval during April and May: a railway bridge, some petroleum storage facilities, and a molasses storage vessel. In the discussion approving the targets it was concluded:

   a. This will meet the President's desire for some noise level and for some action in the immediate future.
   b. These are relatively soft targets. They will not hurt the Cubans terribly much. (Unfortunately, this is usually the case with soft targets—the ones that really hurt are hard and require extensive planning.)
   c. These targets will not be attacked before April 22, if it looks like the American prisoners will be released on that date.
   d. The Special Group should be aware of the consequences of these raids. For example, raids from outside may prompt Cuban firings near or at American ships.

Sabotage of Cuban shipping came up again in the discussion, as did intelligence operations and attacks both from inside and outside Cuba. Notes of the session concluded that Desmond FitzGerald "feels that the President wants some action. Dez [sic] is working on a program which will show continuous motion. The soft targets, which are generally unimportant, will be first because they require the least preparation. As time goes on, however, we will be hitting some harder and more important targets."[20]

Covert activity—including the problems posed by the March 30 announcement of the crackdown on exile raids—dominated the discussion during a Special Group meeting that same day, April 11. "With respect to external operations to be mounted by exile groups, it was agreed that this poses a real dilemma," read notes of the meeting. The publicly announced crackdown on the raids had made it "increasingly difficult" to plausibly disavow responsibility for them without appearing to be either ineffective in controlling them or of being suspected of "active involvement in the operations."[21]

In an April 18 memo to the Special Group, the new Coordinator of Cuban Affairs, Sterling Cottrell, offered a "Proposed New Covert Policy and Program Towards Cuba," which called for placement of explosive devices with time delays on Cuban ships; surface attacks by "maritime assets" on Cuban ships in Cuban waters; externally mounted hit-and-run raids against land targets in Cuba; and support for internal resistance elements in carrying out a variety of sabotage and harassment operations. He concluded with the observation that "when the policy and guidelines of the overall sabotage program are established, it will be possible pro-gressively to develop up to a limit additional covert assets and support capabilities. However, materially to increase the pace of operations, a period of four to six months is required."[22]

Two days later, on April 20, President Kennedy told a meeting of the National Security Council that he "wanted to raise the pressure somewhat in Cuba. He felt that we could hardly carry out a mild policy in Cuba at a time the Communists are carrying out an aggressive policy in Laos."[23] By April 23 Bobby Kennedy was proposing three studies on Cuba: "a. A list of measures we would take following contingencies such as the death of Castro or the shooting down of a U-2. b. A program with the objective of overthrowing Castro in eighteen months. c. A program to cause as much trouble as we can for Communist Cuba during the next eighteen months."[24] There is no indication any of the studies were ever prepared.

By late April the proposed new policy/program for Cuba had come up for discussion before the Special Group with no decision taken but "preliminary reactions," which were summarized by Tom Parrott:

a. The proposition for dealing with selected exile groups is a good one, but the method of dealing with them will have to be more carefully defined.

b. There is no objection to limpets, subject to further technical studies.

c. Surface attacks on Cuban ships do not appear particularly attractive, nor do shore-based attacks of a similar nature.

d. Externally mounted hit-and-run attacks against land targets appear worthwhile. The operations in this category which can be run in May, will be discussed with higher authority. Refineries and power plants seem to be particularly good targets. Operations of this kind will be especially valuable if done in conjunction with other resistance activities.

e. Internal resistance should be stimulated, again in conjunction with related operations.[25]

There were other problems. Jose Miro Cardona resigned as president of the exile Cuban Revolutionary Council, blasting U.S. government inac-tion against Cuba. Several other affiliated organizations and personalities also quit the council, initially created as the front for the Bay of Pigs inva-sion. The council, known originally as the Democratic Revolutionary Front, continued in its exile-front role post–Bay of Pigs, receiving a $137,000 U.S. monthly subsidy, with another $103,000 monthly going to seven other exile groups, including some affiliated with the council. The council's money flow stopped with the resignations, effectively ending its usefulness.[26] As Hurwitch put it, "the exile community in Miami became restless; their political leaders could not survive stagnation."[27]

The groping for a coherent Cuba policy continued for several more weeks, with discussions of contingency plans for Castro's death or defection from the Soviet bloc, the response to a Cuban shoot-down of a U-2 reconnaissance plane overflying the island, and the prospects of forging exile unity.

The indecision at the top clearly was taking its toll on the secret war soldiers, as indicated in a CIA paper taking note of "two rather thoroughly worked out sabotage proposals" rejected by the Special Group. "In order to alleviate the problem of agent morale, which cannot be kept constantly at an optimum level in the face of repeated turndowns, the Agency now proposes to follow a new system." It would develop plans for multiple, rather than individual, sabotage targets, and submit them to the Special Group in hopes of getting "approval for one or more of them for planning purposes. With this in hand, they can then proceed with more detailed planning."[28]

Two weeks later a May 28 meeting of the National Security Council's Standing Group again reflected the differing views over Cuba policy. Bundy insisted the United States didn't have the ability to overthrow Castro. McCone, who supported stepped-up covert operations, argued that increasing economic hardship on Cuba would cause the Cuban military to oust the dictator. McNamara wanted to know what specific economic or covert policies would get rid of Castro. Bobby Kennedy argued that the United States must do something against Castro, even if "we do not believe our actions would bring him down."[29]

Finally, on June 8, the CIA presented a *Proposed Covert Policy and Integrated Program of Action toward Cuba* to the Standing Group.[30] President Kennedy approved the program, including accelerated "sabotage and harassment," on June 19. The stated objective was "to encourage dissident elements in the military and other power centers of the regime to bring about the eventual liquidation of the Castro/Communist entourage and the elimination of the Soviet presence from Cuba." Power plants, transportation facilities, fuel production and storage operations, and production processing and manufacturing plants were the priority sabotage targets. "Higher Authority [Kennedy] showed a particular interest in proposed external sabotage operations" and wanted to know how soon they could begin, said FitzGerald of the high-level meeting that approved the plan. Kennedy was told they would begin by the "dark-of-the-moon period" in July.[31]

The major components of the program were:

A. Covert collection of intelligence, both for U.S. strategic require-ments as well as for operational requirements . . .

B. Propaganda actions to stimulate low-risk simple sabotage and other forms of active and passive resistance . . .

C. Exploitation and stimulation of disaffection in the Cuban military and other power centers . . .

D. Economic denial actions . . .

E. General sabotage and harassment.

F. Support of autonomous anti-Castro Cuban groups to supplement and assist in the execution of the above courses of action . . .

Cited as "sabotage considered appropriate" under the category of "general sabotage and harassment" were:

(1) Simple low-risk sabotage on a large scale stimulated by propaganda media (approved and being implemented).

(2) Sabotage of Cuban ships outside Cuban waters (approved and being implemented).

(3) Externally mounted hit-and-run attacks against appropriately selected targets.

(4) Support of internal resistance elements, providing material and per-sonnel to permit them to undertake a variety of sabotage and harassment operations.

"During the first six months of 1963, little, if any, sabotage activity against Cuba was undertaken," noted the Church Committee, but after President Kennedy's approval of the new covert program, "specific intel-ligence and sabotage operations were submitted to the Special Group for authorization. On October 24, 1963, thirteen major sabotage operations, including the sabotage of an electric power plant, an oil refinery, and a sugar mill were approved for the period from November 1963 through January 1964."[32]

Stepped-up sabotage and harassment activity meant renewed pressure on JMWAVE, where Shackley already was having difficulties with the sta-tion's paramilitary operations. "There were always problems," he said, adding "you need to divide it into several pieces in talking about paramilitary operations." They included the dropping of supply caches for people inside, infiltrating teams for intelligence purposes and, finally, sabotage. It was the latter—known as "boom and bang"—that was most frustrating. "On the one side," said Shackley, "were the people in Washington, Bobby Kennedy, and so forth, who wanted to go after the big targets, strike major economic blows. People were looking at Matahambre [the copper mine in western Cuba] and Nicaro [nickel facility in eastern Cuba]. But some big targets did not lend themselves to boom and bang. They were inland. Target selection for the big targets was a real problem."[33]

The alternative, said Shackley, was "to go after low economic targets, but do more of them . . . the pinprick approach. If you do enough, it will have the same effect. They [Cubans] will have to deploy resources and it will cost them as much as big targets. Bridges close to the coast, storage areas, fires in sugarcane fields; that was the other part of the equation. But we also seemed to have a lot of difficulty making pinprick operations go with a lot of regularity. There were enough problems we had to ask ourselves, 'is there something wrong with our operation . . . our formula?'"

Among the problems, and a perennial complaint heard among various officials involved in covert activities, was the propensity of Cubans to talk too much, comprising operations. As an example, Shackley said, if you "put some guys into Oriente Province, they would drop out of sight in Miami. Then word would go out, 'oh, that group is on a mission.' The guys disappear then everybody starts clacking their mouths. So we took a look at the decision-making process."

Around this time word came down from Washington for more sabotage. Shackley huddled with Dave Morales, the station's paramilitary chief. "We spent a whole day talking about what can we do about giving away information. We had a guy on our staff who had been talking about using the UDTs [underwater demolition teams] more exclusively. It had value and we would have gone for it before but it had very high risk," said Shackley. "We took the guy with our assets and put them in the boonies; put the guy to work training them. We put him together with fifteen or sixteen of these guys, outstanding, very well educated, who handled equipment well. He trained them all over South Florida."

The group that emerged, said Shackley, was "totally separate from everything else we had working." It was a "tightly compartmentalized" unit, said Shackley, with himself, Morales, and the UDT specialist the only Americans at JMWAVE even aware of it. The result was a series of hit-and-run raids on Cuba using small, fast boats and, apparently, even small aircraft. Once trained and ready for action, said Shackley, "we had to find a vehicle for attribution" when they staged an attack. The elite group's public face became Commandos Mambises, a shadowy organization which news accounts reported as based in Central America. The name came from Cuban rebels who fought against Spain in the late nineteenth century. Rafael Martinez Pupo, a wealthy Cuban-exile businessman living in Guatemala—who Shackley described as a Morales friend and onetime Central American distributor for Uncle Ben's rice—emerged as the group's spokesman and public financier.[34] Martinez Pupo identified the group's action leader as a mysterious Cuban known only as "Ignacio."

Although Shackley did not identify the UDT specialist, it may have been Gordon Campbell, the deputy station chief. He was also the head of maritime operations and worked under the cover of Marine Engineering of Homestead, near the JMWAVE station.[35] Campbell is identified as Keith Randall in the "tell all" book by Bradley Ayers. Many Cuban exiles insist that Grayston Lynch, the paramilitary CIA contract employee who went on the beach with the Bay of Pigs invasion force, served as the case officer for Commandos Mambises. But Shackley was adamant in two separate interviews that Lynch had "nothing to do" with the operation. It appears the confusion may have resulted from a successor group to the original Mambises that was devoted to intelligence collection.

Commandos Mambises first surfaced publicly during the last half of August 1963, a bit behind FitzGerald's July "dark-of-the-moon" timetable. One sea and two air attacks were attributed to the group the last two weeks of August. They included the offshore shelling of a metal processing plant on the north coast of Pinar del Rio Province by two fast boats and a rocket raid from the air on an oil installation at Casilda in Las Villas Province. The Commandos Mambises apparently were not responsible for the third raid attributed to them: the aerial strafing and bombing of a sugar mill in Camaguey Province. A *Miami Herald* account of the raid on the metal processing plant observed that "because the raid appeared unusually well-equipped and planned, as compared with similar strikes this year, Cuba blamed the U.S. and 'puppet Central American governments.'"

The story added that the boats "escaped under cover of heavy machinegun fire from a larger mother ship which launched them" and "the three strikes—each on a strategic target, each in a different province, and each well-directed—indicated a stepped-up campaign of such mosquito strikes.

"Refugee sources in Miami said they did not know Martinez Pupo and had not heard of the Mambises. They commented only that the raiders seemed to have unusually good equipment and that it was the first time a raid had been carried out so successfully which had not been followed by a full-scale press conference."[36]

In Guatemala Martinez Pupo was doing his job. He walked into news agency offices in Guatemala City with a communiqué—presumably written by JMWAVE in Miami—announcing the first attack and declaring the Mambises operated from a secret base in the Caribbean with cells established in Cuba. Martinez Pupo's communiqués were subsequently relayed to media in Miami through Salvador Lew, a Cuban exile newscaster who worked as a paralegal for David Walters, a prominent local attorney active in the Democratic Party. Lew later escorted Fidel's sister, Juanita Castro, on a hemisphere tour secretly arranged by JMWAVE after her June 1964 defection.[37] He became a prominent commentator on Cuban radio in Miami and, eventually, was appointed by President George W. Bush in 2001 as director of Radio-TV Marti, the U.S. government–financed anti-Castro propaganda station.

The CIA's Office of National Estimates under Sherman Kent prepared a memorandum for McCone assessing Castro's reaction to the stepped-up sabotage activity. The memo concluded: "Castro would take a very serious view of continuing acts of sabotage. His reaction would almost certainly include a general increase of internal security controls and defensive capabilities, political moves against the US, and requests to the Soviets for assistance in defense. In addition, there might be direct acts of retaliation against Cuban exile bases. The chances of Cuban-inspired sabotage against US installations would probably increase."[38]

But Washington was pleased with the new operation. McGeorge Bundy told the Special Group members in a September 23 memo: "As you know, in August the U.S. Government directed two 'exile' raids against targets in Cuba. From the evidence, now available, it appears that our security, with respect to the U.S. participation in these operations, was excellent. While there will always be public speculation as to the extent of U.S. involvement in raids of this type, I think we would all agree readily that it is important that there be only speculation, and no direct knowledge. . . . I think there are two important, if obvious, security lessons we have learned from the August raids—one, that it is in the nature of the problem that many people probably have to know something about such raids; and two, that these people apparently can maintain adequate security."[39]

News accounts indicate the group carried out three more successful raids before the end of 1963, including an October 1 attack on a lumber mill in Oriente Province; the destruction—by infiltrators into the island a month previously—of a floating barge and crane at Isabela de Sagua in Las Villas Province; and the December 23 sinking of a Russian-made Cuban patrol boat docked at the Isle of Pines. But an October 21 mission to Cabo Corrientes, off Pinar del Rio's southwest coast, to rendezvous with two commandos infiltrated a week earlier as part of a caching and infiltration mission, was far from successful, resulting in what became a potential international incident. The operation was a trap by Castro forces who opened fire on the raiders. Two were killed, one wounded, and four captured. As the *Rex*, the mission's mother ship, fled the area, Cuban planes mistakenly strafed the nearby *J. Louis*, a Liberian-registered, U.S.-owned bauxite-laden freighter en route from Jamaica to Texas.

Castro followed up a few days later with a news conference identifying the *Rex* as a CIA vessel and disclosing that it was then docked at the South Florida port of West Palm Beach. The news sent reporters scurrying up and down Florida's east coast, producing a flurry of speculative stories about the *Rex* (which also operated as the *Explorer II*), the *Leda*, and the *Vilaro*, all so-called mystery ships sailing from Florida ports. Various port officials acknowledged that the ships came and went without the usual customs and other bureaucratic restraints and said they had been asked not to disclose information about the vessels. Shackley, in an early December cable to Washington, said the *Rex* and the *Leda* "would undergo at earliest opportunity [a] paper sale from current corporations to cut-out corporations who would re-register vessels under different flag, change names, change home port, change port of call, repaint, and make whatever modifications possible in superstructure silhouette."[40]

The Mambises were subsequently heard from December 23, with the Isle of Pines attack. A Cuban government communiqué charged that the action "constitutes the first act of aggression by the United States since President Lyndon Johnson took office." The Isle of Pines attack had been on a list of eleven "Proposed infiltration/exfiltration operations into Cuba during November 1963," submitted by the Cuban affairs coordinator to the Special Group on November 8. Identified as Operation 3117, it was described as a "UDT operation designed to sink or damage a Kronstadt or other Cuban patrol craft while in anchorage in Ensenada de la Siguanes, Isle of Pines. The attack will be made by swimmer teams using limpets."[41]

The next raid attributed to the Mambises didn't come until September 1964, when the group claimed to have successfully sabotaged a seventy-foot Russian-built Cuban ship used for diving operations off the Isle of Pines. The communiqué again came from Martinez Pupo, through Lew in Miami, and declared "as Cuban patriots who dislike the gifts of the Soviets, the Commandos Mambises sabotaged the ship with the purpose of reminding Fidel Castro that the war of liberation is on and that his days as oppressor of the Cuban masses are numbered." Given the fact that the Mambises operated out of Florida by JMWAVE and U.S.-directed raids on Cuba had been curtailed, it seems certain that this operation was unauthorized or done by freelance exile raiders under the Mambises banner.

Apart from the Mambises, which provided Washington with its biggest "boom and bang," Shackley said JMWAVE attempted "in theory" to carry out about fifteen operations a month during 1962 and 1963. With each operation came interminable reports to Washington. "We had to send a report every month; account for everything in excruciating detail when they [the teams] came back," said Shackley. That included intelligence collection operations, sabotage, arms caches, and hit-and-run raids. The station also supported "team leaders and unit commanders of organized guerrilla teams in the rural areas of Pinar del Rio," composed mostly of former Batista army soldiers. "We got a guy out of the refugee flow who had leadership potential," said Shackley. "We trained him and put him back in."[42]

By the time of President Kennedy's November 22 assassination, JMWAVE station had planned eighty-eight missions to Cuba during the year, fifteen of which were canceled. Of the remaining seventy-three missions, only four directly involved sabotage. Ten others involved direct encounters with Cuban security forces.[43]

CHAPTER 10

ACCOMMODATION OR ASSASSINATION

O n November 22, 1963, one of history's ultimate triangulations occurred, stretching from Dallas, through Cuba, to Paris. In Dallas Lee Harvey Oswald fired the shot that fatally wounded President Kennedy. Simultaneously, in Cuba French journalist Jean Daniel lunched with Fidel Castro, a day after an all-night interview during which Daniel had delivered a conciliatory message from Kennedy. And in Paris, Nestor Sanchez, a CIA case officer, offered a poison pen device for use in a plot against Castro to Rolando Cubela, a disaffected Cuban military officer.

Kennedy's death that day, and the combination of circumstances surrounding it, created a cottage industry of conflicting conspiracy theories, which still thrives today despite—and in part because of—the Warren Commission's finding that Oswald acted alone. But there are still those who remain convinced that Kennedy was killed by Cuban agents in retaliation for ongoing U.S. efforts to overthrow or assassinate Castro. Others are just as convinced the killing was a plot by disgruntled Mafia, anti-Castro Cuban exiles, and/or renegade CIA agents angered by Kennedy's handling of the Cuba issue. These are theories fed—depending on the point of view—by the documented evidence of, on one hand, ongoing CIA and Mafia attempts to kill Castro and, on the other, Kennedy's failure to remove him with the Bay of Pigs invasion or during the missile crisis coupled with secret tentative steps toward rapprochement that he made before his assassination.

Both "tracks"—covert action and accommodation—continued after Kennedy's death, but slowly withered away under President Johnson's increasing preoccupation with Vietnam, his distaste for the Kennedy brothers' obsession with Castro and Cuba, and his particular antipathy toward Bobby Kennedy.

The fitful steps toward rapprochement continued over a period of about two years, beginning in early 1963 and effectively ending in late 1964, although declassified documents indicate Castro wanted to talk again as late as April 1965. One of the most comprehensive accounts of the failed effort at détente appeared in the October 1999 edition of *Cigar Aficionado*.[1] Written by Peter Kornbluh, a senior analyst at the nonprofit National Security Archive in Washington, the article drew from declassified documents obtained under the Freedom of Information Act. The 1963–64 time frame of the rapprochement effort does not include the ballyhooed secret meeting between Kennedy aide Richard Goodwin and Che Guevara during an August 1961 hemisphere meeting in Punta del Este, Uruguay. Castro told a Havana audience, which included Goodwin, during an October 2002 international conference on the missile crisis that he had not even been aware of the Goodwin-Guevara meeting until after the fact.[2] Goodwin, it should be noted, was one of the principal architects of Operation Mongoose, planning for which was already under way at the time of his meeting with Guevara.

The CIA's involvement in Castro assassination plots extended over a lengthier period, from August 1960 to June 1965. The 1976 Church Committee report revealed "concrete evidence of at least eight plots involving the CIA to assassinate Fidel Castro" during the 1960–65 period, but it went on to say[3] it found no conclusive evidence that Eisenhower, Kennedy, or Johnson, the three presidents in office during that period, had knowledge of the assassination plotting. Whether they did or not remains a point of considerable speculation. Many agency people were convinced that, at the least, Bobby Kennedy knew of the plots, and most probably President Kennedy did as well. Kennedy loyalists, including Arthur Schlesinger, were just as adamant that neither of the Kennedys was aware of the assassination schemes. Some questions remain about Eisenhower's possible knowledge of plots on his watch, but it seems clear that Johnson did not know.

Accommodation

New York attorney James Donovan had just returned from another trip to Havana, where he had met with Castro again on January 25, 1963, this time in an effort to negotiate the release of twenty-two U.S. citizens still imprisoned in Cuba. A month earlier, Donovan, fronting as the lawyer for a private citizens' committee—but in reality a behind-the-scenes U.S.-government negotiator directed by Bobby Kennedy—had successfully gained freedom for the 1,113 Bay of Pigs invasion brigade members still jailed in Cuba in exchange for a $53 million ransom in food and medicines. And it was more than three months after the missile crisis agreement that enraged Castro because of the Soviets' unilateral decision to withdraw the missiles.

On January 26, 1963, Bob Hurwitch, Donovan's State Department contact, recorded in a memorandum for the files what he described as Donovan's "most cordial and intimate meeting to date" with Castro. Comandante Rene Vallejo, Castro's personal physician and confidante who had trained at Massachusetts General Hospital in Boston, served as interpreter. At one point, Hurwitch noted, "during an impromptu visit to a medical school, Castro led 300 medical students in chanting, 'Viva Donovan.'"

According to the Hurwitch memo, "Donovan told Castro his difficulties lay in his dependence on the Soviets. Castro only grunted in reply." But the final two items of the nine-point memo must have been what really caught Washington's attention. They read:

> 8. At the airport just before Donovan's departure, Vallejo broached the subject of re-establishing diplomatic relations with the U.S.
> 9. Castro warmly re-issued the invitation that Donovan return to Cuba with his wife for a week or so (possibly the first week in March). Castro indicated he wanted to talk at length with Donovan about the future of Cuba and international relations in general.[4]

Two days later, Sterling Cottrell sent a copy of the Hurwitch memo to Secretary of State Dean Rusk, along with a covering memo telling Rusk that CIA Director John McCone had similar information. When the president was given the information, he responded that it "looked interesting."[5] As Donovan prepared to return to Havana in early March, Gordon Chase, an aide to Bundy, the president's assistant for national security, wrote in a memo to his boss that Hurwitch had suggested Donovan tell Castro: "As far as I understand U. S. policy, only two things are non-negotiable, (1) Cuba's ties with the Sino-Soviet Bloc and (2) Cuba's interference with the hemisphere." Bundy responded to Chase three days later, "The President does not agree that we should make the breaking of Sino/Soviet ties a non-negotiable point. We don't want to present Castro with a condition that he obviously cannot fulfill. We should start thinking along more flexible lines. The above must be kept close to the vest. The President, himself, is very interested in this one."[6]

Donovan was back in Havana in early April. The CIA debriefed him after his return to Washington. McCone, in an April 10 memo to President Kennedy, reported: "The main thrust of Donovan's discussion [with Castro] . . . was political and can best be evaluated by Doctor Vallejo, a close personal advisor of Castro who was present at the meetings. Vallejo said Castro knew that relations with the United States are necessary and Castro wanted these developed. However, there are certain Cuban Government officials, communists, who are strongly opposed, even more than certain people in the United States. These officials are under close surveillance. They have no great following in Cuba; but if they rebelled at this time, Cuba would be in chaos. He believed that Donovan and Castro could work out a plan for a reasonable relationship between the two countries." McCone concluded by noting "Donovan has the confidence of Castro, who believes Donovan is sincere with no official ties to the United States Government."[7] President Kennedy met privately with McCone the same day, expressing great interest in McCone's memo and "raised questions about Castro's future within Cuba, with or without the Soviet presence. McCone said the matter was under study and he proposed to send Donovan back on April 22 to secure freedom of the remaining prisoners and also keep the channel of communication open."[8]

McCone returned to the subject in another memorandum five days later, suggesting Castro had a dilemma with how to proceed in reaching an accommodation with the United States. "Castro's talks with Donovan have been mild in nature, conciliatory and reasonably frank," wrote McCone. "Of greater significance is Dr. Vallejo's private statements to Donovan that Castro realizes he must find a rapprochement with the United States if he is to succeed in building a viable Cuba. Apparently Castro does not know how to go about this, therefore the subject has not been discussed with Donovan."[9]

Castro soon found a way in Lisa Howard, an assertive and tenacious ABC News reporter who scored a major coup by obtaining an interview with the Cuban leader. The April 22 interview didn't air until May 10, but Richard Helms, then head of the CIA's clandestine services, recorded her observations from CIA debriefings in a three-page memorandum, dated May 1, to McCone on the subject: "Interview of U.S. Newswoman with Fidel Castro Indicating Possible Interest in Rapprochement with the United States."[10]

"It appears," wrote Helms, "that Fidel Castro is looking for a way to reach rapprochement with the United States Government, probably because he is aware that Cuba is in a state of economic chaos. Castro indicated that if a rapprochement was wanted President John F. Kennedy would have to make the first move." Helms offered an early indication of what a mixed blessing the Howard connection became for Kennedy administration officials dealing with the issue. His memo concluded: "Liza [sic] Howard definitely wants to impress the U.S. Government with two facts: Castro is ready to discuss rapprochement and she herself is ready to discuss it with him if asked to do so by the U.S. Government."

The next day Marshall Carter, deputy CIA director, sent a memo to Bundy on behalf of McCone, who was out of town, cautioning "about the importance of secrecy in this matter," adding that McCone "feels that gossip and inevitable leaks with consequent publicity would be most damaging. He suggests that no active steps be taken on the rapprochement matter at this time . . . and that in these circumstances emphasis should be placed in any discussions on the fact that the rapprochement track is being explored as a remote possibility and one of several alternatives involving various levels of dynamic and positive action."[11]

A month later, on June 5, Helms followed up with another memo about numerous signals indicating Castro's desire for rapprochement. The following day the Special Group discussed "various possibilities of establishing channels of communication to Castro." Members agreed it was a "useful endeavor," but took no action.[12]

Little apparently happened until September 1963. William Attwood, a onetime journalist-turned-diplomat then working as an adviser with the UN delegation, volunteered his services—aided and abetted by Lisa Howard, an old journalistic acquaintance—in advancing the cause of rapprochement. Attwood's offer led to the most intensive period of the rapprochement effort, marked by more enthusiasm on the part of Howard and Attwood than the administration. At the suggestion of Averill Harriman,[13] undersecretary of state for political affairs, Attwood wrote a memo proposing "a discreet inquiry into neutralizing Cuba on our terms. It is based on the assumption that, short of change of regime, our principal political objectives in Cuba are: a. The evacuation of all Soviet bloc military personnel, b. An end to subversive activities by Cuba in Latin America, c. Adoption by Cuba of a policy of non-alignment."

The best time to begin that "discreet inquiry," suggested Attwood, was the upcoming session of the UN General Assembly and he was the one to do it. "As a former journalist who spent considerable time with Castro in 1959, I could arrange a casual meeting with the Cuban Delegate, Dr. [Carlos] Lechuga. This could be done socially through mutual acquaintances [Lisa Howard]," Attwood wrote. "I would refer to my last talk with Castro, at which he stressed the desire to be friends with the U.S., and suggest that, as a journalist, I would be curious to know how he felt today. If Castro is ready to talk, this should provide sufficient reasons for Lechuga to come back to me with an invitation." Attwood then cited three reasons why he "should undertake this mission."[14]

The memo wound up first with Stevenson, then with Harriman. Stevenson said he liked the idea and offered to take it up with the president, adding, "Unfortunately, the CIA is still in charge of Cuba." Harriman said he was "adventurous enough" to be interested and urged Attwood to see Bobby Kennedy. Harriman's suggestion resulted in a September 24 meeting with Bobby Kennedy. In the meantime, Attwood had spoken with President Kennedy and "got his agreement to go ahead with the initiative." But "for some reason Stevenson was not keen on my seeing Robert Kennedy, but I trusted Harriman's instincts. Bob had been deeply involved in our Cuban relations and would expect to be consulted about this gambit; also, he had his brother's ear as did no one else."

By the time of his September 24 meeting with Bobby Kennedy, Attwood had already spoken with Lechuga informally at Lisa Howard's cocktail party. Lechuga suggested it might be useful for Attwood to go to Havana, but Bobby Kennedy thought a visit to Havana "was too risky—it was bound to leak—and if nothing came of it the Republicans would call it appeasement and demand a congressional investigation. But he thought the matter was worth pursuing at the U.N. and perhaps even with Castro some place outside Cuba."

The maneuvering continued with contacts between the eager Howard and Attwood on the one side and Lechuga and Rene Vallejo on the other. Bundy told Attwood that Gordon Chase, one of Bundy's deputies, would be his contact at the White House. Vallejo contacted Howard, telling her that Castro "would like a U.S. official to come and see him alone" and offered to send a private plane to Mexico to fly the official to a private airport near Varadero.[15] On November 5 the subject came before the Special Group, which "thought it inadvisable to allow Mr. Attwood, while on the UN staff, to get in touch with Castro." Helms suggested "it might be possible to 'war game' this problem and look at it from all possible angles before making any contacts." A week later Bundy told Attwood to inform Vallejo "it did not seem practicable to us at this stage to send an American official to Cuba and that we would prefer to begin with a visit by Vallejo to the U.S. where Attwood would be glad to see him and listen to any messages he might bring from Castro." Bundy also noted that without any indication of a willingness by Cuba to make some policy changes "it is hard for us to see what could be accomplished by a visit to Cuba."[16] Attwood finally spoke directly with Vallejo by telephone on November 18 from Howard's apartment. Vallejo said he was not able to come to New York but instructions would be sent to Lechuga to discuss "an agenda" for a later meeting with Castro.[17] Chase reported the conversation in a memo to Bundy the following day and concluded by noting "the ball is now in Castro's court."[18] On November 18, the day Attwood spoke with Vallejo, Kennedy gave a speech in Miami on Cuba's future. In the speech Kennedy said Cuba had become "a weapon in an effort dictated by external powers to subvert the other American republics. This and this alone divided us. As long as this is true, nothing is possible. Without it, everything is possible." Arthur Schlesinger Jr., who helped draft the speech, said later that Kennedy's language was intended to convey to Castro the real potential for normalization between the United States and Cuba.[19]

If that was the intended message, Rolando Cubela, the disaffected Cuban military officer code-named AMLASH, received a different message. He was meeting in Paris with Nestor Sanchez, his CIA case officer, when Kennedy was killed in Dallas. "At that meeting," said a U.S. Senate Committee report, "the case officer referred to the President's November 18 speech in Miami as an indication that the President supported a coup. That speech described the Castro government as a 'small band of conspirators' which formed a 'barrier' which 'once removed' would ensure United States support for progressive goals in Cuba. The case officer told AMLASH that FitzGerald had helped write the speech."[20]

With Kennedy's assassination, said Attwood, "the Cuban exercise was quietly laid to rest by our side."[21] It may have been put on hold, but it was not yet laid to rest. On November 25 Chase offered his thoughts in a memo to Bundy, saying Attwood's "Cuban exercise is still in train" but "events of November 22 would appear to make accommodation with Castro an even more doubtful issue than it was. While I think that President Kennedy could have accommodated with Castro and gotten away with it with a minimum of domestic heat, I'm not so sure about President

Johnson" who "would probably run a greater risk of being accused, by the American people, of 'going soft.' In addition, the fact that Lee Oswald has been heralded as a pro-Castro type may make rapprochement with Cuba more difficult—although it is hard to say how much more difficult."[22]

Chase offered three alternative courses for Attwood, and recommended that if Lechuga called Attwood to arrange a meeting, "Attwood should schedule such a meeting for a few days later and call us immediately. However, if Lechuga does not call him, Attwood should take no initiative until he hears from us."

If this course was decided on, said Chase, "the sooner the better. In view of his [Attwood] and [Adlai] Stevenson's activist tendencies in this matter, they will approach him and assure him that we feel the same way and that we are still prepared to hear what Castro has on his mind. . . . While November 22 events probably make accommodation an even tougher issue for President Johnson than it was for President Kennedy, a preliminary Attwood-Lechuga talk still seems worthwhile from our point of view—if the Cubans initiate it."

In a second memo to Bundy the same day, Chase raised the question of Lisa Howard's role and suggested it was a good time to ease her out of the picture. "Her inclusion at every step so far, frankly, makes me nervous."[23]

Meanwhile, Lechuga told Lisa Howard he had received authorization from Castro to meet with Attwood and "wondered whether things were still the same." Chase reported in a December 2 memo to Bundy: "The ball is in our court; Bill [Attwood] owes Lechuga a call. What to do?"[24]

Chase followed up the next day with another memo to Bundy recommending Attwood meet with Lechuga and hear what he had to say. He cautioned "complete discretion," adding "in this regard, we are glad that Lisa Howard is now out of the picture. She should be given no intimation that further U.S. contact is taking place." Chase also suggested delivering a tough message to Cuba along the lines of "if you don't feel you can meet our concerns, then just forget the whole thing; we are quite content to continue on our present basis." He wondered if Attwood was "the man to convey the message"; then he concluded the UN adviser probably was good enough but would benefit from "a good, stiff brainwashing and education in Cuban affairs before he meets with Lechuga."[25]

Chase's recommendation to meet with Lechuga was overruled. On December 4, according to Attwood, "Lechuga approached me in the Delegates' Lounge to say he had a letter from Fidel himself, instructing him to talk with me about a specific agenda. I called Chase, who replied all policies were now under review and be patient. . . . On the twelfth, I told Lechuga to be patient and that so far as I knew, we weren't closing the door. Neither of us knew then that it would be six years before we would meet again—in Havana."

President Johnson, while visiting the U.S. delegation to the UN on December 17, told Attwood at lunch that "he had read my chronological account of our Cuba initiative 'with interest.' And that was it. I was named ambassador to Kenya in January, and during my Washington briefings I saw Chase, who told me there was apparently no desire among the Johnson people to do anything about Cuba in an election year."

Attwood wrote in his 1987 book that it "seems pointless to raise" what part "our Cuban gambit" played in Kennedy's assassination; then he promptly raised it, hinting at a possible role by the CIA, frustrated Cuban exiles, and other adventurers "like Frank Fiorini, alias Frank Sturgis."[26]

Even with Attwood gone, the irrepressible Lisa Howard wouldn't let the issue of accommodation disappear. Returning from another reporting assignment in Cuba, she carried a "verbal message" from Castro to President Johnson, which began, "Please tell President Johnson that I earnestly desire his election to the Presidency in November" and "if there is anything I can do (aside from retiring from politics), I shall be happy to cooperate." The message continued, "if the President feels it necessary during the campaign to make bellicose statements about Cuba or even to take some hostile action—if he will inform me, unofficially, that a specific action is required because of domestic political considerations, I should understand and not take any serious retaliatory action." Castro said he hoped to resume the dialogue begun by Attwood. He realized that "political considerations may delay this approach until after the November elections." But, he said he did not see any areas of contention that "cannot be discussed and settled within a climate of mutual understanding. . . . This hostility between Cuba and the United States is both unnatural and unnecessary—and it can be eliminated."[27]

Howard was insistent upon delivering the message personally to President Johnson. Bundy and Chase were just as adamant that she not deliver it, and to make sure, Bundy circulated a blunt internal memo to seven White House aides he thought Howard might try to approach. It read:

A newspaperwoman named Lisa Howard is back from a long trip to Cuba and says she has a personal message from Castro for the President. She is an extraordinarily determined and self-important creature and will undoubtedly knock at every door we have at least five times. It is quite impossible that she can see Castro and the President without writing about her peacemaking efforts at some stage, and I see nothing whatever to be gained by letting her play this game with us.

My impression is that it took her six weeks to get past Castro's defenses, and the question is whether we can do better.

I should add that Miss Howard has been offered every opportunity to report her findings and information to an appropriate officer of the Government. Her determination to give her message only to the President is all that prevents her from completing her letter-carrier's task.[28]

Howard never managed to get through the White House defenses, although she compensated by later enlisting the support of Adlai Stevenson, much to the consternation of Bundy and Chase.

Chase, in a memo to Bundy, noted "the latest developments add at least two new factors to the situation which make Lisa Howard's participation scarier than it was before. One, for the first time during the Johnson Administration, Lisa has been used to carry a message from the U.S. to Cuba. Before this, the Johnson Administration had relatively little to fear from Lisa since, essentially, we were just listening to her reports on and from Castro. Two, Lisa's contact on the U.S. side is far sexier now [Stevenson], than at any time in the past [Attwood and Chase]." Chase then made it clear he favored removing Howard "from direct participation in the business of passing messages."[29]

Other efforts throughout 1964 to restart the rapprochement dialogue—mostly initiated by Cuba and all unsuccessful—included one with the Spanish government acting as intermediary; a Castro interview with *New York Times* correspondent Richard Eder, which the State Department's Bureau of Intelligence and Research called Cuba's "strongest bid to date for a U.S.-Cuban rapprochement"; and a plan to approach Che Guevara, through a British intermediary, when Guevara visited the UN in December of that year.[30]

What may have been a final Cuban effort came in April 1965, when Celia Sanchez, Castro's longtime companion, called Donovan and "told him that Castro would like to talk to him. Castro asked if Donovan would come down to Cuba. There appeared to be some urgency . . . the ball is now with State." State's proposed response—which Bundy okayed—was to have Donovan call Sanchez back and tell her that he was busy and needed to have more information before he could make it to Havana. There is no indication the overture progressed further.[31] Castro did manage to get the Johnson administration's attention five months later when Cuba opened the tiny north coast port of Camarioca for a mass exodus of some 5,000 refugees to the United States, a prelude of what was to come with Mariel in 1980. Camarioca led to the December 1965 initiation of the so-called Freedom Flights, an organized flow that brought nearly 300,000 refugees from Cuba to the United States over the next seven years.

Assassination

As tentative steps toward accommodation were under way, so were plots to assassinate Castro, as detailed in two key documents: The Church Committee's *Alleged Assassination Plots Involving Foreign Leaders,* published in 1975 and the CIA Inspector General's 1967 *Report on Plots to Assassinate Fidel Castro,* declassified in 1993.

Although the Church Committee reported it found evidence of "at least eight plots" by the CIA to assassinate Castro, it agreed that some of the plots "did not advance beyond the stage of planning and preparation."[32] It also qualified its findings by acknowledging that "the plots against Fidel Castro personally cannot be understood without considering the fully authorized, comprehensive assaults upon his regime, such as the Bay of Pigs invasion in 1961 and Operation MONGOOSE in 1962."[33]

In fact, two of the three most substantive efforts aimed at Castro's assassination—both involving the Mafia—coincided with the Bay of Pigs planning and Mongoose. Both assassination plots were closely held separate tracks, unknown to most of the participants in the Bay of Pigs and Mongoose. As recorded earlier, Jake Esterline, the CIA's Cuba Project chief, learned only accidentally of the first Mafia assassination plot when he refused to authorize funds without being told what they were financing. The second major attempt was essentially a resurrection—or continuation—of the first Mafia-related effort.

A third serious attempt involving assassination centered on Rolando Cubela, a rebel student leader who had fought against Batista. Cubela had some experience in assassinations, reportedly having been involved in the assassination of Batista's military intelligence chief in 1956.[34] Regarded by many as somewhat unstable, Cubela had an intermittent relationship with the CIA from 1961 through June 1965. The CIA contended that the agency's relationship with Cubela involved a coup attempt that was not designed as an assassination, although they also acknowledged that Castro could have died during the coup. Cubela's two successive case officers testified before the Church Committee that Cubela was never asked to assassinate Castro, but Cubela believed assassination to be the first step in a coup. "Both officers were clearly aware of his desire to take such action," said the Church Committee.[35]

The Senate committee report as it related to plots against Castro relied heavily on the detailed CIA inspector general's investigation ordered eight years earlier by then CIA Director Richard Helms in response to a column by Drew Pearson that appeared in newspapers on March 3, 1967. The column began: "President Johnson is sitting on a political H-bomb—an unconfirmed report that Sen. Robert Kennedy may have approved an assassination plot which then possibly backfired against his late brother."[36]

The apparent source of the story was Edward Morgan, an attorney for John Rosselli, a key mob figure in both Mafia-linked plots to kill Castro. After the column appeared, President Johnson asked the FBI to interview Morgan, who hinted at Castro's involvement in President Kennedy's assassination. Johnson received the FBI report on March 22, the same day he happened to be meeting with Helms. He asked Helms for a detailed account of the CIA's plots to assassinate Castro. Helms ordered Jake Earman, the CIA's inspector general, to do the report. The completed report was delivered to Johnson on May 10, 1967.[37] "We were running a damn Murder Incorporated in the Caribbean," Johnson told an interviewer in 1971.[38]

"It became clear very early in our investigation that the vigor with which schemes were pursued within the Agency to eliminate Castro personally varied with the intensity of the U.S. Government's efforts to overthrow the Castro regime," the IG [inspector general's] report noted. "We can identify five separate phases in Agency assassination planning, although the transitions from one to another are not always sharply defined. Each phase is a reflection of the then prevailing Government attitude toward the Cuban regime."[39]

The five phases cited were:

a. Prior to August 1960: All of the identifiable schemes prior to about August 1960, with one possible exception, were aimed only at discrediting

Castro personally by influencing his behaviour or by altering his appearance.

b. August 1960 to April 1961: The plots that were hatched in late 1960 and early 1961 were aggressively pursued and were viewed by at least some of the participants as being merely one aspect of the over-all active effort to overthrow the regime that culminated with the Bay of Pigs.

c. April 1961 to late 1961: A major scheme that was born in August was called off after the Bay of Pigs and remained dormant for several months, as did most other Agency operational activity related to Cuba.

d. Late 1961 to late 1962: That particular scheme was reactivated in early 1962 and was again pushed vigorously in the era of Project MONGOOSE and in the climate of intense administration pressure on CIA to do something about Castro and his Cuba.

e. Late 1962 until well into 1963: After the Cuban missile crisis of October 1962 and the collapse of Project MONGOOSE, the aggressive scheme that was begun in August 1960 and revived in 1962 was finally terminated in 1963, but both were impracticable and nothing ever came of them.

The report added: "We cannot overemphasize the extent to which responsible Agency officers felt themselves subject to the Kennedy administration's severe pressures to do something about Castro and his regime. The fruitless, and in retrospect, often unrealistic plotting should be viewed in that light."

Interestingly, the Cubela connection was cited as part of the IG's report on assassination plots against Castro, even though agency officials testified before the Church Committee that they did not consider it an assassination plot. Cubela's ongoing ties with the agency—and subsequent involvement with a U.S.-funded exile operation headed by Manuel Artime—are explored further in chapter 13.

The IG report made no mention of what the Church Committee called "the first action against the life of a Cuban leader sponsored by the CIA" in July 1960. A Cuban working with the agency in Havana had told his case officer he expected to be in touch with Raul Castro. The Havana Station cabled headquarters and field stations the night of July 20, inquiring about intelligence needs that might be met during the contact. The headquarters duty officer contacted both Tracy Barnes, [Bissell's deputy] and Col. J. C. King. Based on their instructions, the headquarters duty officer cabled back a response on July 21 saying, "Possible removal top three leaders is receiving serious consideration at HQS," and asked whether the Cuban was sufficiently motivated to risk "arranging an acci-dent" involving Raul Castro. A $10,000 payment was authorized "after successful completion." The cable was signed "by direction of J. C. King," who had previously suggested "elimination" of Castro. Soon after, another cable arrived in the Havana Station, signed by Barnes, telling the case officer to "drop the matter." The Cuban had already gone to contact Raul Castro. He returned soon thereafter, saying he had not had the opportunity to arrange an accident.[40]

Only a month later, in August 1960, Bissell met with Sheffield Edwards, the CIA's security director, setting in train the first Mafia-linked effort to assassinate Castro. Edwards turned to Robert Maheu, an ex-FBI agent who had done work for the CIA in the past, to find a Mafia contact. Maheu, authorized by his "clients" to pay $150,000 for Castro's removal, came up with John Rosselli, who in turn, enlisted Sam Giancana. Both Rosselli and Giancana declined payment. Santos Trafficante, another Mafia figure with ties to Havana, was brought into the plot later. So was Tony Varona, a Cuban exile who, coincidentally, happened to be a mem-ber of the exile front group created for the Bay of Pigs invasion. James O'Connell, head of the CIA security office's support division, became the CIA case officer for the operation. As of late September, only Bissell, Edwards, and O'Connell were aware of the plot to use gangster elements to assassinate Castro.

About this time Edwards, with Bissell present, briefed CIA Director Allen Dulles and his deputy, Gen. Charles Cabell, "on the existence of a plot involving members of the syndicate. The discussion was circumspect; Edwards deliberately avoided the use of any 'bad words.' The descriptive term used was 'an intelligence operation.'" Edwards was to tell the IG investigators, however, that he was sure Dulles and Cabell both under-stood the nature of the operation.

Small poison pills became the eventual assassination weapon of choice. The first batch, prepared by the CIA's Technical Services Division, wouldn't dissolve in water, so a new batch was made. The second batch of pills then went from O'Connell, to Rosselli, to Trafficante, and then, apparently, to Juan Orta, who worked in Castro's office. But Orta got "cold feet," according to the gangsters. In fact, Orta already had fallen from favor and lost his access to Castro. He was to take asylum in the Venezuelan embassy a week before the Bay of Pigs. When Orta failed to make contact with Castro, Trafficante put the plotters in touch with the controversial and ambitious Varona, who claimed to have a contact inside a restaurant frequented by Castro. Money and pills were delivered to Varona, but no one seems to know whether the pills ever got to Cuba. If they did, they never made it to Castro. Edwards, according to the IG's report, "is sure there was a complete stand down after that; the operation was dead and remained so until April 1962. He clearly relates the origins of the operation to the upcoming Bay of Pigs invasion, and its termination to the Bay of Pigs failure." Others involved suggested, however, that it remained an ongoing, but temporarily sidetracked operation.

Whatever the case, the Mafia-linked plot was resurrected, this time with Rosselli and Varona playing the key roles without the participation of Giancana and Trafficante. The CIA's intrepid Bill Harvey was now the man in charge and was to run it as part of a larger CIA "Executive Action" program known as ZR/RIFLE.

"The Inspector General's Report divides the gambling syndicate operation into Phase I, terminating with the Bay of Pigs, and Phase II, continuing with the transfer of the operation to William Harvey in late 1961," according to the Church Committee. "The distinction between a clearly demarcated Phase I and Phase II may be an artificial one, as there is considerable evidence that the operation was continuous, perhaps lying dormant for the period immediately following the Bay of Pigs."[41]

While the Church Committee and IG reports differed in some lesser details—in part because the Church Committee had the IG's report to work with and testimony from a wider range of people—the broader outlines are the same in both accounts.

Bissell asked Harvey in early 1961, well before Harvey became involved with Cuba, to establish a general capability, which became known as Executive Action, within the CIA for "disabling foreign leaders, including assassination as a 'last resort.'" ZR/RIFLE became the cryptonym. "Harvey's notes reflect that Bissell asked him to take over the gambling syndicate operation from Edwards and that they discussed the 'application of ZR/RIFLE program to Cuba' on November 16, 1961." Bissell didn't dispute that in his testimony to the Church Committee but said the operation "was not reactivated, in other words, no instructions went out to Rosselli or to others . . . to renew the attempt, until after I left the Agency in February 1962." Richard Helms succeeded Bissell as head of the agency's clandestine operations.

In early April 1962 Harvey asked Edwards, on "explicit orders" from Helms, to put him in touch with Rosselli. By this time Operation Mongoose was well under way, and Harvey headed Task Force W, the CIA

Jake Esterline, the Central Intelligence Agency's (CIA) project director for what became the Bay of Pigs invasion, takes a break at the agency's old offices in temporary buildings adjacent to the reflecting pool below the Lincoln memorial in Washington. *Jake Esterline*

Esterline (left) became a guerrilla warfare expert with the Office of Strategic Services (OSS) during World War II. He was sent to the China-Burma theater of war to train guerrillas to fight the Japanese. Here Esterline is pictured at a guerrilla camp in Tengchung, China, with an unidentified visiting correspondent. This experience, coupled with later postings in the CIA's Western Hemisphere Division, made him a natural choice to be one of the chief planners for operations against Cuba. *Jake Esterline*

Marine colonel Jack Hawkins, paramilitary chief and amphibious operations expert for the Bay of Pigs invasion, is pictured here circa 1956. Hawkins was captured and imprisoned in the Philippines by the Japanese during the early stages of World War II. He later escaped and worked with Filipino guerrillas in Mindanao before his exfiltration to Australia by submarine. *Jack Hawkins*

Hawkins (left) and Esterline together in Washington in 1996 reviewing declassified documents during their first meeting since the ill-fated Bay of Pigs invasion. *Author's Collection*

Richard Bissell (right) with Sen. Frank Church during the 1975 Church Committee hearings about assassination plots against foreign leaders. Bissell, as the CIA's deputy director for plans, controlled CIA operations against Cuba through the Bay of Pigs disaster. Bissell ignored Hawkins and Esterline's warning that the changes to the invasion plans would likely lead to failure. *Miami Herald*

President Kennedy's aides Theodore Sorensen (left) and Arthur Schlesinger Jr. recall the October 1962 Cuban Missile Crisis at a missile display in Havana. They were in Cuba at a conference marking the fortieth anniversary of the missile crisis. *Author's Collection*

Sam Halpern started with the CIA's Cuban operation in the fall of 1961. He was executive assistant to Bill Harvey, who headed the CIA's Task Force W for Operation Mongoose and, subsequently, to Desmond FitzGerald, who headed the CIA's Special Affairs Staff, responsible for post-Mongoose covert operations against Cuba. The date of the picture unknown. *Sam Halpern*

Building #25 on the University of Miami's secluded, 1,572-acre South Campus, served as the CIA's JMWAVE station from late 1961 until 1968. This photograph was taken in 1964. For a time, this command center for U.S. operations against Cuba was the largest CIA station in the world outside of the Langley, Virginia, headquarters. The station operated under the cover name of Zenith Technical Enterprises, Inc. *Miami Herald*

The late Ted Shackley, pictured here in 2001, ran the CIA's JMWAVE station from early 1962 to 1965. Later he headed the CIA station in Saigon during part of the Vietnam War. *Tom Spencer*

These four small U.S. Navy boats on a barge in Miami's Biscayne Bay were rumored to be headed to JMWAVE for use in the not-so-secret war against Cuba. This photograph was taken in August 1963. *Miami Herald*

A collage of anti-Castro propaganda material published by several CIA-subsidized exile organizations after the Bay of Pigs. *Author's Collection*

Left to right, Erneido Oliva, Jose "Pepe" San Roman, and Manuel "Manolo" Artime, all leaders of the Bay of Pigs invasion brigade, display their joy shortly after returning to Miami in December 1962 after spending twenty months as Cuban prisoners. *Miami Herald*

President Kennedy is presented with Brigade 2506 colors on December 29, 1962, in the Miami Orange Bowl. This was part of the welcome-home ceremony for 1,113 Bay of Pigs prisoners who were ransomed for $54 million in food and medicine. At the ceremony, Kennedy promised to return the flag to the brigade in a "free Havana." The flag is presented to Kennedy by Oliva (right), the brigade's second in command. Artime, the Cuban Revolutionary Council's representative to the brigade, is in the center. *Miami Herald*

Cuban Revolutionary Council member Anthony "Tony" Varona was involved in both CIA-Mafia plots to assassinate Castro. *Miami Herald*

Rolando Cubela, code-named AMLASH, was a fighter in the war against Batista and, after Batista's fall, a member of Fidel Castro's inner coterie. After becoming disillusioned with Castro's revolution, he became a CIA "asset" from 1961 to 1965. Cubela wanted to assassinate Castro, and the CIA supplied him with assassination tools. But the plans never panned out, and he was arrested in Cuba in 1966. This picture is believed to have been taken before 1959 when he was a leader of the Revolutionary Student Directorate fighting Batista. *Miami Herald*

Pictured are seven leaders of Artime's U.S.-supported "autonomous group" that operated against Cuba from bases in Nicaragua and Costa Rica in 1964 and 1965. The paramilitary group's decline began in September 1964 when they mistakenly attacked a Spanish freighter headed for Havana, killing several crew members. Artime is in the center of the picture. His deputy, Rafael Quintero, is second from the left. The others are unknown. *Rafael Quintero*

Quintero, far right, and Artime, second from right, point out targets in Cuba to unidentified members of the group at one of their Central American camps. *Rafael Quintero*

Quintero (right) and Segundo Borges, chief of the infiltration teams for Artime's Central American operation, discuss strategy at one of the group's Costa Rican camps in 1964. *Rafael Quintero*

The shoulder-patch emblem of the CIA-run Cuban-exile group Commandos Mambises. *Sam Halpern*

The CIA recruited Carlos Obregon, currently a Miami businessman and a onetime member of the Revolutionary Student Directorate, in 1961. He became an infiltration team leader, and this photograph was taken circa 1966 in Cuba's Las Villas Province. *Carlos Obregon*

Oliva (right), second in command of the Bay of Pigs invasion brigade, and Rafael del Pino, who was a Castro pilot at the Bay of Pigs fighting against the brigade, embrace in 1989 after del Pino's defection. *Erneido Oliva*

component of Mongoose. Harvey met Rosselli in Miami, telling him to maintain his Cuban contacts but not to deal with Maheu or Giancana. The poison pill scheme was reactivated, with Varona again enlisted, through Rosselli, as the deliveryman. Harvey gave the pills to Rosselli in Miami on April 21, 1962. Rosselli told the Church Committee that he told Harvey that the "Cubans" (Varona) planned to use the pills on Fidel and Raul Castro and Che Guevara, and that Harvey had approved.

Varona wanted arms and equipment as a quid pro quo for doing the job. Harvey enlisted the Miami Station to help, although Shackley said he was not aware he was part of an assassination plot. "Harvey was, in his way, highly professional," said Shackley. "He kept things compartmental-ized and I wasn't part of the operation."[42] Harvey and Shackley rented a U-Haul truck under an assumed name, loaded it with explosives, detona-tors, rifles, handguns, radios, and boat radar valued at some $5,000, and delivered it to a Miami parking lot. The truck keys were given to Rosselli, who watched the delivery with O'Connell, from across the street. The truckload was finally picked up. Nothing happened. In May Rosselli told Harvey the pills had been delivered to Cuba. Nothing happened. In Sep-tember Rosselli told Harvey that Varona was preparing to send in another three-man team to "penetrate Castro's bodyguard" and that the pills, referred to as "the medicine," were still "safe" in Cuba. Still nothing hap-pened. Harvey ended the operation in mid-February 1963.[43]

Even as the second phase got under way in April 1962, the residue of an incident in the first phase came back to haunt the operation and caused Bobby Kennedy to become aware of the assassination plot. In October 1961 Giancana was in Miami and wanted Maheu to arrange for a bug of the Las Vegas hotel room in which his girlfriend, Phyllis McGuire of the singing McGuire Sisters, was staying. Giancana believed she was cheating on him with Dan Rowan of the Rowan and Martin comedy team. A maid walked into the room while the bug was being installed, and the local sheriff's office was called. Maheu fixed the matter with local authorities, but word had already reached the FBI, which decided to seek prosecution under wiretapping statutes. But word eventually reached the attorney general, Bobby Kennedy. Lawrence Houston, the CIA's general counsel, and Sheffield Edwards, the security director, briefed Kennedy on May 7, 1962. Edwards said Kennedy was briefed "all the way." Houston said that after the briefing, Kennedy "thought about the problem quite seriously." The attorney general said that he could not proceed against those involved in the wiretapping case. "He spoke quite firmly, saying in effect, 'I trust that if you ever try to do business with organized crime again—with gangsters—you will let the Attorney General know before you do it." Houston quoted Edwards as replying that this was a reasonable request, but Kennedy was not told the plot had been reactivated.[44] At Kennedy's request Edwards wrote a memorandum for the record of the incident a week later.[45]

Some months after the McGuire bugging incident, the FBI discovered that Giancana's girlfriend, Judith Campbell Exner, had been calling President Kennedy from Giancana's home phone. President Kennedy and Giancana were sharing the same girlfriend in bed, and each knew it. President Kennedy was made aware of the FBI discovery and ended his relationship with Exner. But the incident prompted renewed FBI interest in the McGuire bugging episode. FBI Director J. Edgar Hoover wanted a full explanation from the CIA as to why it resisted prosecution, which led to the Houston and Edwards briefing of Bobby Kennedy.[46] Exner, who died in 1999, gained minor celebrity status with tell-all tales of her eighteen-month affair with President Kennedy, but her credibility suffered from the conflicting accounts she offered. Giancana was murdered in the basement kitchen of his Illinois home on June 19, 1975. Rosselli disappeared from his South Florida home July 17, 1976. Fishermen found his body eleven days later, stuffed in a drum in a Miami area bay.

Two other assassination plots surfaced in early 1963, both of which fell in the "nutty schemes" category. The first involved James Donovan, although he did not know it. The idea was to have Donovan present Castro with a skin-diving suit dusted "with a fungus that would produce a disabling and chronic skin disease" and "a breathing apparatus contaminated with tubercle baccili." Dr. Sidney Gottlieb, a CIA scientific adviser, said that the plan had progressed to the point of actually buying a diving suit and readying it for delivery, but he didn't know what happened to the plan or the suit. Sam Halpern, who also was privy to the plot, first said it was dropped because it was impracticable and later recalled that Donovan had already given Castro a skin-diving suit on his own initiative. There was conflicting testimony as to whether the plan was initiated by Harvey or FitzGerald.[47] Ted Shackley, like many CIA personnel, believed the Kennedys were aware of the various assassination plots. As an indication of their knowledge, Shackley cited conversations he had with Donovan "who had been talking with the Kennedys, and Bobby wanted to know what Castro did, details about skin-diving and other things."

A second plot, even more mind-boggling, which originated with Fitz-Gerald, would have had Castro assassinated by an exploding seashell. "The idea," according to the IG's report, "was to take an unusually spectacular sea shell that would be certain to catch Castro's eye, load it with an explosive triggered to blow when the shell was lifted, and submerge it in an area where Castro often went skin diving." FitzGerald went so far as to purchase two books on Caribbean mollusca. But the idea was given up as impracticable when it was found that "none of the shells that might conceivably be found in the Caribbean area was both spectacular enough to be sure of attracting attention and large enough to hold the needed volume of explosive." In addition, the midget submarine they would have had to use to plant the shell had too short an operating range for the operation.[48]

Sam Halpern was another among the many CIA officers who firmly believed the Kennedys were aware of the Castro assassination plots. Halpern said he never talked to his bosses about it but "I believe my bosses were honest people, like Des FitzGerald. . . . It was from Des that I got very clearly time and time again, that's what these guys wanted," meaning Castro's assassination and the Kennedys. Halpern cited a Monday morning when FitzGerald walked into the office with a coffee table book on Caribbean seashells and asked Halpern to have the technicians blow up a picture of one of the shells. Halpern asked, "Are you kidding or something? What's going on?" FitzGerald responded, "You don't know the pressure I'm under . . . that kind of stuff." FitzGerald, who was socially connected with the Kennedy crowd, "wouldn't do those things on his own. He wasn't a cowboy. He was a damn well-disciplined officer and knew what the hell was going on."[49]

Halpern also recounted for the Church Committee the time in October of 1961, shortly after he became involved in Cuba and Richard Bissell was his boss. "Mr. Bissell said he had recently—and he didn't specify the date or the time—he had recently been chewed out in the Cabinet Room of the White House by both the President and the Attorney General for, as he put it, sitting on his ass and not doing anything about getting rid of Castro and the Castro regime. His orders to both [name blacked out] and to me were to plan for an operation to accomplish that end. . . . There was no limitation of any kind. Nothing was forbidden, and nothing was withheld. And the objective was to remove Castro and his regime."[50]

Halpern said later that "when I asked Dick Bissell about what does 'get rid of,' mean, he said 'you can read the English language as well as I can. Get rid of, means get rid of,' so that's why I went along with the AMLASH operation which was in '63."[51]

Tom Parrott was another who said he did not believe "for one second" the oft-repeated contention by Arthur Schlesinger that the Kennedys did not know of the assassination attempts against Castro.

"I'm convinced that Bobby knew plenty about it and was the engine behind it to a considerable extent. Not necessarily directly, by saying you go out and assassinate Castro but saying, you know, 'Why don't you get off your duff and do something? We don't care what you do.' He knew perfectly well, I'm convinced. Now, I don't suppose you're going to find any piece of paper where he obviously says that. How much the president knew, I just don't really know. But somehow I have the feeling that he knew more than he was admitting or more than his sycophants were admitting."[52]

No conclusive evidence has been found to show that either President Kennedy or his brother, Bobby, the attorney general, had prior knowledge of the assassination plots. The same applies for Presidents Eisenhower and Johnson, whose administrations were also encompassed in the Church Committee report. The committee concluded, however, that it found "the system of executive command and control was so ambiguous that it is difficult to be certain at what levels assassination activity was known and authorized. This situation creates the disturbing prospect that Government officials might have undertaken the assassination plots without it having been uncontrovertibly clear that there was explicit authorization from the Presidents. It is also possible that there might have been a successful 'plausible denial' in which Presidential authorization was issued but is now obscured. Whether or not the respective Presidents knew of or authorized the plots, as chief executive officer of the United States, each must bear the ultimate responsibility for the activities of his subordinates."[53]

CHAPTER 11

"LET CUBANS BE CUBANS"

Among the least known, least understood, most creative, and most controversial of the many covert U.S. activities targeting Cuba involved "giving the Cubans their heads," as Assistant Secretary of State Ed Martin phrased it. Martin's October 1962 proposal built on the two-track policy "to engage Cubans more deeply . . . in efforts of their own liberation" suggested a month earlier by Walt Rostow, chairman of the State Department's Policy Planning Council. Shortly after Martin's proposal, the missile crisis exploded and the idea was put on ice, to be resurrected and ultimately approved in June 1963 as the cornerstone of the new post-Mongoose covert policy targeting Cuba.

As Martin envisioned it, the autonomous program would provide the "selected exile group with funds, arms, sabotage equipment, transport, and communications equipment for infiltration operations in order to build a political base of opposition within. We would provide the best technical advice we could. Our role would essentially be that of advisors and purveyors of material goods—it would be the exile group's show. We would insist that hit and run raids or similar harassing activities that clearly originate from outside Cuba and do not reflect internal activity [within Cuba] not be engaged in."[1]

Sam Halpern described the program more succinctly: "The next thing we knew, the word was 'let Cubans be Cubans.' Let the Cubans do their own thing. But the Cubans didn't have any money. So, the CIA's got money. Give 'em money. We gave them money. We told 'em where to buy arms, ammunition. We didn't give it to 'em. They went out and bought their own. They decided what they wanted. They picked their own targets, then they told us what their targets were. We provided them intelligence support. . . . We didn't have anything to do with what they were up to. They just told us what they were going to do and we said, 'Fine. We're not stopping you.' And we didn't."[2]

As with virtually every other covert activity aimed at Cuba in the post–

Bay of Pigs period, Bobby Kennedy was the new program's eager engineer. The CIA, at least at the operational level, was the reluctant conductor. The only two groups ultimately to benefit from "giving the Cubans their heads" were the (MRR), led by Manuel Artime, and the Cuban Revolutionary Junta (JURE) headed by Manuel Ray. They were referred to in official documents as the "autonomous groups." Declassified documents indicate that a third exile group, Comandos L, was considered for funding but never approved. (It has been reported, apparently erroneously, that the Artime organization operated under the code name of Second Naval Guerrilla. Neither the CIA's Halpern nor Artime's deputy, Rafael "Chi Chi" Quintero, had ever heard this code name. Nor was such a reference found in any of the many declassified documents now available.[3])

Artime had been the political representative of the Cuban Revolutionary Council, the exile group organized and subsidized by the CIA to front for the Bay of Pigs Brigade. He landed with the invaders and was among those captured and imprisoned in Cuba until December 1962. He was known as the CIA's "Golden Boy," but as far as the so-called autonomous operations were concerned, Artime was Bobby Kennedy's "Golden Boy." Manuel Ray, public works minister early in Castro's government before defecting, was thought to have a large underground following within Cuba. He had become a favorite of many in the Kennedy administration, particularly White House aide Arthur Schlesinger Jr. Under White House pressure Ray was belatedly added to the Cuban Revolutionary Council on the eve of the Bay of Pigs invasion, but was not part of the invasion force. He was regarded as too liberal by many conservative exiles, and some within the CIA, who saw him as an advocate of *Fidelismo sin Fidel* or Fidelism without Fidel.

Martin recommended that the autonomous program begin only with Ray's JURE, noting the "problems would multiply" if more groups were involved. "In sum," warned Martin, "we should be cautious about grandiose schemes, a 'major' U.S. effort, and deep commitments to the exiles. We should experiment in this new venture on a small scale with patience and tolerance for high noise levels and mistakes." It was a prescient warning.

Approved by the president on June 19, 1963, as part of the CIA's broader Integrated Covert Action Program for Cuba, the "rules of engagement" for the autonomous operations were:

(1) It is the keystone of autonomous operations that they will be executed exclusively by Cuban nationals motivated by the conviction that the overthrow of the Castro/Communist regime must be accomplished by Cubans, both inside and outside Cuba acting in consonance.

(2) The effort will probably cost many Cuban lives. If this cost in lives becomes unacceptable to the U.S. conscience, autonomous operations can be effectively halted by the withdrawal of U.S. support; but once halted, it cannot be resumed.

(3) All autonomous operations will be mounted outside the territory of the United States.

(4) The United States Government must be prepared to deny publicly any participation in these acts no matter how loud or even how accurate may be the reports of U.S. complicity.

(5) The United States presence and direct participation in the operation would be kept to an absolute minimum. Before entering into an operational relationship with a group, the U.S. representative will make it clear that his Government has no intention of intervening militarily except to counter intervention by the Soviets. An experienced CIA officer would be assigned to work with the group in a liaison capacity. He would provide general advice as requested as well as funds and necessary material support. He may be expected to influence but not control the conduct of operations.

(6) These operations would not be undertaken within a fixed time schedule.[4]

Bobby Kennedy wasn't waiting for the president's formal approval to get the autonomous program on track. In early December 1962, even before the missile crisis dust had settled, he called Quintero for a visit to Hickory Hill, the Kennedy estate in McLean, Virginia. "He had a plan in mind," Quintero said. "He wanted a separate operation. My feeling was that this man was a man working behind the scenes, who wanted personal knowledge, not just what he was told by a government agency. He was very knowledgeable. He could talk about people and places on the map." He asked Quintero who could unite the Cuban opposition. Quintero, a longtime Artime friend and collaborator, suggested Artime was the man.[5]

The Bay of Pigs prisoners were released later the same month, among them Artime and Erneido Oliva, the brigade's second in command. Oliva had served in both Batista's army and Castro's army before being spirited out of Cuba in August 1960 to join the brigade training camps in Guatemala. During the battle at the Bay of Pigs he had distinguished himself in defeat. As Oliva walked from the plane after arriving in Homestead, Florida, from Cuba, Enrique Ruiz Williams, a wounded prisoner released earlier, called: " 'Erneido, come, I have somebody who wants to say hello to you.' There was a portable telephone, and when I took it, it was Bobby Kennedy," said Oliva. "He welcomed me to the United States and, in my broken English, I said I was looking forward to meeting him."

Two days later, Oliva, Artime, and other brigade leaders were in Washington meeting with administration officials to prepare for the official December 29 welcoming ceremony for the returned prisoners in Miami's Orange Bowl. Bobby Kennedy was among those they met. The brigade leaders continued their treks back and forth between Miami and Washington after the ceremony, conferring with Pentagon and CIA officials about Cuba. During a mid-January visit to Washington, Oliva and Artime were invited by Bobby Kennedy to Hickory Hill, where the trio discussed the end of Mongoose and potential new anti-Castro efforts. Bobby told them of the Kennedy administration's plan to incorporate brigade members into the U.S. military for training and revealed the basic outline for what was to become Artime's $6- to $7-million effort in Central America. "Artime would be in charge of the paramilitary operation from a country in Central America, not identified at that time, and Oliva in charge of the conventional force," said Oliva. "What Artime was doing, what Oliva was doing, the projects were supposed to mesh. . . . The plans were that at a given time, when Artime's operation gets stronger against Castro, and along with the people inside Cuba, then my officers will get together with the enlisted personnel at Ft. Jackson and organize a unit."

Shortly after the Hickory Hill meeting, Artime and Quintero started laying the groundwork and lobbying Central American officials for the new anti-Castro operation. Oliva and 207 other brigade members were sworn in March 11, 1963, as commissioned officers in the U.S. Army and assigned to Fort Benning, Georgia, for training. President Kennedy formally designated Oliva as the representative for Cuban-Americans in the U.S. military. In addition to the Fort Benning officer group, they included several thousand Cuban enlisted men—many of whom had been recruited during the missile crisis—stationed at Fort Jackson, South Carolina. As their representative, Oliva's liaison at the Pentagon was Alexander Haig Jr.

To accentuate the link between them, Artime visited Oliva at Fort Benning in the spring of 1963 to recruit some of the Cuban officers there for his Central American operation. Oliva said he told Artime, "You can take them if they want to go." Among those at Fort Benning who resigned their commissions and signed on with Artime were Felix Rodriguez and Gustavo Villoldo, both later to gain notoriety as the CIA agents who helped the Bolivian military track down Che Guevara in October 1967. Artime invited Oliva to become the Central American operation's military commander. Oliva declined, preferring to remain in the U.S. Army.[6]

The first clear indication of approval for agency involvement with the autonomous groups came in a CIA paper dated May 16, 1963, although formal presidential approval didn't come for another month. The paper on sabotage in Cuba noted "approval has been granted for Agency support to selected exile groups which are largely autonomous. The first, and most promising, of these is represented by Artime. His planned survey trip to Central America was delayed because of a feeling that he might represent a possible asset in connection with Haiti." However, Artime was now ready to go to Central America, and "at the conclusion of his survey, in about a month, the Agency will bring an over-all plan of operation for approval by the Special Group."[7]

The task of finding a location in Central America where the Artime group could operate fell mainly to Rafael Quintero. Among the most dedicated and tenacious in the anti-Castro fight, Quintero had been with Artime's MRR in the Sierra Maestra against Batista. He fled Cuba for Miami in November 1959. In December he went to Mexico to join Artime after Artime's defection. Returning to Miami in March 1960, Quintero was number twenty-seven to sign up for the Bay of Pigs. His first stop for that operation was Useppa Island, off Florida's gulf coast, for radio communications training. Next he moved to the Guatemala training camps. Returning to Miami in November, he spent a month delivering supplies to the resistance in Cuba before his own infiltration into the island to work with the underground in the period before and after the Bay of Pigs. He returned to Miami in September 1961. Three months later he was back in Cuba, coming out for the final time in April 1962. Then, at Bobby Kennedy's behest, he went to Latin America to enlist support for the release of the Bay of Pigs prisoners. After his return from Latin America, he began working for the agency again in Miami, ferrying weapons into and people in and out of Cuba, until Artime's release from prison.

Quintero's search for a camp location first focused on Nicaragua. In early 1963 he spent "like three months going to Nicaragua every week looking for a site for the camps. . . . We spent a long time picking out a site . . . a convenient site that Luis Somoza [Nicaraguan president] had to approve. We picked out two or three places that they rejected. At the same time, Artime started lobbying people in Costa Rica . . . President [Francisco] Orlich. And that was easy, because he decided that his brother's farm was going to be the place that we could build a camp." Meanwhile, the people in Washington "were getting a little bit disturbed because we were taking a little bit too much time doing this."

It wasn't easy. "On the Atlantic Coast of Nicaragua there was nothing," said Quintero. "We didn't have any type of communication . . . only boats or planes. They didn't have any roads at that time. It was hard to get everybody together in Nicaragua to say, 'well, we're going to fly over this area tomorrow.' You needed to get the plane. You needed to get the pilot. And the weather in Nicaragua is very rough for a small airplane. At 12 o'clock everything is closed. You cannot fly because the clouds are too low and the Nicaraguan pilots were not that good. Anyway, it took some time to finally say this is the place where we are going to go."

The "place" for one site was Monkey Point, at the tip of a peninsula near El Bluff. "We go see the head of the province and he said 'I've got another place you can use.'" It was up the coast near Puerto Cabezas, from where the Bay of Pigs invaders set sail. Things were much easier there. "The commander of the area was very good, very helpful, and we didn't have any problems." Monkey Point was a swamp, Quintero recalled, "so we have to build all that. It took us a lot of time and equipment. We had to build the camp. We have to build a dock. We have to prepare an airfield. It was totally swamp when we went there. It was very well located, but Somoza didn't want us close to any area where people were living."

By late 1963 the camps were up and running. In Nicaragua the maritime operation was at Monkey Point. The commandos—numbering about ninety people—were at Puerto Cabezas. In Costa Rica the infiltration teams were at the Orlich farm in Sarapiqui. A radio operators' base and a weapons barge were at Tortuguero. "So we are talking now about five bases plus one other camp because we had the communications center in San Jose. So we had six places that we had to look out for, secure, and get people for," said Quintero. There also was a refueling base in the Dominican Republic. The total number of exiles in the Central American camps eventually reached about three hundred.

Although they had a common border, Costa Rica and Nicaragua were not on the friendliest of terms. As a result, an effort was made to keep the Nicaraguan and Costa Rican operations as separate as possible. Neither country was told what was going on within its neighbor's borders. "We have more camps and more sophisticated equipment in Costa Rica, but we have more people in Nicaragua," said Quintero. "The Monkey Point base was a big base with a lot of people. . . . We have a couple of airplanes there and the boats, two operational boats, and we have a couple of mother ships."[8]

There are indications Washington provided some assistance for both Artime and Ray to find operational locations. One declassified document carried only the heading, "Talking Points to be Used in Conversation with Foreign Minister Oduber Concerning Cuban Exile Activity," which was prepared to lobby Costa Rican foreign minister Daniel Oduber on behalf of both the anointed exile leaders. The document begins, the United States considers both men "responsible and dedicated Cuban patriots" who "approach the problem of freeing their country somewhat differently: Artime looks to the eventual mounting of guerrilla and sabo- tage operations inside Cuba while Ray's emphasis is on the employment of politico-psychological means within Cuba to encourage defections in the Communist regime and thus to erode the power structure." More significantly, it read the "provision of assistance to these two men is, of course, a matter for the Costa Rican Government itself to decide. For our part, however, we would not discourage such support or assistance." It noted that the U.S. government "does not control Artime or Ray," and added, somewhat ingenuously: "Our information is that they obtain assistance from democratic Latin American individuals and organizations who wish to see the establishment of democracy in Cuba."[9]

A declassified chronology of the autonomous operations based on policy discussions at Special Group meetings, showed that by July 9, 1963, Man- uel Ray's JURE was getting a monthly subsidy of $10,000. Payment to Artime's MRR was not noted but the chronology did report that his oper- ation had "moved forward rapidly in the past three weeks," with Nicara- gua "supplying a base, cover, and logistical support for the operation. In addition, a description was given of the Costa Rican political base worked out by ARTIME."[10]

The chronology entry for July 16, 1963, a week later, reported "the question of disappointingly premature publicity concerning our autono- mous operations with ARTIME was raised. The discussion centered on means of counteracting this premature publicity and several suggestions to do so were made. There was no suggestion of changing the autonomous operation concept." The CIA's Desmond FitzGerald reported on the problem at a meeting of the National Security Council's Standing Group. A summary record of the meeting reads: "There was a discussion of the widespread press reports that the U.S. was backing Cuban exiles who are planning raids against Cuba from Central American States. One news article shown the Attorney General was headed 'Backstage with Bobby' and referred to his [Bobby Kennedy] conversations with persons involved in planning the Cuban raids." The article, written by Hal Hendrix, appeared in the *Miami News* on July 14, 1963.[11]

Another story by Hendrix appeared two days later under the heading: "Top Exile Fighter Quits U.S. for Base." It was an interview with Artime in which he said he was leaving the United States to direct an anti-Castro guerrilla army from a headquarters somewhere in Central America. The story said, "Artime denied vigorously reports circulating here and in Washington that he is being supported and financed by Attorney General Robert Kennedy. 'I have no association with the attorney general,' Artime asserted." Artime added that his support was coming from "some Latin governments, some wealthy Latin Americans and some Latin Political parties" who have helped provide financing and weapons.[12]

The first story by Hendrix, headed "Backstage with Bobby," could have quite possibly come from CIA sources, perhaps even Ted Shackley in Miami, with whom Hendrix was well acquainted. The CIA—especially its operational personnel such as Shackley—was not enthusiastic about the autonomous operations. "The whole operation was set up as a result of Artime's discussion with the Kennedys," Shackley said in an interview. "I was asked my opinion on it and I said it was a lousy idea. They had basically been out of Cuba too long and were not aware of the operational realities in Cuba," which had grown considerably more difficult by 1963. In addition, said Shackley, "Artime didn't have the managerial skills to run this. It was not cost effective to provide them with the support mechanism they would need for being successful." The JMWAVE station in Miami had given Artime a two-week "tutorial" to try and make him "a competent manager of a large clandestine program," said Shackley. "It was clear at the end of it that it was not going to work. After that, our role in Miami was support when Artime was in Miami. I would meet him, but it was an RFK operation," one which Shackley described as "an exercise in futility."[13]

Shackley had even less regard for the other autonomous operation headed by Manuel Ray. "Ray captured attention . . . because he was further to the left and sold the Kennedys. His [CIA] case officer was Al Rodriguez and I told him the thing was a poor effort, a waste of time. The [JMWAVE] station had nothing to do with Ray. He never did anything."[14] Disdain for the autonomous groups within the bureaucracy wasn't limited to the CIA. John Crimmins, by then the coordinator for Cuban affairs, said he was "strongly opposed to them. I never forgave Des [Fitz-Gerald] for pushing for the autonomous business. For someone who didn't like the thing, he was very convincing about the virtues of the autonomous approach."[15]

It was obvious, said Quintero, that the CIA was a reluctant supporter of the autonomous groups. "I remember the first meeting Artime and I had with the CIA guys, when we start planning for Central America. The guy told him, 'This is not as if we chose a name out of a hat for you to be in charge of this operation. It has gone very high and you were picked out to be the guy who is going to run this operation.' That guy [who made the decision] was Bobby Kennedy, who we had met and who was interested in doing something when almost everything else was dead here."[16] And with Bobby Kennedy in charge, it would take more than bureaucratic unhappiness to halt the program.

At the same time, word of Artime's operation was getting around. CIA Director John McCone, in a July 20 memo, advised the attorney general that according to an agency representative in Miami, Jose "Pepin" Bosch, the Cuban-born Bacardi rum boss, had met with Luis Somoza, who "told him of U.S. support for anti-Castro operations from Nicaragua. Bosch said that during a meeting with Somoza on 15 July Somoza indicated that he had received a green light from the Attorney General Robert F. Kennedy to mount anti-Castro raider and resistance operations from Nicaraguan bases. Somoza said that the Attorney General wanted him to work with Manuel Artime, Erneido Oliva and the brothers Jose and Roberto PEREZ-San Roman in implementing anti-Castro operations. Somoza told Bosch that he would use these men but wanted to maintain flexibility, which would also allow him to work with other promising Cuban exiles. Somoza said the Attorney General agreed that he should have full flexibility to handle the matter as he saw fit."[17]

Somoza may have had an ulterior motive, as can be seen from the August 8 entry in the CIA chronology of the autonomous groups, which reads in part: "A status report on ARTIME's operation was discussed,

particularly Luis SOMOZA's efforts to push planned harassment operations in the hope that Castro might launch an offensive against Nicaragua
which SOMOZA believed would bring forth U.S. intervention." Somoza's
efforts encouraged Artime to shift the bulk of his operations to Costa Rica
"without breaking with Somoza."[18] Luis Somoza was by then no longer
president, but he still exercised political power directly, or through Rene
Schick, his handpicked successor.

Meanwhile, Ray continued to operate from South Florida and Puerto
Rico despite the mandate that autonomous group activities were supposed to be "mounted outside the territory of the United States." Declassified documents indicated Ray tried unsuccessfully to get a campsite in
Costa Rica, but finally did get a small base in the Dominican Republic.
Eloy Gutierrez Menoyo, another veteran of the war against Batista, who
defected in January 1961, also had a base in the Dominican Republic,
grouping three organizations: his own Second National Front of the
Escambray, Alpha 66, which he had helped organize earlier in Miami, and
remnants of Ray's old Peoples Revolutionary Movement (MRP). Menoyo
did not receive funding under the autonomous program benefiting Ray
and Artime, although he was held in higher esteem by U.S. officials than
were many other militant exile leaders. Declassified documents hint that
he might have received limited support from the Defense Department.
For example, a memo for the record of the January 9, 1964, Special Group
meeting showed that the Department of the Army requested and received
approval for two "clandestine intelligence operations." One was for "the
establishment of a clandestine net using the Second National Front of the
Escambray."[19] After dropping from sight in mid-1964, Menoyo led a
four-man band that infiltrated Cuba from the Dominican Republic in late
December 1964. Others of his organization were apparently to follow, but
Menoyo and his three companions were captured in late January 1965
near Baracoa in eastern Cuba. A filmed interrogation of the four was presented on Cuban television February 3, 1965, in which Menoyo "con-
fessed" that he had worked earlier with the CIA in sabotage operations
after being trained by the agency to "handle explosives, read maps and
assemble some weapons with which I was not familiar, such as the 30-
caliber machinegun."[20]

By November "Artime and the MRR has [sic] made substantial progress
and expects to mount his first operations in December," according to the

CIA chronology entry, based on a White House meeting to review the Cuban program. Ray was now receiving $25,000 of support monthly, "although he has not progressed to the point that ARTIME has. Higher Authority [the president] concurred that the program continue." Concern about control reemerged, as McCone "emphasized that to a very considerable extent they [the autonomous groups] were uncontrollable and forecast that once ARTIME was in business we might expect some events to take place which were not exactly to our liking."[21] McCone was proven right in dramatic fashion ten months later when Artime's group mistakenly fired on a Spanish freighter off the Cuban coast, killing several crewmen and igniting a major diplomatic flap.

But in late 1963, the problem was more mundane: getting the program operational. "It's difficult to say when we finally became operational, because we had so many problems," said Quintero. "We had logistical problems. We had political problems with the camps. It was very difficult trying to deal with the government of Costa Rica and them not knowing what we were doing in Nicaragua, and the Nicaraguan government not knowing what we were doing in Costa Rica. I would say it was early 1964 before we had a base you could get the infiltration teams, the commandos and all the maritime operations running. . . . You could get people in and out [of Cuba] from a maritime point of view." Another problem, said Quintero, was CIA reluctance. "The CIA wasn't really very happy with the operation. It was something Bobby Kennedy made them do so they had to support us, but they didn't do it willingly. It was another battle that you had to fight."

For Artime and Quintero, there were also the regular monthly meetings with their CIA case officer, Henry Heckscher. Heckscher had been involved with the Bay of Pigs, and Quintero had first met him on Useppa Island and later saw him in the Guatemala training camps. He was later the CIA station chief in Chile at the beginning of Salvador Allende's presidency in 1970. "Henry was reluctant to work with us because somebody dropped it in his lap, and he didn't want it," said Quintero. "But he was a very professional man, and he felt we were wasting our time with what we were doing; that it would only work if we could have some professional advice. He talked to Artime very much about trying to get a brain trust behind him that would tell him what to do, how to do it and when to do it."

The meetings, said Quintero, usually lasted two days and were held in various U.S. cities, among them San Francisco, Atlanta, San Juan, and

Washington, but never Miami. "First we explained the budget for that month; second all the plans we have. We made all the recommendations and what we thought about them. We gave a report of how training was going and explained what plans we have for the coming month. And we had a lot of logistical problems, as you can imagine. To build a camp in the middle of nowhere in the jungle is not an easy task. Then there were all the political problems. That took almost 90 percent of Artime's time, trying to keep Orlich and Somoza satisfied. You know how all these people . . . you know how all the governments are. They want money." In Costa Rica, the Artime group shared an airstrip on the farm with Orlich's brother. "We were using it for our program and he was using it for his own program," said Quintero. And "his program" apparently involved smuggling whiskey and other contraband. "One of the guys we were dealing with in Nicaragua was Ivan Alegrett, who was the consul in Miami. He was kicked out as consul for drug problems, and when he got to Managua, Somoza named him the head of immigration, so you can imagine."[22]

Eventually, things began falling into place. Tito Mesa, a Cuban exile friend of Artime's, had set up a front company, Maritima Bam, S.A., in Panama for the operation's business transactions. (The BAM represented Artime's initials in reverse, Manuel Artime Buesa.) CIA funding was channeled from Switzerland to the Coconut Grove Bank in Miami under the name of Walter Oppenheimer, who was actually Artime.[23] November brought the big enchilada in the form of a barge loaded with 110 tons of arms, ammunition, explosives, and other military equipment. The Defense Department carried out this operation with the approval of the Special Group, "in a manner designed to preclude attributability to the United States, and to attribute the origin of the arms and their means of delivery to European commercial firms." Even the Artime group thought the arms were purchased and transferred from Germany. The operation involved a complex plan under which the CIA obtained a barge, which was picked up in Baltimore by a Navy tug, then towed to the Naval Ammunition Depot in Yorktown, Virginia, where the CIA delivered the arms shipment for loading. The barge was then towed to an area near the Naval Amphibious Base at Little Creek, Virginia, where it was picked up by another vessel that towed it during darkness to a designated spot in international waters off Costa Rica's Atlantic Coast. The tow vessel departed as the CIA maintained surveillance of the anchored barge from a smaller boat nearby until it was retrieved by Artime's men and towed up the jungled Tortuguero River where it was anchored.[24] There the stationary barge, guarded by a seventeen-member security team, became the arms and ammunition storage facility during the course of the Artime operation. When a weapon was needed, said Quintero, it was picked up from the barge.

Only a month or so before that, Erneido Oliva, now at Fort Still, Oklahoma, had been given the go-ahead, after heavy lobbying of Bobby Kennedy and Oliva's Pentagon contacts, to draft a plan to incorporate all the Cubans in the U.S. Army into a single unit. "Remember, I was a pushy guy. I kept calling and said, 'Hey, what are we going to do?' until October, I think, when they called me and said, hey, 'prepare something.'" Oliva is convinced that had President Kennedy lived, the Cuban unit was a force that would eventually have been used against Cuba in conjunction with Artime's operation, despite Kennedy's no-invasion pledge.

Oliva thinks it quite possible that Artime would have provoked a confrontation that would have drawn a reaction from Castro and, in turn, brought a U.S. response.[25] This idea might not be so far-fetched, given that Luis Somoza appeared to be thinking along the same lines. In fact, Castro said in October 2002, at a fortieth anniversary missile crisis conference in Havana, that one of the reasons he had been so resistant to the withdrawal of the Soviet IL-28 bombers from Cuba was the possibility they might have been needed to bomb exile bases.[26]

President Kennedy's assassination brought a halt to CIA-directed sabotage, but it had little immediate impact on the autonomous operations. President Johnson was briefed at a December 19 meeting in the White House on the agency's covert programs. According to the CIA chronology, "in the course of the briefing which included the autonomous operations, Higher Authority asked the cost of these operations and he was informed the total was about $5,000,000. He also asked the cost of Cuban operations for the current year and was informed it was about $21 or 22 million."[27]

Six weeks after becoming president, Johnson was presented with an exhaustive review of the covert action program against Cuba that defined the autonomous operations as "intended to provide a deniable activity, a means of supplementing and expanding our covert capability and a means of taking advantage of untapped political and resistance resources of the exile community." The review, declassified in 2001 but still partially censored under the JFK Assassination Records Review Act, went on to describe the program as "one that now includes [censored] autonomous groups whose credibility as to autonomy is strengthened by the facts that:

> They are led by men whose prominence and status in the Cuban exile community makes plausible their access to funds, equipment and manpower quite independent of the U.S.;
> [Censored] are based in the Caribbean area outside of U.S. territory;
> [Censored] have natural, willing allies in power in several Latin American countries;
> [Censored] are Cuban and employ Cuban nationals exclusively;
> Every item of financial and logistic support has been handled in a manner as to provide maximum protection against proof of CIA or U.S. participation.
> The initial aim of these operations is to strengthen the will to resist by increasing the tempo of subversion and sabotage largely maintained until now by CIA; the eventual aim is to take the fight from the coastline to the interior of Cuba.
> The disadvantage of our autonomous operations is that it is necessary to accept a lower order of efficiency and control than would be considered acceptable in CIA-run operations.[28]

In fact, the review appeared to be somewhat premature. Neither of the autonomous groups had yet become operational, and Ray had not yet found a country to host his operation.

Shortly before President Kennedy's assassination, a new element entered into the equation and reopened debate on the administration's Cuba policy. An arms cache was discovered November 1 on a Venezuelan beach. An investigation determined the cache was left by Cuban agents and meant to aid Venezuelan guerrillas in an effort to disrupt upcoming national elections. With a good case now to be made before the Organization of American States [OAS] for further isolating the Castro government, the new Johnson administration was forced to decide whether to pursue an overt "clean hands" policy or to continue its two-track policy of political pressure and covert action. If U.S.-sponsored covert action continued, it could damage the case for isolation and make Washington vulnerable to accusations of hypocrisy before an OAS Foreign Ministers meeting convoked for July by Venezuela under the Rio Treaty.

At an April 7, 1963, White House meeting to review covert action against Cuba, an informal decision was made to continue a stand-down of CIA-controlled sabotage activities imposed in January, a decision influenced by the upcoming OAS meeting as well as the Soviets' prospective turnover of SAM [surface-to-air missile] missile sites on the island to Cuba. It was decided that nothing should be done about the Artime and Ray autonomous groups which were about to become operational.[29] Two days later, Bundy, Richard Helms, and an unidentified third person met to share their concerns about the Artime and Ray operations and these operations' implications for the upcoming OAS meeting. They concluded that Artime could not be dissuaded from mounting his first action and briefly considered using a U.S. Navy destroyer to halt the operation, before abandoning the idea altogether. "Mr. Bundy capsuled the problem by saying his worry was whether an Artime attack would give the U.S. a hypocritical image when out of the other side of its mouth the U.S. was plumping for votes at the OAS to outlaw subversion and armed attack."[30]

This was the latest in the ongoing debate between the pros and cons of the autonomous groups. Desmond FitzGerald had defended them in a March 6, 1964, letter to Bundy reviewing the CIA's covert action program against Cuba. In his appraisal of the autonomous groups, FitzGerald said:

As you know, again as part of the June plan, we are supporting two 'autonomous' exile groups headed respectively by Manuel Artime and Manolo Ray. In both cases we have gone to maximum lengths to preserve the deniability of U.S. complicity in the operation. Artime, who now possesses the greater mechanical and paramilitary apparatus, has required a good deal of hand-feeding although still within the context of deniability. He will probably not be ready for his operations against Cuba before April or May of this year. He possesses most of his hardware and maritime equipment and has negotiated geographical and political bases in Central America. Manolo Ray has been handled on a much more independent basis. We have furnished him money and a certain amount of general advice. He does not possess the physical accoutrements that Artime has and is probably not as well equipped in terms of professional planning. Ray has a better political image inside Cuba among supporters of the revolution and has recently acquired, according to reports, some of the other left-wing exile activist groups such as Gutierrez Menoyo and his Second Front of the Escambray. He is said to be ready to move into Cuba on a clandestine basis late this spring. His first weapon will be sabotage inside Cuba, apparently not externally-mounted hit-and-run raids.

If U.S. policy should demand that the 'autonomous' operations be suspended, we could of course cut off our support immediately. Artime and his group might or might not disintegrate at once. Manolo Ray almost certainly would continue. Both groups are based outside the United States and our only real leverage on them is through our financial support but withdrawal of this support would probably be fatal to their operations in time. A cutoff of this support, even though this support has been untraceable in a technical sense, would have a considerable impact within the exile community. U.S. support is rumored, especially in the case of Artime, and the collapse of the only remaining evidence of exile action against Castro would hit the exile community hard which is what it in turn would do to its favorite target, U.S. policy. The exile of today, however, appears to have lost much of his fervor and, in any case, does not seem to have the capacity for causing domestic trouble which he had a year or two ago. The Central American countries in which the exile bases exist would be greatly confused, although we have carefully never indicated to the governments of these countries any more than U.S. sympathy for the 'autonomous groups.'[31]

The FitzGerald letter was submitted to the Special Group on March 30 along with a memorandum entitled "Status Report on Autonomous Cuban Exile Groups," to alert the members that both Ray and Artime were about ready for action. On May 13 Artime's commandos hit the Puerto Pilon sugar mill in Cuba's southern Oriente Province. It was the first action after more than a year of preparation, damaging warehouses and reportedly destroying seventy tons of sugar, valued at about one million dollars. Five days later, on May 18, Ray departed for his long-awaited infiltration into Cuba, amid what one CIA report called "a major publicity campaign sparked by the *New York Times*."[32]

The *Times* ran front-page stories by Tad Szulc that focused on Ray for three consecutive days. The first appeared May 19 with a dateline from "Somewhere in the Caribbean." It featured an interview with Ray about his aims and ran under the headline: "Ray Plans to Use Cuban 'Will' As Means to Overthrow Castro." The second article, on May 20, was headlined "Anti-Castro Fight Starts New Phase." In it Szulc proclaimed "the most important single operation now being undertaken is that of the Revolutionary Junta. The leader of the junta, Manuel Ray, was reported today to be somewhere in the Caribbean, presumably preparing to land secretly in Cuba in order to initiate what he has described as the long and painstaking process of hammering together an effective underground organization." The third, on May 21, was headlined "Exiles Proclaim Anti-Castro War and Urge Revolt." It referred to proclamations issued by the organizations headed by Ray and Gutierrez Menoyo and went on to say that "both proclamations were timed for the arrival on the island today of Manuel Ray, the top leader of the Revolutionary Junta, and Maj. Eloy Gutierrez Menoyo, the Second Front commander." Szulc's story was accompanied inside the paper with the text of Ray's proclamation and a profile of Ray.

The articles prompted a three-page May 23 cable from Shackley's JMWAVE station in Miami to Washington with the subject: "Impact in the Miami Area of Recent Tad Szulc Articles on Manuel Ray Rivero." It began by saying "the following roundup on the impact in the Miami area of Tad Szulc articles in the *New York Times* of 19, 20, and 21 May 1964, which have been oriented in a direction which fully propagandizes Manuel Ray Rivero . . . and his anticipated accomplishments in Cuba . . ." It went on to say "the majority of the exile colony has interpreted the *New York Times*'s exhaustive coverage to be a reflection of U.S. intent to modify Ray's existing public image and simultaneously to make it clear to all Cubans that Ray has become a chosen instrument around which the U.S. plans to carry out not only the liberation but the reconstruction of Cuba."[33]

The *New York Times* was not alone in resorting to a bit of jingoism. " 'War On,' Refugees Proclaim," read a May 21 page-one headline in the *Miami Herald*. A day earlier, on May 20, another page-one headline declared: "Cuba Girds for Raids By Exiles." And on May 17, one *Miami Herald* article began with considerable hyperbole, as it turned out:

Two Cuban exiles, one a soft-spoken idealist and the other a machete-slim fighter, today are in or near Cuba to fight or die. Both were veterans of the Cuban revolution against Dictator Fulgencio Batista, and now of the fight against Premier Fidel Castro.

Manuel Ray, an engineer who would rather build than kill but organizes both exceptionally well, plans an internal resistance movement which he hopes will snowball into open fighting or possibly a coup.

Eloy Gutierrez Menoyo, who hates oppression and loves battle with equal vigor, plans guerrilla warfare which he hopes will succeed in the pattern Castro himself once set."

The article concluded:

The promised time for the jumpoff of Ray and Menoyo into Cuba comes at the end of a week during which the Cuban exile community has gorged itself on rumors to the burping point.

However, it has served to make U.S. officials more uncomfortable than anyone else.

As reports of command raids, impending uprisings, infiltration and all manner of heroics ricocheted around Miami, officials privately worried for two reasons:

RUMORS and exaggerations inflame the exiles, causing them to uproot themselves from jobs and homes, and add to the sizable problem of resettlement.

THE IMPLICATION of such reports being distributed here that the U.S. may be secretly involved, which the officials emphatically deny.

Fuel was added to exile excitement by a raid last week by Manuel Artime's Movement for Revolutionary Recovery, which attacked a sugar mill on the south coast of Oriente Province.

CHAPTER 12

FADING FAST

May 20, 1964, proved to be more of a last gasp than another new beginning in the anti-Castro campaign. Neither Ray nor Menoyo lived up to their advance billings, their efforts ending in ignominy, not triumph. Menoyo, at least, reached Cuba. Ray, after his much-ballyhooed departure, succeeded only in reaching Anguilla Cay in the Bahamas. There, on May 30, the boat he planned to use for the final infiltration run to Cuba developed motor trouble. JURE representatives scurried to find a replacement boat along with an additional supply of drinking water, but British authorities (the Bahamas was yet a British possession) got there first, seizing a cache of weapons and explosives and arresting Ray and his crew of seven. They were taken to Nassau where each paid a minimal $14 fine for illegal entry and were released. Ray's "crew" included two *Time-Life* photographers, Andrew St. George and Tom Duncan, suggesting to some that his ill-fated adventure may have been more of a publicity photo op than the opening battle in a new war.[1] Ray was down but not yet out. Menoyo, as noted earlier, dropped from sight for several months, resurfacing in late January 1965 when Cuban authorities announced his capture, along with three companions, in Oriente Province. He served eighteen years in a Cuban prison, returning to Miami after his release to become an advocate of accommodation.

In Washington the new Johnson administration was having trouble making up its mind about the autonomous groups. Much of the ambivalence centered on the upcoming mid-July 1964 OAS meeting to deal with the Cuban arms cache found in Venezuela. The hope was that the meeting would result in tightening Cuba's hemisphere isolation, leading to military intervention if additional caches were found or similar activities continued. Second, there were widespread reports that the Soviets were about to turn over SAM sites to the Cubans. If that happened, there was fear Castro might counter a sabotage raid with an effort to shoot down a U-2 overflight. Still another worry was the reaction of the Cuban exile community if support for the autonomous groups was terminated. These arguments were set forth in a June 3, 1964, report by the CIA: *A Reappraisal of Autonomous Operations*.[2] The author was not identified, but presumably it was heavily influenced, if not written, by Desmond Fitz-Gerald. The paper's slant clearly favored continuation of support for the autonomous operations, despite the State Department's contrary view and widespread anathema for the program among many of the CIA operational people involved with it.

"It has been suggested that a reappraisal of autonomous operations would be in order if, as a result of an OAS resolution on the Venezuelan arms cache, aggression is to be redefined to include subversion," said the study. "It is argued that the U.S. should, if it is to exploit the OAS resolution, not itself engage in the proscribed activities. The U.S. would have to adopt a 'clean hands' position vis-à-vis Cuba and this state of cleanliness must be maintained indefinitely if the U.S. is to remain in a position to apply sanctions against Castro should he be again caught red-handed."

The reappraisal then discussed considerations that would affect U.S. support for the autonomous groups. It opened with the assumption "that it remains U.S. policy to get rid of Fidel Castro by acceptable means. If this premise is correct the first task of the policymaker in framing the issues herein presented, is to balance the two courses of action proposed—i.e. (a) a continuation of autonomous operations and (b) an exclusive reliance on OAS sanctions in terms of their effectiveness in achieving our basic purpose."

When the CIA's integrated covert action program began, the appraisal noted, it had been agreed that it should be given an eighteen-month test, but "despite the truncated nature of the program it appears to us that there have been many indications of success." Cited among the successes was the establishment of a "direct correlation between the series of minor sabotage operations during the late part of 1963 and a rise in internal resistance by sabotage. The Pilon raid [by Artime] and news of Ray's plans to return to Cuba has again set off military alerts and other internal measures not observed in Cuba since the October 1962 missile crisis."

The appraisal made the case for continuation of the two approaches, covert and "clean hands," without choosing either. "Having already denied ourselves unilaterally controlled raiding actions and having taken precaution not to leave our fingerprints on the autonomous operations, may we not proceed along both tracks in their current direction, denying stoutly our involvement in the illegal activities of achieving our national purpose?" the report asked, followed by an answer. "We are certain to be accused of responsibility for other exile activities in which we are not involved. Our innocence will be as difficult to establish as would be our involvement in the case of our autonomous operations."

The reappraisal expressed fear that suspension of support for the autonomous program would assuredly become known in the exile community, and seen as "a further indication that the U.S. is no longer interested in the active liberation of Cuba and is moving in the direction of rapprochement and accommodation with the Castro regime." The potential for adverse domestic political and international repercussions was raised, with particular interest in impact on the Nicaraguan and Costa Rican governments "who have afforded these groups base facilities on their soil." Ending support might provoke the groups to "step up these raids, in defiance of U.S. wishes if necessary" and could even lead to "a choice of activities on the part of these groups that would have a higher 'noise level' than at present." Finally, the report argued, a consequence of the "clean hands" principle would affect all covert activities, not just sabotage raids.

The appraisal concluded:

> Termination of U.S. support for the autonomous groups will not necessarily assure the cessation of externally mounted commando raids on Cuba. In fact, it is likely that the first reaction of the autonomous groups will be to conduct 'higher level' activities than at present including, perhaps, revelations of past U.S. support. There may also be exile raids with which we have no connection, e.g., the SNFE or Alpha 66—for which the U.S. would automatically be blamed.
>
> Adoption of the 'legal track' would have ramifications for covert operations extending far beyond autonomous raiding actions. Maritime infiltration/exfiltration for intelligence and caching operations, both autonomous and unilateral CIA, would have to be included in the ban if the 'clean hands' principle is to be applied in a consistent and meaningful manner.
>
> The cessation of autonomous commando operations—the only remaining external sabotage activity since unilateral CIA operations were stood down in January 1964—would effectively kill the remaining chances of carrying out the objectives of the Integrated Covert Action Program initiated in June 1963.
>
> While the cost would be high, it might well be worth the sacrifice if the U.S. is prepared for armed intervention in Cuba if the OAS will unequivocally support it.

A day later, on June 4, Chase told Bundy that the more he saw of the autonomous operations "the less I like them. . . . These raids probably double our very poor chances of overthrowing Castro."[3] The Special Group put the issue on the agenda for its June 18 meeting. In advance of the meeting, Chase offered some thoughts to Bundy. "There are," he said, "a number of disadvantages to the status quo. . . . At best these raids will make it tougher to keep the lid on Cuba between now and [U.S. elections in] November. This is just the sort of thing that can evoke a highly irrational response from Castro. As things stand, Castro seems convinced that we are tied to the raids—as indeed we are." Chase also raised the possibility that the raids could "touch off a U-2 shootdown and a first class Caribbean crisis." Finally, he told Bundy, the State Department believes the "autonomous raids would make more difficult the enforcement language in the OAS resolution, i.e., our own hands should be clean." Alternatively, Chase suggested, "(a) We can make a real effort to stop the raids. . . . (b) We can search harder for an alternative to the U-2. . . . (c) Using our support as leverage, we can try to discourage the exile groups from making raids of the higher noise-level variety. . . . (d) We can cut off all U.S. ties with these exile groups."[4]

The Special Group took the easy way out, choosing to maintain the status quo, as "none of those present appeared to feel that it was either realistic or practical to sever connections with or to withdraw support from the two principal émigré organizations, those of ARTIME and RAY. It was agreed that ARTIME should be convinced that his greatest value was in his survival as a continuing psychological threat in being."[5]

Chase also advised Bundy that "Manolo Ray recently asked the U.S. Government for three things—(a) a special grant, (b) our influence with the Puerto Ricans getting them to allow Ray to move a boat from Puerto Rico, and (c) our assistance in getting the Dominican Republic to allow Ray to establish a base in that country." There is no indication whether any of the three requests were acted on, but later documents indicate Ray did establish a base in the Dominican Republic sometime in the latter part of 1964.[6]

In July the OAS condemned Cuba for aggression. A State Department analysis summarized the OAS action: "planting an arms cache in Venezuela in connection with a Cuban supported plan to overthrow the Venezuelan Government—and resolved to impose sanctions against the Castro regime. Reaction to the move in the free world ranged from enthusiastic support in most of Latin America to skeptical deprecation in parts of Western Europe." The analysis predicted the sanctions would "help to disrupt subversive activities in Latin America and to further discourage Castro from pursuing these activities" but "have little immediate effect upon the Cuban economy." On balance, the OAS action was seen "as a substantial victory for the US and Venezuela."[7]

With attention focused on preparation for the OAS meeting, Ray made at least two more aborted infiltration attempts of Cuba. He recounted his efforts in a visit to G. Harvey Summ, head of the Miami office for the State Department's coordinator of Cuban affairs. The visits apparently were an attempt to persuade the U.S. government "that his recent failures have not deterred him in his dedication and determination to attempt light spark of internal resistance against Castro forces." He told Summ that as he left for Cuba from Key West on July 11, the Coast Guard had stopped him, which caused him to abandon his attempt. Summ responded that the Coast Guard was doing its duty, and "one could speculate that had he proceeded on July 11 he might have run into some other kind of bad luck." Ray could avoid such difficulties in the future, Summ said, by "operating from somewhere else." Ray was to attempt another infiltration from Key West on July 13. He said he had gotten within five to eight miles of the Cuban coast, when one of his boat motors broke and could not be repaired. He returned to Florida. "Obviously disappointed at failure, Ray nevertheless maintained that he would soon try again. Not sure of how or from where," Summ reported to Washington.[8]

Ray's failure to meet the expectations he had created led to a significant loss of credibility among exiles and defections from his organization. The JURE survived until 1968, but nothing indicated it ever did anything. Neither was there ever any sign of the broad underground network in Cuba that Ray claimed to have. He did, apparently, eventually establish a base in the Dominican Republic and acquire the *Venus*, a 110-foot Panamanian-registered vessel that became the object of an internal JURE dispute. Ray reportedly received U.S. funding of $75,000 for October–December 1964 to underwrite relocation of the group's activities outside U.S. territory.[9]

Intelligence reports indicate he again planned to infiltrate Cuba in December 1964 to reconnoiter for a commando raid early in 1965. As had become routine with Ray, it didn't happen. The infiltration was rescheduled for February 1965. Still nothing happened. "All the men at JURE's camp in the Dominican Republic are a little disgusted because they do not think that Ray will ever go to Cuba. They have given him 5

February as a deadline," read one intelligence report. The report author added his own comment: "If Ray does not leave for Cuba by this date, he will probably lose all his men. They are all anxious to see action but Ray has been giving them nothing but promises and plans."[10]

Shortly after, Jose Ricardo Rabel, the captain of the *Venus*, along with other crew members, plotted to take control of the vessel, two Boston Whalers, and all the weapons at the Dominican base, and carry out a raid of their own. A few days later, according to an intelligence report, "Ray, who thinks the plotting has subsided, gave Rabel $1,000 on 30 January to cover boat expenses, and $50 to each man at the base."[11] The payoffs apparently quelled the revolt.

Artime was bedeviled by problems of a different nature. Rumors circulated of his possible misuse of U.S. funding, prompting a look at the group's finances. The results were reported in a July 16, 1964, CIA memorandum to the 303 Committee (as the Special Group was now called). No evidence of fraud was found, but the memo provided a revealing look into Artime's operation. From June 1963, when the program was approved, until June 30, 1964, a total of $4,933,293 had been spent in support of his operation. At the time of the memo, Artime was receiving "a monthly subsidy of $225,000 for normal operating expenses. Unusual or extraordinary costs such as purchase of additional boats and construction equipment or major ship repairs are funded separately as required." The memo said the figure for the monthly subsidy was based in part on "a payroll of $95,000 for 385 men, subsistence of $27,000 based on $3.00 per day per man for some 300 men in training camps, $47,000 for aviation and maritime operations and maintenance, $15,000 for camp maintenance in both Costa Rica and Nicaragua, and $12,000 travel expenses."

The investigators concluded, "Except for financial losses sustained as a result of poor management, the funds have probably been applied for the purposes for which they were intended." The memo noted that Artime was in charge of a multimillion dollar operation, and "his compensation on a GS-13 scale appears equitable in those conditions. We have found no hard intelligence to support the allegation that ARTIME is leading a life of ostentation and affluence. We have found no evidence of defalcation." It added, however, that the "possibility is ever present in a program of this magnitude and under the existing rules of engagement."[12] Rafael Quintero recalled years later that he and Tito Mesa, the exile businessman who handled the operation's finances, estimated about $7 million had been spent during the life of Artime's autonomous operation.[13]

Meanwhile, an influential new player emerged in early summer 1964 among the exile "action" groups vying for U.S. backing. Known as RECE, the Spanish acronym for Cuban Representation in Exile, its godfather was Jose "Pepin" Bosch, wealthy chief of the Bacardi rum company. He had bankrolled a worldwide referendum, with forty thousand Cubans participating, to select a five-member "war board." The most prominent members were its chief, Ernesto Freyre, an exile lawyer instrumental in negotiating release of the Bay of Pigs prisoners, and Erneido Oliva. Disillusioned with President Johnson's decision to suspend the program for Cubans in the U.S. military, Oliva resigned his army commission in May to become chief of RECE's military operations committee.

A profile of Oliva in the *Miami Herald* shortly after he became RECE's military chief began by noting that "if his success can be measured by the respect he commands within the oftimes internally torn Cuban exile colony, Fidel Castro's days are numbered." It described him as "a professional soldier who preaches brotherly love with the conviction of a man of the cloth . . . emerging as the newest of a handful of leaders upon whom Cuban exiles hang their hopes for a return to the island."[14]

Born of a black working-class Cuban family in the town of Aguacate, between Havana and Matanzas, Oliva joined the Cuban army under Batista, but wasn't tainted by action against Castro. When Batista fell, Oliva was in Panama as an instructor at what was later known as the U.S. Army's School of the Americas. He had returned to Cuba in mid-December 1958 to get married, but was back in Panama when, early on New Year's Day of 1959, he heard the news of Batista's flight. Oliva and Grace, his new bride, returned home from a New Year's Eve party, only to be awakened by a 4 A.M. telephone call from a School of the Americas' secretary alerting him to events in Cuba. He said, "OK," and went back to sleep, awakening again ten minutes later when the import of what he had heard dawned on him.

Hearing nothing from Havana, Oliva said he continued working as an instructor until sometime in February, when "Raul Castro learned there was a Cuban officer in Panama. When they called [the school] and asked, 'Who is there?' And they said 'a lieutenant of the Constitutional Army and he's an instructor.' The secretary told me that they said I had to come back right away; they didn't want any Cuban officers in Panama." The school told him he had only two choices: return to Cuba or go into Panama City and ask for asylum. Oliva discussed the situation with his new wife, deciding to return to Cuba "because there is nothing that I have to be afraid of." He left Grace in Panama. On his return to Cuba in late February, he had to stop first in Costa Rica. There, "someone spotted me in the airport and asked 'Where are you going?' and I said I was going back to Cuba. And they said, 'No, you are not. You are a war criminal.' There were other Cubans in the airport and when they saw me they started shouting, 'war criminal, to the wall,' and I said, 'Guys, I am going to Cuba.' The police had to come and pull me from there and take me to the plane. That was a show."

When he arrived in Havana, Oliva was taken to a small security room in the airport and questioned about what he was doing back in Cuba. He told his questioner he had been called back by Raul Castro, or his chief of staff. They told him they would check him out, and "I thought, 'Oh, my God, I am in trouble.'" His luggage was searched and his Cuban military uniforms discovered. He showed them an identification card from the U.S. Army's school in Panama. He was kept at the airport from 4 P.M. to 10 P.M., then taken to La Cabana, the fortress on the Havana waterfront where summary executions of Batista army men, some of which Oliva had seen on television in Panama, had been taking place.

"That's what was in my mind," Oliva recalled, "but instead they took me to the headquarters and there was Che Guevara; that was the first time I had ever met him. He was really very kind to me, so I don't have any complaints. He welcomed me and said, 'We don't want to have any relationship with the Americans. I have here a report that you are a professional soldier, but never have fought against us . . . blah, blah, blah, so, no problem. But instead of being a first lieutenant, you are now a second lieutenant because you have not done anything for this revolution. Batista promoted you to first lieutenant, so now you are a second lieutenant.'" Oliva was assigned to a military base in Managua, a few miles south of Havana, where he worked with Juan Almeida—who had fought with Castro in the Sierra Maestra—advising an artillery battalion.

Oliva had cautioned his wife to remain in Panama until he called her because of the still uncertain course of events in Cuba. About two weeks after his arrival in Managua, Almeida called him to his headquarters where Grace was waiting, because "she said she was desperate" in Panama. Soon the difficulties began, said Oliva. From Managua, he was assigned to the revolution's new agrarian reform program, "and I saw the Communists taking over. Everywhere I went the party clique was in charge. I said, 'This is it,' and I started working with the underground."

In August 1960 Castro's revolutionary government purchased 105mm howitzers from Italy. Instructors were needed to train troops in the use of these cannons, and Oliva had artillery experience. He was told he would be transferred to a base at San Antonio de los Banos as an instructor. "I said no. I already had in my mind I might be fighting against them someday so I didn't want to train them." In the meantime, Castro created a militia, with Jose Fernandez as its director, and ordered all those officers who had graduated from the military academy to go there as instructors "so there was no way out." Oliva submitted his resignation to Fernandez—who later led the militia forces against the invaders at the Bay of Pigs. Fernandez wouldn't accept his resignation. "What I did was desert, not report anyplace. I stayed for a month in Havana, going to a different motel every night, and that was something for thirty days."

He left his wife and two-month-old daughter with his wife's parents in Aguacate, because "my duty was not to serve with these people." He was finally able to get his papers from the U.S. embassy with help from a man named Robertson of the Christian Democratic Movement and other Americans, presumably from the CIA. Oliva left Cuba on August 19, 1960, and "one week later I was with the brigade in Guatemala." He quickly rose to become commander of the "black team," 150 men trained in guerrilla warfare, who then were to be divided into small groups of twelve to fifteen each and to be dropped into Cuba. Oliva was to be assigned his own group and jump into Pinar del Rio Province to establish a guerrilla base, but the plan subsequently evolved from a guerrilla operation into an invasion, and Oliva became the deputy commander.[15]

After joining RECE, Oliva continued to preach exile unity, or at least coordination among the many factions, and to favor conventional, as opposed to guerrilla, warfare. "With Oliva, the exile action groups take on a new dimension of thinking for how to get rid of Castro," said the *Miami Herald* profile. "His ideas clearly favor a large, well-trained exile force, presumably to be used in an invasion of the island, although he doesn't say it in so many words." A CIA intelligence cable reported that Pepin Bosch had told a source that RECE had the promise of "full military support . . . from a Latin American government for major command and guerrilla type operations against Cuba" if RECE could get a U.S. government pledge that it would not exert diplomatic pressure against the unnamed country for such support.[16]

Declassified documents indicate Oliva complained that U.S. government pressure was preventing Latin American governments from providing financial and logistical support to RECE. A July 6 memo from Chase to Bundy reported that "the Attorney General has not yet talked to Oliva for the purpose of cooling him off," apparently referring to Oliva's unhappiness with the obstacles Washington was putting in his way.[17]

Another Chase-to-Bundy memo the next day reported that "support for Oliva will be an agenda item at the next Special Group meeting. Peter Jessup [a National Security staffer] says that the meeting is on the AG's calendar but feels that a call from you may help ensure that the AG will attend." The same memo noted that Oliva had met with Bill Bowdler, an NSC staffer for Latin America, and "was interested in two things (a) our reaction to the question of . . . obtaining operating facilities outside of the U.S., and (b) our willingness to give assistance to Oliva." Bowdler also reported that "State will prepare a paper for the Special Group meeting which will bring the matter to a head; it will probably include discussion of possible methods we can use to turn down Oliva."[18] This was a clear indication that the Johnson administration viewed continuing U.S. support for exile activist groups such as those headed by Ray, Artime, and now Oliva as a policy of diminishing returns. And that Bobby Kennedy had lost his clout.

Oliva also made an effort to revive the link with Artime established in their January 1963 meeting with Bobby Kennedy at his Hickory Hill residence. According to a source identified as an "Artime confidant" in a CIA intelligence cable, the two met June 30 at Oliva's request. The source said that Oliva had told Artime he had recently spoken with Thomas Mann, the assistant secretary for inter-American affairs and expected to "receive support for his conventional warfare program." Artime told Oliva he had no problem with his conventional warfare plan and morally supported him, but Artime "would continue in his own 'little' way with his unconventional war." The "Artime confidant" reported that Jose Alegrett, the Nicaraguan vice consul in Miami, was "attempting to obtain a Nicaraguan base for Oliva."[19]

On August 6 Freyre and Oliva publicly presented RECE's first progress report since the mid-May formation of its so-called war board. In a follow-up cable to Washington, Summ observed that RECE "went out of way to imply" U.S. government approval. In response to a question about RECE's relationship with Washington, according to Summ's cable, Ernesto Freyre "replied that he had to maintain patriotic discretion in all military activities of this nature, but that he could say that RECE felt highly satisfied with all steps it had taken in Washington."

Of the three specific items announced at RECE's public presentation, as recorded in Summ's cable, the most significant was establishment of a Cuba Liberation Force under Oliva. It had been announced earlier that Bay of Pigs veterans Hugo Sueiro and Jose Morales Cruz were to become Oliva lieutenants. The liberation force would be open to other Cubans with military experience, whether it be with the U.S. Army and the Bay of Pigs, or in Cuba under either Castro or Batista. (Oliva formed a similar group, the Cuban-American Military Council (CAMCO), in the late 1990s, after his retirement as deputy commander of the Washington, D.C., National Guard.) The other two noteworthy announcements at the public presentation were the naming of a seventeen-member finance committee, headed by Pepin Bosch, to raise money for RECE, and a "human resources census" with a detailed questionnaire "oriented toward military/guerrilla background."

Summ concluded in his cable that "RECE activities to date unimpressive . . . other than improved fund-raising which may result from creation finance committee, no visible signs meaningful forward movement. Military plans hazy at best. Plan for census seems meaningless if as appears likely no definite plan in mind for utilization of resources. Year and a quarter after Bosch first broached idea of referendum, and after two months of its own existence, best RECE has to offer seems to be unwarranted implication that it enjoys USG [U.S. government] approval." Summ also reported that he had been told by a reliable source that Oliva joined RECE because "he could not remain in US Army because he saw no hope that plan for action to liberate Cuba, demanded by brigade members in Army, would be forthcoming. RECE offered hope that some kind of action plan would develop."[20]

By the end of August 1964 activist exile activities were still simmering but were hardly boiling. The only group that had done anything to fulfill the high hopes building since the beginning of the year and peaking in May, was Artime, with a single raid on the sugar mill in Cuba's Oriente Province. He added a long anticipated, but less substantial, hit-and-run attack on August 31 against a Soviet radar station at Cabo Cruz on Cuba's southeast coast. A wire service report from Panama quoted Artime as telling a press conference that it was a fifty-five-minute attack by raiders in two boats who had landed on a reef a mile away and walked to the radar station, which was manned by three Russians.[21] Artime's forces were to hit again two weeks later, this time in an attack that marked the beginning of the end for his Central American operation.

CHAPTER 13

LAST HURRAH

An early hint that something had gone terribly awry came in the Associated Press dispatch from Panama at 6:30 P.M., September 14, 1964. It quoted "a Cuban exile source" as saying that anti-Castro commandos had attacked a Cuban flag vessel the previous night in the Caribbean, then added ominously: "There was speculation . . . the commandos may have struck a Spanish freighter."[1]

Artime's MRR raiders, aboard two power launches, had been lying in wait off Cuba's northeast coast for the *Sierra Maestra*, one of Cuba's largest merchant ships. Suddenly, the night of September 13, they opened fire, thinking they had it in their sights. Instead of the *Sierra Maestra* departing Cuba laden with sugar, they hit the *Sierra Aranzazu*, a 270-foot Spanish freighter bound for Havana with a cargo of cork, cognac, textiles, toys, and garlic. The attack set off a series of explosions and fires aboard the ship, killing the captain, first mate, and chief engineer. Eight crewmen were injured.[2] The *Sierra Maestra* had passed through the Panama Canal the previous week, bound for China with ten thousand bags of sugar. "It was a mistake, a big mistake," said Rafael Quintero, Artime's deputy. "I talked to the crew that did the operation. They all saw *Sierra Maestra* and actually the *Sierra Maestra* was supposed to be around that area. . . . It was at night, and people were anxious to see what they wanted to see. They saw the people with the berets."[3]

The incident set off an even bigger diplomatic explosion in Washington, one that dragged on for months, forcing Artime to suspend activity until after the November presidential elections in the United States. By this time, too, Artime's group was really the only force Washington had left in terms of serious covert action against Cuba. Ray's operation had proven to be more illusory than real, and RECE was still struggling to find financing and other support. Even so, it was only a matter of time before Artime's U.S. funding would be curtailed. The cutoff was delayed long enough, however, for Artime's troops to be further tainted by the public eruption of several scandals related to the Central American camps, and for the CIA secretly to establish contact between Rolando Cubela—a longtime, but temperamental, star "asset" inside Cuba—and Artime's group. This was a busy and controversial six months.

In the midst of the frenzy, Oliva and Ernesto Freyre toured Central America in an ongoing effort to drum up support for RECE, the only other exile group still considered to have some sympathy and possible potential. An intelligence cable, with information attributed to a "Cuban exile who has high-level political contacts in Central America," reported that the two RECE officials had visited Panama, Nicaragua, and Costa Rica in early October. In Panama they reportedly asked President Marco Robles for "airstrips for jet training," but Robles put them off. In Nicaragua an interview was arranged with Luis Somoza but there was no indication that support was forthcoming. The cable advised that they had also met with Artime's personal secretary but Artime himself was unavailable. And in Costa Rica "they saw no one with any authority."[4]

Washington had, in any event, bigger problems to confront. The attack on the *Sierra Aranzazu* immediately put the bureaucrats in damage control mode. Castro and, more importantly, the Spaniards were angry. Costa Rica and Nicaragua were nervous. The Soviets were annoyed. Even the Dominicans became entangled with the problem, as the Spaniards suspected the raid was launched from Dominican territory. Within hours after the attack became known, amid speculation that Cuban exiles were involved, White House aide Gordon Chase sent a memo to his boss, McGeorge Bundy, the president's national security assistant. "It seems clear . . . Cuban exiles attacked the Spanish ship. . . . This is not a deep dark secret, although it will probably be tough for anybody to prove," said Chase. He added that the State Department's "press position will probably be a factual accounting indicating our helpfulness in the search and rescue operation and the fact that we really don't know the full story on exactly who made the attack. Naturally we deplore this sort of attack on the high seas."[5]

Others quickly got into the act, among them Cubans on both sides of the Florida Straits. The Secret Continental Anti-Communist Organization (OSAAA), a previously unknown exile group, surfaced for the first—and last—time to claim responsibility for the raid, promising that all ships trading with Cuba, no matter which flag they were under, would be subject to attack. Artime's MRR said it was not involved and that accusations against it were an attempt to discredit the organization. Comandos L, another activist exile group that had attacked a British freighter in 1962 and a Russian freighter in 1963, said it "didn't exclude the possibility" of carrying out similar actions in the future "for the cause of Cuban Liberation." Manolo Ray suggested Castro might have engineered the attack to discredit his foes. Secretary of State Dean Rusk, responding to Spanish protests and Cuban accusations, said the "mystery" raiders did not come from the United States. Spain said it considered the United States morally responsible. Castro, not unexpectedly, charged that the attackers were Cuban counterrevolutionaries "equipped, paid and directed by the Central Intelligence Agency."[6]

Simultaneously with the *Sierra Aranzazu* incident, Gen. Anastasio "Tacho" Somoza, Nicaragua's strongman as head of the country's National Guard and sole military force, was scheduled to be at Baltimore's Friendship Airport as part of a trip to the United States. His old friend, Col. J. C. King, still head of the CIA's Western Hemisphere Division, arranged to meet him at the airport. A two-page script regarding Artime was prepared for King's conversation with Somoza. The script started with the admission "that we have reason to believe that Artime may have been involved in the shocking business of the Spanish ship." It expressed concern that Artime's involvement would become public and "a serious embarrassment" for Nicaragua, but the United States would understand if Somoza decided to close Artime's bases there. It cautioned Somoza not to tell Artime about "our conversation" because his reaction "could be seriously disadvantageous to us and to Nicaragua." If Somoza were to ask about further U.S. support for Artime, King's reply would be "if we were giving support to Artime," King would be "personally sure that we would seriously consider terminating it, if Artime's involvement in the Spanish ship incident became public." The suggested script concluded by saying "the above approach to Somoza and our own approach to Artime are based on three factors: 1) we want to do what we can to avoid public involvement of Artime with the Spanish ship incident; 2) we intend at an appropriate time to dissolve our relationship with Artime; but 3) we do not want to precipitate any messy situation with him in the next few weeks."[7] Among other considerations, U.S. presidential elections were only weeks away.

In October the Soviets expressed their concern. Llewellyn Thompson, the State Department's ambassador-at-large, circulated a memo on October 6 advising that Soviet ambassador Anatoly Dobrynin had come "to talk to me entirely on a personal basis about Cuba." More specifically, he wanted to talk about the raids and the "training of emigrant groups in Central America and elsewhere, and some rumors that some Central American countries might take some forceful action before the end of the year. In the course of the conversation, he mentioned the Artime group and another exile leader whose name he thought was Olivo [sic]." Thompson responded that the United States opposed hit-and-run raids and noted "how embarrassing it was to us that a Spanish ship had been attacked." Thompson also said he "had not heard the rumor of a Central American supported action and did not think it to be true." Dobrynin said he didn't see how a Spanish ship could be attacked with all the air and sea power the United States had in the area. Thompson "pointed out that we could scarcely get into position of escorting ships to Cuba in view of our overall policy." Dobrynin then said the Soviet Union had been "relatively quiet about the activities directed against Cuba" because it didn't want to "inject the issue into the American political campaign."[8]

The Dominicans were the next to complain. A cable from U.S. Ambassador William Tapley Bennett in Santo Domingo said the country's top officials had told him "they have recently had a very hard-nosed approach from the Spanish Ambassador, who gave it to them hot and heavy with respect Sept 13 attack on Spanish vessel 'Sierra Aranzazu' and possibility attackers may have been based on Dom territory." Bennett said the Dominican government had asked for the most complete report possible on the incident to help them in replying to the Spaniards. In conclusion Bennett said he was in favor of providing them information "as Department believes appropriate. Aside from being cooperative with a friendly govt., it could be useful in opening Dominican eyes to type of problems they may run into through involvement in Cuban adventurism and might encourage them to take more sober attitude with respect activities Cuban exiles in Dom. territory."[9]

John Crimmins, the coordinator for Cuban affairs, was about to finish an "investigation" of the *Sierra Aranzazu* incident and said the Spaniards had asked for an evaluation of the various reports that had been furnished them. Gordon Chase, in a November 10 memo to Bundy, noted that the "general pitch he [Crimmins] will probably use is to take into account such facts as (a) that we want to give the Spanish the minimum necessary to keep them from thinking that we are trying to deceive them and (b) that the Spanish, themselves, probably evaluate Artime as the prime suspect." Among the points Chase said Crimmins might make to the Spaniards were: it couldn't be ruled out that the Cubans themselves did it, but it was more probably the exiles; there are a number of exile groups that have the capability; the most likely suspect is Artime; and (if pressed) by a process of elimination, the attack seems to have come from the Dominican Republic.[10]

On November 21 Crimmins circulated a memo on the investigation into the *Sierra Aranzazu* affair. "The weight of the evidence has inevitably (but not conclusively) fallen on Artime's MRR," Crimmins wrote, in the heavily censored declassified document. He cited six specific conclusions, which he recommended be passed on to the Spaniards in an informal, secret memorandum. They were:

1. Because conclusive proof is lacking, we cannot completely eliminate the hypothesis that the attack was made by the Cuban Government, either through error or as a provocation.
2. We are almost certain, however, that the attack was carried out by a Cuban exile group.
3. We estimate that several exile groups probably had, alone or in combination, a technical and organizational capability to carry out such an attack.
4. These include the Artime group (the MRR), the Menoyo group (SNFE-Alpha 66-MRP), the Ray group (the JURE), and the student group (DRE).
5. Of these groups, we estimate that the most probable suspect is the MRR, but we have not been able to establish this firmly.
6. We are certain that US territory was in no way involved in the attack.[11]

As his rationale for thinking the MRR was the most likely suspect, Crimmins said "the trend of the reporting [FBI and CIA] is certainly in that direction. So far as we can determine, the MRR has the best—although not the only—capability. The MRR had been more active than the other possibilities in recent months [Pilon, Cabo Cruz]. There were strong rumors immediately after the attack that the MRR was going to make an announcement, a sequence which was in the pattern of the Pilon and Cabo Cruz incidents."[12]

Two developments about this time provided a much welcome distraction from the *Sierra Aranzazu*, but created new problems of their own. For Artime the positive development, one that would give him a reprieve, was buried in a November 5 memorandum from the CIA to the 303 Committee on the future of his operation. The memo alerted the high-level White House group that Artime had established a "potentially significant" contact the previous month with Rolando Cubela's dissident group inside Cuba. As a result, the agency suggested a delay on any decision to cut off Artime's support "until we have the opportunity to evaluate potential of the internal group."[13]

The more immediate, more negative, and much more visible problem for Artime was the rash of news stories beginning to appear about the same time, primarily in the *Miami Herald*, focusing on scandals in his Central America camps. "Exiles Target of Probe by Costa Rica," proclaimed a November 21, 1964, page-one headline. Datelined San Jose, Costa Rica, the story reported: "President Francisco Orlich had confirmed authorities began an extensive probe after discovery of about $50,000 worth of contraband whisky [sic]. According to reports here and in neighboring Panama, Cuban exiles associated with the anti-Castro organization called Revolutionary Recovery Movement (MRR) are linked with the whisky and possibly other contraband shipments filtering into the country." Artime, who had just returned to Miami from Costa Rica when the story appeared, issued a statement denying "any smuggling activities have been carried out by any member of the Movement for Revolutionary Recovery. It is an attempt by the Communists to smear me."

Unfortunately for Artime, the *Herald* article was only the beginning. Continuing news coverage not only focused on alleged scandals but also tore away the thin veneer of secrecy that still surrounded the training camps in Costa Rica. Another story reported, "no other exile organization is so well financed and so well equipped as Artime's. His forces, sporting a four-ship navy and free movement in Central America, have had commando capability for approximately one year. Their score: destruction of one sugar warehouse containing 70,000 sacks of sugar May 13 and an attack, extent of damage unconfirmed, on a radar station August 30."[14] That was followed by a headline proclaiming "MRR Says Exile Shot at Camp," over a story which said Artime's MRR acknowledged that a "missing Cuban refugee father of two was shot to death" in one of its Central American training camps. "The strange death of Roberto Trujillo Rodriguez, kept secret four months, is being investigated to determine whether the shooting was an accident or a criminal act, MRR officials said."[15]

The almost daily drumbeat of doom kept up for the rest of December. "Costa Rican Boots Anti-Fidel Camps," declared a December 5 headline. The story began: "President Francisco J. Orlich has ordered the elimination of military training camps—including any manned by Cuban exiles—in the northeastern area of Costa Rica. The order did not specify Cuban exile camps, but was a blanket instruction to dismantle all such camps discovered by security police."[16] The order appeared to be more bark than bite, a move responding to the politically embarrassing contraband scandal that erupted a few weeks earlier. It was clear that the camps were being used as a cover for smuggling, but no solid evidence ever emerged linking the MRR to the contraband. And the airstrip the Artime organization used was on property owned by President Orlich's brother. "We were both using the same strip," said Quintero. "We were using it for our program and he was using it for his own program."[17] Nor did the camps shut down following Orlich's order. They did not close for another three months, and then only because of a cutoff of U.S. financing. Still, the stories continued. A five-part series written by Al Burt of the *Miami Herald* in mid-December contained great detail about the camps' origins and operations. Most of the information was close to the mark, although off on some specific details, such as Bobby Kennedy's key role.[18] Coupled with the sinking of the *Sierra Aranzazu*, the negative publicity generated by the Artime operation at the end of 1964 most likely would have prompted Washington to suspend funding much earlier than it finally did had it not been for AMLASH, the CIA's code name for the Cubela caper.

The Revolutionary Student Directorate (DRE) of which Cubela was the second-ranking leader, and Castro's 26th of July Movement had been rivals in the guerrilla campaign against Batista. Cubela had become close to Castro since the triumph of the revolution and at the time of the Artime contact he was the only serious prospect the CIA had to ignite a coup attempt. The agency made its first contact with the temperamental Cubela when he visited Mexico City in March 1961 for a leftist-sponsored Latin America Conference on National Sovereignty, Emancipation, and Peace. A longtime friend of Cubela's had arranged a meeting for him with an officer in the Mexico City CIA station to sound out his views on the situation in Cuba. The meeting was inconclusive but led to other meetings out of which grew operation AMLASH. Intermittent contact was maintained from early 1961 until September 1963, with little of substance emerging other than talk of Cubela's defection. Several meetings were held in Helsinki during midsummer 1962 as Cubela attended a conference in Finland. There "the original objective of defecting Cubela was quickly changed to recruiting him in place." An agent's report of the first meeting in Helsinki read, "Cubela stated many times during the course of this and subsequent meetings that he was only interested in involving himself in a plan of significant action, and which was truly designed to achieve rapidly his desire to help Cuba."[19]

Nestor Sanchez became Cubela's CIA case officer in 1963, just as Artime's autonomous operation was getting organized. According to Sanchez, Desmond FitzGerald, in charge of the agency's Special Affairs Staff, had divided Cuba responsibility between "internal" and "external" operations. Sanchez was put in charge of the internal, which meant developing activities inside Cuba, "essentially Cubela." Henry Heckscher had the external side, "essentially Artime." The agency, said Sanchez, was not allowed to make any "tactical decisions," only provide financing. "Bobby Kennedy was running everybody he could get his hands on," remembered Sanchez. "It was damned messy. The Kennedys didn't trust anybody, especially the CIA and the Pentagon. The Kennedys thought anything the agency was associated with smelled."[20]

By the time Sanchez became Cubela's case officer AMLASH was getting more attention. Using an assumed name, Sanchez first met Cubela in September 1963 at the Pan American Games in Porto Alegre, Brazil. Another meeting took place the next month in Paris. Cubela insisted upon "meeting with a senior U.S. official, preferably Robert F. Kennedy, for assurance of U.S. moral support for any activity Cubela undertook in Cuba." FitzGerald had a planned October 29 visit to Paris for other business and agreed to meet with Cubela "as personal representative of Robert F. Kennedy," although nobody told Kennedy about the meeting.[21]

Helms, FitzGerald's boss as the head of clandestine services, speculated before the Church Committee that the reason they had not consulted the attorney general was because "this was so central to the whole theme of what we had been trying to do . . . [find someone inside Cuba who might head a government and have a group to replace Castro]. This is obviously what we had been pushing, what everybody had been pushing for us to try to do, and it is in that context that I would have made some remark like this." Helms said he told FitzGerald to "go ahead and say that from the standpoint of political support, the United States government will be behind you if you are successful. This had nothing to do with killings. This had only to do with the political action part of it."[22]

FitzGerald, using an alias, met with Cubela in Paris on October 29. Sanchez acted as interpreter. In a memorandum for the record of the meeting, FitzGerald said he told Cubela that the United States would help "any anti-Communist Cuban group which succeeds in neutralizing the present Cuban leadership and assumes sufficient control" to request U.S.

assistance. Added comment in the CIA inspector general's report on assassination plots and attributed to those involved, but not part of the written record, said Cubela "spoke repeatedly of the need for an assassination weapon," specifically a "high-powered rifle with a telescopic sight . . . that could be used to kill Castro from a distance." FitzGerald responded that the "U.S. simply does not do such things." Cubela persisted, through intermediaries, in his demand for the high-powered rifle, but finally said he would settle for some other "technical means of doing the job that would not automatically cause him to lose his own life." That's when the poison pen device was concocted, using Black Leaf 40, a nicotine sulphate, a "deadly poison that can be administered orally, by injection or by absorption through the skin." Sanchez returned to Paris on November 22 to deliver the pen/syringe device to Cubela and tell him how it worked.[23] In testimony before the Church Committee, Sanchez said Cubela "did not think much of the device," but Sanchez could not remember whether he took it with him or threw it away. There was conflicting testimony on whether the device was to be used in an assassination attempt against Castro or for Cubela's own protection.[24] Sanchez also described for the committee the context in which Cubela raised the topic of assassination: "You also must recognize that AM/LASH was a rather temperamental man whose temperament was of a mercurial nature and whereas he may have said something like this [assassination] in one fit of pique, he would settle down and talk about organizing a regular military coup in the next breath."[25]

In March and June 1964 the JMWAVE station in Miami dispatched two separate arms caches to Cuba for Cubela as part of the ongoing AMTRUNK operation, which was targeted at military officials. In May Cubela let it be known he wanted a silencer for a Belgian FAL submachine gun as soon as possible. But it first had to be modified and there wasn't time to do it for the June cache. Cubela was subsequently notified that it was not feasible to make a silencer for a FAL. By late 1964 Cubela was increasingly insistent that assassination was a necessary first step in a coup. In a memorandum, Sanchez suggested Cubela be put in touch with Artime. The memo said: "AM/LASH was told and fully understands that the United States Government cannot become involved to any degree in the 'first step' of his plan. If he needs support, he realizes he will have to get it elsewhere. FYI: This is where B-1 [Artime] could fit in nicely in giving any support he would request."[26]

The CIA's seven-page November 5 memo to the 303 Committee is essentially a review of the Artime operation until that time and the agency recommendations for the operation, concluding with the recommendation to continue it in conjunction with Cubela. Following the *Sierra Aranzazu* incident, Artime suspended operations until after President Johnson's victory in the November presidential election. Despite news reports to the contrary, the agency said Artime had "maintained close contact and good relations" with top officials in both Nicaragua and Costa Rica, "where he continues to receive their complete cooperation and support." Enrique Peralta, Guatemala's military president, had invited him to a meeting. "President Robles of Panama has promised Artime his full cooperation and any support he may need," and "President Reid of the Dominican Republic provided Artime a forward operating base in his country. Artime is in the process of surveying the base site." The memo then got to the crux of the matter.

"As a result of the publicity Artime received over the past year for his anti-Castro activity and the fact that at present he is considered the strongest of the active Cuban exile groups, an internal dissident group established contact with him and proposed joining forces," the CIA reported. "An emissary from the internal dissident group met with one of Artime's representatives in Europe in early October 1964 and proposed a 'summit' meeting between Artime and their 'top guy' as soon as the latter can travel to Europe, probably between 15 and 30 November 1964."

The CIA memo reported that Artime and his aides had come to the conclusion that the internal dissidents included at least a half-dozen prominent revolutionary figures, among them Efigenio Ameijeiras, Juan Almeida, and Faustino Perez, all of whom were with Castro aboard the *Granma* when it sailed from Mexico to Cuba in late 1956 to begin the guerrilla campaign against Batista. "Reports from independent sources confirm the discontent of this particular group," the memo reported. "In late 1963 an Agency representative had several meetings with a Cuban officer [Cubela] closely associated with this group who reported their anti-regime feelings and plans for a coup against Castro with the support of this group. It is known that the emissary who established contact with Artime's representative is a confidant of this officer."[27]

In urging continued support for Artime in light of the Cubela connection, the CIA argued:

Whereas the incident of the *Sierra Aranzazu* raised serious doubts about the desirability of continued support to Artime, the contact of Artime by a potentially significant internal dissident group introduces an entirely new dimension to the problem. It is believed that within sixty to ninety days a reasonable evaluation of the potential and plans of the internal group can be made. Therefore, it appears desirable to defer any final decision on support (if any) to Artime until we have the opportunity to evaluate the potential of the internal group. It is assumed that the internal group established contact with Artime because of their belief that his paramilitary capability is based on close relations with the United States. Hence, if Artime is to maintain his attractiveness and continue developing this contact, it is necessary for Artime to maintain a good façade in terms of his paramilitary capability. While we feel it is desirable to give Artime every opportunity to develop an operation with the internal group, we believe the groundwork should be laid for a phase out of support to the paramilitary aspect of the program. Artime will be unhappy with any decision to terminate support regardless of how such a decision is implemented, but we believe a negotiated phase out dovetailed with support to develop the internal operation will reduce the number of problems and best protect the deniability of United States complicity in the operation, provided Artime cooperates.

It recommended:

a. Artime concentrate on developing the internal operation, maintaining his paramilitary posture to the degree necessary to preserve his attractiveness to the internal group.

b. Support to Artime at approximately the present level be continued for the next sixty to ninety days in order to give Artime an opportunity to develop an operation with the dissident internal group which has sought him out.

c. Should it be considered vital in order to maintain his attractiveness to the internal group and hold his own group together, permit Artime to conduct one raid and plan but not execute at least one more during this period.

The November 5 memo gave no indication how contact between Artime and Cubela might have been contrived to put them together "in such a way that neither of them knew that the contact had been made by the CIA." There also is a discrepancy as to when the initial contact with the Artime group was made. The Church Committee report said "documents in the AM/LASH file establish that in early 1965, the CIA put AM/LASH in contact with B-1 [Artime], the leader of an anti-Castro group."

The November 5 memo said the contact was made in October 1964. A chronology in the CIA inspector general's 1967 report on assassination plots, said that Artime "received information through Madrid" on August 30, 1964, "that a group of dissident members of the Castro regime desired to establish direct contact" with him. On October 7, 1964, "an Artime associate [Quintero] went to France for a meeting with an intermediary from the dissident group."

Then, on November 13, the CIA chronology cites a contact report of a meeting in Washington with Artime: "Artime agreed to talk to AMLASH-1 [Cubela] if it turns out that he is the contact man for the dissident group. Artime thinks that if AMLASH-1 is the chief of the dissident group we can all forget about the operation." Three weeks later, on December 4, a request was prepared "for $6,500 as an extraordinary budget expenditure for the travel of Artime for maintaining contact with the internal dissident group's representative in Europe during November and December 1964. There is no direct indication in the file that the request was approved, but indirect evidence indicates that it was. Artime did travel to Europe and maintained the contacts."

Sanchez, the CIA's AMLASH case officer, met Cubela again in Paris on December 6–7. On December 10 he reported in a memo: "Artime does not know and we do not plan to tell him that we are in direct contact with Cubela [one and one-half lines censored; presumably referring to assassination/coup plot]. . . . Cubela was told and fully understands that U.S. Government cannot become involved to any degree in the 'first step' of his plan. If he needs support, he realizes he will have to get it elsewhere. FYI: This is where Artime could fit in nicely in giving any support Cubela would request." A parenthetical note follows with comment from the investigators, which says: "Sanchez explained to us that what had happened was that SAS [CIA's Special Affairs Staff] contrived to put Artime and Cubela together in such a way that neither knew that the contact had been engineered by CIA. The thought was that Artime needed a man inside and Cubela wanted a silenced weapon, which CIA was unwilling to furnish to him directly. By putting the two together, Artime might get his man inside and Cubela might get his silenced weapon—from Artime. CIA did not intend to furnish an assassination weapon for Artime, and did not do so."[28]

Washington obviously considered an internal coup the last-best hope it had of unseating Castro; so much so that by year's end representatives of the CIA, Defense, and State had prepared "A Contingency Plan for a

Coup in Cuba" and what the U.S. response would be. They sent it to the Joint Chiefs of Staff. A December 30, 1964, cover letter signed by Cyrus Vance noted, "Bundy has been advised . . . and requested to inform the President of the existence of the plan on a suitable occasion." As foreseen in the plan, the U.S. response would vary depending on whether it had "up to forty-eight hours" advance notice of the coup. If so, it would then send in a "special team" to make a decision on whether to provide support; otherwise "a longer time would be required." The plan laid out the criteria that had to be met for U.S. support:

(1) Have some power base in the Cuban army or militia in order to survive.

(2) Be prepared to establish a provisional government, however rudimentary, with some sort of public claim to political viability to provide an adequate political basis for covert U.S. action (not required if Soviet troops were clearly fighting Cuban patriots).

(3) Neutralize the top echelon of Cuban leadership.

(4) Seize and hold significant piece of territory, preferably including Havana, long enough to permit the United States plausibly to extend support and some form of recognition to the provisional government.

The contingency plan emphasized, "The US does not contemplate either a premeditated full scale invasion of Cuba (except in the case of Soviet intervention or the reintroduction of offensive weapons) or the contrivance of a provocation which could be used as a pretext for such action."[29]

Quintero, the MRR representative who made the initial contact with the internal dissidents and was the first to meet with Cubela, said the link began with Alberto Blanco, one of the dissidents on the Cuban embassy staff in Madrid. Quintero said he went to Mallorca to talk with a ship captain about hijacking a passenger liner as Portuguese rebels had done three years earlier with the *Santa Maria* off the coast of Brazil. When he got back to Madrid from Mallorca, "Cuco" Leon, a former Cuban legislator who was friendly with Somoza, told him "there's a bigger thing here than that . . . a big comandante in Cuba, they're planning a plot against Cuba." The hijacking plan was canceled "in order not to get any kind of publicity that could hurt the operation with Cubela." The August 30 meeting with Blanco was arranged for Paris, beginning the MRR relationship with the Cubela dissidents.

Quintero said he had a second meeting in December in Rome with Cubela himself to "finalize the military plan." Artime held his first meeting with Cubela in Madrid on December 27, 1964. Cubela and Artime met a second time in Madrid on December 30, 1964. That, said Quintero, is "when everything was set up. All this was told to our CIA contacts in our monthly meeting; all that we were doing, because even if we didn't have to get approval, we were supposed to tell them what we were doing because we were spending money and they wanted to know what we were doing with it." One reason they decided to go ahead with Cubela, said Quintero, was that the MRR objective was the overthrow of Castro "and we knew at a given moment that the commando operations, infiltration and maritime operations were not going to overthrow the government. So we have to go for the king, and basically the king here was the elimination of Castro. That's when we came up with the Cubela operation."[30]

The CIA chronology records both December meetings between Artime and Cubela. At the second meeting "Cubela told Artime that he had requested a silencer for a FAL rifle from the Americans, which they had not been able to provide. Artime agreed to furnish either a silencer for a FAL or a comparable rifle with silencer. If Artime obtained a silencer for a FAL, Cubela would personally carry it back to Cuba with him. If Artime had to settle for some other type of silenced rifle, he would cache it in Cuba for Cubela."[31] Quintero said the MRR provided the silencer by making it themselves and then sending it to Europe for Cubela to retrieve.[32]

According to Quintero, the plot finally agreed on was a combined assassination-coup attempt at Varadero, the beach resort on Cuba's north coast, where the annual 26th of July ceremonies were scheduled in 1965. "All the Cabinet was going to be there, and Fidel. That's how the idea came up. Fidel was going to make his speech. At the time he was giving his speech, Cubela was supposed to kill him with the rifle." Artime and several dozen of his commandos would land simultaneously, cutting off the road and taking the Cabinet ministers hostage. "We were supposed to take over Varadero and the whole thing would start there and then the people from the Central Army Command could rise up against the government," said Quintero. Artime even had an inventor friend in Miami "building some small helicopters that were to be used in the operation," according to Quintero.

Varadero was the key location for two reasons: It had only one road to and from the mainland that could be taken over by a few people and

Calixto Garcia, commander of Cuba's Central Army, which included Varadero, was said to be a member of the internal dissident group. "Calixto
Garcia was for us the most important guy in this whole group because he
had command of troops," said Quintero. "And that's when the idea of the
Varadero operation came up because he was in Matanzas and in charge of
Varadero, so he could support us in this coup d'etat or whatever you want
to call it." An element of the plot involved the infiltration of Quintero
into Cuba before it was executed. "He [Cubela] was going to kill Castro
but the condition he made was that somebody from outside had to be
with him. Artime said I was going to be the person. Then we got him the
silencer." Tentative details of the plot and the composition of a provisional government were worked out at the December 30 meeting in
Madrid between Artime and Cubela. "As a matter of fact, when they had
this meeting all the names came up to the table. They talked about making some kind of government and there were three persons. Along with
Cubela, the other ones were going to be Artime and the other person
would have to come from one of the names on the table," said Quintero.[33]

A January 6, 1965, CIA memorandum to the 303 Committee, recorded
the following account of the December 30 meeting between Artime and
Cubela:

> During a six-hour meeting, Cubela stated that three groups are involved in
> a coup against Fidel Castro and plan to use troops to seize power. The
> three groups are: One from the Directorio Revolutionario (DR), led by
> Cubela himself; one from the 26 July Movement led by Efigenio Ameijeiras
> Delgado, Vice-Minister of the Armed Forces for Special Affairs; and
> another separate 26th of July Movement group headed by Cmdte. Guil-
> lermo Garcia Frias, Commander of the Western Army. (The Western
> Army, whose area includes Havana, has approximately half the active
> strength of the entire Cuban Army.) The loyalty of this army to Garcia is
> not presently known. . . .
>
> Artime and Cubela reached tentative agreement on cooperation in the
> execution of a coup against the top leadership of the Castro regime and
> the creation of a junta to replace Fidel Castro. Cubela stated he would not
> oppose Artime as president of the junta. In addition, Artime's group . . .
> would be allowed two other representatives in the junta, provided Artime's
> selections were made from prisoners presently interned on the Isle of
> Pines. The dissident group would be given representation in the junta
> equal to Artime's. The major role to be allotted to the MRR in the junta is
> due to the dissidents' belief that Artime and the MRR are favorably

regarded by the United States; by according them a major role the dissidents, even though tarnished by collaboration with Castro, hope to gain United States support. . . .

One of the points emphasized by Cubela was the need for more frequent commando raids in order to raise the morale and spirit of resistance of the people inside Cuba. He expressed the view that these raids reassure the people inside Cuba that active resistance to Castro continues. . . . Artime and Cubela made arrangements to meet once again at the end of January, before Cubela returns to Havana, in order to work out final details, including timing. . . .

Despite the rather optimistic view of the above reported discussions, we cannot forecast the chances of success since the operation is primarily dependent upon the resoluteness of a few key officers and the loyalty of their officers and men at the critical time.

The January 6 CIA memo again argued for continued support of Artime, citing as reasons:

While the operation has been relatively secure as long as our subsidies allowed Artime to keep full control of his group, it is doubtful the same degree of security can be maintained once subsidies are terminated. All agencies should be prepared, therefore, for a number of security breaches involving press stories regarding covert United States support to the MRR. . . .

The internal dissidents appear to count heavily on Artime's involvement with them as a guarantee of United States benevolence once they seize power. If publicity is given to the discontinuance of our covert relationship with Artime, it is possible that the dissidents will drop, or at least delay, their plans to upset the Castro regime. . . .

There are a number of technical problems involved in terminating the Artime relationship. Many of these have to do with contractual obligations which will continue after the termination and which CIA will have to continue to meet for a limited period of time. Sufficient funds are available to handle these problems.

The memo concluded by recommending that Artime's funding be continued until the end of February 1965, nearly two more months.[34]

The CIA's relationship with Artime remained a rocky one, however. The memo had begun by citing his "reluctantly acquiescing" to a request to cancel a commando raid in early December. Later in the month, while

Artime was in Europe "Quintero was strongly admonished not to attempt such a raid." He was told, however, there was "no objection to carrying out the intelligence infiltration operation which Artime told his men was of primary importance." Quintero continued to hedge on the commando raid, saying he had "firm orders from Artime to carry it out," even though they both were "well aware that failure to heed our admonition would wholly jeopardize their support by the United States Government." Artime returned from Europe on December 31, 1964, apparently ordering the raid to go ahead, but first told the mother ship and two Swift boats to put into the Dominican Republic for repairs. An intercepted message indicated the repairs had been carried out at sea and the raid against Casilda, on Cuba's south coast near Trinidad, would be carried out the night of January 5, 1965.[35]

Two memos from Chase to Bundy on January 5 indicate White House displeasure with Artime. The terse first message read, "The Artime raid scheduled for tonight has been called off because of weather." Bundy had scrawled at the bottom: "Bet 5–1 it never goes, McB." Chase's handwritten response said, "You're on, and John Crimmins says he wants a piece of the action. (The next attempt, by the way, is scheduled for tonight.)"[36] The second memo reported "the weather was bad on New Year's Eve, Artime had mechanical difficulties, and raid scheduled for that night did not materialize. However, Artime intends to pull off his attack tonight despite our strong expressions of disapproval." It added that Artime "apparently feels that an attack is mandatory to maintain the morale of his people and to maintain the confidence of a dissident group inside Cuba."[37]

There is little indication of any activity by Artime's group during the rest of January, although the capture of Menoyo in Cuba raised concerns in the White House. "John Crimmins commented that this is a bad thing," said Chase in a memo to Bundy. "It will be a big blow to anti-Castro morale in Cuba. . . . It shows how efficient the Cuban Government is. Menoyo is an old experienced guerrilla fighter who, in the past, has impressed John with his intelligence, security and carefulness."[38] On February 2 a cable arrived in CIA headquarters from Paris. Although the name is blacked out, it presumably came from Sanchez, Cubela's case officer, and reported that "Cubela and [name blacked out] returned Paris January 31. Met 1 February. Cubela states full agreement reached with Artime and he well satisfied with arrangements which he outlined for our information (along same lines as reported by Artime). . . . Artime providing package in Madrid which Cubela plans carry back in personal luggage." The package apparently referred to the silencer sent to Cubela. Another message on February 11, said "Cubela is to receive one pistol with silencer and one Belgian FAL with silencer from Artime's secretary. Both weapons come from U.S. and now in Madrid." And this on February 12: "Artime reported on final meeting with Cubela: Artime had three packages of special items made up by his technical people and delivered to Cubela in Madrid. Cubela seemed satisfied."[39]

Washington became even more irritated with the Artime operation in early February. A Chase-to-Bundy memo reported the MRR, with Artime in Europe, had called off a plan to go into Cuba, seize a couple of hostages, and hold them as an exchange for Menoyo. But the group went ahead with an effort to bring out some of its own people, which ended in disaster. "The exfiltration effort failed," Chase reported. Two agents were captured and the boats involved "were sighted and chased vigorously by Cuban air and sea forces. Only an inordinate amount of luck allowed the boats to escape to Nicaragua." Chase suggested the likely implications of the episode. "First, the two captured agents will undoubtedly spill their guts. Needless to say, we will, of course, deny any implication. Second, the conduct of the operation may have been conducted from a Miami radio station in spite of our policy statements to the effect that no U.S. territories would be used in the conduct of such raids. We are still checking this one out. Third, State has just about had it with the Artime group and seems to be leaning in favor of an immediate cut-off of ties with Artime. Of possible bearing on this decision will be the outcome of the Artime/internal dissident talks which took place recently."[40]

State had indeed "had it" with Artime and his operation. And with Lyndon Johnson in the White House there was no longer need to worry about whether Bobby Kennedy disagreed. In a stiff February 23 memo to the "Members of the 303 Committee," the department "strongly" recommended a three-point course of action:

1. Artime will be notified without delay that, in conformity with previous statements made to him, US support for his group will be terminated as of February 28, with phasing out of US assistance to be carried out as quickly as possible.
2. Artime will be notified immediately, with respect to his dealings with Cubela concerning the "internal operation," that (a) it is our firm estimate that under present circumstances such an operation is impractical,

    unrealistic and almost certain to fail; (b) we cannot be certain that the participation by internal Cuban elements is not a provocation and a trap; and (c) in any case, we want it clearly understood that we cannot and will not make any commitments in advance concerning US support for such an operation.

3. Through both diplomatic and Agency channels, the Nicaragua, Costa Rican and Dominican Governments will be informed discreetly, but clearly, that (a) we are in no way supporting Artime; (b) he is on his own; (c) any arrangements made with, or facilities provided to, Artime by the Governments concerned are strictly between them and him; and (d) we would understand and would have no objection if the Governments concerned were to refuse assistance to him or withdraw present assistance from him.[41]

Much as a pesky gnat that won't go away, the question of how to deal with the RECE exile group popped up again during the increasingly intense debate over the future of the Artime operation. Whether to provide U.S. funding for RECE had been a subject of ongoing discussion. John Crimmins, the coordinator of Cuban affairs, had requested input from his colleagues, among them Gordon Chase. Chase responded that, "basically, I do not think that the Cuban exiles have much to offer the U.S. by way of significantly helping us to solve our Cuban problems. This factor," said Chase, "coupled with the long history of highly troublesome, relatively unfruitful U.S./exile relations, leads me to the conclusion that the burden of proof rests, in very great measure, on those who argue in favor of starting a program of support (large or small) for RECE." Starting a program for RECE, observed Chase, "at a minimum will cost us some money and time and which, at a maximum, will cause us a Pandora's Box-full of typical exile problems." He concluded by noting "there are questions regarding the desirability of using RECE even *if* things hot up and even *if* we want to step up the pressure on Cuba: What will RECE be able to do in the crunch that we will not be able to do better? Can they make better propaganda? Conduct more effective covert operations?"[42]

From here, the record of events becomes murkier. What is clear, however, is that abrupt termination of the Artime operation called for by the State Department was not approved as recommended. Most, if not all, U.S. funding was cut off, but apparently not as of February 28. Newspaper accounts, reinforced by Quintero's recollections that they received a one-month notice, indicate the camps began to shut down by mid-March.

The Artime-Cubela operation continued for several more months with the MRR's cash on hand, said Quintero. The one declassified record available dealing with the subject is a heavily censored March 4, 1965, memo from Chase to Bundy in advance of that day's Special Group meeting. Regarding the Artime operation, Chase noted, "State is pressing to cut off Artime, largely because of his irresponsible activity. [About two lines blocked out.] . . . Vance may express the view that a cutoff will drive Artime up the wall and that he will go off and do something that could cause us real trouble vis-à-vis our present conflict with the East. For example, he might go off and sink a Soviet ship. [About two lines blocked out, presumably Vance's proposal.] . . . The advantage of this would be twofold—First, it would keep Artime quiet; second, his residual power to hurt us, when we finally do cut him off, will be reduced." There is no clue to what Vance might have proposed, but it could have been a more gradual phase-out of support and a continuation of the Cubela plot.[43]

The recurring question of support for RECE again was anticipated to be on the agenda. "One question which will arise today is whether or not to start giving some low-risk support to RECE," wrote Chase. "While State and DOD, at the working levels, originally were in favor of it, they seem to have changed their position. . . . State does not want to compromise its position on Artime (i.e., If you give aid to RECE, how can you stop aid to Artime?) State and DOD will probably propose that, in turning down RECE, we give them $17,000. . . . Arguments in favor of giving them the money are: (a) it will lessen the shock of giving RECE a negative reply, (b) they will not look bad among exiles (we don't want them to look bad because they are 'good guys'), and (c) part of RECE's problem has not been their fault. We have not been able to give them as prompt an answer as they would have liked. I continue to be in favor of not getting involved with RECE; I agree that $17,000 is a small price to pay for a kiss-off."[44] A record of the meeting itself was not found.

On March 14, the *Miami Herald* ran a page-one story under the headline: "Exile Camps Closed; Move Is Called Tactical Shift." It read, in part:

"The Cuban exile organization, Revolutionary Recovery Movement, has lost a major portion of its financial support and been forced to close commando camps in Central America. MRR commandos have been returning to Miami for the past week. In Miami, MRR spokesmen claimed the closing of the camps in Nicaragua and Costa Rica represented only a change in tactics. They said it simply meant they would concentrate on subversion. Returning commandos told a different story. They said 'operational assistance' had been lost a few weeks ago, and that this week they were told there would be no more 'salary' checks ($175 and up per month)."

The story cited the contraband scandal, the attack on the *Sierra Aranzazu*, the capture of two MRR infiltrators and their subsequent confessions on Cuban television, disorganization, and the unexplained death of one commando as reasons for the shutdown. Lending credence to the belief that support for the Cubela operation continued, the story said, "MRR spokesmen in Miami contended the commando camps were only suspended while the organization concentrated on activities inside Cuba."[45]

Quintero, while not recalling the exact dates, remembered the final days. "We knew it was coming," said Quintero. "We more or less had the feeling that it was coming." He and Artime got the word at a meeting with Heckscher, their CIA case officer, at a "safe house" in Alexandria, Virginia. Telling the commandos in the camps was the difficult part, said Quintero. "We expect that people will say, 'Well, let's do the last one and let's go to Cuba.' But Artime was able to convince the people that we were going to keep everything. You know that Artime was a very good talker, and he was able to convince the guys that he was going to keep the boats and keep the people together. . . . Even if the Americans can't help us, we're going to go on our own. He was able to relieve most of the people. He kept people believing they were really going to stay." In fact, said Quintero, "he left some people in El Bluff [Nicaragua], and he built a house, supposedly for Somoza. And we put a waterproof basement in that house, and put about half the weapons we had taken to Nicaragua in there. We only turned back to the CIA about half of them and the other half we kept. It didn't really make a big difference. Those weapons weren't going to last that long . . . anyway we did it . . . it was permissible."

In Nicaragua, said Quintero, Gen. Anastasio "Tacho" Somoza, head of the country's National Guard, "told us to think about trying to keep it [the operation] going. But Artime knew he wasn't going to be able to because of the problems between the Costa Ricans and the Nicaraguans. We had all the weapons in a barge there in the middle of the river in Costa Rica, and we really didn't want to take that over to Nicaragua. We had taken some of the weapons from there to Nicaragua, but the big stuff, the main stuff, was still in the barge. We just took a few we were using and the ones we were using for training to Nicaragua." The two Swift boats belonging to the MRR were brought back to Naples, Florida, and, under Quintero's supervision, sent off to the Cuban exiles fighting in the Congo.[46]

On June 23, 1965, CIA "headquarters sent a cable to stations concerned, directing termination of contact with members of the Cubela group." It read, in part:

"Convincing proof that entire AMLASH group insecure and that further contact with key members of group constitute menace to CIA operations against Cuba as well as to the security of CIA staff personnel in Western Europe.

"Under the circumstances headquarters desires that contact with key members of the group be eliminated as rapidly as possible, and that assets who may be in contact with individual members of the group or peripherally involved in AMLASH conspiracy be warned of danger implicit in these associations and directed to eliminate contacts ASAP."[47]

According to author Thomas Powers, the CIA apparently learned from listening devices that Cubela had been talking too much about his plotting during visits to Europe. Even a CIA officer in Rome picked up talk of Cubela's boasting from Cuban contacts he maintained on his own. The CIA ordered all contact broken and warned Artime that Cubela was not to be trusted.[48]

Curiously, it wasn't until March 1, 1966, eight months later, that Cuba announced that security police had arrested "two military officers for alleged counterrevolutionary activities involving the U.S. Central Intelligence Agency. They were identified as Maj. Rolando Cubela and Maj. Ramon Guin." Cubela was found guilty and sentenced to thirty years in prison, after Castro asked for leniency.[49] Cubela was released after serving less than half his sentence. He now lives in Spain and is said to visit Miami occasionally.

The CIA belatedly prepared a report in 1976 on the AMLASH Operation for the Church Committee, relating to any possible link to President Kennedy's assassination. It noted that transcripts of Cubela's 1966 trial "contain no references to his activities prior to 1964, i.e., before President Kennedy's assassination. The transcripts suggest that, to the Cubans' knowledge, AMLASH/1 was not in touch with the CIA before November 1964. Nor did the book which Castro provided Senator McGovern in 1975, which purported to be an inventory of all known plots against Castro's life, contain any allegation of AMLASH/1 anti-Castro activity prior to late 1964. The book mentions travel by AMLASH/1 to Madrid 'where he was recruited by CIA agents.' This travel occurred in November 1964. The above two instances strongly suggest that Castro was not aware that AMLASH/1 had any contact with CIA prior to November 1964; i.e, one year after President Kennedy's death."[50]

CHAPTER 14

LBJ CASHES OUT

The end of the AMLASH operation in late June 1965, and with it that of Artime's autonomous group, brought an effective close to nearly six years of covert war against Cuba. The dispatch of infiltration teams for intelligence gathering, psychological, propaganda, and other more passive and peripheral activities continued sporadically for nearly three more years, along with the occasional uncontrolled free-lance exile efforts. But officially sanctioned assassination plots, sabotage, and hit-and-run raids were gone. The so-called autonomous groups were dead. While it is now apparent Johnson didn't have much enthusiasm for the secret war, the circumstances existing when he took office made change inevitable. The Venezuelan arms cache issue that was headed to the OAS for debate meant lowering the volume of U.S. covert activities. Vietnam was heating up. And in early January 1964, violent anti-American rioting in Panama diverted attention from Cuba to a more immediate crisis. In late April 1965 civil war exploded in the Dominican Republic. Even more importantly, the mutual antipathy between Johnson and Bobby Kennedy meant that the most influential advocate for an aggressive covert action program against Cuba had lost his voice.

The changing atmosphere in Washington after Kennedy's assassination became quickly apparent to those on the front lines of the secret war. "There was less enthusiasm after Johnson became president," said Shackley, the JMWAVE chief. "We were still putting out plans but not getting agreement for paramilitary activity. As a result, we were having trouble keeping the troops motivated. We never got any specific orders to shut down. We just started cutting back, getting out of some of our leases," added Shackley, who departed Miami in mid-1965.[1]

Bradley Ayers, the Army Ranger captain detached to JMWAVE for training purposes, told a similar story. "While the nightmarish events continued to unfold in Dallas and Washington in the days following the assassination, we tried to continue our work as it had been before the

237

President's death," recounted Ayers. "Two things became obvious almost immediately. One, at our operational level there was a total vacuum of policy. As a result, virtually all paramilitary activity remained frozen, and no one could even guess when or in what way station operations would be resumed. Two, an undercurrent of suspicion and paranoia developed at headquarters as a result of the official and semiofficial witch hunts that were being conducted throughout various government agencies. As conspiracy rumors swept the nation—many of them connecting the assassination with Fidel Castro and the Cubans—the CIA, especially the Miami station, found itself in a particularly sensitive position."[2]

At CIA headquarters Sam Halpern remembered that after Johnson became president, "the pressure gradually disappeared, just stopped. Suddenly we weren't getting telephone calls anymore that said we had to get rid of Castro. We felt it in terms that there was nobody screaming at us every day of the week. It wasn't the same after Johnson took over. He had other things to think about."[3] The same thing happened at the coordinator of Cuban affairs office where John Crimmins remembered "before the assassination, [McGeorge] Bundy would call every other day, either pleased or indignant about something. Under Johnson, I'd get a call a week, then a call every two weeks from Gordon Chase [Bundy's aide]. That just sort of withered away, petered out."[4]

Rafael Quintero also sensed the difference. After President Kennedy's assassination, said Quintero, "Bobby still kept putting pressure on but as soon as Johnson took over you could see it, you could feel that things were not the same as before. There was not that support as before. We knew it was going to be the end of it. You read any of Johnson's speeches and you'll see he doesn't mention Cuba at all. I guess he was too busy with the Vietnam problem. . . . The Cuban problem wasn't important enough." Henry Heckscher, their CIA case officer, "sort of let us know," said Quintero. "He told us this guy [Johnson] is not going to continue with this operation. He's not that kind of guy. And at the time there were a lot of people against it. They didn't think after Kennedy that it was going to last very long. It was a nonissue for Lyndon Johnson. The only guy that kept it alive was Bobby Kennedy." Quintero said he supported Bobby Kennedy in his 1968 presidential bid, and "I firmly believe, and I'm probably the only Cuban who believes, that if he had been elected president he would have done something regarding Castro, something final."[5]

As vice president, Johnson had played virtually no role in formulating foreign policy, let alone dealing with Cuba. Once he became president he was more disposed to listen to his advisers, particularly those in the State Department, who opposed the covert Cuba policy but previously had been silenced by Bobby Kennedy. "Nothing underscored Johnson's limited role in foreign policy-making more than his silence during White House deliberations on the Cuban missile crisis in October 1962," wrote historian Robert Dallek. "During the two weeks that JFK held meetings on how to settle the greatest post-1945 crisis in Soviet-American relations, LBJ was a shadow figure, expressing few opinions and asserting himself only on the afternoon of October 27, when the President was not present."[6]

Johnson started thinking about Cuba when he became president, however, as indicated by a December 1 conversation with Senator J. William Fulbright, a conversation which also reflected concerns about Vietnam. Johnson asked Fulbright what he should be doing about Cuba. Fulbright said he didn't think "we ought to stir that up any. I think this election sounds good—what I heard of it today—in Venezuela. I think the goddamned thing ought to be let alone, as of the moment. I think if you stir it up . . ."

> Johnson interrupted: They're shipping arms all over the damned hemisphere. [Helms had shown him a Cuban rifle two days before that had been seized as part of the Venezuelan arms cache.]
>
> Fulbright: *That* we ought to stop. I thought you meant about going into Cuba.
>
> Johnson: No, I'm not getting into any Bay of Pigs deal! No, I'm just asking you what we ought to do to pinch their nuts more than we're doing. Why don't you give me a one-page memo on what you'd do, if you were President, about Cuba?
>
> Fulbright: You mean, exclusive of any direct interference?
>
> Johnson: I mean what you'd do, if you were President, about Cuba. Inclusive or exclusive of anything. Just what you'd do. And get your good brain to working. I'd like to look at it and see.

Johnson then asked about Vietnam, to which Fulbright responded: "I just think that is a hell of a situation. . . . I'll be goddamned if I don't think it's hopeless."[7]

As president, Johnson's first serious formal session on Cuba policy came December 19, 1963, with a high-level briefing in the White House. The meeting generated an advance flood of papers from various agencies

and departments, recommending everything from a presidential statement supporting the internal dissidents to tightening the economic
embargo, sabotage air strikes, and accelerating efforts at rapprochement.
The CIA, in a status report, defined U.S. policy as one of isolating Cuba
"from the Western Hemisphere and the rest of the Free World and to exert
maximum pressures, short of open and direct US military intervention,
to prevent the consolidation and stabilization of the Castro-Communist
regime." The agency's covert action program, according to the report,
"is designed to support other governmental measures to proliferate and
intensify the pressures on Castro to encourage dissident elements, particularly in the military, to carry out and eliminate Castro and the Soviet
presence in Cuba." The report saw the "ultimate objective" as replacing
the Castro regime "with one which will be fully compatible with the goals
of the US and will cooperate with US efforts to establish friendly and sta-
ble regimes throughout Latin America."

The CIA report acknowledged that current U.S. programs "at their
present levels" were not likely to "result in the early overthrow of the
Castro/Communist regime," thus it "would seem timely to examine what
additional covert and overt measures can be taken to quicken the pace of
events." Among these measures, it cited, "expanding and intensifying the
category of sabotage and harassment at least for the next year." To do so,
two courses of action were suggested: (1) relax the crackdown on non-
CIA controlled Cuban exile maritime raids and air strikes from U.S. territory while urging the British to do likewise from the Bahamas, and (2)
authorize CIA autonomous groups to conduct air strikes against major
economic targets such as power plants and oil refineries. The advantages
and disadvantages of each were offered. Still, the CIA concluded: "In the
last analysis . . . there are only two courses which would eliminate the
Castro regime at an early date: an invasion or a complete blockade."[8]

McGeorge Bundy, who had remained in the White House as Johnson's
national security assistant, laid out for his new boss a comprehensive,
twenty-two-page paper on Cuba policy in advance of the December 19
meeting. Its elemental nature clearly indicated the new president had only
a basic knowledge of the Kennedy administration's Cuba policy. In contrast to the CIA's status report, Bundy said, "the bare minimum of our
policy is a Cuba which poses no threat to its neighbors and which is not
a Soviet satellite. In moving towards this objective we have rejected the
options of unprovoked U.S. military intervention in Cuba and an effec-

tive, total blockade around Cuba—primarily because they would risk another US/USSR confrontation."

Bundy outlined what he called "offensive and defensive" measures against Cuba within the new policy framework of January 1963. "Offensively," said Bundy "our ultimate minimum target is to remove the Soviet satellite from the Hemisphere." Success was hoped for "by concentrating on three intermediate targets—intensifying Cuba's already-serious economic difficulties; increasing the cost and unpleasantness to the Soviets of maintaining Cuba; and stimulating direct and indirect internal resistance to the regime. Our chief weapons for achieving these offensive targets are two—isolation measures and covert measures."

The covert measures, said Bundy, "covered essentially six areas." The first four were identified as (1) intelligence gathering for "both U.S. strategic and operational requirements"; (2) CIA-controlled propaganda directed at Cuba; (3) cooperation with the State Department and other agencies to "deny Cuba commodities which it urgently needs"; and (4) identification and establishment of "contact with potentially dissident non-Communist elements in the power centers of the regime" in an effort at stimulating an internal coup. And, added Bundy, "we currently are in direct contact with several people in Cuba who may be of significance." The remaining two "offensive measures" were the four small-scale CIA-controlled sabotage operations (Commandos Mambises) "for the purpose of stimulating resistance and hurting Cuba economically," and aid for "the autonomous groups and individuals, who will probably be ready to begin infiltration and sabotage in mid-January, and who will not necessarily be responsive to our guidance."

Bundy acknowledged that the covert program's "potential for bringing about a basic change in Cuba is still largely unknown" and was limited by current policy that "prevents covert air attacks on Cuban targets and prevents free-lance exile raids on Cuba from U.S. territory." Bundy concluded his Cuba primer by telling the president that "the general consensus in the Government is that we should try to find ways of stepping up our pressures against the Castro regime." He cited seven possible ways to do so: air attacks, unleashing of exiles, military feints, low-level flights, free world shipping to Cuba, public presidential statement, and talks with Soviets and Cubans (in an attempt to drive a wedge between them).[9]

The December 19 White House briefing brought together such ranking officials as George Ball and U. Alexis Johnson of the State Department, Treasury Secretary Douglas Dillon, Deputy Defense Secretary Roswell

Gilpatric, along with ranking representatives of the CIA, USIA, and the National Security Staff. Bobby Kennedy was conspicuously missing. Desmond FitzGerald recorded that "the President appeared interested in the number of agents inside Cuba but made no particular comment concerning the program until the subject of economic denial was introduced." He wanted to know what additional measures could be taken. In a discussion of "promoting disaffection among the Cuban military, the President said it did not seem we had gone very far along this line." FitzGerald responded that "the program being presented was, with the exception of the economic denial item, entirely a covert program and, if run at full capacity, would tax the capabilities of the clandestine services—in other words, if new and broader measures against Cuba were to be undertaken, they would have to be within the overt field."

The discussion turned to sabotage, harassment, and a proposed raid against the refinery at Matanzas, on Cuba's north coast. "After hearing the pros and cons, the President stated that he did not feel that the present time was a good one to conduct an operation of this magnitude which carried less than 50 percent chance of success," but said planning should continue. "Recognizing that a cessation of raids would have a bad morale effect within Cuba, he agreed that low risk operations, with admittedly lower economic and psychological impact, should be conducted."[10]

A memo for the record of the same meeting by Gen. Earle Wheeler of the Joint Chiefs of Staff reflected again that the president had particular interest in the exploitation of discontent within the Cuban military. FitzGerald told him it was a "long term undertaking. While there are disaffected Cuban military men in important posts, they have not, to date, made any contacts with each other nor formed any sort of group." FitzGerald added that Castro's overthrow from within would have to be supported by the Cuban military to have any chance of success. During discussion of sabotage and harassment, reported Wheeler, "the President expressed his reluctance to undertake high risk actions at this time for two reasons: (1) Current attempts to get OAS agreement to various actions directed against Cuba might be jeopardized; and, (2) The Soviets seem to be watching closely the new administration's policies toward Cuba, and it might influence unfavorably the success of our efforts to achieve further reductions in Soviet military personnel in Cuba." The meeting concluded with "discussion of further actions we might take to increase pressure and harassments at an appropriate time. . . . While the President did not express disapprobation, neither did he express approval. In fact, no real decisions were taken at this meeting which must be regarded, I think, as being an important orientation session."[11]

Nine days into the New Year Bundy advised the president that "three small-scale sabotage operations have been approved by the Special Group, but this recommendation is based on a routine continuation of broad policy guidance which I think you may wish to review." The three operations involved a coastal warehouse and pier, a naval or patrol vessel in a harbor, and a fuel barge in coastal waters. Bundy noted that all three operations had been approved three months earlier, including one that was rescheduled because of high seas. He said the operations were comparable to "the small attack on a Cuban naval patrol in late December which Castro promptly blamed on you." That apparently referred to the Commandos Mambises's December 23 sinking of a Russian-made Cuban patrol boat docked at the Isle of Pines, since renamed the Isle of Youth. Bundy said that operation was planned before Kennedy's assassination and "not cancelled thereafter because it seemed to fall within the guidance you expressed in your . . . review of the Cuban problem." The policy question faced now, observed Bundy, is: "If we condone these even small sabotage operations, Castro will certainly know it. Equally, if we call them off, he will know it, and so will the Russians. We thus have an opportunity to choose."

Bundy said he didn't think "the choice should be made on momentum alone. I therefore recommend a Cabinet-level review of the whole principle of covert sabotage against Cuba. I know that Rusk has never liked it and that McNamara thinks it does very little good. McCone and the CIA are for it, and so are most of the middle-level officers dealing with the Castro problem. I myself consider the matter extremely balanced, but before hearing full argument, my guess is that in your position I would stop sabotage attacks on the ground that they are illegal, ineffective, and damaging to our broader policy. I might then wish to make a little capital from this decision with the Soviet Union."[12] The raids were never approved.

Two new sabotage proposals were brought before a Special Group meeting the next day, January 10, for approval. The first targeted a petroleum refinery and storage facilities near Santiago, in eastern Cuba. It was rejected. The second proposed target was a sawmill located on the north coast of Oriente Province. "The attack," said the proposal, "is to be conducted by a commando team which will place incendiaries and demolitions at critical locations throughout the installation. A second target, which may be attacked as security factors permit, is a large floating crane which has been anchored in the area and which appears to be used in loading ore from a near-by mine. This operational proposal with its two targets was approved subject to the concurrence of higher authority. Also, it was the consensus of the Group that the views of higher authority should be obtained on what is desired generally in the field of sabotage activities in Cuba." The memo for the record of the meeting shows Bobby Kennedy attended while the sabotage proposals were discussed.[13] There is no indication the CIA went ahead with the second proposal. Although no document was found specifically suspending CIA-controlled sabotage operations, other documents suggested a suspension of such operations was imposed in January and the program was eventually terminated.[14] That would mean the December 23, 1963, raid by the Commandos Mambises was the last CIA-controlled sabotage operation of the secret war.

One of the early indicators that Johnson leaned to curtailment of the Cuba program came in mid-to-late January and related to the Cubans in the U.S. military. Erneido Oliva, the deputy commander of the Bay of Pigs and by then a commissioned officer in the U.S. Army, had come to Washington from Fort Sill, Oklahoma. He wanted to know where his proposal—with Bobby Kennedy's endorsement—to unite all Cubans within the military into a cohesive unit stood. Oliva was in his hotel when Bobby Kennedy's secretary called. She said a friend of the attorney general's would pick him up and take him to the White House where Kennedy was in an important meeting with President Johnson. Kennedy met Oliva outside the White House, telling him "the President has made his decision, final decision" to end the Special Presidential Program for Bay of Pigs veterans in the U.S. military, a program President Kennedy had announced the previous March designating Oliva as its special representative. A few minutes later Kennedy and Oliva were taken into the White House library, "and Johnson came in and he flatly told me my program with the Cubans had to be terminated. Bobby didn't say anything. You know they didn't get along well. He told me before that he had tried to persuade him . . . but he didn't try and persuade the president of the United States in front of me. He was only listening, his head bowed, pretty sad." Oliva said the meeting lasted sixteen minutes and at its end President Johnson asked them to go to the Pentagon.

There, McNamara, Vance, Califano, and Haig were waiting. McNamara delivered the same message the president had delivered in the White House. Oliva was then asked to visit the military bases where Cubans were stationed, accompanied by Califano and Haig, to inform them of the decision. The Cubans were to be told they could remain in the military if they wished, but not as part of a special program. "At the beginning I said, 'No, no, I am not going anyplace. I am not helping you do anything. That's it.' I was fed up with the whole thing. But Haig, who was really like a friend at the time, persuaded me to recognize the importance of it. If Haig and Califano go around to every base to get together with forty, fifty, Cuban officers and they didn't see me, they would say, 'What is going on?' This is why they needed me." Haig, Califano, and Oliva made the visits in February. Oliva resigned from active duty in May to join RECE.[15]

Later in January the CIA prepared an exhaustive review—and defense—of the current covert action program against Cuba. It again cited the six areas as part of its interdependent courses of action program approved the preceding June. They were: (1) covert collection of intelligence; (2) propaganda actions to stimulate low-risk simple sabotage; (3) economic denial; (4) exploitation and stimulation of disaffection in the Cuban armed forces and other power centers of the regime to encourage these elements to carry out a coup against the Castro/Communist factions; (5) general sabotage and harassment; and (6) support of autonomous anti-Castro Cuban exile groups. The review noted that item five, general sabotage and harassment, "has been the subject of continual review since the inception of the program and is the primary subject of this paper." The CIA said it believed "there is sufficient evidence to show that sabotage raids, despite the risk involved, are a necessary stimulus to internal action which will need to be continued for a considerable period to permit the tempo of internal acts to reach a point where it can become self-contained." It argued that ending the raids would send the wrong message to both those inside Cuba and the rest of Latin America where it would be seen as a switch from "aggressive action against the Castro regime to one of 'coexistence' and eventual accommodation." It also anticipated "a new surge of domestic political agitation on the part of the numerous Cuban exiles who have political connections within the U.S." In conclusion, it recommended that "the covert program be continued in at least its present form and scope."[16]

The new president received his baptism of fire in dealing with the Cuba problem beginning on "a quiet Sunday afternoon, February 2, 1964," in the Dry Tortugas, a small group of islands off the Florida Keys. The Coast Guard spotted four Cuban fishing boats in U.S. territorial waters. The four boats and their thirty-six crew members were intercepted and escorted to Key West the next day. "Two of the Cuban captains admitted that they knew they were fishing inside U.S. waters," Johnson wrote in *The Vantage Point*, a first-person account of his presidency. "We also learned that before they left Cuba the crews were told they had been selected for an 'historic venture.' Their assignment was to 'test U.S. reactions.' In other words, the incursion of the Cuban boats was a deliberate confrontation." The confrontation set off a week of frenzied and confrontational diplomacy. Cuba maintained the fishing boats were in international waters, accusing the United States of "piracy" and "vandalism." On February 5 the Swiss ambassador in Havana, as the representative of Washington's interests in the absence of diplomatic relations, was called in and told that Cuba was cutting off the water supply to the Guantánamo Naval Base. It would remain off until the fishermen were released. This action had long been anticipated and contingency plans were made. Tankers began hauling water from Florida, and Johnson made two other decisions: to provide the base with a self-sufficient water supply and to cut back gradually and eventually end the employment of all Cubans on the base. On February 21 a Florida court dropped charges against the Cuban crews, fined the captains $500 each, and released all of the fishermen. Castro ordered the water turned back on the same day. He was told that it was no longer needed.[17]

John Crimmins, the coordinator of Cuban affairs, recalled the incident as "the first indication of Johnson's approach" to the Cuba problem. "There was a big furor. . . . The press was all upset. . . . Some voices said we have to do something forceful about this, but he was very prudent and careful, no cowboy stuff, very low key. He didn't want to provoke anything. It was not the end of the world."[18]

A month later the CIA received a reading on the Cuban reaction to the Guantánamo affair from a source described as "a medium level Cuban government official, who has proved to be a mature, intelligent and astute observer" and another from "a high level government official who is definitely in a position to know Fidel Castro's expressed views on the matter under discussion." McCone passed the intelligence report on to Rusk, McNamara, and Bundy. It reported that Castro "sincerely desires to enter into negotiation with the United States with the aim of reducing tension" but "reacts with strong irritation or 'rage' to events which increase tension between the United States and Cuba," a reaction particularly evident in the case of the four fishing boats. "Despite Castro's basic concern that the situation not get out of hand, his prestige was obviously at stake in the eyes of the Cuban populace. His irritation at American handling contributed to the forces shaping his response. He was constrained to take action to restore his prestige, and related to a high regime official that he saw three courses of action open to Cuba." They were to dispatch Cuban MIGs to harass the USS *Oxford*, stationed in waters off Havana; fire at a U-2 plane as it flew over Cuba; and cut off the water supply to Guantánamo. The intelligence report said that at no time did Castro and leading *Fidelistas* show concern about a possible U.S. invasion because the Soviet Union would intervene to prevent such action. "Curiously enough . . . Castro and his principle lieutenants more or less lost sight of . . . U.S. reactions" while "imagining what the reaction of Khrushchev would be to the incident. They were convinced that 'Nikita' would be panicked at the thought that Guantanamo might confront him with an unpleasant situation vis a vis the United States, and top Cuban leaders generally gave themselves over to amusement at the situation and commented 'Nikita must be soiling himself with fright.' "[19]

Sometime in early February apparently, Cyrus Vance, the secretary of the Army who had been designated by President Kennedy under the June 1963 covert action program as the executive agent for the entire federal government in dealing with Cuba, came up with his own ideas for the future of covert action.[20] Vance's original document was not found, but a February 12, 1964, note on covert activities circulated by Peter Jessup of the White House National Security staff, referred to a paper as "pretty much a Vance idea and his motivation seems to be to get a fish-or-cut-bait decision. Mr. McNamara disliked an earlier longer paper but is fond of this one. FitzGerald registers no dissent because he is of the fish-or-cut-bait school." The implication is that Vance wants either a much more aggressive program of covert action or an end to it. The Jessup memo said that despite the "extreme wariness of higher authority [the president] at this time," the suggested types of action in the Vance proposal "do include some items of a controversial nature such as placing un-activated devices in ships of foreign flags and then warning the consignee. . . . Equally hairy is the proposal for kidnapping and physical harassment of Peking-oriented trainees while attributing same to Kruschev [sic] supporters." The memo noted, however, "that if a decision is reached (following examination of the Cuba review) to step up activity, such action would come up as a separate operation to the Special Group."[21] The Special Group met two days later, with the Vance proposals on the agenda. Vance reported that "he could speak for the Secretary of Defense; his attitude had turned toward a much harder line," but no other detail of the proposed program was included in a memorandum for the record of the meeting. During a more general discussion on covert activities, "the following points were emphasized: Continued covert action received support although divergence on the level of activity was registered. There was a consensus that the present level of operations was no longer effective in attaining the basic objective of toppling Castro but harassment might keep the regime off balance. There was an area of disagreement on proofs of effectiveness of current and past measures. Mr. Bundy summarized the dilemma by noting that the high risk, dangerous operations are the rewarding ones and the low noise, innocuous operations prove to be unrewarding."[22] Even though the Vance–Defense Department proposal was not found, subsequent events make it obvious it was not approved.

Desmond FitzGerald, in a revealing March 6, 1964, letter to Bundy, summed up the disappointing status of covert activities in the context of the program approved the preceding June. The excerpts below are from FitzGerald's letter, written the same day he and Helms met with Bundy, while covert action was still being reviewed. Wrote FitzGerald:

> The sabotage raids, built into the program as a sort of firing pin for internal unrest and to create the conditions for a coup, which was to be the main force leading to Castro's defeat, ran only from August to December and only five were actually conducted. The effectiveness of those five raids is debatable; there are strong proponents on both sides of the argument. Regardless of how that debate might come out, however, five rather low-key raids followed by the present three-month hiatus, the latter clearly noted by pro- and anti-Castroites alike, adds up to a program of much smaller dimension than originally envisioned which could not be expected to have had the desired detonating effect.
>
> At the present time, as a result of a number of circumstances well known to you, Castro is in a strong upswing and the spirit of resistance within Cuba is at a very low point indeed. In my estimation, a covert program at this time designed to overthrow Castro is not realistic. Acceptance of risks and noise level of a greater magnitude than we had in mind in June would be needed to stand a chance in view of the developments since last June. This then raises the question of what should happen now to the vari-

ous bits and pieces of the June program. I would like to mention these separately and refer to some of the considerations typical to each.

The sabotage raids are conducted by Cuban exile groups [apparently refers to Commandos Mambises] trained in Florida and entirely subject to our planning and control. There are three of these groups totaling approximately 50 men. To place them in position and recover them there requires an extensive maritime apparatus in Florida, which likewise serves intelligence agent infiltrations and exfiltrations. To maintain the raiding capability on a stand-by basis is expensive but, more importantly, the raiding groups themselves have a relatively short shelf life; if not employed their morale deteriorates and some of the members, usually the best motivated, drop out. Replacements can be acquired and trained but their caliber and morale is in large part determined by the morale of the exile community as a whole. We probably can retain the present raiding groups at roughly their current capabilities for another month or two, although the well-known Cuban volatility is capable of causing sudden and more rapid deterioration.

In short, we will need to know within a reasonable time whether we should continue to effect repairs to and keep in being our sabotage raiding apparatus. The dismemberment of these raiding teams could be accomplished without too much shock to the exile community. It would be noticed, but, if done carefully, particularly if it coincided with the commencement of 'autonomous' operations, it should not cause undue repercussions and polemics against U.S. policy.

The remainder of the letter dealt with the Ray and Artime autonomous groups, plus Menoyo's activities; the possible consequences of suspending autonomous operations; "a capacity which is increasing, to sabotage Cuban ships in foreign ports"; economic warfare; contact with and subversion of Cuban military and other ranking officials; and intelligence collection.

In conclusion FitzGerald asked for advice as to "which of the above lines of action we should continue, which we should try to retain as a shelf capability and which to abandon. (Of course, intelligence collection would continue.) As parts of an integrated national program designed to get rid of Castro, they seemed to us to make sense; as separate pieces they can serve to exert some braking effect on Castro's program, but that is about all."[23]

Decision day came April 7 with a White House meeting convened to discuss the covert program against Cuba. Among those present, in addition to the president, were Bundy from the White House; Rusk, Under-secretary Alexis Johnson, Assistant Secretary Tom Mann, and John Crimmins from the State Department; McNamara and Vance from the Defense Department; General Taylor from the Joint Chiefs; and McCone, Helms, and FitzGerald from the CIA. Again, Bobby Kennedy was not listed among the attendees. The seven items on the agenda which required "discussion and decision at a higher level," were familiar: (1) collection of intelligence; (2) covert propaganda to encourage low risk forms of active and passive resistance; (3) cooperation with other agencies in economic denial; (4) attempts to identify and establish contact with potential dissident elements inside Cuba; (5) indirect economic sabotage; (6) CIA-controlled sabotage raiding; and (7) autonomous operations. Approval was recommended for the first five items. It was noted after the last two items that "opinion was divided and it is recommended that higher authority hear their arguments."[24]

At the meeting, Rusk came down hard against CIA-controlled raids, arguing that "two things presently militate against a resumption of the program: (a) the pending OAS matter with respect to the Venezuelan arms cache which may be strengthened by discovery of arms in the Argentine [sic] as well as in Brazil, and (b) the prospective turnover of the SAM sites by the Russians to the Cubans in April or May." Bundy also said he had "come to the conclusion that it is unlikely an effective sabotage program will be conducted." Policy makers, he said, "each time for good reasons, had turned sabotage operations on and off to such an extent that a program of the type envisioned in the June paper simply does not . . . appear feasible." McCone defended the program, arguing that "five relatively low-key operations" since the previous June "didn't constitute a test of the program." McNamara said, "It was his opinion that the covert program has no chance of success in terms of upsetting Fidel Castro." Rusk recommended "that we keep the raiding assets in being for the next two months and that the question be discussed again following the resolution of the OAS events and the Cuban use of the SAM sites. The President accepted this recommendation."[25] By contrast, the Church Committee report said, "According to the minutes of the Special Group meeting on April 7, 1964, President Johnson decided to discontinue the use of CIA-controlled sabotage raids against Cuba."[26] That does not appear to be the case. Nor was it a Special Group meeting on April 7, but a special high-level White House meeting. Although no document was found confirming the Church Committee report, neither was documentary evidence found of any further CIA-controlled sabotage raids. Such raids were "stood down" the previous January and apparently never resumed.

Two weeks later Gordon Chase followed up with a memo to Bundy, responding to his request that "the staff think about studies which can be done now but which might bear fruit in 1965." Chase suggested that "one aspect which could profit from further study between now and November" was the question of rapprochement with Castro. "To get the most out of such a study," said Chase, "the drafters should probably start with the hypothesis that in January, 1965, the U.S. Government decides that the Castro regime is here to stay and that it is desirable to try to reach an acceptable rapprochement with Castro." Chase then suggested several questions for the drafters to address.[27] Nothing indicated any follow-up. An April 23 speech by Undersecretary of State George Ball, which was widely touted by Johnson administration officials, appeared to signal the subtle shift in policy toward Cuba that was occurring. "Foreign policies are rarely full-armed like Minerva," Ball began. "More often they evolve in response to events and circumstances. In such cases there is the danger that the assumptions on which policies are founded may become obscured." That had happened with policy toward Cuba, said Ball. "Some of the public discussion that has surrounded that policy has involved misapprehensions on a number of fronts; misapprehensions as to the nature of the danger posed by the present and potential activities of the Castro Government, misapprehensions as to the range of policies available to counter that danger, and misapprehensions as to the objectives that we can expect to accomplish by the policies employed."[28]

The main weapons left in Washington's covert arsenal after April 7 were the Ray and Artime autonomous operations over which the United States had no tactical control. Both Cuban leaders by then had stoked the emotional fires leading up to May 20, Cuba's Independence Day. Artime had just carried out the first raid against the Cabo Cruz sugar mill. Ray was poised to fulfill his promise of returning to Cuba to light the flame of his supposedly formidable underground ground network, which proved an illusion. Some fifteen journalists from major newspapers in the United States and London poured into Miami. "Most of the exiles believe that Castro's end is near and that an undefined 'something' big is on its way—a something which is expected to solve all their problems and allow them to return to liberated Cuba in the next 30 or 60 days," said a May

21 CIA report prepared by JMWAVE in Miami.[29] Little did the exile community know that President Johnson already had made the decision to cut bait, rather than fish. Ray, his credibility destroyed, sputtered ineptly along until sometime in 1965. Artime's group shot itself in the foot with the mistaken attack on the Spanish freighter, but then managed to stay on life support via the Cubela plot, a long shot at best. For all practical purposes the secret war had sputtered to an end by June 1965. Or so everyone thought.

Suddenly, Adm. William Raborn, the newly named CIA director, made an abortive effort to resurrect the program, just as the Artime-Cubela plot gasped its last. In a June 26 memo to the president, Bundy advised him that Raborn "has recommended reactivation of a paramilitary effort against Cuba. . . . Tommy Thompson, Cy Vance and I are against the recommendation, but, along with Raborn, we have agreed to report the matter to you in case you want to pursue it further." Among the operations Raborn proposed were: (1) maritime raids by commando teams against coastal targets; (2) use of an underwater demolition team to blow up ships in Cuban ports; (3) night attacks on major Cuban merchant vessels while in Cuban territorial waters; (4) air bombing of selected targets in Cuba by covert aircraft; and (5) deception operations designed to give the impression of imminent invasion by U.S. forces. "The trouble most of us see in such operations," said Bundy, "is that their international noise level outweighs their anti-Castro value. Especially with the Dominican problem before us, most of us do not recommend visible violent actions against Cuba. I believe this is also the opinion of Dean Rusk and Bob McNamara. But if you feel differently, we can have the matter examined again."[30] Johnson obviously did not feel differently. The only thing left to do was clean up the residue from six unsuccessful years trying to dump Fidel.

Desmond FitzGerald's Special Affairs Staff, an independent unit handling Cuba at CIA headquarters, reverted back to being a part of the Western Hemisphere Division in 1965. Shackley left Miami in mid-June 1965, after beginning the scale-down of what had been the frontline command post for the secret war. By late 1966 a further substantial cutback and reorganization of JMWAVE was under way. "Many covert entities were terminated and personnel reassigned," according to the Miami Station review of operations.

By early 1968 "it became apparent that as a result of sustained operational activity . . . in the Miami area over a period of years the cover of the Miami Station had eroded to a point that the security of our operations was increasingly jeopardized," added the station review. "This erosion was more significant following the *Ramparts* exposure of CIA operations and the possibility that the location of our Station on property leased from the University of Miami might be especially embarrassing to the University." It was clear. The South Campus station was obsolete, the CIA had outstayed their welcome, and the University of Miami wanted them to leave.

The decision was made to deactivate JMWAVE and replace it with a smaller operation "which would be better able to respond to current needs." By then CIA personnel at the station—still operating under commercial cover—had been reduced from a peak of some four hundred to one hundred fifty.

The new station began operation—this time under official cover—with about fifty persons in August 1968 at a U.S. Coast Guard facility in what then was described as a "run-down" part of Miami Beach. Today the area is part of the booming South Beach nightlife scene. The station housed, according to the review document, "a new and much smaller media operation. . . . Intelligence collection was expanded to include the Bahamas and Lesser Antilles. Increased emphasis was given to third-country Cuban operations [agent recruitment and technical operations against Cuban embassies abroad] under the guidance of the new Station. The Cuban émigré organizations supported by the Station were drastically reduced and activities were phased down. [Word blacked out] responsibility for the residual covert operations was transferred to Headquarters and the remaining Cuban émigré operations were terminated."[31]

The secret war against Castro had come full circle. Jake Esterline returned to Miami in early 1968 to preside over the reorganization, reduction, and relocation of JMWAVE. He had been deputy chief of the Western Hemisphere Division when he volunteered for the Miami job. "I felt a sense of obligation to the Cubans after the failure of the Bay of Pigs," said Esterline. "If it was going to be done, I wanted to see it done right. I thought, 'Really, my heart will always be with these people, these Cuban exiles in all these years, starting with the Bay of Pigs, and I don't want to see them cast in the cold.' " In returning to Miami, he posed as a business consultant working for a company called Consultech, operating from a small office located—ironically—on the John F. Kennedy Causeway. In addition to arranging for the station's relocation, Esterline further reduced its assets, closing front companies, canceling lingering leases, and the most difficult of all, laying off the several hundred Cubans still on the payroll, while trying to avoid an embarrassing public scandal. "Obviously the agency didn't want a big explosion in South Florida in terms of dropping everybody. Some of the diehard ones who felt they had to get to Castro were very unhappy. They accepted the fact . . . but were not happy that we were giving up the fight, in their words. Well, I wasn't very happy about that either." But, said Esterline, "in that context one recognized the inevitability that the total U.S. involvement in Vietnam precluded anything being done in terms of Castro. Since the missile crisis, there didn't seem to be anything new and different that would warrant any diversion from Vietnam."[32]

EPILOGUE

The legacy of the unsuccessful six-year secret war against Fidel Castro—a legacy that belongs mostly to the Kennedy brothers—is not an admirable one. Among the war's many negative consequences were the consolidation of Castro's hold on Cuba, contributing to the Soviet decision to install offensive missiles on the island and spawning a cadre of Cuban exile terrorists perpetrating murder and mayhem far in excess of their relatively small numbers.

Historian Robert Dallek, in his biography of John F. Kennedy, rightly wrote that "the Bay of Pigs failure followed by repeated discussions of how to topple Castro show Kennedy at his worst—inexperienced and driven by Cold War imperatives that helped bring the world to the edge of a disastrous nuclear war." In a more debatable observation, Dallek added that "the almost universal praise for his restraint and accommodation in the missile crisis, followed by secret explorations of détente with Havana more than make up for his initial errors of judgment. Indeed, a second Kennedy term might have brought resolution to unproductive tensions with Castro and foreclosed more than forty years of Cuban-American antagonism."[1]

The praise for the president's "restraint and accommodation" doesn't take into account that Operation Mongoose, the program of covert action and overt saber rattling, most certainly contributed to the Soviet decision to install the missiles. And the argument that a second Kennedy term "might have brought resolution to unproductive tensions" and ended forty years of antagonism, is purely speculative; just another what-if in a landscape littered with what-ifs related to Cuba. What if Kennedy hadn't changed the landing site for the Bay of Pigs? What if he had not curtailed the air cover? What if U.S. troops had been ordered in as the exile invasion collapsed? What if he had called the invasion off? What if an assassination attempt against Castro had succeeded? What if the Kennedys, rather than becoming obsessed with removing Castro after the Bay of Pigs defeat, had forgone Mongoose and the other covert programs? There might not even have been a missile crisis. The list goes on.

Richard Goodwin, the Kennedy aide who met secretly with Che Guevara at Punta del Este, Uruguay, in August 1961—even as he was presiding over the task force that created Mongoose—wrote in his memo to Kennedy of his meeting that Guevara "wanted to thank us very much for the invasion—that it had been a great political victory for them—enabled them to consolidate—and transformed them from an aggrieved little country to an equal."[2]

In fact, the Kennedy vendetta against Cuba mirrored, in some ways, the methods employed by America's Cold War enemies. In a speech a week after the Bay of Pigs collapsed, Kennedy argued that communism relied "primarily on covert means for expanding its sphere of influence—on infiltration instead of invasion, on subversion instead of elections, on intimidation instead of free choice, on guerrillas by night instead of armies by day."[3] Similar methods, in part, were used during both the Bay of Pigs and Mongoose operations.

At the international conference in Havana marking the fortieth anniversary of the missile crisis, Robert McNamara remarked that he "didn't think Mongoose was worth a damn, but I didn't say 'don't do it.' " One of the major themes underlying the two days of discussions at the conference was the role of Mongoose as a catalyst for the missile crisis. Symbolic of the Cuban's emphasis on Mongoose was the publication, coinciding with the conference, of a book entitled *Operacion Mangosta: Preludio de la Invasion Directa a CUBA (Operation Mongoose: Prelude for the Direct Invasion of Cuba)* by Jacinto Valdes, a researcher for State Security's Center for Historic Research. Both the Russian and the Cuban delegations left little doubt that they saw in Operation Mongoose—as the book title suggests—the prelude for a U.S. invasion.

Arthur Schlesinger Jr., who also opposed the Bay of Pigs invasion, offered his view of Mongoose as "silly and stupid," while acknowledging that "it's well understood that as a consequence of Operation Mongoose that the Cubans had a legitimate fear of an American invasion." Richard Goodwin said, "it was clear what the President wanted, and the attorney general, whom I assume spoke the President's mind, but much less charmingly, was 'what could we do about getting rid of a Communist government in Cuba?' And out of that came Operation Mongoose . . . the success of that operation can be seen right here."

Ted Sorensen, a Kennedy speechwriter, told Castro he knew nothing about, and had nothing to do with, Mongoose, but apologized anyway. He noted that "President Kennedy, following the Bay of Pigs, approved policies to isolate Cuba, to weaken Cuba as a Soviet outpost in the Western Hemisphere, to diminish its economy, to exclude it from other Latin American regional activities; to de-fang it so to speak, as a military base for the Soviet Union, but it was not his intention to destroy Cuba, much less to kill its leaders . . . to the extent that Operation Mongoose exceeded these non-violent objectives of the President, and speaking only for myself, not the U.S. government, not even for President Kennedy, long since dead, to the extent that these non-violent objectives were exceeded by operations of Mongoose, Mr. President, I apologize."[4]

If ever there was a classic case of unintended consequences, it came from the residue of the covert war and its out-of-work veterans. Many, but not all, had been on the CIA's payroll in some fashion. Others, such as soldiers of fortune like Frank Sturgis/Fiorini, were attracted by the opportunity to ply their trade. Many of those who had worked for the CIA had learned how to fire a weapon, use an explosive, operate a boat, and in some cases, fly a plane. Much of the unused stock of C-4 and other such material was readily available at the right places in Miami and apparently found its way into the hands of would-be terrorists. Explosions rocked Miami with regularity. At least half a dozen exile terrorist organizations emerged, among them Cuban Power, Cuban National Liberation Front, Omega 7, Christian Nationalist Movement, and a coalition called the Coordination of United Revolutionary Organizations (CORU).

A report from the Metro-Dade County Organized Crime Bureau file on terrorism dated June 18, 1979, and posted on the Internet, started by saying that since May 25, 1977, "there had been 24 bombings and attempted bombings" in the U.S. and Puerto Rico. "San Juan," said the report, "has had 43 Cuban exile terrorist incidents since 1970. Of these, 41 were bombings and 2 were shooting murders. New York City has had 25 of these terrorist incidents since 1970. . . . In one 24-hour period in December 1975 a Cuban exile terrorist placed 8 bombs in the Miami, Florida area. Most of these bombs were placed in Government buildings such as Post Offices, Social Security Office, the State Attorney's office in Miami, and even in the Miami FBI office." This outburst occurred during a visit by William D. Rogers, the assistant secretary of state for inter-American affairs, apparently as a protest to the Ford administration's tentative overtures toward rapprochement.

"For the first few years of the Castro regime," said the report, "the

United States Government obviously was assisting Cuban exiles in their fight to topple the communist regime of Cuba. The U.S. Government supported the ill-fated Bay of Pigs invasion in 1961, and later supported other Cuban exile groups in their missions against Cuba. Because of this U.S. support there was no terrorism as such until the end of the 1960s, when the various Cuban exile groups began to realize that the U.S. Government was withdrawing support for their anti-Castro cause."[5]

Among the more notorious actions attributed to veterans of the secret war were the June 1972 Watergate burglary that eventually ended Richard Nixon's presidency; the October 1976 midair bombing of a Cuban airliner off the coast of Barbados, killing all seventy-three aboard, including Cuba's entire junior fencing team; the 1976 assassination of former Chilean ambassador Orlando Letelier and Ronni Moffitt, an American colleague, when the car driven by Letelier was blown up by a bomb as they entered Washington's Sheridan Circle; the apparent political assassinations of several high-profile Miami exile figures, most among the Cuban community's more moderate voices; the 1964 firing of a bazooka at the UN as Che Guevara prepared to address the organization; a bomb blast that took both legs of popular Miami Spanish-radio journalist Emilio Milian, who had denounced exile terrorism and intimidation. The reign of terror continued sporadically in Miami throughout much of the 1970s and into the 1980s.

Among the most notorious of the extremists were Orlando Bosch, a pediatrician by profession but terrorist by trade who had no documented CIA link, and Luis Posada, who, according to a 1991 *Miami Herald* story, "learned the finer points of demolitions from a friend on the CIA payroll. The agent then supplied him with explosives—the cheap stuff that stained your hands—to use in Cuba." Although a member of the Bay of Pigs Brigade, he sat out the invasion in Guatemala with a never-deployed battalion. Both Bosch and Posada were implicated in the deadly 1976 Cuban airliner bombing and jailed in Venezuela. But the DISIP, Venezuela's intelligence agency under President Carlos Andres Perez, had come under heavy Cuban exile influence. One of its ranking officers was Posada, who was working with the unit at the time he was implicated in the airliner bombing. Posada escaped, with help, and Bosch, after nine hunger strikes, was acquitted and deported back to the United States. After his escape, Posada fled to Central America where he worked in security for Presidents Jose Napoleon Duarte of El Salvador and Vinicio Cerezo of Guatemala.[6] Posada was held responsible for bombs placed in several Havana hotels during 1997, one of which killed an Italian guest. He was later convicted and jailed in Panama for plotting an assassination attempt against Fidel Castro during a visit there, but was pardoned in August 2004 and fled to Honduras.

Bosch has a lengthy history of terrorist acts, including firing a .57 mm recoilless rifle at a Polish freighter docked at the Port of Miami, a crime for which he was convicted, along with two members of his Cuban Power group. *Granma,* Cuba's state newspaper, published a list in 1980 of nearly fifty terrorist acts in which it claimed Bosch participated, either directly or indirectly. In one of the more absurd episodes, Bosch was arrested for towing a torpedo in a trailer along a busy South Florida roadway. In 1983 the Miami City Commission declared "A Dr. Orlando Bosch Day."

Not all the unemployed veterans of the secret war turned to terrorism. Some joined the fight against communism in the Congo. Others went to Vietnam. Felix Rodriguez and Gustavo Villoldo, working for the CIA, helped track down Che Guevara in the Bolivian jungles. Rafael Quintero worked with Ollie North's "off-the-shelf" resupply operation for U.S.-backed, anti-Sandinista guerrillas in Central America after Congress shut off their funding. This project led to the Iran-Contra scandal. While it's easy to agree with Dallek's assessment that Cuba policy showed Kennedy "at his worst," many exiles, among them Erneido Oliva and Rafael Quintero, remain convinced that the last best hope for the overthrow of Castro died with the Kennedys.

Finally, following are some personal observations and assumptions based on extensive research—interviews, declassified documents, reading of published material—and a limited firsthand knowledge of the 1959–1965 period encompassed by this book.

One gets a sense that a potential overt invasion/intervention by U.S. forces was implicit if the opportunity presented itself in all four of the separate identifiable phases of the secret war against Castro—the Bay of Pigs, Mongoose, the post-Mongoose period from the missile crisis to Kennedy's assassination, and post-assassination activity, mainly by the exile-led and U.S.-funded autonomous groups.

But only at the time of the Bay of Pigs does it appear the overthrow of Castro might have been successful without an accompanying overt and immediate U.S. military action. The scenario appears to have been that if the invasion brigade could seize and hold a beachhead on Cuban territory for several days, the exile political front would be flown in, declare itself a provisional government and request foreign military assistance. The only other time U.S. intervention was considered—with unknown and perhaps disastrous consequences—was during the missile crisis.

Instead, as is now known, in return for withdrawing the missiles from Cuba, Kennedy pledged to Khrushchev that the U.S. would not invade the island. Despite the Pentagon's apparent eagerness to find a pretext for an invasion, there is no indication the Kennedys were seriously contemplating U.S. military intervention during Mongoose. The exception: an internal rebellion within Cuba which they had hoped Mongoose would provoke. By the end of the missile crisis, such a rebellion was remote at best, given the decimation of organized anti-Castro resistance as a result of the Bay of Pigs, the increased Soviet Bloc role in Cuba, Castro's still-substantial popular support and an increasingly proficient Cuban security apparatus, augmented by the so-called Committees for the Defense of the Revolution (CDR), the block-by-block spy groups whose formation Castro announced in September 1960.

All of these factors make the rationale for the final two phases of the secret war—apparently still largely based on the hope of fomenting internal revolution that might provoke U.S. military intervention—even more puzzling. They may, however, help explain why President Kennedy embarked on the back-channel effort to normalize relations, as Castro's durability became increasingly evident, despite declining popular support.

In conclusion, it is interesting to note—mostly from declassified U.S. government documents—the assessments of Castro's popularity and his regime's increased control from the late 1960 through late 1963 period. The declassified documents serve to dramatize the futility of sparking an internal revolt, a premise on which U.S. covert programs that followed the Bay of Pigs were based. All of the documents—except the first on the early exodus into exile—were available to policy planners. In hindsight, one wonders if they were even read, let alone heeded.

Castro, when he seized power, unquestionably had the overwhelming majority of Cubans with him. But doubts arose quickly with the summary executions of some six hundred "war criminals" within the first three months of his rule, some of whom had certainly been guilty of heinous crimes under Batista. Regardless of the victims' wrongs, the spectacle of them going to the wall without due process was unnerving for many.

Batista supporters began to flee almost immediately after Castro took over, although the number of Cuban refugees generally was minimal in the early days of the Castro Revolution. By the middle of 1962 large-scale political and economic disenchantment had set in, with some three thousand potential internal dissidents arriving every week in Miami, a flood curtailed when air service was shut down during the missile crisis. By one estimate, about 215,000 Cubans emigrated to the United States between the latter part of 1958 and early 1963.[7]

On December 6, 1960, the U.S. embassy, in a lengthy cable from Havana to Washington, reported "during the past three months the popular support of the Castro regime has dropped markedly." Conceding that there were no precise figures, it estimated "Castro's dedicated support stands somewhere between 15 and 25 percent" with the remaining percentage divided between "a firm opposition and a wavering bloc of some 40 to 50 percent," with a continued downward trend. The cable added: "The government is determined to suppress the opposition at any cost. It has accumulated a substantial quantity of military hardware from the Soviet bloc and is making great efforts to train the military in their use. . . . It is not likely that the Castro regime will fall without considerable bloodletting and destruction of property."[8]

Two days later, on December 8, 1960, a Special National Intelligence Estimate declared Castro "remains firmly in control of Cuba. His overall popular support has declined . . . but as a symbol of revolutionary change he retains widespread support, particularly among the poorer classes. . . . In less than two years the Castro regime has consolidated its hold over Cuban society. New institutions have been created, and others, which have resisted the regime's domination, have been eliminated or revamped." It concluded by saying "we believe that during the period of this estimate [six months] Castro's control of Cuba will be further consolidated," adding that any major threat to his regime was "likely to be offset by the growing effectiveness of the state's instrumentalities of control."[9]

And as Marine Col. Jack Hawkins, chief of the Bay of Pigs paramilitary staff, concluded in his after-action report less than three weeks after the failed venture: "Further efforts to develop armed internal resistance, or to organize Cuban exile forces, should not be made except in connection with planned overt intervention by United States forces."[10]

On November 3, 1961, the day Operation Mongoose—a program designed to provoke an internal uprising in Cuba—was unveiled at a White House briefing, Sherman Kent, chairman of the board of National

Estimates, began a memo to Allen Dulles, then the CIA director, by saying: "The Castro regime has sufficient popular support and repressive capabilities to cope with any internal threat likely to develop within the foreseeable future. . . . At the same time, the regime's capabilities for repression are increasing more rapidly than are the potentialities for active resistance." Kent went on to say: "Fidel Castro's personal prestige and popularity were indispensable to the regime in the earlier stages of its development. None of his lieutenants could have inherited the personal authority which he then exercised. His loss now, by assassination or by natural causes, would certainly give an unsettling effect, but would probably not prove fatal."[11]

On March 21, 1962, another National Intelligence Estimate on Cuba made the following key points:

> (1) Forces available to the regime to suppress insurrection or repel invasion have been and are being greatly improved, with substantial Bloc assistance through provision of material and instruction; (2) Castro and the Revolution retain the positive support of at least a quarter of the population; (3) There is active resistance in Cuba, but it is limited, uncoordinated, unsupported, and desperate. The regime, with all the power of repression at its disposal, has shown that it can contain the present level of resistance activity; (4) The regime's apparatus for surveillance and repression should be able to cope with any popular tendency toward active resistance. Any impulse toward widespread revolt is inhibited by the fear which the apparatus inspires, and also by the lack of dynamic leadership and of any expectation of liberation within the foreseeable future.[12]

On June 14, 1963, five days before President Kennedy approved a new, integrated covert action program to topple Castro, another National Intelligence Estimate on Cuba, declared: "After a period marked by bitterness on Castro's part and by restraint on the part of the Soviets, the two parties now appear to have agreed to emphasize the consolidation of the Castro regime. We believe that the current situation within Cuba favors this consolidation. The mere passage of time tends to favor Castro as Cubans and others become accustomed to the idea that he is here to stay and as his regime gains in experience. It is unlikely that internal political opposition or economic difficulties will cause the regime to collapse. All our evidence points to the complete political dominance of Fidel, whose charismatic appeal continues to be the most important factor in the forward drive of the Cuban revolution."[13]

EPILOGUE

And from a December 12, 1963, CIA "status report" on Cuba, three weeks after President Kennedy's assassination: "We believe that apathy and resentment are now widespread in Cuba," but cautioning that "while they might complicate Castro's problems, they do not represent a serious threat to him or his regime." The assessment added: "In sum, our present policy can be characterized as one of low risk and low return: we are unlikely to experience a direct confrontation with the U.S.S.R. or to engender political strains with allied or neutral nations. On the other hand, we are still far from accomplishing our objectives of toppling the Castro regime . . . current U.S. programs at their present levels are not likely, barring unforeseen events such as the sudden death of Castro, to result in the early overthrow of the Castro-Communist regime."[14]

This assessment remained valid more than four decades later.

NOTES

Introduction

1. *Alleged Assassination Plots Involving Foreign Leaders. An Interim Report of the United States Senate Select Committee to Study Government Operations,* (New York: W. W. Norton, 1976), 71.

2. Ibid., 9.

3. Ibid., 9.

4. Ibid., xxxi.

5. Jake Esterline interview by author May 20–21, 1995.

6. Jake Esterline, audiocassette tape dictated for, and transcribed by, author November 1997.

7. *Foreign Relations of the United States (FRUS), Cuba, 1958–1960, Volume VI,* (Washington, D.C.: U.S. Government Printing Office, 1991), Doc nos. 64, 173; 271, 281.

8. John Dorschner and Roberto Fabricio, *The Winds of Change,* (New York: Coward, McCann & Geoghegan, 1980), 284–285, 313–314, 338, 367.

9. *Alleged Assassination Plots,* 11–12.

10. reign Relations of the United States (FRUS), *Cuba, 1961–63, Volume X,* (Washington, D. C.: U.S. Government Printing Office, 1997). Doc no. 57; 302–303.

11. Ibid., Doc no. 159; 306–307.

12. Ibid., Doc no. 205; 481–483.

13. Ibid., Doc no. 291; 710–718.

1. The Beginnings

1. Aleksandr Fursenko and Timothy Naftali. *"One Hell of a Gamble,"* (New York: W. W. Norton, 1997), 15–16.

2. Theodore Draper, *Castro's Revolution: Myths and Realities,* (New York: Frederick A. Praeger, 1962), 56–57, 107.

3. Andres Suarez, *Cuba: Castroism and Communism, 1959–1966,* (Cambridge, MA: M.I.T. Press, 1967), 18.

4. *FRUS, VI,* Doc no. 377; 639–640.

5. Ibid., Doc no. 423; 740–746.

6. Taylor Commission, April 22, 1961, 3. From declassified reports [National Security Archive, Washington. D. C.]. Report partially declassified in 1977 and published as *Operation Zapata,* (Frederick, MD: University Publications of America, 1981).

7. Peter Kornbluh, ed., *Bay of Pigs Declassified. The Secret CIA Report on the Invasion of Cuba,* (New York: New Press, 1998), 47–48.

8. *FRUS, VI,* Doc no. 623; 1178–1184.

9. Wayne S. Smith, *The Closest of Enemies,* (New York: W.W. Norton, 1987), 64.

10. Philip W. Bonsal, *Cuba, Castro and the United States,* (Pittsburgh: University of Pittsburgh Press, 1971), 175.

11. Jake Esterline interview by author, May 20–21, 1995, and audiocassette tape dictated for, and transcribed by, author November 1997.

12. Jack Hawkins, letters to author, January 19, 2002, and December 12, 2002.

13. Peter Wyden, *Bay of Pigs: The Untold Story,* (New York: Simon & Schuster, 1979), 331.

14. Ralph Weber, ed., *Spymasters: Ten CIA Officers in Their Own Words,* (Wilmington, DE: Scholarly Resources, 1999), 43–45; Evan Thomas, *The Very Best Men: Four Who Dared,* (New York: Simon & Schuster, 1995), 87.

15. James G. Blight and Peter Kornbluh, eds., *Politics of Illusion: The Bay of Pigs Invasion Reexamined,* (Boulder, CO: Lynne Rienner Publishers, 1998), 83.

16. Jake Esterline, audiocassette tape dictated for, and transcribed by, author September 1998.

17. Esterline, interview by author, June 10–11, 1995.

18. Jack Hawkins, *Clandestine Services History. Record of Paramilitary Action Against the Castro Government of Cuba. 17 March 1960–May 1961,* (National Security Archive, Washington, D.C.; declassified 1997).

19. Kornbluh, *Bay of Pigs Declassified,* 27.

20. Kornbluh, *Bay of Pigs Declassified,* 30.

21. *Operation Zapata,* Memo no. 1; 4–5.

22. Ibid., 6.

23. Hawkins, *Record of Paramilitary Action,* 9.

24. *Operation Zapata,* Memo no. 1; 6

25. Richard M. Bissell Jr., Jonathan E. Lewis, and Francis T. Pudlo, *Reflections of a Cold Warrior,* (New Haven, CT: Yale University Press, 1996), 156–157.

26. *FRUS,* X, Doc no. 9; 10–16.

27. Taylor Commission, April 24, 1961 (From declassified report, National Security Archive, Washington, D.C.), 9.

28. Esterline, from audiocassette tape provided author, November 1997.

29. CIA Inspector General, *Report on Plots to Assassinate Fidel Castro, May 23, 1967, (National Security Archive; declassified 1993)*, 14.

30. Bissell, *Reflections*, 157.

31. Michael R. Beschloss, *The CrisisYears: Kennedy and Khrushchev 1960–1963*, (New York: Edward Burlingame Books, 1991), 134.

32. Jack Pfeiffer, *Transcript of Oral Interview of Richard Bissell Jr.*, (Farmington, CT; October 17, 1975), 16.

33. Bissell, *Reflections*, 157.

34. *FRUS, X*, Doc no. 339; 807–809.

35. Esterline, from audiocassette tape dictated for author, November 1997.

36. Esterline interview by author May 20–21, 1995.

37. Esterline, from audiocassette tape dictated for author, September 1998.

2. Evolution of a Disaster

1. Jake Esterline, from audiocassette tape dictated for, sent to, and transcribed by author, November 1998.

2. Jack Hawkins, letter to author, August 27, 2001.

3. Ibid.

4. Ibid.

5. *Bay of Pigs 40 Years After: A Documents Briefing Book for an International Conference: March 22–24, 2001, tab No. 2, item no.18* . [Briefing Book prepared by National Security Archive, Washington, D.C., which cohosted conference with University of Havana, Cuba.].

6. Bissell, *Reflections,* 183.

7. Wyden, *Bay of Pigs,* 170.

8. Esterline, interview by author, June 10, 1995.

9. Pfeiffer, *Bissell Transcript*, 41.

10. Bissell, *Reflections*, 171.

11. Hawkins, letter to author, October 3, 2002.

12. Ibid., November 16, 2002.

13. *FRUS, X*, Doc no. 98; 221–222.

14. Wyden, *Bay of Pigs,* 168–169.

15. *Bay of Pigs 40 Years After*. Havana. March 22–24, 2001. From conference videotape transcribed by author.

16. Hawkins, letter to Peter Kornbluh, National Security Archive, March 3, 1998.

17. Ibid., letter to author, March 7, 2002.

18. Haynes Johnson, *The Bay of Pigs: The Leaders' Story of Brigade 2506*, (New York: W.W. Norton, 1964), 75–76.

19. Alexander Haig Jr. with Charles McCrarry, *Inner Circles: How America Changed the World.* (New York: Warner Books, 1992), 106–107.

20. Erneido Oliva. *"General Oliva's Story,"* unpublished manuscript, excerpts provided author, 1998.

21. Jack Pfeiffer, *Transcript of Oral Interview with Jacob D. Esterline,* St. Croix, U.S. Virgin Islands, November 10–11, 1975, 33–34.

22. Oliva, interview by author, March 22, 2000.

23. Hawkins, letter to author, June 10, 2001.

24. Jim Flannery, letter to author, June 2002.

25. *FRUS, X,* Doc no. 193; 412–417.

26. Allen Dulles, *The Craft of Intelligence,* (New York: Signet, 1965), 175–176.

27. Arthur Schlesinger Jr., *A Thousand Days: John F. Kennedy in the White House,* (London: Mayflower-Dell, 1967), 206–207.

28. Oliva interview.

29. General Charles P. Cabell, *A Man of Intelligence: Memoirs of War, Peace, and the CIA.* (Colorado Springs, CO: Impavide Publications, 1997), 366–374.

30. Bissell, *Reflections,* 184–185.

31. Esterline, tape recordings, November 1997 and September 1998.

32. Manuel Chavez, *The Berman Connection,* (unpublished memoirs of a retired Air Force Intelligence Officer attached to the Miami CIA station in the early 1960s).

33. Justin Gleichauf, telephone interview with author, May 29, 2002.

3. Fixing Blame

1. Tom Parrott, interviews with author, May 19, 1999, and March 4, 2002.

2. Bissell, *Reflections,* 191. From Box 138, Box 244, Princeton University. Used by permission of Princeton Library.

3. Operation Zapata. The "Ultrasensitive" Report and Testimony of the Board of Inquiry on the Bay of Pigs. Memorandum No.1. Narrative of the anti-Castro Cuban Operation Zapata. #75. (Frederick, MD: University Publications of America, Inc., 1981), n29.

4. Parrott interview.

5. *Operation Zapata,* 43.

6. Letter is part of documents declassified in 1998 with *CIA Inspector General's Report* (Kirkpatrick Report) as provided by National Security Archive, Washington, D.C.

7. *Miami Herald,* "Bay of Pigs Report Bares Split in CIA," February 28, 1998.

8. Ibid.

9. Peter Grose, *Gentleman Spy: The Life of Allen Dulles,* (Boston: Houghton Mifflin, 1994), 535.

10. Parrott interview.

11. Weber, ed., *Spymasters*, 68–69.

12. Ibid., 136–137.

13. *Miami Herald*, "Bay of Pigs Report Bares Split in CIA," February 28, 1998.

14. Jake Esterline did talk with Peter Wyden for his 1979 book on the Bay of Pigs. Esterline is identified in the book as Jake Engler, the CIA cover name he often used. Hawkins, in a memo provided the author in 1996, said he had "declined for 35 years to make any remarks at all to any writer or reporter about the Bay of Pigs—until recently when I decided to report a few facts. I have never read any quotation of me in these 35 years which has any basis in fact."

15. Hawkins, memo to author, February 27, 1997, *Covert Operations Against the Castro Government of Cuba. January, 1960–April, 1961.*

16. Parrott, letter to author, February 20, 2002.

17. Hawkins, memo to author, February 27, 1997, *Covert Operations Against the Castro Government of Cuba.*

18. Ibid.

19. *Miami Herald*, "Revisiting the Failure at the Bay of Pigs," June 9, 1996.

20. Lawrence Freedman, *Kennedy's Wars: Berlin, Cuba, Laos, and Vietnam*, (New York: Oxford University Press, 2000), 133.

21. Jim Flannery, letter to author, June 2002.

22. Jake Esterline, cassette tape sent to author, September 1998.

23. Seymour M. Hersh, *The Dark Side of Camelot*, (Boston: Little, Brown and Company) 186.

24. Jack Hawkins, telephone interview with author, April 1998.

25. Jim Flannery provided copy to author of unpublished paper on the Bay of Pigs written in 2000 for his grandchildren.

26. Thomas, *The Very Best Men*, 245.

27. Freedman, *Kennedy's Wars*, 133.

28. *Operation Zapata*, 40.

29. Bissell, *Reflections*, 143.

30. Weber, ed., *Spymasters*, 50.

31. Schlesinger, *A Thousand Days*, 206–207.

32. Hawkins, undated paper provided author.

33. Esterline, interview by author, June 10–11, 1995.

4. Bobby Takes Charge

1. *FRUS, X*, Doc no. 158; 304–306

2. C. David Heymann, *RFK*, (New York: Dutton, 1998), 256.

3. *FRUS, X*, Doc no. 166; 313–314

4. Edwin O. Gutman and Jeffrey Shulman, ed., *Robert Kennedy in His Own Words,* (New York: Bantam Press, 1988), 239–240.

5. Bissell, *Reflections,* 201.

6. *FRUS, X,* Doc no.157; 302–304; italicized sentence underscored and exclamation point added by Kennedy in his own hand.

7. Ibid., Doc no. 157; 302–304.

8. Ibid., Doc no. 184; 397.

9. Ibid., Doc no. 163; 310–318.

10. Ibid., Doc no. 163; 310–312.

11. *Operation Zapata,* 52–53.

12. Heymann, *RFK,* 255–256.

13. *FRUS, X,* Doc nos. 205, 206 and 207; 481–489.

14. Ibid., Doc no. 214; 518–520.

15. Ibid., Doc no. 223; 554–560.

16. *Alleged Assassination Plots,* 136.

17. Arthur Schlesinger Jr., *Robert Kennedy and His Times,* Vol. I. (Boston: Houghton Mifflin Company, 1978), 493.

18. *FRUS, X,* Doc no. 250; 631–633.

19. Ibid., Doc no. 256; 640–641.

20. Ibid., Doc no. 258; 645–646.

21. Parrott interview.

22. Dino Brugioni; Robert F. McCort, ed., *EYEBALL TO EYEBALL,* (New York: Random House, 1990), 59–60.

23. Parrott, letter to author, October 2, 2002.

24. *FRUS, X,* Doc no. 269; 664–665.

25. Ibid., Doc no. 270; 666–667.

26. Ibid., Doc no. 271; 668–672.

27. Ibid., Doc no. 272; 673–674.

28. Ibid., Doc no. 273; 675–677.

29. Robert Hurwitch, State Department Cuba Desk Officer, 1960–64, *Most of Myself,* unpublished memoirs, 129–130.

30. *Alleged Assassination Plots,* 138.

31. Richard N. Goodwin, *Remembering America,* (Boston: Little, Brown and Company, 1988), 445.

5. Mongoose

1. Hurwitch, unpublished memoirs, 130.

2. Response to question asked Schlesinger by author, who attended conference as invited observer.

3. Richard Helms with William Wood, *A Look over My Shoulder: A Life in the Central Intelligence Agency*, (New York: Random House, 2003), 205, 209–210.

4. Blight and Kornbluh, eds., *Politics of Illusion*, 117.

5. Sam Halpern, interviews with author, August 19, 1996, and July 13, 2001.

6. Ibid.

7. Ibid.

8. *FRUS, X*, Doc no. 283; 696–699.

9. Ted Shackley, interviews with author, April 9, 1998, and September 18, 2002.

10. Bissell, *Reflections*, 203.

11. Parrott interview.

12. Halpern interview.

13. Bissell, *Reflections*, 201.

14. Halpern interview.

15. Parrott interview.

16. Alexander Haig Jr., interview with author, April 29, 2002.

17. *FRUS, X*, Doc no. 281; 691–695.

18. Halpern interview.

19. *FRUS, X*, Doc no. 286; 701–702.

20. Ibid., Doc no. 288; 704–705.

21. Ibid., Doc no. 291; 710–718.

22. Ibid., Doc no. 292; 719–720.

23. Halpern interview.

24. *FRUS, X*, Doc no. 309; 765.

25. Ibid., Doc no. 304; 745–747.

26. From Documents Briefing Book prepared by The National Security Archive, Washington, D. C., for Bay of Pigs/Mongoose Conference, St. Simon's Island, Georgia, May 31–June 2, 1996.

27. Halpern interview.

28. *FRUS, X*, Doc no. 305; 747–748.

29. Bissell, *Reflections*, 201.

30. *Alleged Assassination Plots*, 334.

6. "Nutty Schemes"

1. Hurwitch, unpublished memoirs, 131.

2. Ronald Steel, *In Love with Night: The American Romance with Robert Kennedy*, (New York: Simon & Schuster, 2000), 79.

3. Parrott interview.

4. *Alleged Assassination Plots*, 142.

5. Cecil B. Currey, *Edward Lansdale: The Unquiet American,* (Washington, D.C: Brassey's, 1998), 244.

6. Parrott interview.

7. Blight and Kornbluh, eds., *Politics of Illusion,* 116.

8. *Alleged Assassination Plots,* 143.

9. Halpern interview.

10. *Alleged Assassination Plots,* 144.

11. Documents Briefing Book prepared by The National Security Archive (not to be confused with U.S. Government's National Archives) for Bay of Pigs conference, Havana, March 22–24, 2001.

12. Anna Nelson, Lisandro Perez, eds., *CUBAN STUDIES 32,* University of Pittsburgh Press, Pittsburgh, PA, 2001.

13. JFK Assassination Records Review Board [ARRB] papers; National Archives, Washington, D.C., JCS Central Files 1962, Box 29.

14. Jon Elliston, *Psywar on Cuba,* (Melbourne, Australia: Ocean Press, 2000), 114–116.

15. *FRUS, X,* Doc no. 365; 896–897.

16. Ibid., Doc no. 370; 922.

17. Chavez, unpublished memoirs, 362–363.

18. Documents Briefing Book prepared by the National Security Archive for Bay of Pigs conference, Havana, Cuba, March 22–24, 2001.

19. JFK ARRB, National Archives, Washington D.C. Memorandum for Record. Minutes of Special Group (Augmented) on Operation Mongoose, September 27, 1962.

20. JFK ARRB, National Archives, Washington, D.C. Memorandum for Record. Minutes of Special Group (Augmented) on Operation Mongoose, October 16, 1962.

21. JFK AARB, National Archives, Washington, D. C. Memorandum for Record. Minutes of Special Group (Augmented), October 26, 1962.

22. *Foreign Relations of the United States (FRUS), Cuba Missile Crisis and Aftermath, 1961–1963, Volume XI,* (Washington, D.C.: U. S. Government Printing Office, 1996), Doc no. 274; 681–687.

23. Ibid., Doc no. 306; 748–750.

24. Ibid., Doc no. 309; 754–755.

25. Documents Briefing Book prepared by The National Security Archive for Bay of Pigs conference, Havana, Cuba, March 22–24, 2001.

26. Ibid.

27. Elliston, *Psywar,* 169–174.

28. CIA Inspector General's "Report on Plots to Assassinate Fidel Castro," 9–13.

7. Mongoose Redux

1. Halpern interview.

2. *FRUS, X,* Doc no. 314; 771–772.

3. Documents Briefing Book prepared by The National Security Archive for international conference on Bay of Pigs, Havana, Cuba, March 2001.

4. Ibid.

5. Church Committee testimony of Sam Halpern, June 18, 1975. Declassified, 1994. Copy provided by The National Security Archive.

6. Shackley interview.

7. Parrott interview.

8. Halpern interview.

9. *FRUS, X,* Doc no. 325; 791–792.

10. Ibid., Doc no. 331; 800–801.

11. Carlos Lechuga, *Cuba and the Missile Crisis,* (Melbourne, Australia: Ocean Press, 2000), 24–26.

12. Jean Daniel, "UNOFFICIAL ENVOY: An Historic Report from Two Capitals," *The New Republic,* December 14, 1963, 15–20.

13. Memo, Hughes to Acting Secretary, 12/13/63, #64, National Security/ Country file, Box 17, LBJ Library.

14. Fursenko and Naftali, *"One Hell of a Gamble,"* 150.

15. General Anatoli I. Gribkov and General William Y. Smith, *Operation Anadyr. U.S. and Russian Generals Recount the Cuban Missile Crisis,* (Chicago: edition q, inc., 1994), 91.

16. Fursenko and Naftali, *"One Hell of a Gamble,"* 179–180.

17. Lechuga, *Cuba and the Missile Crisis,* 25.

18. *FRUS, X,* Doc no. 340; 822–823.

19. Ibid., Doc no. 343; 826–827.

20. *Miami Herald,* "Castro Tells of Regret in '62 Crisis," October 20, 2002.

21. FRUS, X, Doc no. 344; 827.

22. Ibid., Doc no. 353; 846–850.

23. Ibid., Doc no. 353; 846–850.

24. Ibid., Doc no. 354; 850–851.

25. Ibid., Doc no. 360; 878–884.

26. Ibid., Doc no. 361; 885.

27. Ibid., Doc no. 367; 899–917.

28. Ibid., Doc no. 367; 907.

29. *Alleged Assassination Plots,* 147.

30. *FRUS, X,* Doc no. 377; 939–940.

31. Ibid., Doc no. 380; 944–946.

32. Ibid., Doc no. 380; 944–946.

33. Ibid., Doc no. 378; 940–941.

34. Gribkov and Smith, *Operation Anadyr*, 108–109.

35. FRUS, *X*, Doc no. 382; 947–949.

36. Shackley interview.

37. Ibid.

38. *FRUS, X*, Doc no. 398; footnote #2, 973.

39. Shackley interview.

40. *Bay of Pigs 40 Years After*. Documents Briefing Book prepared by The National Security Archive for Bay of Pigs conference, Havana, Cuba, March 22–24, 2001.

41. Blight and Kornbluh, *Politics of Illusion*, 130.

42. *FRUS, X*, Doc no. 386; 957–958.

43. Ibid., Doc no. 390; 963–966.

44. Ibid., Doc no. 413; 1043–1044.

45. Ibid., Doc no. 420; 1052.

46. Ibid., Doc no. 431; 1067–1068.

47. Halpern interview.

48. *FRUS, XI*, Doc no. 8; 11–13.

49. Chang and Kornbluh, eds., *The Cuban Missile Crisis, 1962*, 1992 edition, 52.

50. *FRUS, XI*, Doc no. 19; 45–47.

51. Ibid., Doc no. 21; 72.

52. Rafael Quintero interview, April 15, 2003.

53. Evan Thomas, *Robert Kennedy: His Life*, (New York: Simon & Schuster, 2000), 234.

54. Chang and Kornbluh, eds., *The Cuban Missile Crisis, 1962*, 1992 edition, 224.

55. Hurwitch, unpublished memoirs, 139.

56. *FRUS*, XI, Doc no. 79; 221–226.

57. Ibid., Doc no. 82; 229–231.

58. *Alleged Assassination Plots*, 148*n*.

59. Parrott interview.

60. *Alleged Assassination Plots*. 147–148.

61. *FRUS, XI*, Doc no. 217; 543–545.

62. Ibid., Doc no. 261; 648–651.

63. Hurwitch, unpublished memoirs, 166.

8. Miami: Perpetual Intrigue

1. Shackley interview.

2. *Look* magazine, June 16, 1964.

3. *Miami Herald*, June 2, 1964.

4. Shackley interview.

5. Bradley Ayers, *The War That Never Was*, (New York: Bobbs-Merrill, 1976), 26.

6. Shackley interview.

7. Justin Gleichauf, *Studies of Intelligence*, (Unclassified Edition. Winter-Spring 2001, No. 10), 49–53.

8. Letter sent to White House dated February 12, 1963, declassified under JFK Assassination Records Review Act.

9. Gleichauf, telephone interview, May 29, 2002.

10. John Dorschner, "Casablanca of the Caribbean," *Miami Herald/TROPIC*, April 4, 1976.

11. Documents Briefing Book prepared by The National Security Archive for Bay of Pigs conference, Havana, Cuba, March 22–24, 2001

12. Parrott interview.

13. Ibid.

14. Gleichauf, telephone interview.

15. George Volsky, interview, February 7, 2002.

16. David Corn, *Blond Ghost*, (New York: Simon & Schuster, 1994), 102–103.

17. Carlos Obregon, interview October 17, 1996, and essay written for author November 1996.

18. CIA document Appendix J entitled *The Miami Station;* declassified November 6, 1995, under JFK Assassination Records Act, provided by The National Security Archive (document to which it was appended is not identified).

19. Robert Reynolds, interview, July 12, 2001.

20. Gleichauf, telephone interview.

21. Miami Station document—note #18 above—says 300 persons were assigned. Most published accounts say JMWAVE station had 400 people assigned to it at the peak, although that may have included about 100 assigned to Cuba, but not working in Miami.

22. Miami Station document—note #18 above—neither of the two exiles who offered views of Operation 40 wanted to be identified; operation remains a sensitive and controversial issue in the Cuban community.

23. *Studies of Intelligence,* cited above.

24. Shackley interviews.

25. Ibid.

9. A New Beginning

1. *FRUS, XI*, Doc no. 170; 432–437.

2. Ibid., Doc. 231; 586–590.

3. *FRUS, X,* Doc no. 406; 1025–1032.

4. *FRUS, XI,* Doc no. 14; 22–25.

5. Ibid., Doc no. 216; 541–542.

6. Ibid., Doc no. 261; 648–651.

7. Ibid., Doc no. 264; 656–657.

8. Parrott interview.

9. Halpern interview.

10. *FRUS, XI,* Doc no. 114; 303.

11. Halpern interview.

12. *FRUS, XI,* Doc no. 366; 867.

13. Blight and Kornbluh, *Politics of Illusion,* 130–131.

14. FRUS, *XI,* Doc no. 260; 646–648.

15. Ibid., Doc no. 274; 681–688.

16. John Crimmins, telephone interview, November 2003.

17. Haig, *Inner Circles,* 106.

18. *FRUS,* XI, Doc no. 271; 668–669.

19. JFK ARRB, Record no. 145–10001–104919.

20. *FRUS, XI,* Doc no. 313; 761–762.

21. Ibid., Doc no. 311; 757–758.

22. Ibid., Doc no. 318; 769–772.

23. Ibid., Doc no. 319; 772–773.

24. Ibid., Doc no. 322; 780–781.

25. Ibid., Doc no. 323; 782–784.

26. Ibid., Doc no. 325; 786–788.

27. Hurwitch, unpublished memoirs, 166.

28. JFK ARRB, Record no. 145–10001–10195; CIA paper 5/16/64, "Sabotage in Cuba."

29. *FRUS, XI,* Doc no. 344; 821–823.

30. Ibid., Doc no. 346; 828–834.

31. Ibid., Doc no. 348; 837–838.

32. *Alleged Assassination Plots,* 173.

33. Shackley interview.

34. Ibid.

35. Hinckle and Turner, *Deadly Secrets,* end note #2, chapter 5, 430.

36. *Miami Herald,* August 21, 1963.

37. Corn, *Blond Ghost,* 81.

38. JFK ARRB, Record no. 145–10001–10126.

39. Documents Briefing Book prepared by The National Security Archive for Bay of Pigs conference, Havana, Cuba, March 2001.

40. Corn, *Blond Ghost,* 105.

41. Documents Briefing Book prepared by The National Security Archive, Bay of Pigs conference, Havana, Cuba, March 2001.

42. Shackley interview.
43. Corn, *Blond Ghost*, 112.

10. Accommodation or Assassination

1. Peter Kornbluh, *Cigar Aficionado*, October 1999.
2. Author attended conference as an observer.
3. *Alleged Assassination Plots*, 71.
4. *FRUS, XI*, Doc no. 275; 687–688.
5. Ibid., 687*n*.
6. Peter Kornbluh, Electronic Briefing Book, The National Security Archive website, August 1999, and *Cigar Aficionado*, October 1999.
7. *FRUS, XI*, Doc no. 310; 755–756.
8. Ibid., 756*n*.
9. Ibid., Doc no. 314; 762–763.
10. Kornbluh, Electronic Briefing Book, The National Security Archive website, August 1999.
11. *FRUS, XI*, Doc no. 332; 798–799.
12. Kornbluh, Electronic Briefing Book, The National Security Archive website, August 1999.
13. William Attwood, *The Twilight Struggle: Tales of the Cold War*, (New York: Harper and Row, 1987), 258–259.
14. *FRUS, XI*, Doc no. 367; 868–870.
15. Attwood, *The Twilight Struggle*, 260–261.
16. *FRUS, XI*, Doc no. 377; 888–889.
17. JFK ARRB, Record no. 145–10001–10016.
18. Ibid., Record no. 145–10001–10012.
19. Kornbluh, *Cigar Aficionado*, 97.
20. *The Investigation of the Assassination of President John F. Kennedy: Performance of the Intelligence Agencies,* Book V, Final Report of the Select Committee to Study Governmental Operations with Respect to Intelligence Activities, United States Senate, April 23, 1976, 19–20.
21. Attwood, *The Twilight Struggle*, 263.
22. Memo, Chase to Bundy, 11/25/63, "Cuba—Item of Presidential Interest," Country Country File, NSF, Box 21, LBJ Library.
23. JFK ARRB, Record no. 145–10001–10015.
24. Ibid., Record no. 145–10001–10013.
25. Memo, Chase to Bundy, 12/3/63, "Bill Attwood's Activities," Country File, NSF, Box 21, LBJ Library.
26. Attwood, *The Twilight Struggle*, 263–264.

27. Verbal message from Castro, given to Lisa Howard for President Johnson, 2/12/64, Country File, NSF, Box 21, LBJ Library.

28. Memo, Bundy to seven White House aides, 2/26/64. Country File, NSF, Box 21, LBJ Library.

29. Memo, Chase to Bundy, 7/7/64, "Adlai Stevenson and Lisa Howard," Country File, NSF, Box 21, LBJ Library.

30. Kornbluh, *Cigar Aficionado*, October 1999.

31. Memo, Chase to Bundy, "Castro and Donovan," Country File, NSF, Box 21, LBJ Library.

32. *Alleged Assassination Plots*, 71.

33. Ibid., 6.

34. CIA Inspector General's 1967 "Report on Plots to Assassinate Fidel Castro."

35. *Alleged Assassination Plots*, 87.

36. Copy of Pearson column is contained in CIA IG's "Report on Plots to Assassinate Fidel Castro."

37. Thomas Powers, *The Man Who Kept the Secrets: Richard Helms and the CIA*, (New York: Alfred A. Knopf, 1979), 120–122, 156.

38. Ibid., 57, 347n.

39. CIA IG's "Report on Plots to Assassinate Fidel Castro."

40. *Alleged Assassination Plots*, 73.

41. Ibid., 83.

42. Shackley interview.

43. *Alleged Assassination Plots*, 83–85.

44. CIA IG's "Report on Plots to Assassinate Fidel Castro."

45 *FRUS*, X. Doc no. 337; 807–808.

46. Powers, *The Man Who Kept the Secrets*, 346n.

47. CIA IG's "Report on Plots to Assassinate Fidel Castro."

48. Ibid.

49. Halpern interview.

50. Halpern testimony to Church Committee.

51. Halpern interview.

52. Parrott interview.

53. *Alleged Assassination Plots*, 6–7.

11. "Let Cubans Be Cubans"

1. *FRUS, XI,* Doc no. 14; 22–25.

2. Halpern interview.

3. Authors Warren Hinckle and William Turner, in their book *The Fish Is Red,* and in an updated version entitled *Deadly Secrets,* say, without attribution,

that Manuel Artime's autonomous operation in Central America was code-named Second Naval Guerrilla. Rafael Quintero, Artime's deputy, and Sam Halpern, executive assistant in the CIA office responsible for dealing with the Artime group, told the author that they had never heard of Second Naval Guerrilla.

4. *FRUS, XI*, Doc no. 346; 828–834.

5. Thomas, *Robert Kennedy: His Life*, 235–236.

6. Erneido Oliva, interviews March 22, 2000; March 3 and June 27, 2002.

7. JFK ARRB Record no. 45–10001–10195, CIA paper "Sabotage in Cuba," 5/16/64.

8. Quintero interview.

9. Paper, "Talking Points to Be Used in Conversation with Foreign Minister Oduber Concerning Cuban Exile Activities," #144-a, Country File, NSF, Box 22, LBJ Library.

10. JFK ARRB, Record no. 145–10001–10242.

11. *FRUS, XI*, Doc no. 356; 850–853. Footnote #6, page 852, incorrectly identifies the article as appearing in the *Miami Herald*. It appeared in the *Miami News*.

12. *Miami News*, July 16, 1963.

13. Shackley interview.

14. Ibid.

15. John Crimmins, telephone interview, November 2002.

16. Quintero interview.

17. JFK ARRB, Record no. 145–10001–10124.

18. Ibid., Record no. 145–10001–10242.

19. Ibid., Record no. 145–10001–10168.

20. Transcript, Federal Broadcast Information Service. "Menoyo Interrogation," #93, 2/3/65, Country File, NSF, Box 22, LBJ Library.

21. JFK ARRB, Record no. 145–10001–10242.

22. Quintero interview.

23. Ibid.

24. JFK ARRB, Record no. 145–10001–10229.

25. Oliva interview.

26. Author was present as conference observer.

27. JFK ARRB, Record no. 145–10001–10242

28. Report, "Review of Current Program of Covert Action Against Cuba," 1/9/64, #2, Country File, NSF, Box 24, LBJ Library.

29. Memo, McCone for the Record, "Meetings with the President" 4/7/64, #3, John McCone memoranda file, Box 1, LBJ Library.

30. Memo for the Record, Helms and Bundy meeting on Artime and Ray, #94A. Cuba Country file, NSF, Box 22, LBJ Library.

31. JFK ARRB, Record no. 145–10001–10033.

32. Ibid., Record no. 145–10001–10032.

NOTES

33. Intelligence Information Cable, #5, 5/23/64, Country File, NSF, Box 22, LBJ Library.

12. Fading Fast

1. House Select Committee on Intelligence, Vol. X: Anti-Castro Activists and Organizations, XIV, 140–141; Intelligence Information Cable, #20, 6/4/64, Country Files, NSF, Box 22, LBJ Library.

2. JFK ARRB, "A Reappraisal of Autonomous Operations," 6/3/64, Record no. 145–10001–10032.

3. Memo, Chase to Bundy, "Raids by Artime-Special Group Meeting," 6/4/64, #40, Country File, NSF, Box 22, LBJ Library.

4. Memo, Chase to Bundy, "Special Group—Autonomous Exile Groups," 6/18/64, #97, Country Files, NSF, Box 22, LBJ Library.

5. JFK ARRB, Record no. 145–10001–10242.

6. Memo, Chase to Bundy, "Special Group—Autonomous Exile Groups," 6/18/64, #97, Country File, NSF, Box 22, LBJ Library.

7. Research Memorandum, INR—Hughes to Secretary of State, "Significance of July OAS Meeting," 9/14/64, #37, Country File, NSF, Box 25, LBJ Library.

8. Incoming Telegram, Cuban Coordinator/Miami to Secretary of State, 7/21/64, #15, Country File, NSF, Box 22, LBJ Library.

9. House Select Committee on Intelligence, VOL. X: Anti-Castro Activists and Organizations, XIV, 140–141.

10. Intelligence Information Cable, 1/26/65, #30, Country File, NSF, Box 22, LBJ Library.

11. Ibid.

12. JFK ARRB, Memo, "Financial Support to the Autonomous Group Headed by Manuel Artime." 7/16/64. Record no. 145–10001–10241.

13. Quintero Interview.

14. *Miami Herald*, "Exiles Look to Oliva for Hope," 6/21/64.

15. Oliva interview.

16. Intelligence Information Cable, 6/5/64, #42, Country File, NSF, Box 22, LBJ Library.

17. Memo, Chase to Bundy, "Major Oliva to Meet Bowdler," 7/6/65, #134, Country File, NSF, Box 22, LBJ Library.

18. Memo, Chase to Bundy, "Special Group—Support for Oliva," 7/7/64, #135, Country File, NSF, Box 22, LBJ Library.

19. Intelligence Information Cable, 7/2/64, #48, Country File, NSF, Box 22, LBJ Library.

20. Cable, Summ to Secretary of State, 8/12/64, #102, Country File, NSF, Box 22, LBJ Library.

21. Cable, UPI from Panama, 8/31/64, #47a, Country File, NSF, Box 22, LBJ Library.

13. Last Hurrah

1. Associated Press cable, Panama, 9/14/64, #108a, Country File, NSF, Box 22, LBJ Library.

2. *Miami Herald*, September 16, 1964.

3. Quintero interview.

4. Cable, "RECE Visit," 10/23/64, #67, Country File, Cuba, Box 22, LBJ Library.

5. Memo, Chase to Bundy, 9/15/64, #112, "Artime's Raid," Country File, NSF, Box 22, LBJ Library.

6. Press accounts appearing in *Miami Herald*, September 15 to September 25, 1965.

7. Draft, Proposed Script for Conversation with Somoza on Artime, 9/16/64, #51, Country File, NSF, Box 22, LBJ Library.

8. Memo, Thompson to Secretary of State et al., 10/6/64, #14, Country File, NSF, Box 22, LBJ Library.

9. Cable, US Embassy to State Department, 11/9/64, #9a, Country File, NSF, Box 20, LBJ Library.

10. Memo, Chase to Bundy, 11/10/64, #9, Country File, NSF, Box 20, LBJ Library.

11. Memo, Coordinator of Cuban Affairs, "Conclusions of Investigation of Spanish Ship Incident," 11/21/64, #124-b, Country File, NSF, Box 22, LBJ Library.

12. Ibid.

13. Memo for 303 Committee, 11/5/64, #53, "Future of the Autonomous Group Headed by Manuel Artime," Country File, NSF, Box 22, LBJ Library.

14. *Miami Herald*, November 22, 1964.

15. Ibid., December 4, 1964.

16. Ibid., December 5, 1964.

17. Quintero interview.

18. *Miami Herald,* five-part series beginning December 12, 1964.

19. CIA IG's "Report on Plots to Assassinate Fidel Castro."

20. Nestor Sanchez interview by author, March 7, 2002.

21. CIA IG's "Report on Plots to Assassinate Fidel Castro."

22. *Alleged Assassination Plots*, 87.

23. CIA IG's "Report on Plots to Assassinate Fidel Castro." The Church Com-

mittee report, as do some other accounts, erroneously report that FitzGerald returned to Paris on November 22 with Sanchez to deliver the pen. Sanchez alone delivered it.

24. *Alleged Assassination Plots*, 88–89.

25. Ibid., 87*n*.

26. Ibid., 89.

27. Memo for 303 Committee, 11/5/64, #53, "Future of the Autonomous Group Headed by Manuel Artime," Country File, NSF, Box 22, LBJ Library.

28. CIA IG's "Report on Plots to Assassinate Fidel Castro."

29. JFK ARRB, Record no. 202–10002–10117, JCS Central Files 1963.

30. Quintero interview.

31. CIA IG's "Report on Plots to Assassinate Fidel Castro."

32. Quintero interview.

33. Ibid.

34. Memo, to 303 Committee, 1/6/65, #62, "Activities of Manuel Artime Buesa . . ." Country File, Cuba, Box 22, LBJ Library.

35. Ibid.

36. Memo, Chase to Bundy, 1/5/65, #61, Country File, Cuba, Box 22, LBJ Library.

37. Memo, Chase to Bundy, 1/5/65, #62, "Artime," Country File, Cuba, Box 22, LBJ Library.

38. Memo, Chase to Bundy, 1/26/65, #81 "Cuba—Miscellaneous," Country File, Cuba, Box 22, LBJ Library.

39. CIA IG's "Report on Plots to Assassinate Fidel Castro."

40. Memo, Chase to Bundy, 34 2/9/65, #65, "Cuba—Activities of Artime Group," Country File, Cuba, Box 22, LBJ Library.

41. Memo, State to 303 Committee, 2/23/65, #66a, "Artime Group," Country File, Cuba, Box 22, LBJ Library.

42. Memo, Chase to Crimmins, 2/18/65, "U.S. Government Relations with RECE," #70, Country File, Cuba, Box 22, LBJ Library.

43. Memo, Chase to Bundy, 3/4/65, #1, Country File, Cuba, Box 24, LBJ Library.

44. Ibid.

45. *Miami Herald*, March 15, 1965.

46. Quintero interview.

47. CIA IG's "Report on Plots to Assassinate Fidel Castro."

48. Powers, *The Man Who Kept the Secrets*, 152.

49. CIA IG's "Report on Plots to Assassinate Fidel Castro."

50. JFK ARRB, Doc no. 145–10001–10211.

14. LBJ Cashes out

1. Shackley interview.

2. Ayers, *The War That Never Was*, 182–183.

3. Halpern, telephone interview, October 31, 2002.

4. Crimmins, telephone interview, November 2002.

5. Quintero interview.

6. Robert Dallek, *Flawed Giant,* (New York: Oxford University Press, 1998), 18–19.

7. Michael Beschloss, *Taking Charge,* (New York: Simon & Schuster, 1997), 87.

8. CIA Memo, "Cuba—A Status Report," 12/12/63, #28, Country File, NSF, Box 24, LBJ Library.

9. Memo, Bundy to the President, 12/15/63, #33, Country File, NSF, Box 24, LBJ Library.

10. Memo for Record, "Meetings with the President, 23 November 1963–27 December 1963," 12/19/65, John McCone Memoranda, Box 1, LBJ Library.

11. JFK ARRB. Record no. 202–10002–10010, Taylor Papers.

12. Memo, Bundy to the President, 1/9/64, #1, Country File, NSF, Box 24, LBJ Library.

13. JFK ARRB, Record no. 145–10001–10168.

14. Joseph A. Califano Jr., *The Triumph and Tragedy of Lyndon Johnson: The White House Years,* (New York: Simon & Schuster, 1991). A notation says "soon after Johnson became President, he ordered a stop to all covert activity to eliminate or overthrow Castro." 295*n.* Califano at the time was a Pentagon aide involved with Cuba. The reference could be to either a January 1964 suspension or, more likely, an April 7, 1964, meeting in the White House. Califano did not respond to an interview request.

15. Oliva interview.

16. CIA, "Review of Current Program of Covert Action Against Cuba," 1/25/64, #2, Country File, NSF, Box 24, LBJ Library.

17. Lyndon Baines Johnson, *The Vantage Point,* (New York: Holt, Rinehart and Winston, 1971), 184–187.

18. Crimmins, telephone interview, November 2002.

19. JFK ARRB, Record no. 145–10001–10111.

20. Haig, *Inner Circles,* 109.

21. JFK ARRB, Record no. 145–10001–10157.

22. Ibid., Record no. 145–10001–10221.

23. Ibid., letter, FitzGerald to Bundy, Record no. 145–10001–10003.

24. Memo for Discussion, 4/7/64, #205, NSF, McGeorge Bundy Files, Box 2, LBJ Library.

25. Memo for Record, "Meeting at the White House; Review of Covert Program Directed against Cuba," 4/7/64, #3, John McCone Memoranda, Box 1, LBJ Library.

26. *Alleged Assassination Plots,* 177.

27. Memo, Chase to Bundy, 4/22/64, #51, NSF, Country File, Box 18, LBJ Library.

28. George Ball speech, 4/23/64, Roanoke, Virginia; copy from author's personal files.

29. JFK ARRB, Record no. 145–10001–10115.

30. Memo, Bundy to the President, 6/26/65, #17, NSF, Country File, Box 24, LBJ Library.

31. The Miami Station, Appendix J. See note #18, Chapter Eight.

32. Esterline interview.

Epilogue

1. Robert Dallek, *An Unfinished Life: John F. Kennedy 1917–1963*, (Boston: Little, Brown and Company, 2003), 709.

2. FRUS, X, Doc no. 257; 642–645.

3. Freedman, *Kennedy's Wars*, 147.

4. From notes by author who attended conference as an observer.

5. From website: www.Cuban-exile.com.doc.

6. *Miami Herald*, "The Shadow Warrior," November 10, 1991.

7. Richard R. Fagan, Richard A. Brody, and Thomas J. O'Leary, *Cubans in Exile: Disaffection and the Revolution,* (Stanford, CA: Stanford University Press, 1968), 17, 62.

8. *FRUS, VI*, Doc no. 617; 1149–1163.

9. Ibid., Doc no. 620; 1168–1174.

10. Jack Hawkins, "Record of Paramilitary Action Against the Castro Government of Cuba."

11. *FRUS, X*, Doc no. 271; 668–672.

12. Ibid., Doc no. 315; 772–776.

13. *FRUS, XI*, Doc no. 347; 834–846.

14. *Miami Herald*, "1963 Report on Cuba Has Familiar Ring," October 15, 1998.

BIBLIOGRAPHY

Books

Abel, Elie. *The Missile Crisis.* Philadelphia: J.B. Lippincott, 1966.

Andrew, Christopher. *For the President's Eyes Only: Secret Intelligence and the American Presidency from Washington to Bush.* New York: HarperCollins, 1995.

Attwood, William. *The Reds and the Blacks: A Personal Adventure.* New York: Harper and Row, 1967.

Attwood, William. *The Twilight Struggle: Tales of the Cold War.* New York: Harper and Row, 1987.

Ayers, Bradley Earl. *The War That Never Was: An Insider's Account of CIA Covert Operations against Cuba.* Indianapolis: Bobbs-Merrill, 1976.

Bamford, James. *Body of Secrets.* New York: Doubleday, 2001.

Belsito, Frank. *CIA: Cuba and the Caribbean. (CIA Officer's Memoirs).* Reston, VA: Ancient Mariner Press, 2002.

Berle, Adolf A. *Power.* New York: Harcourt Brace & World, 1967.

Beschloss, Michael R. *The Crisis Years: Kennedy and Khrushchev, 1960–63.* New York: Edward Burlingame Books, 1991.

Beschloss, Michael R. *Reaching for Glory: Lyndon Johnson's Secret White House Tapes, 1964–65.* New York: Simon & Schuster, 2001.

Beschloss, Michael R. *Taking Charge: The Johnson White House Tapes, 1963–64.* New York: Simon & Schuster, 1997.

Bethel, Paul. *The Losers: The Definitive Account by an Eyewitness of the Communist Conquest of Cuba and the Soviet Penetration in Latin America.* New Rochelle, NY: Arlington House, 1969.

Bird, Kai. *The Color of Truth. McGeorge Bundy and William Bundy: Brothers in Arms.* New York: Simon & Schuster, 1998.

Bissell, Richard M., Jonathan E. Lewis, and Frances T. Pudlo. *Reflections of a Cold Warrior: From Yalta to the Bay of Pigs.* New Haven, CT: Yale University Press, 1996.

Blight, James G., and Philip Brenner. *Sad and Luminous Days: Cuba's Struggle with the Superpowers after the Missile Crisis.* Lanham, MD: Rowman & Littlefield Publishers, 2002.

Blight, James G., and Peter Kornbluh, eds. *Politics of Illusion: The Bay of Pigs Rexamined.* Boulder, CO: Lynn Reinner Publishers, 1998.

Blight, James G., and David A. Welch, eds. *Intelligence and the Cuban Missile Crisis.* London: Frank Cass, 1998.

Bonachea, Rolando E., and Nelson P. Valdes, eds. *Revolutionary Struggle: 1947–58.* Vol. 1 of *Selected Works of Fidel Castro.* Cambridge, MA: MIT Press, 1972.

Bonsal, Philip W. *Cuba, Castro, and the United States.* Pittsburgh: University of Pittsburgh Press, 1971.

Bourne, Peter G. *Fidel: A Biography of Fidel Castro.* New York: Dodd, Mead, 1986.

Bove, Mike. *Flight 13: Thirteen Years with Castro.* New York: Vantage Press, 1973.

Breuer, William B. *Vendetta! Castro and the Kennedy Brothers.* New York: John Wiley & Sons, 1997.

Brugioni, Dino A. *Eyeball to Eyeball: The Inside Story of the Cuban Missile Crisis.* Edited by Robert F. McCort. New York: Random House, 1990.

Bundy, McGeorge. *Danger and Survival: Choices About the Bomb in the First Fifty Years.* New York: Random House, 1988.

Califano, Joseph A., Jr. *The Triumph & Tragedy of Lyndon Johnson: The White House Years.* New York: Simon & Schuster, 1991.

Chang, Laurence, and Peter Kornbluh, eds. *The Cuban Missile Crisis.* New York: New Press, 1992.

Cline, Ray S. *Secrets, Spies and Scholars.* Washington: Acropolis Books, 1976.

Corn, David. *Blond Ghost: Ted Shackley and the CIA's Crusades.* New York: Simon & Schuster, 1994.

Currey, Cecil B. *Edward Lansdale: The Unquiet American.* Washington, DC: Brassey's, 1998.

Dallek, Robert. *Flawed Giant: Lyndon Johnson and His Times 1961–73.* New York: Oxford University Press, 1998.

Dallek, Robert. *An Unfinished Life: John F. Kennedy 1917–63.* Boston: Little, Brown, 2003.

Diez Acosta, Tomas. *October 1962: The 'Missile' Crisis as Seen from Cuba.* New York: Pathfinder, 2002.

Dinerstein, Herbert S. *The Making of a Missile Crisis: October 1962.* Baltimore: Johns Hopkins University Press, 1976

Dominguez, Jorge I. *To Make a World Safe for Revolution: Cuba's Foreign Policy.* Cambridge, MA, Harvard University Press, 1989.

Dorschner, John, and Roberto Fabricio. *The Winds of December.* New York: Coward, McCann & Geoghegan, 1980.

Draper, Theodore. *Castro's Revolution. Myths and Realities.* New York: Frederick A. Praeger, 1962.

Draper, Theodore. *Castroism: Theory and Practice.* New York: Frederick A. Praeger, 1965.

Dubois, Jules. *Fidel Castro. Rebel—Liberator or Dictator?* Indianapolis: Bobbs-Merrill, 1959.

Dulles, Allen. *The Craft of Intelligence.* New York: Signet Books, 1965.

Eckstein, Susan Eva. *Back from the Future: Cuba Under Castro.* Princeton, NJ: Princeton University Press, 1994.

Elliston, Jon, ed. *Psywar on Cuba: The Declassified History of U.S. Anti-Castro Propaganda.* Melbourne, Australia: Ocean Press, 1999.

Escalante, Fabian. *The Secret War: CIA Covert Operations Against Cuba 1959–62.* Melbourne, Australia: Ocean Press, 1995.

Fagan, Richard R., Richard A. Brody, and Thomas J. O'Leary. *Cubans in Exile: Disaffection and the Revolution.* Stanford, CA: Stanford University Press, 1968.

Falcoff, Mark, ed. *The Cuban Revolution and the United States: A History in Documents 1958–60.* Washington, DC: U.S. Cuba Press, 2001.

Faria, Miguel A., Jr. *Cuba in Revolution: Escape from a Lost Paradise.* Macon, GA: Hacienda Publishing, 2002.

Fonzi, Gaeton. *The Last Investigation.* New York: Thunder's Mouth Press, 1994.

Franklin, Jane. *Cuba and the United States: A Chronological History.* Melbourne, Australia: Ocean Press, 1997.

Franqui, Carlos. *Diary of the Cuban Revolution.* New York: Viking Press, 1976.

Freedman, Lawrence. *Kennedy's Wars: Berlin, Cuba, Laos, and Vietnam.* Oxford, UK: Oxford University Press, 2000.

Fursenko, Alexsander, and Timothy Naftali. *One Hell of a Gamble: Khrushchev, Castro, and Kennedy 1958–64.* New York: W. W. Norton, 1997.

Garthoff, Raymond L. *Reflections on the Cuban Missile Crisis.* Washington, DC: Brookings Institution, 1989.

Geyer, Georgie Anne. *Guerrilla Prince: The Untold Story of Fidel Castro.* Boston: Little, Brown, 1991.

Goodsell, James Nelson, ed. *Fidel Castro's Personal Revolution in Cuba: 1959–73.* New York: Alfred A. Knopf, 1975.

Goodwin, Richard N. *Remembering America: A Voice from the Sixties.* Boston: Little, Brown, 1988.

Gribkov, Gen. Anatoli I., and William Y. Smith. *Operation Anadyr: U.S and Soviet Generals Recount the Cuban Missile Crisis.* Edited by Alfred Friendly Jr. Chicago: edition q, 1994.

Gross, Peter. *Gentleman Spy: The Life of Allen Dulles.* New York: Houghton Mifflin, 1994.

Guthman, Edwin O., and Jeffrey Shulman, eds., *Robert Kennedy: In His Own Words.* New York: Bantam Books, 1988.

Halperin, Maurice. *The Rise and Decline of Fidel Castro.* Berkeley: University of California, 1972.

Haig, Alexander M., Jr., and Charles McCarry. *Inner Circles: How America Changed the World, a Memoir.* New York: Warner Books, 1992.

Hawkins, Jack. *Never Say Die*. Philadelphia: Dorrance, 1961.

Helms, Richard, and William Hood. *A Look over My Shoulder: A Life in the Central Intelligence Agency*. New York: Random House, 2003.

Heymann, C. Davis. *RFK: A Candid Biography of Robert F. Kennedy*. New York: Dutton, 1998.

Higgins, Trumbull. *The Perfect Failure: Kennedy, Eisenhower, and the CIA at the Bay of Pigs*. New York: W.W. Norton, 1987.

Hinckle, Warren, and William W. Turner. *Deadly Secrets: The CIA-MAFIA War Against Castro and the Assassination of J.F.K*. New York: Thunder's Mouth Press, 1992.

Hinckle, Warren, and William W. Turner. *The Fish Is Red: The Story of the Secret War Against Castro*. New York: Harper and Row, 1981.

Hougan, Jim. *Spooks*. New York: Bantam Books, 1978.

Huberman, Leo, and Paul M. Sweezy. *Cuba: Anatomy of a Revolution*. New York: Monthly Review Press, 1961.

Huberman, Leo, and Paul M. Sweezy. *Socialism in Cuba*. New York: Monthly Review Press, 1969.

Hunt, E. Howard. *Undercover: Memoirs of an American Secret Agent*. London: W. H. Allen, 1975.

Hunt, Howard. *Give Us This Day*. New Rochelle, NY: Arlington House, 1973.

Jackson, D. Bruce. *Castro, the Kremlin, and Communism in Latin America*. Baltimore: Johns Hopkins University Press, 1969.

Johnson, Haynes. *The Bay of Pigs: The Leaders' Story of Brigade 2506*. New York: W. W. Norton, 1964.

Johnson, Lyndon Baines. *The Vantage Point: Perspectives of the Presidency 1963–69*. New York: Holt, Rinehart and Winston, 1971.

Jones, Kirby, and Frank Mankiewicz. *With Fidel: A Portrait of Castro and Cuba*. Chicago: Playboy Press, 1975.

Karol, K. S. *Guerrillas in Power: The Course of the Cuban Revolution*. New York: Hill & Wang, 1970.

Kennedy, Robert F. *Thirteen Days: A Memoir of the Cuban Missile Crisis*. New York: W. W. Norton, 1969.

Kenner, Martin, and James Petras, eds. *Fidel Castro Speaks*. New York: Grove Press, 1969.

Kirkpatrick, Lyman B., Jr. *The Real CIA*. New York: Macmillan, 1968.

Kornbluh, Peter, ed. *Bay of Pigs Declassified: The Secret CIA Report on the Invasion of Cuba*. New York: New Press, 1998.

Langley, Lester D. *The Cuban Policy of the United States: A Brief History*. New York: John Wiley & Sons, 1968.

Leamer, Laurence. *The Kennedy Men: 1901–63*. New York: William Morrow, 2002.

Lechuga, Carlos. *Cuba and the Missile Crisis*. Melbourne, Australia: Ocean Press, 2001.

Llerena, Mario. *The Unsuspected Revolution: The Birth and Rise of Castroism*. Ithaca, NY: Cornell University Press, 1978.

Lopez-Fresquet, Rufo. *My Fourteen Months with Castro*. Cleveland, OH: World Publishing, 1966.

Lynch, Grayston L. *Decision for Disaster: Betrayal at the Bay of Pigs*. Washington, DC: Brassey's, 1998.

MacGaffey, Wyatt, and Clifford R. Barnett. *Twentieth Century Cuba: The Background of the Castro Revolution*. Garden City, NY: Anchor Books, 1962.

Mahony, Richard D. *Sons & Brothers: The Days of Jack and Bobby Kennedy*. New York: Arcade Publishing, 1999.

Mallin, Jay, Sr. *Covering Castro: Rise and Decline of Cuba's Communist Dictator*. Washington, DC: U.S.*Cuba Institute Press and Transaction Publishers, 1994.

Mallin, Jay, Sr. *Fortress Cuba: Russia's American Base*. Chicago: Henry Regnery, 1965.

Martin, David C. *Wilderness of Mirrors*. New York: Harper and Row, 1980.

Matthews, Herbert L. *Castro: A Political Biography*. London: Alan Lane The Penguin Press, 1969.

Matthews, Herbert L. *The Cuban Story*. New York: George Braziller, 1961.

Matthews, Herbert L. *Revolution in Cuba*. New York: Charles Scribner's Sons, 1975.

May, Ernest R., and Philip D. Zelikow. *The Kennedy Tapes: Inside the White House During the Cuban Missile Crisis*. Cambridge, MA: Belknap Press of Harvard University, 1997.

Mazarr, Michael J. *Semper Fidel: America and Cuba, 1776–88*. Baltimore: Nautical and Aviation Publishing Company of America, 1988.

Miller, Warren. *90 Miles From Home: The Truth from inside Castro's Cuba*. Greenwich, CT: Fawcett Publications, 1961.

Mills, C. Wright. *Listen Yankee: The Revolution in Cuba*. New York: Ballantine Books, 1960.

O'Connor, James. *The Origins of Socialism in Cuba*. Ithaca, NY: Cornell University Press, 1970.

Persons, Albert C. *Bay of Pigs*. Birmingham, AL: Kingston Press, 1968.

Phillips, David Atlee. *The Night Watch*. New York: Ballantine Books, 1977.

Powers, Thomas. *Intelligence Wars: American Secret History from Hitler to Al-Qaeda*. New York: New York Review of Books, 2002.

Powers, Thomas. *The Man Who Kept the Secrets: Richard Helms and the CIA*. New York: Alfred A. Knopf, 1979.

Prados, John. *Presidents' Secret Wars: CIA and Pentagon Covert Operations Since World War II*. New York: William Morrow, 1986.

Quirk, Robert. *Fidel Castro*. New York: W. W. Norton, 1993.

Rabe, Stephen G. *Eisenhower and Latin America*. Chapel Hill: University of North Carolina Press, 1988.

Ranelagh, John. *The Agency: The Rise and Decline of the CIA. From Wild Bill Donovan to William Casey.* New York: Simon & Schuster, 1986.

Ratliff, William E. *Castroism and Communism in Latin America, 1959–76.* Washington, DC: American Enterprise Institute for Public Policy Research, 1976.

Ratliff, William E., ed. *The Selling of Fidel Castro: The Media and the Cuban Revolution.* New Brunswick, NJ: Transaction Books, 1987.

Reeves, Richard. *President Kennedy: Profile of Power.* New York: Simon & Schuster, 1993.

Rivero Collado, Carlos. *Los Sobrinos del Tio Sam.* La Habana, Cuba: Editorial de Ciencias Sociales, 1976.

Ridenour, Ron. *Back Fire: The CIA's Biggest Burn.* Havana, Cuba: Jose Marti Publishing House, 1991.

Robbins, Carla Anne. *The Cuban Threat.* New York: McGraw-Hill, 1983.

Rodriguez, Felix I., and John Weisman. *Shadow Warrior: The CIA Hero of a Hundred Unknown Battles.* New York: Simon & Schuster, 1989.

Rodriguez, Juan Carlos. *The Bay of Pigs and the CIA.* Melbourne, Australia: Ocean Press, 1999.

Rusk, Dean, as told to Richard Rusk. *As I Saw It.* New York: W. W. Norton & Company, 1990.

Russo, Gus. *Live by the Sword: The Secret War Against Castro and the Death of JFK.* Baltimore: Bancroft Press, 1998.

Sarte, Jean-Paul. *Sarte on Cuba.* New York: Ballantine Books, 1961.

Schaap, Dick. *R.F.K.* New York: Signet Books, 1967.

Schlesinger, Arthur M., Jr. *Robert Kennedy and His Times. Volume I.* Boston: Houghton Mifflin, 1978.

Schlesinger, Arthur M., Jr. *Robert Kennedy and His Times. Volume II.* Boston: Houghton Mifflin, 1978.

Schlesinger, Arthur M., Jr. *A Thousand Days: John F. Kennedy in the White House.* London: Mayflower-Dell Paperback, 1967.

Shesol, Jeff. *Mutual Contempt: Lyndon Johnson, Robert Kennedy, and the Feud That Defined a Decade.* New York: W.W. Norton, 1997.

Smith, Wayne. *The Closest of Enemies.* New York: W. W. Norton, 1987.

Sorensen, Theodore C. *Kennedy.* New York: Konecky & Konecky, 1965.

Steel, Ronald. *In Love with Night: The American Romance with Robert Kennedy.* New York: Simon & Schuser, 2000.

Suarez, Andres. *Cuba: Castroism and Communism, 1959–1966.* Cambridge, MA: MIT Press, 1967.

Suchlicki, Jaime, ed. *Cuba, Castro, and Revolution.* Coral Gables, FL: University of Miami Press, 1972.

Sutherland, Elizabeth. *The Youngest Revolution: A Personal Report on Cuba.* New York: Dial Press, 1969.

Szulc, Tad. *Fidel: A Critical Portrait.* New York: William Morrow, 1986.

Szulc, Tad, and Karl Meyer. *The Cuban Invasion: The Chronicle of a Disaster.* New York: Ballantine Books, 1962.

Tetlow, Edwin. *Eye on Cuba.* New York: Harcourt Brace & World, 1966.

Thomas, Evan. *Robert Kennedy: His Life.* New York: Simon & Schuster, 2000.

Thomas, Evan. *The Very Best Men. Four Who Dared: The Early Years of the CIA.* New York: Simon & Schuster, 1995.

Thomas, Hugh. *Cuba: The Pursuit of Freedom.* New York: Harper and Row, 1971.

Turner, William. *Rearview Mirror: Looking Back at the FBI, CIA, and Other Tails.* Granite Bay, CA: Penmarin Books, 2001.

Valdes-Pena, Jacinto. *Operacion Mangosta: Preludio de la Invasion Directa a CUBA.* Havana, Cuba: Editorial Capitan San Luis, 2002.

Weber, Ralph E., ed. *Spymasters: Ten CIA Officers in Their Own Words.* Wilmington, DE: Scholarly Resources Inc., 1999.

Welch, Richard E., Jr. *Response to Revolution: The United States and the Cuban Revolution, 1959–61.* Chapel Hill: University of North Carolina Press, 1985.

Williams, Bryon. *Cuba: The Continuing Revolution.* New York: Parents' Magazine Press, 1969.

Wise, David, and Thomas B. Ross. *The Invisible Government.* New York: Random House, 1964.

Wofford, Harris. *Of Kennedys & Kings: Making Sense of the Sixties.* Pittsburgh: University of Pittsburgh Press, 1980.

Wright, Peter, and Paul Greengrass. *Spy Catcher: The Candid Autobiography of a Senior Intelligence Officer.* New York: Viking, 1987.

Documentary Books

Alleged Assassination Plots Involving Foreign Leaders: An Interim Report of the Select Committee to Study Government Operations. New York: W. W. Norton, 1976.

British Archives on the Cuban Missile Crisis 1962. London: Archival Publications International, 2001.

CIA Targets Fidel: The Secret Assassination Report. Melbourne, Australia: Ocean Press, 1996.

Foreign Relations of the United States, Cuba, 1958–1960. Vol VI. Washington, DC: U.S. Government Printing Office, 1991.

Foreign Relations of the United States, Cuba, 1961–1963. Vol. X. Washington, DC: U.S. Government Printing Office, 1997.

Foreign Relations of the United States, Cuban Missile Crisis and Aftermath. Vol. XI. Washington, DC: U.S. Government Printing Office, 1996.

History of an Agression: The Trial of the Playa Giron Mercenaries. Havana, Cuba: Ediciones Venceremos, 1964.

BIBLIOGRAPHY

McAuliffe, Mary S., ed. *CIA Documents on the Cuban Missile Crisis: 1962.* Washington, DC: History Staff Central Intelligence Agency, 1992.
Operation Zapata: The "Ultrasensitive" Report and Testimony of the Board of Inquiry on the Bay of Pigs. Frederick, MD: University Publications of America, 1984.

Articles

Bohning, Don. "The Cold Warrior." *Tropic/The Miami Herald*, January 14, 1996.
Branch, Taylor, and George Crile, III. "The Kennedy Vendetta: How the CIA Waged a Silent War against Cuba." *Harper's*, August 1975.
Daniel, Jean. "Unofficial Envoy: An Historic Report from Two Capitals." *The New Republic*, December 14, 1963.
Dorschner, John. "Casablanca of the Caribbean." *Tropic/The Miami Herald*, April 4, 1976.
Gleichauf, Justin. "A Listening Post in Miami." *Studies of Intelligence*, no. 10 (Winter-Spring 2001, unclassified edition): 49–53.
Gleijes, Piero. "Ships in the Night: The CIA, the White House and the Bay of Pigs." *Journal of Latin American Studies*, February 1995.
Kornbluh, Peter. "JFK & Castro: The Secret Quest for Accommodation." *Cigar Aficionado*, October 1999.
Murphy, Charles J. V. "Cuba: The Record Set Straight." *Fortune*, September 1961.
Nelson, Anna. "Operation Northwoods and the Covert War Against Cuba." *Cuban Studies* 32. Edited by Lisandro Perez. Pittsburgh: University of Pittsburgh Press, 2001.

Unpublished Works

Chavez, Manuel J. "The Berman Connection." Memoirs of retired Air Force Intelligence Officer attached to overt CIA station in Miami in early 1960s, 2001.
Flannery, Jim. "Bay of Pigs." Short essay for grandchildren by retired CIA official who served as aide to Richard Bissell at time of Bay of Pigs, December 2000.
Harman, J. S. Memorandum for the Record: "Report on Plots to Assassinate Fidel Castro." 1967. (Published commercially as *CIA Targets Fidel.* Melbourne, Australia: Ocean Press, 1996. With commentary by former head of Cuban State Security.)
Hurwitch, Robert. "Most of Myself, Part II." Unpublished memoirs by a State Department Cuba Desk Officer, 1960–64. 1990.

BIBLIOGRAPHY

Jacobs, Donald P. "An Encore for Zapata? The Kennedy Administration's Military Contingency Plans for an Invasion of Cuba, 1962–63." Master's Thesis. George Washington University, August 1999.

Oliva, Erneido. "General Oliva's Story." Unpublished manuscript, excerpts provided to author, 1998.

INDEX

INDEX

ABOUT THE AUTHOR

Don Bohning retired at the end of 2000 from the *Miami Herald,* where he had been Latin America editor. He joined the *Herald* in July 1959 after graduating with a degree in foreign trade from the American Institute of Foreign Trade (Thunderbird) in Glendale, Arizona, which later became the Graduate School for International Management. After joining the *Herald,* he was first assigned to its Hollywood, Florida, bureau. He became a member of the *Herald*'s Latin America staff in 1964. His coverage responsibilities included the Cuban exile community in Miami. He was named Latin America editor in 1967, a position he held until he retired.

In the course of nearly thirty-seven years as a foreign correspondent and editor for the *Herald,* he visited every independent country in the Western Hemisphere, reporting on such events as the 1973 Pinochet coup in Chile; the 1973 Juan Peron funeral in Argentina; the 1972 Managua, Nicaragua, earthquake; the 1978 Jonestown Massacre in Guyana; the 1986 fall of the Duvalier dynasty in Haiti; the 1983 invasion of Grenada; the 1989 invasion of Panama; negotiation, ratification, and implementation of the Panama Canal treaties; the Jamaica turmoil of the 1970s; the 1979 Non-Aligned Summit in Havana; and the 1969 Rockefeller Mission to Latin America. He also covered the 1976 Republican and Democratic National Conventions as part of the Knight-Ridder Newspapers reporting and editing team. He has won numerous journalistic awards, among them from the Inter-American Press Association, the Overseas Press Club, Columbia University's Maria Moors Cabot Prize, and the first Knight-Ridder Newspapers Excellence Award for news reporting.

A native of South Dakota, Bohning attended Dakota Wesleyan University in Mitchell, South Dakota, from 1951 until graduation in 1955 with a major in political science and a minor in economics. He worked on the university newspaper throughout his four years at Dakota Wesleyan, as well as at the *Daily Republic,* the local newspaper, including a year as a full-time reporter after graduation. He spent two years in the U.S. Army before attending Thunderbird.